Middle and Secondary Classroom Management

LESSONS FROM RESEARCH AND PRACTICE

Fifth Edition

CAROL SIMON WEINSTEIN

Rutgers, the State University of New Jersey

INGRID NOVODVORSKY

University of Arizona

McGraw Hill Education

KH

MIDDLE AND SECONDARY CLASSROOM MANAGEMENT: LESSONS FROM RESEARCH
AND PRACTICE, FIFTH EDITION

Published by McGraw-Hill Education, 2 Penn Plaza, New York, NY 10121. Copyright © 2015 by McGraw-Hill
Education. All rights reserved. Printed in the United States of America. Previous editions © 2011, 2007, and
2003. No part of this publication may be reproduced or distributed in any form or by any means, or stored in a
database or retrieval system, without the prior written consent of McGraw-Hill Education, including, but not
limited to, in any network or other electronic storage or transmission, or broadcast for distance learning.

Some ancillaries, including electronic and print components, may not be available to customers outside the
United States.

This book is printed on acid-free paper.

1 2 3 4 5 6 7 8 9 0 DOC/DOC 1 0 9 8 7 6 5 4

ISBN 978-0-07-802453-5
MHID 0-07-802453-6

Senior Vice President, Products & Markets: *Kurt L. Strand*
Vice President, Content Production & Technology Services: *Kimberly Meriwether David*
Brand Manager: *Allison McNamara*
Managing Editor: *Penina Braffman*
Associate Marketing Manager: *Alexandra Schultz*
Director, Content Production: *Terri Schiesl*
Content Project Manager: *Mary Jane Lampe*
Buyer: *Laura Fuller*
Cover Designer: *Studio Montage*
Cover Image: *Design Pics/Tim Antoniuk*
Compositor: *Laserwords Private Limited*
Typeface: *10.5/12 Times LT Std Roman*
Printer: *R. R. Donnelley*

All credits appearing on page or at the end of the book are considered to be an extension of the copyright page.

Library of Congress Cataloging-in-Publication Data

Weinstein, Carol Simon.
  Middle and secondary classroom management : lessons from research and practice / Carol Simon
Weinstein, Rutgers, the State University of New Jersey, Ingrid Novodvorsky, the University of Arizona.
    —Fifth edition.
  pages cm.
  ISBN 978-0-07-802453-5 (alk. paper)
  1. Classroom management. 2. Education, Secondary. 3. Education, Elementary. 4. Classroom
environment. I. Novodvorsky, Ingrid. II. Title.
LB3013.W46 2015
373.1102'4—dc23
                                                        2013041556

The Internet addresses listed in the text were accurate at the time of publication. The inclusion of a Web site
does not indicate an endorsement by the authors or McGraw-Hill Education, and McGraw-Hill Education does
not guarantee the accuracy of the information presented at these sites.

9/23/16

ABOUT THE AUTHORS

Carol Simon Weinstein is professor emerita in the Department of Learning and Teaching at Rutgers Graduate School of Education. She received her bachelor's degree in psychology from Clark University in Worcester, Massachusetts, and her master's and doctoral degrees from Harvard Graduate School of Education. Dr. Weinstein began her research career by studying the impact of classroom design on students' behavior and attitudes. She pursued this topic for many years, writing about the ways that classroom environments can be designed to facilitate teachers' goals and to foster children's learning and development. Eventually, Dr. Weinstein's interest in organizing classroom space expanded to include classroom organization and management in general. She is the author of numerous chapters and articles on classroom management and teacher education students' beliefs about caring and control. Most recently, she has focused on the need for "culturally responsive classroom management," or classroom management in the service of social justice. In 2006, Dr. Weinstein co-edited (with Carolyn Evertson) the first *Handbook of Classroom Management: Research, Practice, and Contemporary Issues* (Lawrence Erlbaum Associates, Inc.), a compendium of 47 chapters written by scholars from around the world. In 2011, the Classroom Management Special Interest Group of the American Educational Research Association honored Dr. Weinstein by creating "The Carol Weinstein Outstanding Research Award" for the best paper on classroom management presented at the annual conference.

Ingrid Novodvorsky is Director of the College of Science Teacher Preparation Program and Faculty Fellow for Instruction and Assessment at the University of Arizona. She earned a bachelor's degree in Physics and Mathematics, and master's and doctoral degrees in Secondary Education, all from the University of Arizona. Before joining the university, Dr. Novodvorsky taught high-school physics and mathematics. During that time, she hosted student teachers in her classroom and mentored beginning science teacher colleagues. As one of the founding faculty members, Dr. Novodvorsky created a course on classroom management for the Teacher Preparation Program, in recognition that this is a critical aspect of preparing teachers. Her current scholarly work at the university is focused on faculty development for improving instruction and assessment.

DEDICATION

To Fred, Donna, Donnie, Sandy, and Christina: You continue to teach and inspire all who read this book.

And to Hannah, Judah, and Cora: May your teachers be as masterful as these.

BRIEF CONTENTS

CONTENTS

ix

PREFACE

These days, the "hot topics" in education focus on ways to increase academic achievement: implementing core curriculum standards; incorporating technology into the curriculum; reducing the achievement gap among students from different racial, ethnic, and economic backgrounds; and assessing students' learning (partly to enable data-driven instruction, partly to evaluate teacher effectiveness, and partly to assign grades to schools). Except for a continued, even heightened, concern about bullying, discussions of classroom management have receded into the background. Yet, studies consistently show that classroom management plays a critical role—perhaps the *most* critical role—in students' academic achievement. This finding makes sense. Teachers cannot implement core curriculum standards if they are unable to create an orderly, respectful classroom environment; smart phones can disrupt as much as they can instruct; and assessments will only show increases in academic achievement only if students are paying attention when teachers are teaching.

Ironically, the emphasis on achievement sometimes leads to conditions that make classroom management particularly challenging. If scores on standardized tests are what matters most, then content areas not on the test, such as music, art, and physical education, may be allotted less time or even eliminated. If teachers' jobs are at least partly dependent on students' standardized test scores, teachers might forgo engaging, developmentally appropriate activities in favor of "test prep." In short, narrowing the curriculum and requiring teachers to "teach to the test" could lead to boredom and apathy—a situation that inevitably breeds management problems.

Teachers face additional management challenges because of changes in the composition and size of their classes. In the years since the first edition of *Secondary Classroom Management,* classes have become increasingly diverse, with students from a wide range of racial, ethnic, and cultural backgrounds, students who are learning English, and students with disabilities. Diagnoses of attention deficit hyperactivity disorder (ADHD) and autism are escalating dramatically (for reasons that are not entirely clear). The recent economic crisis has resulted in higher levels of poverty and homelessness and created a climate of uncertainty, anxiety, and fear. An alarming number of children come to school with emotional and psychological problems. As school budgets have been slashed, schools have been closed, and class sizes have increased. Now more than ever, teachers need to know how to establish classrooms that are supportive, inclusive, caring, and orderly.

Unfortunately, beginning teachers frequently report that their teacher education programs did not prepare them for the challenges of classroom management. They call for more preparation in areas such as communicating with parents; responding to inappropriate behavior; working in diverse, multicultural settings; and helping students with special needs. They complain about courses that are too removed from the realities of schools and crave examples of real teachers dealing with the challenges of real students in real classrooms. *Middle and Secondary Classroom Management: Lessons from Research and Practice* is designed to address these concerns.

ORGANIZATION OF THE TEXT

As the subtitle of this book indicates, we have integrated what research has to say about effective classroom management with knowledge culled from practice. We do this by highlighting the thinking and the actual management practices of five real teachers: Fred Cerequas (social studies), Donna Chambliss (language arts), Donnie Collins (mathematics), Sandy Krupinski (chemistry), and Christina Vreeland (English). These five teachers not only teach different subjects but also work in school districts that differ substantially in terms of race, ethnicity, and socioeconomic status. Christina is a novice teacher, whereas the others are all quite experienced, and Donna teaches in a middle school. Readers will come to know these five teachers—to hear their thinking on various aspects of classroom management and to see the ways they interact with students. Their stories provide real-life illustrations of the concepts and principles derived from research.

Part I of the book introduces these teachers and the fundamental concepts and principles that guide the book. In Part II, we focus on the management tasks involved in *building a respectful, productive environment for learning*—from designing the physical space, building positive teacher-student relationships, creating community, and teaching norms to knowing your students, working with families, and using time efficiently. In Part III, we turn to strategies for *organizing and managing instruction*. We address topics that are often omitted in classroom management texts but are actually crucial, such as motivating students and managing some of the instructional formats commonly used in secondary classrooms—independent work, recitations and discussions, and small-group work (including cooperative learning). Parts II and III both emphasize strategies for preventing behavior problems. In Part IV, we discuss what to do when prevention isn't enough and describe ways to intervene when problems arise.

The goal of *Middle and Secondary Classroom Management* is to provide clear, practical guidance that is based on research and the wisdom of practice. We have tried to balance the need to provide breadth and depth of coverage with the need for a book that is accessible, engaging, and reasonable in length. (In fact, this new edition is considerably shorter than the previous one.) For the sake of readability, we consistently use "we" and "us" even when describing incidents that involved only one of the authors.

THE FIFTH EDITION: WHAT'S THE SAME? WHAT'S DIFFERENT?

This edition retains several pedagogical features that instructors and students have found useful. In almost every chapter, readers can find the following:

- *Pause and Reflect* boxes to promote engagement and comprehension.

- *Activities for Skill Building and Reflection* that are divided into three sections: "In Class, "On Your Own," and "For Your Portfolio."

- An annotated list of books and articles in *For Further Reading.*
- A list of *Organizational Resources* describing agencies that can provide additional information.
- *Practical Tips* boxes with useful classroom management strategies.
- Marginal icons that alert readers to content focusing on cultural diversity.
- *Meet the Educator* boxes that highlight the work of well-known educators whom beginning teachers are likely to meet during inservice workshops or lectures.

The most significant change in this new edition is the introduction of Donna Chambliss, an eighth-grade language arts teacher in an urban middle school. Additionally, we have made a number of other changes (many in response to feedback from users of the fourth edition):

- Chapter 1 introduces three styles of management (authoritative, authoritarian, and permissive), expands the discussion of "warm demanders," and considers teachers' need for social-emotional intelligence and self-care.
- Chapter 2 discusses assigning seats at the beginning of the year.
- Because users of the book found Chapter 3, "Building Respectful, Caring Relationships" too long, it has been divided into two chapters, one on teacher-student relationships (Chapter 3) and one on peer relationships (Chapter 4).
- Chapter 5, "Establishing Expectations for Behavior," now includes a *Practical Tips* box on the use of technology.
- Chapter 6, "Knowing Your Students and Their Special Needs," has been substantially pared down to focus on classroom-management aspects of student diversity and a section on hearing loss has been added.
- The chapter on "Making the Most of Classroom Time" has been moved from Part III, "Organizing and Managing Instruction," to Part II, "Establishing an Environment for Learning."
- The chapters on "Managing Independent Work" and "Managing Recitations and Discussions" have been combined and streamlined (Chapter 10), and the material has been reorganized.
- Chapter 11, "Managing Small-Group Work" includes a discussion of what to do when students don't want to participate in a group activity and prefer to work alone.
- Chapter 12, "Responding Effectively to Inappropriate Behavior," has more discussion of Positive Behavioral Intervention and Supports (PBIS) and addresses the question of teachers' responsibility when they learn through social media that students have engaged in inappropriate or even illegal activity off campus.
- As always, all chapters have been updated to reflect recent scholarship and current concerns; there are more than 100 new references.

Finally, because many teacher education programs now require prospective teachers to demonstrate that they possess the knowledge and skills that teachers need in order to be effective, we have created a table showing the competencies addressed in each chapter. (This table appears at the end of the preface.) These have been taken from Charlotte Danielson's book, *Enhancing Professional Practice: A Framework for Teaching* (2007). Danielson's framework identifies those aspects of a teacher's responsibilities that have been documented through empirical studies and theoretical research as promoting students' learning. In other words, they define what teachers should know and be able to do. Danielson was one of the developers of Praxis III, the last in a series of professional assessments for beginning teachers from the Educational Testing Service (ETS). Praxis III measures actual teaching skills and classroom performance and is used to make licensing decisions in a number of states. Danielson's framework is based largely on the Praxis III criteria.

ELEMENTARY CLASSROOM MANAGEMENT: A COMPANION TEXT

This edition of *Middle and Secondary Classroom Management* parallels the sixth edition of *Elementary Classroom Management: Lessons from Research and Practice* (Weinstein & Romano, 2014), so that instructors teaching courses with both elementary and secondary teacher education students can use the two books as a package. Although the principles and concepts discussed are the same, the teachers on which the companion book is based all work at the elementary level, and the "lessons from research" are based largely on studies conducted in kindergarten through sixth grade.

ACKNOWLEDGMENTS

Once again, we express our gratitude to the teachers featured in this book. They allowed us to observe in their classrooms and shared their wisdom, frustrations, and celebrations during countless hours of interviews. In the interest of full disclosure, three points about the structure of the book need to be made. First, the portraits of Christina, Donna, Donnie, Fred, and Sandy are composites derived from material that was collected over a number of years. In other words, we have created a portrait of each teacher by describing incidents that occurred in different years with different students as though they had all occurred in the same academic year with the same classes. Second, we should note that Sandy has recently retired, and Christina is no longer an English teacher but has become the language arts supervisor for her district. Fred and Donnie retired several years ago. (In some cases, we have updated vignettes from these teachers to reflect current technology and events, but we have in no way changed the substance of their interactions or comments.) Donna is currently in her 12th year of teaching. All of the teachers except Donnie had input into this new edition. Finally, because Donna is a new addition to the book, we interviewed her separately about the issues that were collectively discussed with the original "cast of characters." Nonetheless, for the sake of coherence and simplicity, we have integrated her stories with those of the other teachers.

We are also grateful to our McGraw-Hill Project Team: Penina Braffman Greenfield, Managing Editor; Sourav Majumdar, Full-Service Project Manager; MaryJane Lampe, Content Project Manager; Nicole Bridge, Development Editor; and Alexandra Schultz, Marketing Manager. To the individuals who reviewed the previous edition, we express our deep appreciation: Marcia Walker, Trevecca Nazarene

University; Steven Ward, University of Central Arkansas; Kellie Cain, University of the Pacific; Eileen Austin, University of South Florida; Joan Berry, University of Mary Hardin-Baylor. If there are any errors or misstatements, the fault is entirely our own.

Finally, a special thank you to Neil, who understands that, even in retirement, classroom management can remain a passion, and to Chris for providing unfailing support during the revision process.

Carol Simon Weinstein

Ingrid Novodvorsky

Charlotte Danielson
Enhancing Professional Practice: A Framework for Teaching (2nd ed.)
ASCD, 2007

Chapter	1	2	3	4	5	6	7	8	9	10	11	12	13
Domain 1: Planning and Preparation													
Component 1b: Demonstrating Knowledge of Students						√			√	√	√		
• Knowledge of child and adolescent development						√							
• Knowledge of students' special needs						√							
Component 1c: Setting Instructional Outcomes									√				
• Value, sequence, and alignment									√				
• Suitability for diverse learners									√				
Component 1e: Designing Coherent Instruction										√	√		
• Learning activities										√	√		
• Instructional materials and resources										√			
• Instructional groups											√		
Domain 2: The Classroom Environment		√	√	√	√						√	√	√
Component 2a: Creating Environment of Respect/ Rapport			√	√								√	√
• Teacher interaction with students												√	√
• Student interactions with other students				√									
Component 2c: Managing Classroom Procedures					√			√					
• Management of instructional groups					√						√		
• Management of transitions					√			√					
• Management of materials and supplies					√								
• Management of noninstructional duties					√								

Chapter	1	2	3	4	5	6	7	8	9	10	11	12	13
Component 2d: Managing Student Behavior												√	√
• Expectations					√								
• Monitoring of student behavior					√								
• Response to student misbehavior					√							√	√
Component 2e: Organizing Physical Space		√											
• Safety and accessibility		√											
• Arrangement of furniture/use of physical resources		√											
Domain 3: Instruction													
Component 3a: Communicating with Students								√	√	√	√		
• Directions and procedures								√	√		√		
• Expectations for learning									√		√		
Component 3b: Using Questioning/Discussion Techniques										√			
• Discussion techniques									√	√			
• Student participation									√	√			
Component 3c: Engaging Students in Learning								√	√		√		
• Structure and pacing								√					
• Activities and assignments									√				
• Grouping of students									√		√		
• Instructional materials and resources									√				
Component 3d: Using Assessment in Instruction									√	√			
• Feedback to students									√	√			
• Student self-assessment and monitoring of progress									√	√			
• Monitoring of student learning								√		√			

Chapter	1	2	3	4	5	6	7	8	9	10	11	12	13
Component 3e: Demonstrating Flexibility/Responsiveness													
• Lesson adjustment									√		√		
• Response to students									√		√		
• Persistence									√				
Domain 4: Professional Responsibility	√					√							
Component 4a: Reflecting on Teaching	√					√							
Component 4c: Communicating with Families							√						
• Information about the instructional program							√						
• Information about individual students							√						
• Engagement of families in the instructional program						√	√						
Component 4e: Growing and Developing Professionally	√												

PART I

Introduction

When you hear the words "a really good teacher," what comes to mind?

We have asked our teacher education students this question, and invariably they talk about *caring*. A good teacher is a caring teacher, they say, someone who respects and supports students, who doesn't put them down, and who shows genuine interest in them as individuals. Our teacher education students also believe they have the capacity to be that kind of teacher. They envision themselves nurturing students' self-esteem, rejoicing in their successes, and creating strong bonds of affection and mutual respect.

And then these prospective teachers begin student teaching. Over the weeks, the talk about caring begins to fade away, replaced by talk of control and discipline, penalties and consequences. Student teachers lament the fact that they were "too nice" at the beginning and conclude that they should have been "meaner." Some even seem to believe that caring and order are mutually exclusive.

The tension between wanting to care and needing to achieve order is not uncommon among novice teachers. But showing that you care and achieving order are *not* irreconcilable goals. The two actually go hand in hand. Indeed, *one of the main ways in which teachers create an orderly environment is by treating students with warmth and respect.* Common sense tells us that students are more likely to cooperate with teachers who are seen as responsive, trustworthy, and respectful, and research consistently shows this to be true.

At the same time, *one of the ways to show students you care is by taking responsibility for keeping order.* Far from just being "warm and fuzzy," caring teachers are willing to assume the leadership role that is part of being a teacher. For such teachers, caring is not just about being affectionate and respectful; it is also about monitoring behavior, teaching and enforcing norms, and providing needed organization and structure. These teachers understand that students actually crave limits—even though they may protest loudly.

In Chapter 1, you will meet five "good" secondary teachers whose experiences and wisdom form the basis for this book. As you will see, they are able to combine warmth and respect with an insistence that students work hard, comply with classroom norms, and treat one another with consideration. This combination constitutes *authoritative classroom management,* a concept we will explore in the following chapter.

1 CHAPTER

 Managing Classrooms to Nurture
Students, Build Self-Discipline,
and Promote Learning

For many prospective and beginning teachers, entering a middle or high school class-room is like returning home after a brief absence. So little has changed: Desks with oversized arms are still arranged in straggly rows, bells still signal the end of classes, and bulletin boards still display faded copies of bell schedules and fire drill instructions. The familiarity of these sights and sounds makes us feel comfortable and at ease; in fact, it may lead us to conclude that the transition from student to teacher will be relatively easy. Yet, ironically, this very familiarity can be a trap; it can make it difficult to appreciate what a curious and demanding place the secondary classroom really is. Looking at the classroom as if we have never seen one before may help us recognize some of its strange characteristics and contradictions.

Viewed from a fresh perspective, the classroom turns out to be an extremely crowded place. It is more like a subway or a bus than a place designed for learning, and it is difficult to think of another setting (except prison, perhaps) where such large groups of individuals are packed so closely together for so many hours. Nonetheless, amid this crowdedness, students are often not permitted to interact. They "must learn how to be alone in a crowd" (Jackson, 1990, p. 16).

There are other contradictions in this curious place. Middle and high school students are expected to work together in harmony, yet they may be strangers—even rivals—and may come from very different cultural backgrounds. Students are urged to help one another, but they are also told to keep their eyes on their own papers. They are encouraged to cooperate, but they are often in competition, especially if they are concerned about class rank and college admission. They are lectured about being independent and responsible, yet they are also expected to show complete, unquestioning obedience to the teacher's dictates. (This peculiar situation is captured in the cartoon that appears in Figure 1.1.) They are urged to work slowly and carefully, but they are often reminded that 42- (or even 84-) minute periods require adherence to a rigid time schedule.

In addition to these contradictions, Walter Doyle (2006) has pointed out six features of the classroom setting that make it even more complex. First, classrooms are characterized by *multidimensionality*. Unlike a post office or a restaurant, places devoted to a single activity, the classroom is the setting for a broad range of events. Within its boundaries, students read, write, discuss, work on projects, view videos, and listen to lectures. Teachers not only lead whole-class discussions, coordinate small-group activities, and administer tests; they also take attendance, settle disputes, and counsel students with problems. Somehow, the classroom environment must be able to accommodate all these activities.

Second, many of these activities take place at the same time. This *simultaneity* makes the classroom a bit like a three-ring circus. Secondary teachers tend to use whole-group instruction more than their elementary counterparts; nonetheless, it is not uncommon to see a cluster of students working on a project while a few individuals

"I expect you all to be independent, innovative, critical thinkers who will do exactly as I say."

FIGURE 1.1   *Source:* Reprinted by permission of Warren.

write at their desks or on computers and a small group meets with the teacher about materials to include in their portfolios. Still other students may be text messaging about yesterday's soccer game. It is this simultaneity that makes having "eyes in the back of your head" so valuable to teachers.

A third characteristic of classrooms is the rapid pace at which things happen. Classroom events occur with an *immediacy* that makes it impossible to think through every action ahead of time. An argument erupts over a perceived insult; a student complains that a neighbor is copying; a normally silent student makes a serious, but irrelevant, comment during a group discussion. Each of these incidents requires a quick response, an on-the-spot decision about how to proceed. Furthermore, classroom incidents such as these cannot always be anticipated, despite the most careful planning. This *unpredictability* is a fourth characteristic of classrooms. It ensures that being a teacher is rarely boring, but unpredictability can also be exhausting.

A fifth characteristic of classrooms is the *lack of privacy*. Classrooms are remarkably public places. Within their four walls, each person's behavior can be observed by many others. Teachers may feel as though they are always on stage. And such feelings are understandable; with 20 or 30 pairs of eyes watching, it is difficult to find a moment for a private chuckle or an unobserved groan. But the scrutiny goes both ways: Teachers constantly monitor students' behavior as well. And in response to this sometimes unwelcome surveillance, students learn to send text messages, comb their hair, and do homework for another course without (they hope) the teacher's ever noticing. Yet, even if they avoid the teacher's eyes, there are always peers watching. It is difficult for students to have a private interaction with the teacher, to conceal a grade on a test, or to make a mistake without a witness.

Finally, over the course of the academic year, classes construct a joint *history*. This sixth characteristic means that classes, like families, remember past events—both positive and negative. They remember who got yelled at, who got away with being late to class, and what the teacher said about homework assignments. They remember who was going to have only "one more chance"—and if the teacher didn't follow through, they remember that too. The class memory means that teachers must work to shape a history of shared experiences that will support, rather than frustrate, future activities.

Crowded, competitive, contradictory, multidimensional, fast-paced, unpredictable, public—this portrait of the classroom highlights characteristics that we often overlook. We have begun the book with this portrait because we believe that *effective organization and management require an understanding of the unique features of the classroom.* Many of the management problems that beginning teachers encounter can be traced back to their failure to understand the complex setting in which they work.

Past experiences with children and adolescents may also mislead beginning teachers. For example, you may have tutored an individual student who was having academic difficulties, or perhaps you have been a camp counselor or a swim-club instructor. Although these are valuable experiences, they are very different from teaching in classrooms. Teachers do not work one-on-one with students in a private room; they seldom lead recreational activities that participants have themselves selected. Teachers do not even work with people who have chosen to be present. Instead, *teachers work with captive groups of students, on academic agendas that students have not helped to set, in a crowded, public setting.* Within this setting, teachers must carry out the fundamental tasks of classroom management.

DEFINITION, FRAMEWORK, AND GUIDING PRINCIPLES

Classroom management is often thought of as getting students to behave by using rules, rewards, and penalties. But it is much more than that. We define classroom management as the actions teachers take to *establish and sustain a caring, orderly environment that fosters students' academic learning as well as their social and emotional growth.* From this perspective, *how* a teacher achieves order is as important as *whether* a teacher achieves order (Evertson & Weinstein, 2006). Keeping this in mind, let's consider three hypothetical teachers with very different approaches to classroom management (Walker, 2008, 2009).

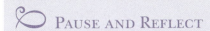

PAUSE AND REFLECT

Before going any further, jot down the words that come to mind when you hear the phrase "classroom management." Then write the answer to this question: "What is the goal of classroom management?" After reading the next section, compare your goal statement with the statement in the book. Are they similar? Different?

- Teacher A thinks that the most important aspect of classroom management is to create a warm classroom environment so that students will enjoy school and feel they are valued. He tries to be sensitive, empathetic, and caring. He makes few academic or behavioral demands on students, believing that they should have the autonomy to make their own decisions. He says, "I realize that students sometimes think I'm a pushover, but I believe that giving them a lot of freedom will help them to develop a sense of responsibility for their own learning and behavior."

- Teacher B believes in running a tight ship where students know exactly how they're supposed to behave and what the consequences will be if they act inappropriately. She holds her students to high standards of academic performance and behavior and thinks it's important to be in absolute control. She shows little warmth or affection for her students, reprimands them in front of their peers, and frequently hands out punishments. She's proud of being a "no-nonsense teacher." She says, "I'm not here to be their friend. I'm here to teach. My students may think I'm strict, even mean, but one day they'll thank me for this."

- Teacher C is similar to Teacher A in that she also believes in creating a warm, caring environment in which students feel comfortable, connected, and valued. She tries to enhance students' sense of autonomy by providing opportunities for them to participate in decision making. She wants her students to behave not out of fear of punishment but out of a sense of personal responsibility. On the other hand, Teacher C resembles Teacher B in that she holds high expectations for student learning and behavior and thinks there must be consequences for inappropriate behavior. Unlike Teacher B, however, she takes the time to provide rationales for classroom rules and never humiliates students in front of their peers.

Borrowing terminology from the literature on parenting (Baumrind, 1978), we can characterize Teacher A as *permissive:* He provides a lot of warmth and affection but little if any leadership, and he makes few demands on his students. In contrast,

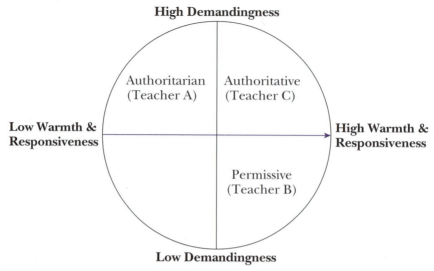

FIGURE 1.2   Three Approaches to Classroom Management

Teacher B is *authoritarian:* She is very demanding—even dictatorial—and exhibits little warmth, sensitivity, or responsiveness to students' needs. Teacher C is *authoritative,* combining the best of A and B: She is not only warm, empathetic, and supportive but also insists that her students work hard, adhere to classroom norms, and treat one another respectfully. Authoritative teachers can also be considered *"warm demanders"* (Bondy & Ross, 2008; Davis, Gabelman, & Wingfield, 2011; Kleinfeld, 1975; Ware, 2006).

Figure 1.2 is a graphic representation of these three types of teachers. Note that we have not discussed teachers who fall in the lower left quadrant (low demandingness and low warmth) because it is unlikely that they have a coherent perspective on classroom management.

Research has indicated that warm-demanding, authoritative teachers are most likely to achieve positive teacher-student relationships, respectful classroom climates, and better academic and social-emotional outcomes for students (Marzano, Marzano, & Pickering, 2003; J. M. T. Walker, 2008, 2009; Wubbels, Brekelmans, den Brok, & van Tartwijk, 2006). These positive outcomes are also seen at the school level. In a research study conducted in Virginia, secondary schools that students perceived to be high in both structure and support (warm-demanding schools) had lower student suspension rates, and the gap between suspension rates of Black and White students was smaller (Gregory, Cornell, & Fan, 2011). For these reasons, a warm-demanding approach to classroom management provides the framework for *Middle and Secondary Classroom Management.* In addition, five principles guide the content and organization of this book. (These are summarized in Table 1.1.)

The first principle is that *successful management fosters self-discipline and personal responsibility.* Let's be honest: Every teacher's worst fear is the prospect of losing control—of being helpless and ineffectual in the face of unruly, anarchic classes. Given this nightmare, it's tempting to create a coercive, top-down management

TABLE 1.1 Six Guiding Principles of Classroom Management
1. Successful classroom management fosters self-discipline and personal responsibility.
2. Most problems of disorder in classrooms can be avoided if teachers foster positive student-teacher relationships, implement engaging instruction, and use good preventive management strategies.
3. The need for order must not supersede the need for meaningful instruction.
4. Managing today's diverse classrooms requires the knowledge, skills, and predispositions to work with students from diverse racial, ethnic, language, and social class backgrounds. In other words, teachers must become "culturally responsive classroom managers."
5. Becoming an effective classroom manager requires social-emotional competence.
6. Becoming an effective classroom manager requires knowledge, reflection, hard work, and classroom experience.

system that relies heavily on the use of rewards and penalties to gain obedience (i.e., an authoritarian approach). Yet such an approach depends on constant monitoring and does little to teach students to make good choices about how to act. Obviously, teachers need to set limits and guide students' behavior, but the goal is an environment in which students behave appropriately not out of fear of punishment or desire for reward but out of a sense of personal responsibility.

The second principle is that *most problems of disorder in classrooms can be avoided if teachers foster positive relationships with students, implement engaging instruction, and use good preventive management strategies.* Let's look at each of these components in order. Positive teacher-student relationships are the very foundation of effective classroom management (Marzano, Marzano, & Pickering, 2003). Extensive research demonstrates that when students perceive their teachers to be supportive and caring, they are more likely to engage in cooperative, responsible behavior and adhere to classroom rules and norms (Hoy & Weinstein, 2006). Similarly, when students find academic activities meaningful, engrossing, and stimulating, they are less inclined to daydream or disrupt. Finally, a pivotal study by Jacob Kounin (1970) documented the fact that orderly classes are more the result of a teacher's ability to *prevent* student misconduct than of particular ways of *handling* it. As a result of Kounin's work, we now distinguish between *discipline*—responding to inappropriate behavior—and *classroom management*—ways of creating a caring, respectful environment that supports learning.

Third, *the need for order must not supersede the need for meaningful instruction.* Although instruction cannot take place in an environment that is chaotic and disorderly, an excessive focus on management can sometimes *hinder* instruction (Doyle, 1986, 2006). For example, a teacher may wish to divide the class into small groups for a cooperative learning activity. Yet her anxiety about the noise level and her fear that students might not work well together could make her abandon the small-group project and substitute an individual worksheet assignment. Academic work that is more intellectually and socially challenging may also be more challenging from a managerial perspective, yet it is crucial that teachers not sacrifice the curriculum to achieve an orderly classroom. As Doyle (1985) comments, "A well-run lesson that teaches nothing is just as useless as a chaotic lesson in which no academic work is possible" (p. 33).

The fourth principle is that *managing today's diverse classrooms requires the knowledge, skills, and predispositions to work with students from diverse racial, ethnic, language, and social class backgrounds. In other words, teachers must become "culturally responsive classroom managers"* (Weinstein, Curran, & Tomlinson-Clarke, 2003; Weinstein, Tomlinson-Clarke, & Curran, 2004). Sometimes, a desire to treat students fairly leads teachers to strive for "color-blindness" (Nieto, 2002), and educators are often reluctant to talk about cultural characteristics for fear of stereotyping. But definitions and expectations of appropriate behavior are culturally influenced, and conflicts are likely to occur if we ignore our students' cultural backgrounds. Geneva Gay (2006) provides a telling example of what can happen when there is a "cultural gap" between teachers and students. She notes that African Americans frequently use "evocative vocabulary" and "inject high energy, exuberance, and passion" into their verbal communication (p. 355). European American teachers may interpret such speech as rude or vulgar and feel compelled to chastise the students or even impose a punishment. Because the students see nothing wrong with what they said, they may resent and resist the teacher's response. As Gay notes: "The result is a cultural conflict that can quickly escalate into disciplinary sanctions in the classroom or referrals for administrative action" (p. 355).

To avoid such situations, we need to become aware of our own culturally based assumptions, biases, and values and reflect on how these influence our expectations for behavior and our interactions with students. By bringing our cultural biases to a conscious level, we are less likely to misinterpret the behaviors of our culturally different students and treat them inequitably. In addition, we must acquire cultural content knowledge. We must learn, for example, about our students' family backgrounds and their culture's norms for interpersonal relationships. Obviously, this knowledge must not be used to categorize or stereotype, and it is critical that we recognize the significant individual differences that exist among members of the same cultural group. Nonetheless, cultural content knowledge can be useful in developing *hypotheses* about students' behavior (Weiner, 1999).

The fifth principle is that *becoming an effective classroom manager requires social-emotional competence* (SEC). If teachers are to promote students' ability to be empathetic, interact in cooperative and respectful ways, control their impulses, resolve conflicts peacefully, and make responsible decisions, they themselves must have a high degree of SEC (Jennings & Greenberg, 2009). Socially and emotionally competent teachers are aware of their emotions and understand their emotional strengths and weaknesses. They also have the capacity to perceive and understand the emotions of others and to recognize the dynamics of classroom situations. When students behave in ways that provoke strong, negative reactions such as anger and despair, teachers with SEC know how to manage their emotions and their behavior so they can deal with the situations constructively and can preserve their relationships with students. In sum, SEC underlies teachers' ability to develop positive relationships with students and to create a caring, respectful classroom environment.

Another important aspect of SEC is teachers' ability to engage in self-care because teaching is a high-stress profession in which relationships (with students, colleagues, administrators, and parents) are pivotal. It is critical that you take care of yourself and support your colleagues; Cody (2013) has provided some suggestions. One first-year teacher we know had this to say about self-care:

> *The best alteration I've made that has had a big impact on my teaching and comfort level in the classroom was giving up caffeine. This was something that definitely took some thought and dedication. However, it's helped me drastically with that daily anxiety hurdle and with my pacing; there was a pretty stark contrast between the caffeinated Mr. T pushing the class at a fairly rigorous pace, and the relaxed, tea-drinking teacher who takes time for more frequent formative checks and feedback. My students seem to prefer this new tone—one of a teacher taking the time to establish a connection and making them feel more directly cared about, rather than the teacher just showing up with a mug and going through the day's lesson. It's been productive, I think, to show the students that I actually took a step to try and make their learning experience better, and to illustrate my commitment to wanting to do my job well.*

Our final principle is that *effective classroom management requires knowledge, reflection, hard work, and classroom experience.* Classroom management cannot be reduced to a set of recipes or a list of "how to's." Similarly, teachers cannot achieve well-managed classrooms by following "gut instinct" or doing "what feels right." Classroom management is a *learned craft.* That means that you must become familiar with the knowledge base that undergirds effective management and then learn to implement this knowledge in actual classroom settings. At the end of each chapter, we provide scenarios and problem-solving activities to assist you in analyzing situations, generating solutions, and making thoughtful decisions, but it is only in the complex setting of the classroom that you will learn to do this in "real time."

LESSONS FROM RESEARCH AND PRACTICE

Middle and Secondary Classroom Management weaves together concepts and principles derived from research with the wisdom and experiences of five real teachers. As you read the chapters that follow, you will learn about the classes they teach and about the physical constraints of their rooms. You will hear them reflect on their rules and routines and watch as they teach them to students. You will find out about the ways they try to respond to problem behaviors. In sum, *this book focuses on real decisions made by real teachers as they manage the complex environment of the classroom.* By sharing their stories, we do not mean to suggest that their ways of managing classrooms are the only effective ways. Rather, our goal is to illustrate how five reflective, caring, but very different individuals approach the tasks involved in classroom management. We introduce the teachers (in alphabetical order) below. Table 1.2 provides an overview of the teachers and the districts in which they teach.

Fred Cerequas: Social Studies

Fred Cerequas ("Ser-a-kwas") works in a school district that has a reputation for being innovative. This well-regarded school district currently has about 9,100 students and is gaining more than 200 a year. The student population is also becoming

TABLE 1.2 Overview of Featured Teachers and Their Districts

Teacher's Name	Subject	District Size (students)	District Students Qualified for Free/Reduced Lunch (percent)	District Ethnic/ Racial Diversity
Fred Cerequas	Social Studies	7,500	12	Predominantly European American
Donna Chambless	Language Arts	52,000	63	Predominantly Latino
Donnie Collins	Mathematics	6,500	80	Approximately half Latino and half African American
Sandra Krupinski	Chemistry	1,650	26	Approximately half European American and half a mix of African American, Latino, and Asian American
Christina Vreeland	English	12,900	13	Predominantly European American

increasingly diverse; it is now 64 percent European American, 20 percent Asian American, 10 percent African American, and 6 percent Latino. More than 50 different first languages are spoken—in particular, Spanish, Gujarati, Hindi, Cantonese,

Fred Cerequas

and Arabic—and the socioeconomic range is striking. Although people think of the community as middle- to upper-middle-class, a sizable number of its children live in low-cost mobile home parks. About 12 percent are eligible for the federal free or reduced-price lunch program. The high school houses 1,800 students in grades 9 through 12.

Fred's route to teaching social studies was circuitous. As the son of factory workers who had to leave school for economic reasons, Fred went into the United States Army after high school. He worked as an information specialist in Alaska, where he had a radio and television show and wrote for several army newspapers. Upon discharge, he began to work his way through college by driving a school bus for high school students. It was then that he discovered he was able to "connect with kids" and decided to earn a teaching certificate. He's taught in the same district for his entire career—a total of 34 years. Far from being burned out, Fred still believes he learns as much from his students as they do from him.

Fred currently teaches five classes a day, including U.S. History I; law, government, and politics; and non-Western history. He articulates his goals for his students by telling the story of Tanida, a senior he had last year. After learning about the problems of women and children in developing countries, Tanida arranged for her classmates to sponsor a little girl in Africa through the organization Save the Children. To Fred, Tanida's efforts represent a combination of knowledge and compassion, and it is this combination that he strives for in his classes. He tells us:

I believe *real* teachers are cultivators. They nurture the seeds of wisdom in their students by helping them become independent, eager learners who combine experience and knowledge with the genuine concern for others that gives life its meaning.

Fred admits that his goals are not easily achieved in today's typical high school, where "the whole system seems geared to efficiency rather than humanity." Nonetheless, Fred is energetic and optimistic, and he demands a lot from his students. Early in the fall, for example, Fred led a discussion on the social institutions common to all cultures. Although students were generally cooperative, about one-half of the class wasn't fully engaged. Fred stopped the lesson and addressed the students' apathy in his characteristically direct, down-to-earth manner:

Listen, we don't study junk in here. What we're doing in here is trying to understand processes of change. *This affects us; this stuff can make a difference in your life.* And if you can be more than just bored seniors, we can do some really important stuff in here.

After class, Fred sat in the teachers' room reflecting on the students' resistance and detachment. He spoke of the skepticism and detachment frequently displayed by students, particularly seniors; he acknowledged the difficulty of convincing them that what they were studying held meaning for their lives. Nonetheless, he vowed to "convert" them. Given Fred's commitment and passion for teaching, we had little doubt that he would succeed. After all, according to Fred, "*Teacher* is not a word that describes what I do for a living; rather, it defines who I am."

Donna Chambliss

Donna Chambliss: Language Arts

Donna teaches eighth-grade language arts in a sprawling, urban district with 97 schools. Of the approximately 52,000 students in this district, 61 percent are Latino, 24 percent are European American, 6 percent are African American, 4 percent are Native American, 2 percent are Asian American, and 3 percent have mixed ethnicity. Approximately 73 percent qualify for the federal free or reduced-price lunch program. Donna's school enrolls approximately 500 students in grades six, seven, and eight, and the school's needs are great. It has no counselors and no librarians, and subjects such as art, music, and languages have been eliminated. Although it was once considered a "tough" school with frequent episodes of violence, they have decreased in recent years as a result of efforts to enhance communication among parents, administration, and teachers.

Donna's path to having her own classroom wasn't straightforward, but in one way or another, she was always involved in teaching:

 There are some things that are just a part of your soul. Teaching is in my soul. I got a chance to do other things—I was a bank teller, a travel agent, a stay-at-home mother—but in every position I found myself teaching people how to do things. When my two daughters were in school, I was so involved in their

education that teachers and administrators kept telling me I should go back to school and get certified. After 15 years of teaching as a volunteer, I did. I always knew I was meant to be a teacher. I have a natural, ongoing curiosity about everything, and I want to impart that to my students.

Donna teaches five 1-hour periods in a row—147 students in all—and works in the library during her 30-minute lunch period on Mondays, Wednesdays, and Fridays. It's a taxing schedule, but Donna's energy and enthusiasm are evident from the moment students enter the room. Also evident is her commitment to creating an environment in which every student is a valued individual. For example, instead of simply saying students' names when calling roll, Donna says "good morning" to each student: "Good morning, Manuel." "Good morning, Desiree." In turn, students respond with "good morning" to Donna (although some can't break the habit of saying "here").

In addition to fostering a welcoming, respectful atmosphere, Donna strives to emulate her high school teachers (in Anchorage, Alaska) who pushed her to think on her own and to understand that there is never just one way to an answer. She says she always found it hard to sit still in classes where teachers "talked at students" for the whole period, so she emphasizes inquiry, collaboration, and project-based instruction. During each hour-long period, Donna is everywhere, directing lessons that are varied and brisk and require students' active participation. One of her major goals is to teach her students "how to link information and to make connections," so her lessons often incorporate social studies (the history of the suffrage movement), art (opportunities for drawing and learning about famous artists), world language (poetry in Italian and Spanish), and geography (she makes frequent reference to the United States and world maps on a wall in her classroom).

Reflecting on the many students she has taught in her seven years of full-time teaching, Donna comments that she especially "loves working with underperforming kids." As she puts it, "I look for the ones who think they can't do it, who have given up, and are just skating by. Then I start talking about something like vampires, and they perk up." Donna acknowledges the difficulties many of her students face: Some are angry, some have special needs that have gone undiagnosed and unsupported until eighth grade, some come from dysfunctional families, and all of them are faced with the pressures of high-stakes standardized testing. Nonetheless, she says:

 These kids are incredible. I'm in awe of them—their willingness to participate, their ability to recall what they've learned, their personal pride. Kids like this challenge me to continue to work hard and to grow. I love it when I hear them say, "You're tough, Miss, but you're the best teacher."

Donnie Collins: Mathematics

Donnie teaches in a mid-sized urban district that serves 6,500 students in 10 schools; 54 percent of the students are Latino and 41 percent are African American. Many of the children come from poor or low-income families, evidenced by the fact that 80 percent of the students qualify for the federal free or reduced-price lunch program. The high school currently accommodates 788 students in grades 9 through 12.

Donnie teaches two 80-minute classes at the high school—Algebra I and a special review course for students who have failed the mathematics portion of the state

Donnie Collins

exam required for graduation. She then drives to a nearby elementary school where she teaches mathematics to eighth-graders in the gifted and talented program.

Being a teacher was Donnie's childhood dream. "As a child I always wanted to play school," she recalls, "and I always wanted to be the teacher, never one of the pupils." Reflecting on this early dream, Donnie acknowledges the influence of her grandmother, who had been an elementary teacher before she opened a beauty school and shop. Although Donnie's parents were farmers, they recognized that farming was not for her. As Donnie puts it, "My calling was to be a teacher."

Donnie acknowledges the influence of two of her own teachers. Her fifth-grade teacher, Mrs. Poole, was intimidating at first, but Donnie soon realized that Mrs. Poole wasn't mean; she was just concerned about students' achievement and well-being. "From Mrs. Poole, I learned about the importance of maintaining discipline, about the need to be firm and fair, and the value of keeping in touch with parents." Later, in high school, Donnie encountered Miss Anchrum, a young math teacher fresh out of college with lots of new ideas about how to make math exciting: "Miss Anchrum made math real, and she would accept nothing less than our best." From her, Donnie learned the importance of motivating students and holding high expectations.

Donnie eventually earned both a bachelor's degree and a master's degree in mathematics, along with certification to teach. But the impact of Mrs. Poole and Miss Anchrum has stayed with her, and her teaching reflects the lessons she learned from them. When asked about her goals, she answers without hesitation:

I want the same things my teachers wanted. I want my students to become creative, independent thinkers; I want them to be able to function effectively in our everyday world; I want them to make a positive contribution to society. When students say, "Oh, Ms. Collins, I don't need to know this; all I need to know is how to count my money," I tell them: "But first you have to *make* the money, and once you've made your money, you have to *keep* it. And you have to know math to do that."

Donnie's goals are not achieved easily. She is frustrated by those students "who can't see beyond today," who cause disruption, and who create problems for those who do want to learn. As she puts it, "Education is just not a priority for many of my students. *Survival* is the priority." Sometimes she has to forgo a math lesson in order to discuss the more immediate problems of her students: conflicts with families, pregnancy, parenting (the high school has a day care center for the children of its students), running away from home, violence in the community, and drugs. With a certain amount of resignation, Donnie comments:

If you try to go ahead with a math lesson when they're all riled up about something that has happened at home or in the neighborhood, you're doomed. There's just no point to it. It's better to put away the quadratic equations and *talk*.

Despite the difficulties, Donnie is still enthusiastic and optimistic about her chosen career. Listening to her speak about the goals she has for her students and the satisfactions she derives from teaching makes it is obvious that the legacies of Mrs. Poole and Miss Anchrum live on in this mathematics teacher.

Sandra Krupinski: Chemistry

Sandy Krupinski teaches in a small, extremely diverse community. The district's three schools serve children who live in large, expensive houses as well as those from low-income apartment complexes. The student population of 1,650 is 53 percent European American, 17 percent African American, 14 percent Latino, and 16 percent Asian American. About 26 percent of the children qualify for the federal free or reduced-price lunch program. The high school currently houses 650 students in grades 7 through 12.

This year, Sandy teaches three classes of chemistry—two college prep and one advanced placement. Her classes are more diverse than in previous years. In her sixth-period class, for example, there are five African Americans, one Latino, one Asian American, and one whose family has come from India. The class also includes a student classified as emotionally disturbed, one with Tourette's syndrome, and one with oppositional defiance disorder.

Sandy's love of science was awakened when she was a student at the very same high school, and teaching seemed to be the obvious, logical career. Her father, a construction worker, and her mother, an office manager for an insurance company, applauded the decision to be a teacher, proud that Sandy would be the first in her family to attend college.

Sandy Krupinski

Sandy is very clear about what she is trying to achieve with her students. She sees chemistry as a vehicle for helping students develop problem-solving skills, self-discipline ("a new experience for some"), and self-confidence:

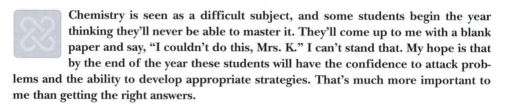

Chemistry is seen as a difficult subject, and some students begin the year thinking they'll never be able to master it. They'll come up to me with a blank paper and say, "I couldn't do this, Mrs. K." I can't stand that. My hope is that by the end of the year these students will have the confidence to attack problems and the ability to develop appropriate strategies. That's much more important to me than getting the right answers.

To achieve this goal, Sandy tries hard to create an accepting, nonthreatening atmosphere in her class. On the first day of school, for example, she asks students to answer four questions: (1) How do you learn best? (2) What do you expect to be excited about in chemistry? (3) What do you expect to be nervous about? and (4) What can I do to help? Their responses are revealing. One student shares his fear of talking in front of the class. Several confide that they are anxious about the difficulty of the course, particularly the need to memorize "lots of itsy, bitsy facts." One girl with limited proficiency in English writes about the fact that her "language is not good," and asks Sandy to speak slowly. When students return on the second day of class, Sandy thanks them for sharing information that will help her to help them and reassures them that she will be patient, that they will proceed slowly, and that she will always be available for extra help outside of class. Afterward, thinking about why she takes the time to do this, Sandy comments, "As I talk about each fear they've expressed, I can actually see their shoulders drop, and I can feel the anxiety level in the class go down."

Sandy may be sensitive to students' anxieties about chemistry, but she still communicates high expectations and a no-nonsense attitude. This year, during an unexpectedly long "vacation" brought about by a fierce blizzard, Sandy e-mailed all of her Advanced Placement students to give them an assignment "so they wouldn't fall behind." Her students weren't surprised; one of them told her, "Oh, Mrs. K., we just *knew* you'd contact us!" Incidents such as this have helped to build Sandy Krupinski's reputation as a teacher who is passionate about chemistry and fiercely committed to students' learning.

Christina Vreeland: English

Christina's district is large and sprawling with 24 schools and 12,900 students. The student body is predominantly European American (61 percent), but the racial and ethnic diversity is steadily increasing (African American, 8 percent; Latino, 10 percent; Asian American, 20 percent; Native American, 1 percent), and 13 percent of the students qualify for the federal free or reduced-price lunch program. Christina is in her

Christina Vreeland

second year of teaching in one of the high schools, which houses 900 students from 10 different towns. Because her school uses block scheduling, Christina meets three 84-minute classes a day—two 10th grade English classes and one basic skills class for students who have failed the state test required for graduation.

Christina grew up in the community, the daughter of a truck driver whose family emigrated from Puerto Rico when he was three, and an office worker raised in a nearby town. Christina attended the state university where she majored in English and minored in Spanish. After receiving her bachelor's degree, she continued on for a master's degree and certification in English Education.

Like Donnie and Sandy, Christina never really considered a career other than teaching. Even as a little girl, Christina "always had to be the teacher and tell everyone else what to do." But it wasn't until her junior year in high school that she began to think seriously about the kind of teacher she wanted to be:

 I had an excellent teacher, Helaine Rasmussen. We had to do a big term paper that year. . . . 20 pages! But Mrs. Rasmussen had former students come in and talk about how they had done the project, and she took us through it step by step, so that everything just seemed to fall into place. We were able to compose this paper we never thought we would be able to do.

Then in my senior year, I had Angela Korodan for honors English. She started off by meeting with us at the end of junior year to give us the summer reading assignments that we had to mail her over the summer. On the first few days of school, we sat in a circle, and talked about ourselves. These were people I had known for a long time, but I still learned things. She talked too; she told us about how she became a teacher, and how she had been a nun.

From Mrs. Rasmussen, Christina learned the importance of being rigorous and systematic. From Mrs. Korodan, she learned about the value of building communication and a sense of community. These are lessons that Christina tries hard to remember now that she is on the other side of the desk.

One of Christina's major goals is to help her students "make a place for reading and writing in their everyday lives." She explains:

 I think that lots of times English teachers are so passionate about literature and analysis of literature that we forget that our students are not preparing to be English teachers. . . . What I need to do is foster the kind of reading and writing that will be useful for *them* and to create the *desire* to read and write.

Despite her idealism, Christina sometimes feels exhausted by all the demands of teaching. One day in midwinter, she expressed some of the doubts she had recently been experiencing:

 For the last few days, I've been questioning, "Why do I want to be here? Why do I say I enjoy this?" And then today, we had a great discussion about the novel we're reading. The kids really got into it. I had kids making important points—I didn't have to ask the leading questions each time. And they had

the *desire* to discuss with each other and to read more. . . . At the end of the class [in the English Department office], the other teachers looked at me and saw me smiling. They knew I'd been feeling overwhelmed. One of them asked, "Why are you so happy?" And I told them, "I just had an experience that renewed my faith in my ability to do this for the rest of my life."

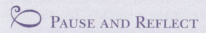 PAUSE AND REFLECT

Now that you've met the teachers, take a minute to think about their personalities and approaches to classroom management. Do you feel a special kinship with any of the five teachers? If your answer is yes, why do you feel this way? Next, reflect on your own middle and high school experiences. Were there any teachers whom you would characterize as especially effective classroom managers? What did they do that made them especially effective? Are there any similarities between these teachers and the teachers you've just read about?

WHAT DO THE STUDENTS SAY?

While working with these five teachers, we became curious about the perceptions of the students in their classrooms. In particular, we were interested in why they thought students were cooperative and well behaved in some classes and uncooperative and ill behaved in others as well as their views of the particular classes we were observing. In each class, the teacher left the room so that the students could talk more comfortably. We explained that we wanted the "student perspective" on classroom management and asked them to explain in writing "why kids behave in some classes," "why kids misbehave in some classes," and "how kids generally behave in this class and why." After students had a chance to write down their thoughts, they shared their responses.

Across classes, students demonstrated extraordinary consistency. Whether they were in 8th grade or 12th grade or in basic skills classes or honors classes, students' responses reflected three main themes. First, students stressed the importance of teachers' *relating to students with caring and respect.* They talked about teachers who "can relate to our teenage lifestyle," who "try to get to know us and understand us," who "create trust," who "help you and explain what they want," and "who work with you, not against you." A student in one of Fred's classes put it this way: "When a teacher takes some time to get to know students and shows some humor or shares a bit of their personal life, students may relate to them better." And one of Christina's students wrote this:

> I want to cooperate in this class because she is not all serious, she can laugh, have fun, and still get all the work done. Students can tell when a teacher wants to help you and teach you, and when they just do it because they have to.

Clearly, not all teachers relate to students in this way. Students wrote about teachers "who put students down," who "don't care," and who are "beyond strict." One student wrote, "If a teacher doesn't think about what the students are feeling, they won't like him/her. Students can always detect those sort of things. Dislike = misbehave." Many students used the word respect in both their written and oral comments, and we pressed them to tell us what "respecting students" looks like. They didn't have difficulty: Teachers respect students when they give them their grades privately, when they come prepared for class, when they "scold a student quietly instead of in class in front of others," when they allow students to give their own opinions, and when they make sure that students treat each other well (e.g., they don't allow kids to talk when another kid is talking). Teachers also show respect when they take time to help students who are confused. Donna's students, for example, emphasized her willingness to "explain everything thoroughly (really thoroughly)" and contrasted her with "teachers who just give you a paper and tell you to do it."

A second theme that students discussed was the need for teachers to set limits and enforce them. This was expressed in a number of different ways: "Teachers need to be a strong authority figure"; "teachers need to tell kids what they expect and give no second tries"; "teachers need to show strength"; "teachers need to be strict (but not mean)"; "teachers need to come off as someone who has control." What these responses clearly convey is students' lack of respect for teachers who are too permissive, who are "too cowardly to take charge," and who "let kids run all over them." One student wrote: "Kids misbehave when the teacher lets them pretty much do whatever they want. If they're disrupting class the teacher will try to go on with her class by maybe trying to speak above the person disrupting the class or ignoring it." This view was reiterated in another student's response: "Usually misbehavior happens in classes when teachers are too lenient. Every class needs to have some time to relax and fool around, but the teacher should know the limit."

The final theme to emerge from students' comments was the importance of *teaching in a way that is motivating and interesting.* One of Donnie's students captured this widely shared perspective:

> *Teachers have to make the class fun, but organized. Have a lot of interaction between students and challenge them. . . . Sometimes teachers are boring. The class drags on and the students lose attention span towards the teacher and the class. If the teacher teaches in an old-fashion [sic] style, the kids become frustrated.*

These ideas were expressed in a number of ways: Teachers need to be knowledgeable and to *love* what they do ("kids can tell"); teachers need to teach in creative ways—not just out of the book; they need to get the whole class involved; they need to relate the material to students' lives. Although a lot of people used the word *fun,* one of Fred's students wrote, "Not everything can be fun; it doesn't have to be fun, but there are ways teachers can make it more interesting and more challenging." For Christina's students, the "cool things Mrs. Vreeland picks for us to do" were especially important because their classes are 84 minutes long.

These themes—*relating to students with caring and respect, setting limits and enforcing them, and teaching in a way that is motivating and interesting*—characterize the behavior of the five teachers featured in this book. As we watched them teach, we were repeatedly struck by the caring and sensitivity they showed to students by their authoritative, "no-nonsense" attitudes and by their efforts to stimulate students' interest and engagement in lessons. Students clearly recognized and appreciated the ability to combine these three characteristics. We will address these themes in the sections of the book that follow.

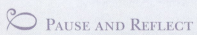

PAUSE AND REFLECT

After listening to these students discuss the characteristics of effective classroom managers—caring and respect, teaching in a way that is motivating and engaging, and firmness (the ability to set and enforce limits)—take a moment to reflect on your own strengths and weaknesses in these three areas. What do you think will be your greatest challenge?

CONCLUDING COMMENTS

Fred, Donna, Donnie, Sandy, and Christina teach different subjects in different settings. Grade levels range from 8th to 12th. Sandy, Fred, and Christina teach classes that are predominantly White (although still quite diverse), Donnie's classes are predominantly African American and Latino, and Donna's classes are predominantly Latino. Fred and Christina work in districts in which about 10 percent of the children are eligible for free or reduced-price lunch compared with 26 percent in Sandy's district, 63 percent in Donna's district, and 80 percent in Donnie's district. Sandy teaches an Advanced Placement class, and Donnie and Christina teach basic skills classes for students who have failed portions of the state test required for graduation. Donnie and Christina teach in schools that have adopted block scheduling, whereas Fred's and Sandy's classes are about 45 minutes, and Donna's are 60 minutes. To be effective, our five teachers must be sensitive and responsive to these differences in age, race, culture, socioeconomic conditions, achievement levels, and class duration.

Despite these differences, Fred, Donna, Donnie, Sandy, and Christina are alike in many ways. Obvious similarities emerge when they talk about the tasks of classroom management. Interestingly, when these five teachers speak about classroom management, they rarely use the words *discipline* or *punishment, confrontation* or *penalty.* Instead, they emphasize mutual respect; they talk about the importance of being organized and well prepared; they stress the need to develop a "caring community," in which all individuals are contributing, valued members (Schaps, 2003; Watson & Battistich, 2006); they speak about involving students and helping them to achieve.

It's important to remember that these teachers are real human beings working in the complex, uncertain environment of the classroom. Christina is in only her second year of teaching, and as she herself admits, she is "a novice when it comes to knowing what works." Fred, Donna, Donnie, and Sandy are experienced, skillful teachers who are extremely effective at preventing misbehavior, but even their classrooms are not free of problems. (In fact, Chapter 12 focuses specifically on the ways all five teachers deal with misbehavior.) Like all of us, these teachers make mistakes; they become frustrated and impatient; they sometimes fail to live up to their own images of the ideal teacher. By their own testimony, they are all still learning how to run more effective classrooms.

It is also important to remember that these five teachers do not follow recipes or prescriptions for classroom management, so their ways of interacting with students often look very different. Nonetheless, underlying the differences in behavior are the same guiding principles. The chapters that follow will try to convey the ways these five excellent teachers tailor the principles to fit their own particular contexts.

SUMMARY

This chapter examined some of the contradictions and special characteristics of classrooms. It argued that effective management requires an understanding of the unique features of the classroom environment and stressed the fact that teachers work with captive groups of students on academic agendas that students have not helped to set. Within this peculiar setting, teachers must work to create a caring, orderly environment that fosters students' learning and social and emotional growth.

Contradictions of the Classroom Environment

- Classrooms are crowded, yet students are often not allowed to interact.
- Students are expected to work together harmoniously, yet they may not know or like each other.
- Students are urged to cooperate, yet they often work in individual or competitive situations.
- Students are encouraged to be independent, yet they are also expected to conform to the teacher's dictates.
- Students are instructed to work slowly and carefully, but they have to be aware of the "press of time" in a 42- (or an 84-) minute period.

Characteristics of the Classroom Environment

- Multidimensionality
- Simultaneity
- Immediacy
- Unpredictability
- Lack of privacy
- History

Three Approaches to Classroom Management

- Permissive (low demandingness/high warmth and responsiveness)
- Authoritarian (high demandingness/low warmth and responsiveness)
- Authoritative or warm demanding (high demandingness/high warmth and responsiveness)

Guiding Principles of the Book

- Most problems of disorder can be avoided if teachers foster positive teacher-student relationships, implement engaging instruction, and use good preventive management strategies.
- The need for order must not supersede the need for meaningful instruction.
- Teachers must be "culturally responsive classroom managers."
- Becoming an effective classroom manager requires social-emotional competence (SEC).
- Becoming an effective classroom manager requires knowledge, reflection, hard work, and classroom experience.

Lessons from Research and Practice

This chapter introduced the five teachers whose thinking and experiences will be described throughout the rest of the book. For an overview of the featured teachers and their districts, see Table 1.2.

- Fred Cerequas (social studies)
- Donna Chambliss (language arts)
- Donnie Collins (mathematics)
- Sandra Krupinski (chemistry)
- Christina Vreeland (English)

Although these five teachers teach different subjects in very different settings, they are alike in many ways. In particular, they speak about classroom management in very similar terms: They emphasize the prevention of behavior problems, mutual respect, involving students in learning activities, and the importance of being organized and well prepared.

What Do the Students Say?

When asked why they behave well in certain classes but not in others, students consistently voiced three themes about teachers who promoted good behavior: relating to students with caring and respect, teaching in a way that is motivating and interesting, and setting limits and enforcing them. We will return to these three themes in subsequent chapters.

ACTIVITIES FOR SKILL BUILDING AND REFLECTION

In Class

1. In a small group, discuss the six characteristics of classroom environments and share your ideas about how these characteristics will affect you as a classroom teacher.

2. As a class, read *Miss Nelson Is Missing* by Harry Allard and James Marshall (1977). This classic children's book is about the "kids in Room 207"—"the worst-behaved class in the whole school"—and their teacher, gentle Miss Nelson. One day Miss Nelson doesn't come to school, and in her place is Miss Viola Swamp, a substitute who soon makes the children long for the days when Miss Nelson was their teacher. Using the three styles of classroom management introduced in this chapter, characterize the approaches used by Miss Nelson and Miss Swamp and reflect on what is needed to create an orderly but respectful environment.

3. In a group, discuss the three approaches to classroom management: permissive, authoritarian, and authoritative (warm demander). Think about teachers you have had who exemplify these three different approaches. What were your reactions to these teachers?

4. Review the biographies of each teacher included in this text. Identify three to four major ways in which the teachers are similar.

On Your Own

1. Think about the questions that Christina was pondering: *"Why do I want to be here? Why do I say I enjoy this?"* What is it that *you* want in your classes? What do *you* find enjoyable (or *think* you will find enjoyable) about teaching? Then consider the implications for classroom organization and management. In other words, if you want students to participate enthusiastically, what will you do to encourage their participation? If you want them to treat one another with respect and kindness, what will you do to create that kind of atmosphere?

2. Reflect on your past experiences with children and adolescents (e.g., tutoring, being a camp counselor). What did you learn from those experiences that might help you in the classroom?

For Your Portfolio

Pretend you are a teacher being featured in this book. What is *your* story? Think about what motivated you to choose a career in teaching and what your goals are. Write down some of the key points you would want included in your own introduction. (This piece of writing can be a useful document to review before interviewing and can serve as inspiration during the often challenging first year of teaching.)

FOR FURTHER READING

Burant, T., Christensen, L., Salas, K. D., & Walters, S. (Eds.) (2010). *The new teacher book: Finding purpose, balance, and hope during your first years in the classroom.* Milwaukee, WI: Rethinking Schools.

   This book was written to inspire new teachers to hold on to the reasons that they became teachers: a deep caring for students, the opportunity to spark student growth and development, and the desire to be involved in work that matters. Chapter topics include getting off to a good start, building a classroom community, and handling discipline issues.

Charney, R. S. (2002). *Teaching children to care: Classroom management for ethical and academic growth, K–8.* Greenfield, MA: Northeast Foundation for Children.

   Based on Charney's experiences as a teacher and informed by work on the *Responsive Classroom* approach, this book illustrates ways of managing classrooms to nurture students' social and intellectual growth. Although the book is geared to elementary school, it is also appropriate for teachers in middle school and junior high.

Cushman, K. (2003). *Fires in the bathroom: Advice for teachers from high school students.* New York: The New Press.

Cushman, K., & Rogers, L. (2008). *Fires in the middle school bathroom: Advice for teachers from middle schoolers.* New York: The New Press.

   For each of these books, the authors conducted extensive interviews of 40 students from urban areas across the country. Students were asked what they wished their teachers knew about them and about how they best learn. A clear message in both books is that when students talk about instruction, what comes up first is how they feel about their teachers and how their teachers make them feel as learners.

Gregory, A., & Ripski, M. (2008). Adolescent trust in teachers: Implications for behavior in the high school classroom. *School Psychology Review, 37*(3), 337–353.

   This study examined the relationship between high school teachers' approaches to discipline and their students' behavior. Findings indicated that teachers who emphasized relationship building were less likely to have students who exhibited defiance.

Sell, S. (2013). Tech4CM. Retrieved from http://tech4cm.wikispaces.com/.

   This site provides links to technology tools for classroom management. The sections on the site correspond to many of the chapters in this text.

Walker, J. M. T. (Ed.) (2009). Authoritative classroom management: How control and nurturance work together. *Theory Into Practice, 48*(2), 122–129.

   This article draws from the research on parenting and child development to describe the three approaches to classroom management presented in this chapter. The author then uses case studies of three classrooms to illustrate how control and nurturance interact to influence student engagement and learning.

Weinstein, C. S. (Ed.) (2003). Classroom management in a diverse society. *Theory Into Practice, 42*(4).

   The articles in this special theme issue of *TIP* address different aspects of classroom management in a diverse society, but all of them reflect the idea that the fundamental task of classroom management is to create an inclusive, supportive, and caring environment.

ORGANIZATIONAL RESOURCES

REACH Center, www.reachctr.org. The REACH center provides curricula and training to promote multicultural and global awareness for elementary, middle, and high school classrooms.

What Kids Can Do, Inc. (WKCD), www.whatkidscando.org. This organization was founded to promote the perception of young people as valued resources, and to advocate for learning that engages students as knowledge creators, not simply test takers. The youth who concern WKCD most are those marginalized by poverty, race, and language.

PART II

Establishing an Environment for Learning

Don't smile until Christmas."

When the two of us went through our respective teacher education programs, that bit of folk advice was all we learned about preventing inappropriate behavior. The idea was to refrain from smiling during the first few months of school so that students would perceive you as stern and serious. Then, according to this way of thinking, they wouldn't dare act up.

Actually, our programs didn't talk much about student behavior at all; the overwhelming focus was on what to teach (curriculum) and how to teach it (instructional methods). On those rare occasions when we did discuss students' behavior, it was always in terms of *discipline*—what to do to individuals *after* an instance of misbehavior had occurred. When we graduated from our programs and entered teaching, our ability to create respectful, productive learning environments was more a matter of good instincts and luck than of any real knowledge.

Fortunately, the situation has changed a great deal over the last 35 years. Teacher education students can now learn research-based principles, concepts, and practices for creating orderly classrooms—and smiling is definitely encouraged. The emphasis has shifted from what to do *after misbehavior occurs* (discipline) to how to *prevent it in the first place.* Discipline is still important because prevention sometimes fails, but educators now talk about the much broader concept of *classroom management* (of which discipline is only one part). As we discussed in Chapter 1, we define classroom management as *the tasks teachers must carry out to establish a learning environment that is caring, inclusive, and productive.*

This section of the book addresses "beginning-of-the-year" tasks. Because most teachers immediately face arranging classroom furniture, Chapter 2 focuses on the physical environment. The chapter is intended to help you design a classroom setting that is safe, functional, and compatible with your academic and social goals. In Chapter 3, we examine ways to develop positive teacher-student relationships so that students feel respected and cared for. Chapter 4 focuses on the importance of promoting positive peer relationships and creating a sense of community. Chapter 5 turns to the task of establishing and teaching expectations for behavior. We stress the fact that shared behavioral expectations are essential if classrooms are to be orderly, productive environments. In Chapter 6, we discuss the importance of getting to know your students—understanding and appreciating the characteristics they all share as well as their individual, unique needs. Chapter 7 explores the benefits that accrue when teachers and families work together and suggests strategies for reaching out to families. Finally, Chapter 8 looks at the amount of time available for instruction and discusses ways to make sure you aren't wasting this previous resource. Throughout these chapters, we learn about the beliefs and practices of our five teachers as well as what research has to say on the topics discussed.

2 CHAPTER

Designing the Physical Environment

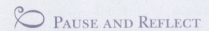

PAUSE AND REFLECT

You have probably spent more than 13,000 hours as a student in elementary and secondary classrooms. Undoubtedly some of these rooms were much more attractive and comfortable than others. Think about what made them that way. For example, was it the bulletin boards or posters? The presence of plants? The type and arrangement of the furniture? The lighting? The size or location of the room? Think about the specific characteristics that made these rooms pleasant environments in which to learn and then reflect on which ones are under the teacher's control. Keep these characteristics in mind as you read this chapter.

Discussions of classroom management at the secondary level often neglect the physical characteristics of the classroom. This is unfortunate because the *physical environment can influence the way teachers and students feel, think, and behave.* Careful planning of this environment—within the constraints of your daily schedule—is an integral part of good classroom management. Moreover, *creating a comfortable, functional classroom is one way to show your students that you care about them.*

The effects of the classroom setting can be both *direct* and *indirect* (Proshansky & Wolfe, 1974). For example, if students seated in straight rows are unable to carry on a class discussion because they can't hear one another, the *environment is directly hindering their participation.* Students might also be affected *indirectly* if they infer from the seating arrangement that the teacher does not really want them to interact. In this case, the arrangement of the desks is sending a message to the students about how they are supposed to behave. Their reading of this message would be accurate if the teacher had deliberately arranged the seats to inhibit discussion. More likely, however, the teacher genuinely desires class participation but has never thought about the link between the classroom environment and student behavior.

This chapter is intended to help you develop *"environmental competence"* (Martin, 2002; Steele, 1973): awareness of the physical environment and its impact and the ability to use that environment to meet your goals. Even when they share space or move from room to room, environmentally competent teachers are sensitive to the messages communicated by the physical setting. They plan spatial arrangements that support their instructional plans. They know how to evaluate the effectiveness of a classroom environment. They are alert to the possibility that physical factors might contribute to behavioral problems, and they modify at least some aspects of the classroom environment when the need arises.

Throughout this chapter, we will illustrate major points with examples from the classrooms of the five teachers you have just met. Donnie, Fred, and Sandy teach their classes in one room this year, although they share their room with other teachers. Christina has to share *and* move; another English teacher uses her room during the first two blocks of the day when Christina has prep period, and she teaches her basic skills class in another room. Donna is the luckiest: She gets to stay in her own room throughout the day and shares it with no other teacher.

SIX FUNCTIONS OF THE CLASSROOM SETTING

All physical settings serve six basic functions: security and shelter, social contact, symbolic identification, task instrumentality, pleasure, and growth (Steele, 1973). These six functions provide a useful framework for thinking about the the classroom and make it clear that designing the physical setting is far more than decorating a few bulletin boards.

Security and Shelter

The most fundamental function of all built environments is to provide security and shelter. Like homes, office buildings, and stores, classrooms should provide protection from bad weather, noise, extreme heat or cold, and noxious odors. Sadly, even this most basic function is sometimes not fulfilled, and teachers and students must battle highway noise, broken windows, and leaky roofs. In those situations, it is difficult to meet any of the other functions. Physical security is a *precondition* that must be satisfied, at least to some extent, before the environment can serve students' and teachers' other, higher-level needs.

Physical security is a particularly important issue in classes such as science, home economics, woodworking, and art where students come into contact with potentially dangerous supplies and equipment. It is essential that teachers of these subjects know about safety guidelines regarding properly handling, storing, and labeling course materials. The National Science Teachers Association has established recommendations for safe storage, safety equipment, and effective layouts as well as student/teacher and student/space ratios in science classrooms (Motz, Biehle, & West, 2007). In her classroom, Sandy tries to anticipate where accidents might occur and to arrange supplies in a way that minimizes risk. For example, when her students are doing a lab that involves two chemicals that are harmful when mixed together, she sets one chemical out and keeps one under her control. In this way, students have to ask her for it ("I'm ready for my nitric acid."), and she can double-check that they are following correct lab procedures.

Physical security is also a matter of special concern if you have students who use wheelchairs, leg braces, or crutches or who have unsteady gaits. Navigating through crowded classrooms can be a formidable and dangerous task. Be sensitive to the need for wide aisles and space to store walkers and crutches when not in use.

Often school environments provide *physical* security but fail to offer *psychological* security—the feeling that this is a good, comfortable place to be. Psychological security is especially crucial for students who live in impoverished, unstable, or unsafe home environments. One way to enhance psychological security is to make sure your classroom contains some "softness." With their linoleum floors, concrete block walls, and formica surfaces, classrooms tend to be "hard" places. But students (and adults) tend to feel more secure and comfortable in environments that contain items that are soft or responsive to their touch. If you are lucky enough to have your own classroom, think about ways that you can incorporate elements of softness into the environment (e.g., plants, an aquarium, fabric, varying textures).

Another way to increase psychological security is to arrange classroom space so that students have as much freedom from interference as possible. In the crowded classroom environment, it is easy to become distracted. You need to make sure that students' desks are not too near areas of heavy traffic (e.g., the pencil sharpener, the front door). This is particularly important for students with attention-deficit hyperactivity disorder (ADHD), a neurobiological disability that interferes with an individual's ability to sustain attention. Students with ADHD have difficulty focusing attention, concentrating, listening, following instructions, and organizing tasks. (See Chapter 6 for additional information on ADHD.) You can help students with ADHD by seating them away from noisy, high-traffic areas, near well-focused students, and as close to you as possible so that it's easy to make eye contact (Carbone, 2001).

You can also enhance psychological security by setting up a few cubicles where students who want more enclosure can work alone or providing folding cardboard dividers (three pieces of heavy cardboard bound together) that students can place on their desks. All of us need to "get away from it all" at times, but research suggests that opportunities for privacy are particularly important for students who are distractible or have difficulty relating to their peers (Weinstein, 1982).

Social Contact

INTERACTION AMONG STUDENTS

As you plan the arrangement of students' desks, you need to think carefully about how much interaction you want among students because different arrangements facilitate different amounts of contact. Clusters of desks promote social contact because individuals are close together and can have direct eye contact with those across from them. In clusters, students can work together on activities, share materials, have small-group discussions, and help each other with assignments. This arrangement is most appropriate if you plan to emphasize collaboration and cooperative learning activities. But it is unwise—even inhumane—to seat students in clusters and then forbid them to interact. If you do that, students receive two contradictory messages: the seating arrangement is communicating that it's okay to interact but your verbal message is just the opposite!

In contrast to clusters, rows of desks reduce interaction among students and make it easier for them to concentrate on individual assignments. This appears particularly true for students who have behavior problems and learning disabilities. Researchers found that on-task behavior dropped by half and disruptive behavior increased by three times when "behaviourally troublesome" adolescents with moderate learning problems moved from rows to tables (Wheldall & Lam, 1987).

Rows also direct students' attention toward the teacher, so they are particularly appropriate for teacher-centered instruction. But there are a number of variations on this theme. For example, you might consider putting desks in horizontal rows. (See Figure 2.1.) This arrangement still orients students toward the teacher but provides them with close "neighbors" on each side. Another variation is shown in Figure 2.2 in

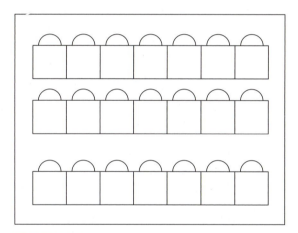

FIGURE 2.1   A Horizontal Arrangement

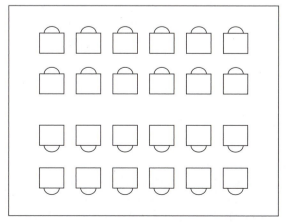

FIGURE 2.2   Rows Facing Each Other

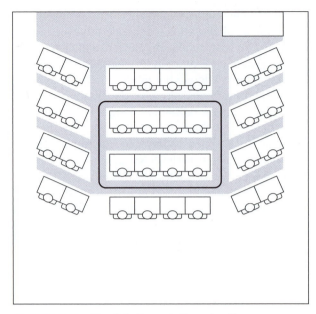

FIGURE 2.3   Fredric Jones's Interior Loop
Arrangement

Source: F. H. Jones, P. Jones, J. L. Jones, F. Jones, & B. T. Jones.
(2007). *Tools for Teaching: Discipline, Instruction, Motivation.* Santa
Cruz, CA: Fredric H. Jones & Associates. Reprinted with permission.

which desks are arranged two deep in rows that face each other with a wide aisle down the middle of the classroom. Because this arrangement allows students to see each other and to interact more easily, it is particularly useful for class discussions. Still another row option (Figure 2.3) has an "interior loop" that allows you close proximity to all students (F. H. Jones, P. Jones, J. L. Jones, F. Jones, & B. T. Jones, 2007).

Fred, Christina, and Donna have all chosen to arrange their desks in rows (see Figure 2.4 for Donna's arrangement); however, all three teachers regularly have students move into other configurations when appropriate (for example, clusters for small-group work). This year, Christina's large classes have led to experimentation with a new arrangement for whole-group discussions (see Figure 2.5):

 I stand in the center of the room, and I tell all the kids to turn their desks to a 45-degree angle, so that they're all facing the center. Then I sit outside the circle; it helps me to keep my mouth shut.

Figure 2.6 illustrates the way Sandy has arranged her classroom. As you can see, the space is divided into a whole-group instructional area where students sit at clusters of trapezoidal tables, and a laboratory or work area. Although she is unhappy that students are packed so closely together during presentations and homework review, Sandy wants to get as many students as possible in a row so that all students are relatively close to the front of the room.

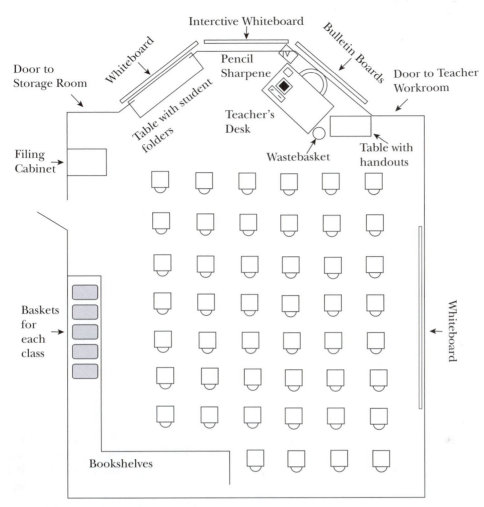

FIGURE 2.4   Sandy's Room Arrangement

In Donnie's classroom, two-person tables have replaced the standard desks she once used. She started out by arranging the tables in groups of two, forming horizontal rows, but continues to try other arrangements as the need arises (see Figure 2.7 for one example). She even allows individual students to move their tables into configurations that they feel are more comfortable. Interestingly, although Donnie's tables are attractive and facilitate small-group work, she actually prefers desks, which she can more easily arrange in a horseshoe.

Christina, Donna, Fred, and Donnie show a willingness to rearrange their rooms that is not typical. Indeed, teachers generally prefer to change the instructional format to fit the existing furniture arrangement rather than changing the arrangement to fit the instructional format (Kutnick, Blatchford, Clark, McIntyre, & Baines, 2005). Thus, teachers who have student desks in rows might opt for paired discussion rather than cooperative learning groups because this will not require moving the furniture. We can

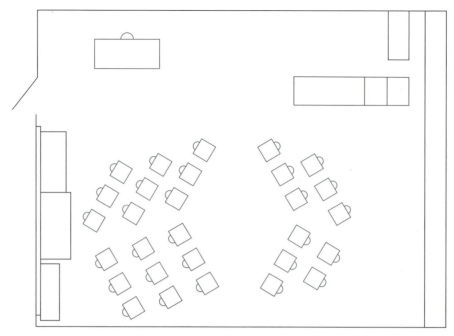

FIGURE 2.5   Christina's Arrangement for Whole Group

Christina's arrangement for class discussions.

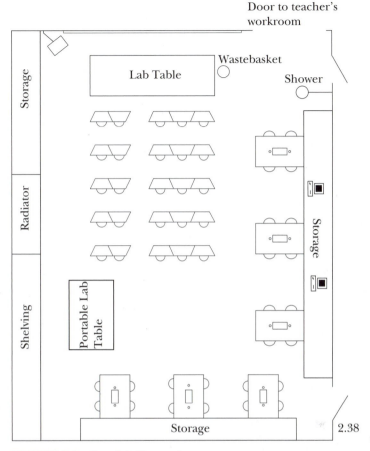

FIGURE 2.6   Sandy's Room Arrangement

understand this reluctance: Moving furniture can result in loss of instructional time, chaos, and confusion. But it doesn't have to be this way. Watching Donna, Christina, Fred, and Donnie's students move their desks or tables into new configurations makes it clear that students can learn to do this quietly and quickly—but they will need to be taught the procedures to follow. (See Chapter 5.)

When considering student interaction and desk arrangement, it's also important to think about whether to assign students to seats. Often students want to sit near their friends, but some individuals have definite spatial preferences as well (e.g., they prefer to sit in a corner, near the window, or in the front row). Donnie and Fred allow students to sit where they wish—as long as they behave appropriately, of course. (And with a smile, Fred advises his students to "sit next to someone smart.") Christina assigns students to seats alphabetically at the start of the year, and changes their seats periodically once she learns their names. Although Sandy allows students to sit where they wish at the start of the school year, she rearranges her collaborative groups at the beginning of every new marking period. Donna assigns seats and changes them every

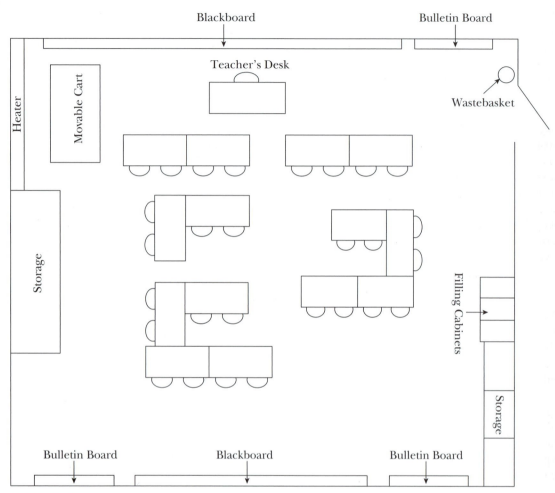

FIGURE 2.7   One of Donnie's Rearrangements

two weeks. "When I change seating assignments, I often put students who I need to observe in the front seats. I'm constantly trying to see their eyes and check on how they are doing."

INTERACTION BETWEEN THE TEACHER AND THE STUDENTS

The way students are arranged can also affect the interaction between teacher and students. A number of studies have found that in classrooms where desks are arranged in rows, the teacher interacts mostly with students seated in the front and center of the classroom. Students in this "action zone" (Adams & Biddle, 1970) participate more in class discussions and initiate more questions and comments.

Educational researchers have tried to tease out the reasons for this phenomenon. Do students who are more interested and more eager to participate select seats in the front, or does a front seating position somehow produce these attitudes and behaviors?

This issue has not been fully resolved, but the weight of the evidence indicates that a front-center seat does encourage participation, and a seat in the back makes it more difficult to participate and easier to "tune out." During a discussion with students in one of Sandy's classes, it was clear that they were aware of this phenomenon. As one student said, "When we're all so close to the front, you know that the teacher can see you real easily. That helps keep you awake!"

Although research on the action zone has examined only row arrangements, it is easy to imagine that the same phenomenon would occur whenever teachers direct most of their comments and questions to the students who are closest to them. Keep this in mind and take steps to ensure that the action zone encompasses your whole class. One suggestion is to move around the room whenever possible. Donna notes, "I sit on desks, I stand in front, I stand in back; they hear my voice from all corners of the room." In addition, make sure to establish eye contact with students seated farther away from you, direct comments to students seated in the rear and on the sides, and periodically change students' seats (or allow students to select new ones) so that all have an opportunity to be up front.

Symbolic Identification

The term *symbolic identification* refers to the information that a setting provides about the people who spend time there. The key questions are these: What does this room tell us about the students—their classroom activities, backgrounds, accomplishments, and preferences? What does the classroom tell us about the teacher's goals, values, and beliefs about education?

Too often, classrooms resemble motel rooms. They are pleasant but impersonal, revealing nothing about the people who use the space—or even about the subject that is studied there. This "anonymity" is exacerbated in middle and high school where six or seven classes may use the space during the day. Nonetheless, it's important to think about ways to personalize your classroom setting. Before using wall space or bulletin boards, however, be sure to negotiate "property rights" with the other teachers who are using the room.

All five teachers attempt to personalize their classrooms within the constraints of their individual circumstances. In Christina's classroom, mobiles of drama masks and literary genres hang from the ceiling. Five brightly colored bulletin boards across the back wall contain photographs of famous writers at their desks with quotations describing the ways they approach—and conquer—the agonies of writing.

Donnie has the use of only two bulletin boards, but she tries to have them reflect her students' activities and accomplishments. She reads the newspaper and regularly posts stories about her current and former students. Sometimes, she takes photographs of her students and displays them in honor of special events (e.g., when a student does particularly fine work or has had outstanding attendance).

Sandy also posts photographs of her students conducting laboratory investigations, although never without explicit permission. Occasionally, Sandy also displays students' outstanding work, but she offers words of caution:

 High school students often don't want their work posted on the bulletin board, because they don't want to "stand out" from their peers in any way. If I do put work up, I make sure to put their names on the *back* of the paper.

Donna displays "goal posters" that her students create at the beginning of the school year. Using colorful markers, students print their names in the center of the paper. Around their names, they write five adjectives that describe themselves and five goals for the year ahead. Those goals include "I want to turn in all of my homework in all my classes." "I want to gain a better relationship with my parents!" "I don't want to get my phone taken away."

You can also personalize classroom space by displaying materials that reflect the cultural backgrounds of the students in your class, especially as they relate to your subject matter. For example, an art classroom could exhibit work by artists from your students' native countries. A science classroom could display posters of scientists from around the world. In a math classroom, "ethnomathematical" displays could explore concepts such as number, graphs, topology, probability, and symmetry in the context of non-Western cultures (e.g., Africa, China, India, the Incas, the Mayans).

In addition, consider ways you can use the environment to communicate something about your *own* cultural background, experiences, and interests. You might want to hang your favorite art prints, display pictures of your family, or exhibit your collection of ceramic frogs. (You probably shouldn't display irreplaceable objects because they may be inadvertently damaged.) Over Christina's desk is a mobile of wooden apples that she made during the summer before her first year of teaching. Donna displays pictures, drawings, and artifacts that her students have given her over the years. She notes, "The kids love my personal wall. I think it makes me seem more approachable and less strict. My wall also reflects my sense of humor and interests away from school." Finally, look critically at commercial materials before posting them on your classroom walls and ask yourself if they really contribute to students' learning (Tarr, 2004). Bulletin boards are prime "real estate," so unless the materials are valuable, it might be better to display students' work or items that you have created.

Task Instrumentality

This function concerns the many ways the environment supports the tasks we need to accomplish. Think about the tasks and activities that will be carried out in your classroom. Will students work alone at their desks on writing assignments? Will they work cooperatively on activities and projects? Will you instruct the whole class from the whiteboard, overhead projector, or video projector connected to a computer? Will you work with small lab groups? Will students complete tasks on computers in the classroom?

For each of these tasks, you need to consider the physical design requirements. For example, if you plan to give whole-group instruction before students work independently (e.g., at lab tables), think about where to locate the instructional area vis-à-vis the work area. Do you want it near a whiteboard or the projection screen? In any case, its location should allow all students to see and hear your presentations without being cramped. You also want the work areas to be organized well so that individuals or small groups do not interfere with one another.

If you have a computer dedicated to noninstructional uses such as recordkeeping, you probably want to locate it on your desk; if you use a computer for presentations, it needs to be located near the video projector or interactive whiteboard (Bolick & Cooper, 2006). If you have computers in your classroom for student use, you also need to think carefully about where to locate the computer workstations although the location of electrical outlets and wiring for Internet access may dictate the placement. If students are going to work in pairs or in small groups, place the stations in an area where clusters of students can gather round without creating traffic congestion and distraction. Also be sure to keep the computers away from water and from chalkboards because dust can cause a problem.

Whatever tasks will occur in your classroom, you need to keep in mind a few general guidelines. These are presented in the Practical Tips Box.

 PRACTICAL TIPS FOR

Arranging a Functional Classroom

- *Frequently used classroom materials should be accessible to students.* Materials such as calculators, scissors, dictionaries, textbooks, staplers, tape, and rulers should be easy to reach. This will minimize the time spent preparing for activities and cleaning up. Decide which materials will be kept in locked or closed cabinets and which will be kept on open shelves. Think about whether materials are accessible to students who use wheelchairs, crutches, or walkers.

- *Shelves and storage areas should be well organized so that it is clear where materials and equipment belong.* It is useful to label shelves so that everyone knows where things go. This will make it easier to obtain materials and to return them. You should also have some sort of a system for the distribution and collection of students' work (e.g., in–out boxes). Materials that students should not access without permission should be stored in locked or closed cabinets.

- *Pathways throughout the room should be designed carefully to avoid congestion and distraction.* Paths to the pencil sharpener, supply closet, and trashcan(s) should be clearly visible and unobstructed. These high-traffic areas should be as far from students' desks as possible. Are pathways wide enough for students who use wheelchairs?

- *The seating arrangement should allow students to have a clear view of instructional presentations.* Students should be able to see instructional presentations without turning their desks or chairs around.

- *The location of the teacher's desk depends on where you will be spending your time.* If you will be constantly moving about the room, your desk can be out of the way, perhaps in a corner. If you will use your desk as a conference area or as a workstation, then it needs to be more centrally located. But be careful: With a central location, you may be tempted to remain at your desk for long periods of time, and this cuts down your ability to monitor students' work and behavior. Moreover, if your desk is in a central location, holding student conferences there may be distracting to other students.

- *Decide where to store your own personal teaching aids and supplies.* If you move from room to room, arrange to have a desk drawer or a shelf in a storage cabinet for your own personal use. At the very least, you will probably need storage for pens and markers, paper clips, a stapler, rubber bands, chalk or whiteboard markers, tape, tissues, attendance forms, and file folders. An alternative strategy is to carry your personal supplies with you, perhaps in a plastic organizer or a movable cart.

Pleasure

The important question here is whether students and teachers find the classroom attractive and pleasing. To the already overworked teacher, aesthetic concerns may seem irrelevant and insignificant (at least until parent conferences or open house night draw near). Yet given the amount of time that you and your students spend in your classroom, it is worth thinking about ways to create a pleasing environment.

In a classic study on environmental attractiveness, experimenters compared interviews that took place in an "ugly" room with those that took place in a "beautiful" room (Maslow & Mintz, 1956). The researchers found that interviewers assigned to the ugly room complained of headaches, fatigue, and discomfort. Furthermore, the interviews *finished more quickly* in the ugly room. Apparently, people in the ugly room tried to finish their task as quickly as possible to escape from the unpleasant setting.

Other studies have demonstrated that aesthetically pleasing environments can have a positive effect on attendance and feelings of group cohesion (Horowitz & Otto, 1973) and on participation in class discussions (Sommer & Olson, 1980). Thus, it is worth thinking about ways to make your classroom more attractive. Christina has six or seven bulletin boards, all decorated in different colors with different borders. Some of them are interactive, such as a vocabulary board on which students post challenging words and define and illustrate their use. Christina also purchased literary themed calendars, cut them apart, laminated them, and displayed the illustrations around the room. Christina commented, "Teachers tease that I have an elementary school classroom in a high school, but the kids seem to enjoy it and it makes me happy."

Growth

Steele's last function is particularly relevant to classrooms because they are settings specifically intended to promote students' development. This function is also the most difficult to pin down, however. Although it's easy to see that environments should be functional and attractive, it's less obvious that they can be designed to foster growth. Furthermore, growth can refer to any number of areas—learning to solve algebra problems, increasing one's self-confidence, learning to cooperate. For simplicity, we restrict our discussion to ways in which the environment can promote students' *cognitive development and academic achievement.*

Psychologists have found that the opportunity to explore rich, stimulating environments is related to cognitive growth. Your classroom should be more than a place where students listen to direct instruction, complete assignments, and demonstrate mastery of skills. It should be a setting that *invites students into the learning experience* (Strong-Wilson & Ellis, 2007)—*to explore, observe, investigate, test, and discover.* This means that in addition to the standard textbooks and supplemental materials, your classroom should contain a wide variety of materials related to your content area, such as works of fiction, replicas of historical documents, math manipulatives or puzzles, science specimens or models, or replicas of artwork.

Donna's classroom is a good example of this recommendation. In addition to the standard language arts posters illustrating writing mechanics, the room also contains materials not directly related to the language arts curriculum. Donna explains:

My students have a limited understanding about where they are in the world, so I have maps up on the walls that I use when we're learning about word origins and when we read about travel to different parts of the world. There's a list of state capitals, some information about the states, and the U. S. Constitution, because I want them to learn more about our country. I also have all the books they use in other classes and math and science posters. I tell them, "We're going to make connections between what you're learning in my class and in reading, in math, in science." I've also created a minilibrary containing fiction and nonfiction books that I think will stimulate their interest and which they're allowed to borrow.

Christina uses her bulletin boards to support the units in her curriculum. For example, she starts off a poetry unit by giving groups of students a copy of a poem cut into the individual words. Students create a new poem with the words and she displays the new and original poems side by side as they continue work in the unit. To introduce the Ray Bradbury author study, she collected a number of artifacts about Bradbury and created a collage for another bulletin board. She noted, "This was an annual unit, so I purchased a large clear plastic poster frame and assembled the collage within. I didn't have to re-create the bulletin board each year; I just took out the framed display and hung it in the middle of a bulletin board."

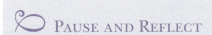

PAUSE AND REFLECT

We have heard middle and high school teachers comment that the six functions of the classroom setting are interesting but more applicable to the elementary classroom. We disagree. Think about how a teacher can use the six functions of the classroom in planning and setting up a classroom environment that is developmentally appropriate for 6th- through 12th-grade students.

THE TEACHER AS ENVIRONMENTAL DESIGNER

If you think about the various roles that settings play, you will realize that the functions not only overlap but also actually conflict. Seating that is good for social contact may be bad for testing, as Donnie can attest: She often prepares two to three versions of a test because students are sitting so close to one another! Similarly, room arrangements that provide students with privacy may be poor for monitoring and maintaining order. As you think about your room and your own priorities, you will have to determine which functions will take precedence over others. You also need to think about what is possible for you to achieve if you are a "nomad" who must move from room to room or share space with other teachers. This section of the chapter describes a process that you can follow as you design your classroom.

Think about the Activities the Room Will Accommodate

The first step in designing a classroom is to reflect on the activities it is to accommodate. For example, if you are teaching a lab science, you may need to accommodate whole-group instruction, hands-on lab work, media presentations, and testing. If you are teaching history, you may want to have small-group research projects, debates, simulations, and role-plays in addition to teacher presentations, class discussions, and seatwork. If you are teaching a world language, you may want to facilitate conversation among students. List these activities in a column, and next to each activity note whether it has any special physical requirements. For example, small groups may need storage space for projects, and lab work may require access to gas lines or water. Also consider which activities involve objects that cannot be moved, such as the projection screen, equipment that needs an electrical outlet, or wiring for Internet access.

Regardless of the activities in your classroom, it is helpful to think of the different spaces in the room in terms of the three learning settings that have been used throughout human history: the campfire, the watering hole, and the cave (Thornburg, 2007). The campfire is the more formal space where an expert shares knowledge with others; this is the space where you present direct instruction. The watering hole is a less formal, social learning space where peers learn from each other; you can create this space in your classroom by allowing students to cluster desks together or by adding areas of comfortable seating where students can gather. Finally, the cave is a private space where students go alone to think about what they have heard or experienced and build understanding. You can create caves for your students by allowing them to separate their desks and providing physical dividers that allow them to isolate themselves for this important thinking.

Remember that there is no one right way to design your classroom. The important thing is to make sure that your spatial arrangement supports the teaching strategies that you will use and the behaviors you want from your students.

Think about Whether the Students in Your Classroom Have Special Needs That Require Environmental Modifications

Also think about the characteristics of the students who will be using the room and whether you need to make any environmental modifications so the classroom is safe and comfortable. Will any students have orthopedic problems that require wide aisles or special equipment and furniture? (For example, Sandy has a portable lab table to accommodate a student who uses a wheelchair.) If any students have hearing impairments, it's desirable to minimize background noise by placing felt or rubber caps on chair and table legs. (Tennis balls work well!) Covering table surfaces with fabric and lining study carrels with acoustical tile or corkboard can also help cut down on noise (Mamlin & Dodd-Murphy, 2002).

Also think about special needs when assigning students their seats. Will you have any students with attention difficulties who may need seats away from distractions? If you have any students with hearing impairments who need to lip-read, locate their seats so they can see your face, and then make sure that you face them when you address the class. If you have any students with visual impairments, they will need seats close to where you will present material (e.g., the projection screen or whiteboard). Make a list of the accommodations you may need to make in your classroom for each of these types of learners and what you might do to benefit all the students in your classroom.

Think about the Needs of Other Adults in the Room

As more and more students with special needs are educated in general education classrooms, it becomes increasingly likely that you will be working with other adults (e.g., special education teachers providing in-class support, paraprofessionals, instructional aides). In fact, a study of 18 elementary schools found that teachers were more likely to have at least one additional adult in their classrooms than to be alone with their students (Valli, Croninger, & Walters, 2007).

Resource teachers or instructional aides require, at a minimum, a place to store materials and equipment and a place to sit, so you will need to decide where these will be. One of Sandy's classes, for example, includes a student with a brain injury who has a full-time personal aide. In this particular case, Sandy prefers the aide to sit in the back of the room—rather than next to the student. She explains:

> **My biggest challenge with James is to make him part of the community, and having the aide sitting right next to him, taking notes for him, makes it harder for him to get integrated into his group. I decided to have another member of his cooperative group take notes for him (on carbonless paper), and they have really begun to connect. The kids learned to listen to him and to accept his contributions, but that wouldn't have happened as easily if the aide had been right there. Sometimes an aide's protection doesn't allow the student to grow, to become more independent, and to become a real, functioning member of the group.**

(We will revisit these issues in Chapter 6, when we discuss co-teaching between general and special education teachers.)

Involve Students in Environmental Decisions

Although a great deal can be done before the start of school, some things can be left undone so that your students can be involved in the design process. If you teach four or five classes in one room, it is obviously impossible to involve everyone in all environmental decisions; however, you might solicit ideas for room design from your various classes, and then select those that seem most feasible. You might also rotate responsibility for some aspect of the environment among your classes (e.g., each class could have an opportunity to design a bulletin board display). Inviting students to participate in environmental decision making not only helps to create more responsive physical arrangements but also prepares students for their roles as active, involved citizens who possess environmental competence.

Try the New Arrangement, Evaluate, and Redesign

In addition to being responsive to students' input on your room arrangement, you can use the six functions of the environment as a framework for evaluating your classroom design. For example, does the desk arrangement facilitate or hinder social contact among students? Do displays communicate information about the subject matter and students' work? Are frequently used materials accessible to students? Does the room provide pleasure? Does it support student growth?

As you evaluate the effectiveness of the classroom setting, stay alert for behavioral problems that the physical arrangement might cause. For example, if a student suddenly becomes inattentive when his seat is moved next to the pencil sharpener, it is likely that an environmental change rather than detention is in order. If the classroom floor is constantly littered despite your appeals for neatness, the underlying problem may be an inadequate number of trashcans and/or inconvenient locations.

SOME THOUGHTS ON HAVING TO SHARE ROOMS

When we sat down as a group to discuss the role of the physical environment in classroom management, it became clear that all of the teachers who have to share classrooms feel extremely frustrated. Christina was blunt about having to teach in two different rooms: "I hate it!" Sandy emphasized the difficulties that are created when access to the classroom is limited:

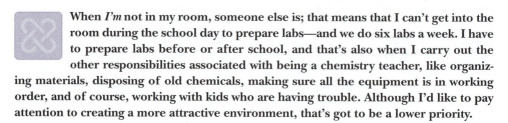

When *I'm* not in my room, someone else is; that means that I can't get into the room during the school day to prepare labs—and we do six labs a week. I have to prepare labs before or after school, and that's also when I carry out the other responsibilities associated with being a chemistry teacher, like organizing materials, disposing of old chemicals, making sure all the equipment is in working order, and of course, working with kids who are having trouble. Although I'd like to pay attention to creating a more attractive environment, that's got to be a lower priority.

The teachers also expressed irritation over other common problems—for example, inadequate storage space (Christina likes to "hoard" things), inappropriate furniture, and insufficient numbers of desks. They traded war stories about materials that disappear (Fred's gone through three staplers this year) and the lack of personal work areas. (It took Sandy three years to get a desk where she could sit during free periods to plan lessons and grade papers; when she finally got one, it was in a storage closet!) They also talked about the problems that arise when the other teachers sharing the room are inconsiderate "roommates" who fail to clean up adequately. Because this was a topic that clearly raised their blood pressure, it seems important to share a few of the lessons they have learned.

Being a Good Roommate

During our discussion, Donnie shared an anecdote that illustrates the kinds of problems that can occur when teachers have to share rooms.

I share the room with a long-term substitute who's supposed to monitor a study hall in my room during second period. He thinks he doesn't really have to watch the kids, so they sit there and write all over the desks. Finally, I couldn't stand it anymore; I took a sponge and cleanser and cleaned all the tables before school began. I taught first period and then turned the room over to him. When I came back for third period, the desks were covered with writing again! I was furious!

Given the other teacher's status as a long-term substitute coming in the middle of the year, Donnie's situation was particularly difficult. In general, however, working out an explicit agreement at the very beginning of the year is important. It should specify how the classroom is to be initially arranged, which boards (bulletin, chalk, or white) are available to each of you, and what storage space you can each use. If, as a new teacher, you are assigned to share a room with an experienced teacher, be sure to have these discussions before you start rearranging the room or taking over board or storage space.

You should also discuss how the classroom should be left at the end of each class period. You and your roommate might agree that desks are to be returned to a standard arrangement, boards are to be erased, materials are to be put away, the floor is to be cleaned, no food is to be in the room, and (of course) no writing is to be on the desks or tables. You also need to agree on a procedure to follow if the agreement is violated, so you don't have to suffer in silence. As Sandy tells us, "It's not enough to have an agreement; you have to follow through. My roommate and I have agreed to hold the kids accountable for the condition of the room. If I come in and find a problem, I tell her about it, and she deals with it the next time she sees those students."

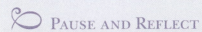

PAUSE AND REFLECT

Think about the problems that arise when teachers have to share rooms. If you are in that situation, what specific items would you want to include in an agreement about how the room is to be left? What procedure would you want to have in place if the agreement is violated?

CONCLUDING COMMENTS

All five teachers agree on the importance of thinking about the physical environment. Fred comments:

> **Some of the ideas—like the action zone, for example—are important for teachers to know about even if they move from room to room and have little control over the classroom. On the other hand, some of the ideas—like psychological security—are hard to put into practice if you're a nomad. But that's okay; thinking about these issues is important anyway. We need to say to new teachers, "Listen, folks, you're going to have to be clever in dealing with this. If you can't add soft, warm fuzzies to your room, then you're going to have to compensate. You're going to have to find other ways of providing psychological security, like making sure your kids feel safe in your classroom because they know they're not going to get hammered."**

As Fred suggests, it is not easy for secondary teachers to create their ideal classroom settings. Nonetheless, we hope this chapter has given you an increased awareness of the physical environment and its impact along with a realistic sense of how you can use the environment to meet your goals. Remember that environmental competence is an integral part of effective classroom management.

SUMMARY

This chapter discussed how the classroom's physical environment influences the way teachers and students feel, think, and behave. It stressed the need for teachers to be aware of the direct and indirect effects of the physical environment. This awareness is the first step to developing "environmental competence." The chapter suggested ways to use the six functions of the environment as a framework for designing a classroom that will support your instructional goals.

Security and Shelter

- Be aware of and implement safety guidelines for dangerous supplies and equipment.
- Be sensitive to the needs of students with physical disabilities and attention problems.
- Add elements of softness.
- Arrange space for freedom from interference.
- Create opportunities for privacy by adding cubicles or folding cardboard dividers.

Social Contact

- Consider how much interaction you want among students.
- Think about whether you are making contact with *all* of your students; avoid a small action zone.

Symbolic Identification

- Personalize your classroom space so that it communicates appropriate information about you, your students, and your subject matter.

Task Instrumentality

- Make sure frequently used materials are accessible to students.
- Make it clear where things belong.
- Plan pathways to avoid congestion and distraction.
- Arrange seats for a clear view of presentations.
- Locate your desk in an appropriate place (off to the side helps to ensure that you will circulate).

Pleasure

- Create an aesthetically pleasing environment through the use of plants, color, and bulletin board displays.

Growth

- Stock your room with a variety of materials related to your as well as other, content areas.
- Create spaces in your classroom where students can interact with materials and with each other. Allow for watering holes and caves as well as the more traditional campfire learning spaces.

Carefully planning the physical environment is an integral part of good classroom management. When you begin to design your room, think about the activities it will accommodate; if possible, invite your students to participate in the design process. Also reflect on whether any of your students have special needs that require environmental modifications. Be sure to provide the necessary seating and storage space for any other teachers or aides who will be in your classroom. Try your arrangement, evaluate it, and redesign as necessary. If you are sharing your room with other teachers, be sure to work out an explicit agreement about how you will share the space and how you and your students will be accountable for maintaining it in good condition.

ACTIVITIES FOR SKILL BUILDING AND REFLECTION

In Class

In small groups, consider the following seating arrangements. For each one, think about the types of instructional strategies for which it is appropriate or inappropriate. The first one has been done as an example.

Arrangement	Appropriate Instructional Strategies for This Arrangement	Inappropriate Instructional Strategies for This Arrangement
Rows	*Teacher or student presentations; audiovisual presentations; testing*	*Student-centered discussions; small-group work*
Horizontal Rows		
Horseshoe		
Small Clusters		
Circle		

On Your Own

Visit a middle or high school classroom, watch two to three class sessions in that classroom, draw a classroom map, and evaluate the physical layout in terms of the six functions of the environment. Use the bulleted items under each of the functions presented in the chapter summary to create a checklist. For example, to evaluate social contact, look for evidence that the classroom arrangement supports the appropriate amount of student interaction and that the action zone encompasses the entire class.

For Your Portfolio

Imagine for a moment that you have a classroom of your own: You don't have to change rooms, and you don't even have to share it with any other teacher! Draw a floor plan of your ideal classroom. (You can go to classroom.4teachers.org to use an online floor-planning tool.) In a brief commentary, explain why you are designing the room this way.

FOR FURTHER READING

Butin, D. (2000). *Classrooms.* Washington, DC: National Clearinghouse for Educational Facilities. Available online at http://www.ncef.org/pubs/classrooms.pdf.
    This article presents ideas for classroom design that are consistent with a view of learning as an active process of engaging students.

Schmollinger, C. S., Opaleski, K. Chapman, M. L., Jociu, R., & Sherri, B. (2002). How do you make your classroom an inviting place for students to come back to each year? *English Journal, 91*(6), 20–22.
    This article presents five English teachers' ideas about how to create an attractive, inviting, and stimulating environment for their students.

Thornburg, D. D. (2007). Campfires in cyberspace: Primordial metaphors for learning in the 21st century. Available online at www.usdla.org/html/journal/JUN01_Issue/article01.html.
    This article presents learning space metaphors (campfire, watering hole, cave, and life) and describes the importance of providing access to each type of learning space in the classroom.

Whitmore, K. F. & Laurich, L. (2010). What happens in the arcade shouldn't stay in the arcade: Lessons for classroom design. *Language Arts, 88*(1), 21–31.

This article describes how to apply the principles of shared space and shared ownership that students experience in video arcades to classrooms. The authors worked with a fifth/sixth grade teacher to increase student access to space in his classroom and, as a result, increased students' access to literacy instruction.

ORGANIZATIONAL RESOURCES

Classroom.4teachers.org and *teacher.scholastic.com/tools/class_setup.* These two sites provide tools for drawing a classroom layout. You can enter your classroom's dimensions and drag icons to explore different arrangements.

Learn NC K–12 Teaching and Learning, www.learnnc.org/lp/pages/BasicEnv1. The University of North Carolina at Chapel Hill School of Education finds the most innovative and successful practices in K through 12 education and makes them available to teachers and students. The site includes articles on the physical climate of the classroom, arranging for independence, working with available space, and sample classroom floor plans.

The Science House, www.science-house.org/resources/safety.htm. This site provides resources and information regarding science classrooms and lab safety.

CHAPTER 3

Developing Positive Teacher-Student Relationships

Some years ago, we supervised a student teacher named Annie, who had been placed in a fourth-grade classroom. One of us had taught Annie in a course on campus, and we had some concerns about her organizational ability. Nevertheless, we weren't prepared for what we saw on the first visit to her classroom. Annie was teaching a lesson on quotation marks. Although it wasn't exactly captivating, it wasn't awful. But her students' behavior *was*. They chatted, rummaged through their desks, and completely ignored the lesson. Furthermore, throughout the period, a steady stream of students walked up to Annie, asked to go to the restroom, and left the room. We watched in disbelief as a student left about every three minutes; at one point, five or six students were out at the same time. Yet Annie never asked students to wait until she had finished teaching or until the previous person had returned.

When the period was over and we met with Annie to discuss the lesson, we asked her to talk about the students' behavior. We wondered how she interpreted the students' lack of interest in her lesson and their obvious desire to leave the room. We also wanted to know why she had never said "no" when a student asked to leave the room. We remember her answer clearly:

I want to show the children that I care about them. I don't want to rule this classroom like a dictator. If I say no when someone asks to go to the bathroom, that would be showing them that I don't respect them.

Annie never did create the atmosphere of mutual respect she desired; in fact, she never completed student teaching. Her commitment "to care"—which she defined as "never say no"—led to a situation so chaotic and so confused that no learning, teaching, *or* caring was possible. Using the terminology introduced in Chapter 1, we can see that in her effort to avoid being *authoritarian* ("a dictator"), Annie actually became too *permissive*. She was unable to develop an *authoritative* approach to classroom management. In other words, Annie never became a "warm demander."

WHY IS SHOWING CARE IMPORTANT?

Over the years, we have thought a lot about Annie and her efforts to establish a respectful, caring environment. Although Annie was ultimately unsuccessful, we understand and applaud the high priority she placed on positive teacher-student relationships. In fact, a recent study found that 15 of 18 excellent classroom managers identified relationship building as *the most important factor in effective classroom management* (Holt, Hargrove, & Harris, 2011). Common sense tells us that students are more likely to cooperate with teachers who are seen as caring, trustworthy, and respectful, and research consistently bears this out (Cornelius-White, 2007; Gregory & Ripski, 2008; Hoy & Weinstein, 2006; Hullena & Hullena, 2010; Osterman, 2000). Recently, a review of 99 studies conducted from 1990 to 2011 concluded that positive teacher-student relationships (characterized by warmth and empathy) are significantly associated with students' engagement in learning activities (Roorda, Koomen, Spilt, & Oort, 2011). This is especially true for older students, even into late adolescence, those who are academically at risk or from disadvantaged economic backgrounds, and those with learning difficulties. In addition, other studies have indicated that positive teacher-student relationships are also critical for Black and Hispanic students, who frequently perceive that their teachers (generally European American) fail to understand their perspectives, accept them as individuals, honor their cultural backgrounds, or demonstrate respect (S. R. Katz, 1999; Nieto & Bode, 2008; Sheets, 1996). Indeed, Angela Valenzuela (1999) argues that the immigrant Mexican and Mexican American high school students she studied in Houston need to feel *cared for* before they can *care about* school.

Another study underscores the key role that positive relationships play in classroom management (Cothran, Kulinna, & Garrahy, 2003). Interviews with 182 adolescents (grades 6 through 12), representing diverse socioeconomic, cultural, and academic backgrounds, revealed students' high regard for teachers who listen well, treat students with respect, and exhibit caring. Sonya made this comment: "If you have a relationship with your students, they're gonna trust you more and they're gonna respect you more and then they'll be nicer to you." When the researchers asked her to elaborate on what she meant by "be nicer to you," she responded this way:

> We like don't mouth off to her. We try not to talk when she is talking and we don't talk back. We try to listen and remember what she is telling us like directions and instructions and we don't talk back to her and we aren't whining about what she wants, what she has planned. (p. 439)

The researchers note that the importance of caring, respectful relationships "is not a common topic in classroom management discussions" (p. 441). They contend that this is unfortunate because teacher caring is a key factor in gaining students' cooperation and their engagement in academic activities.

But gaining cooperation is certainly not the only reason for trying to develop positive relationships with students. If we want adolescents to be seriously engaged in learning, to share their thoughts and feelings, to take risks, and to develop a sense of social responsibility, then we need to organize classrooms so that students feel safe and cared for (Patrick, Ryan, & Kaplan, 2007). Even achieving the most basic goal of having students stay in school depends on developing meaningful relationships: When youths were asked why they dropped out of high school, they frequently stated it was because no one cared about them (National Research Council, 2004).

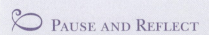

PAUSE AND REFLECT

Before going any further, think about a teacher you had in middle or high school who showed caring and respect for students. In specific behavioral terms, what did this teacher do to communicate that he or she cared about you?

In retrospect, Annie's problem was not the high priority she placed on being caring and creating positive relationships with her students. *Her problem was the way she thought about caring.* Clearly, never saying "no" doesn't work. So what *does?* The next section of this chapter provides specific suggestions, using examples from our five teachers.

WAYS TO SHOW CARE AND RESPECT FOR STUDENTS

Be Welcoming

Beginning teachers are often told not to smile until Christmas so students will perceive them as serious and tough. We don't agree. A smile is a simple, effective way to be welcoming. On the first day of school, Donna stands at the classroom door and greets students with a big smile and a friendly comment: "Good morning! I like that shirt." "Oh, I like those leggings." "Hi. How are you? It's hot in here, guys, sorry." "Wow, great colors on your shirt!" "Welcome aboard. Have a seat anywhere." Later, she calls roll, telling students, "I'm going to call out your name as you were registered. If there's another name you want to be called, let me know." As students raise their hands or say good morning in response to her "Good Morning," Donna asks about siblings or other relatives she might have taught and checks on whether she has pronounced names correctly. In today's diverse classrooms, it's likely that some names will be unfamiliar. Christina finds that writing the phonetic pronunciations in her record book is a real help. She has also noted that some Asian American students are reluctant to correct mispronunciation, fearing that it would be disrespectful.

Donnie also shows an interest in students' names as she welcomes students on the first day of school:

> After introducing herself and explaining how she got her name, Donnie asks the students to tell her about themselves in the same way: "Tell me your name, where you got it from or what it means, if you have a nickname you want me to use, and then choose an adjective to describe yourself. I'm going to write these down so I can learn your names as quickly as possible. But please be patient; it might take a little while."

Another simple way to be welcoming is to connect individually with every one of your students on a regular basis. This may seem impossible when you have 150 or more students. But one simple way to do this is to have each student provide information on an index card, such as birthday, favorite (or least favorite) school subjects, and out-of school activities (e.g., ballet, soccer, piano). For each class, keep the cards in a deck on your desk, and each day, pay special attention to the student whose card is on the top of the deck. For example, greet the student by name at the door, ask him or her to be a special assistant for an activity, or talk with him or her during a free moment. In about a month, you can interact with each student in a way that makes him or her feel special (Bigelow, 2012).

Learn about Students' Lives

In addition to welcoming your students, another way to show care and respect is to learn about their lives. For example, you might ask your students to complete an information sheet that asks about favorite school subjects, after-school jobs, hobbies, or pets, along with anything else they want you to know about them. Attending their sporting events, plays, and concerts is another way of getting to know your students.

Fred begins the process of learning about his students as he takes roll on the first day of school. After pronouncing each student's name, he asks a question (e.g., What's your favorite TV show? What's your favorite kind of music?). This not only allows him to learn about his students but also gives them some confidence about speaking out in class. Fred also conducts class discussions in which he asks students to respond to questions such as:

- What are the best things about being a high school student in the 21st century?
- What are the most memorable world events in your life so far?
- If you were the superintendent of this district, what changes would you make in this high school?

Another idea comes from JoBeth Allen (2008), who was part of a teacher study group in Georgia that used photography to learn about students' families. With a small grant, the study group teachers bought three cameras for each classroom and invited students to photograph what was important to them in their homes and neighborhoods. Students took the cameras home on a rotating basis, and students and family members wrote personal stories, memories, poetry, and letters about the photos.

Be Sensitive to Students' Concerns

In essence, being sensitive to students means thinking about classroom events and activities from a student's point of view. On the first day of school, for example, Christina assigns seats alphabetically so that she can learn students' names as quickly as possible. Realizing that students may be unhappy about the location of their seats or their particular neighbors, she reassures them that seats will be changed periodically.

Keeping grades a private matter between you and an individual student also demonstrates sensitivity. Most adolescents don't want anyone to know they've gotten a failing grade; public announcements are less likely to increase motivation than to generate resentment. Even if you announce only the As, you can embarrass students.

A fifth-grader we know was mortified when her teacher held her test up in front of the whole class and announced that, "Laura was obviously the only one who studied!" And what does an announcement like that convey to the student who normally received Ds, but studied really hard and earned a C? When Sandy gives students' papers back, she tells them to keep their grades to themselves while they are in the room—"no asking, no telling." If they wish to divulge their grades once they've left the room, that's their prerogative.

Because secondary students have a tremendous need to save face, sensitivity also means discussing inappropriate behavior quietly and privately. Public reprimands are humiliating—and research consistently demonstrates that students view public humiliation as an *unacceptable* form of discipline (Hoy & Weinstein, 2006). Moreover, students consider it a very *severe* intervention—not something to be shrugged off lightly. A study of 300 junior high school students in Israel found that students viewed *"shaming or personally insulting a student" as severe as "permanent suspension from school"* and more severe than detention, student-teacher conferences, reporting to the principal's office, and verbal reprimands (Zeidner, 1988). Students also rated public humiliation as significantly more severe than teachers did.

Public humiliation will not only poison your relationship with students but also can have long-term negative effects. A Canadian study (Brendgen, Wanner, Vitaro, Bukowski, & Tremblay, 2007) found that elementary students from kindergarten through fourth grade who were "picked on" by the teacher (defined as behaviors such as scolding, criticizing, or shouting) were more likely to display behavior problems in young adulthood. (See Figure 3.1.)

Donna has witnessed the negative effects of humiliation:

 When kids have been affected by humiliation, it's a struggle to help them rise above it. Middle school students need to feel safe in order to take a risk. Oftentimes the high performing kids are "risk takers"; they take risks with just about anything. I bet those kids have been nurtured by some caring adult.

To preserve the student-teacher relationship, Donnie approaches misbehaving students quietly and sets up a time to meet:

 I'll tell them, "I don't want to take up class time and I don't want to embarrass you. Stop by after school so we can talk privately." If that's not possible, we'll meet during lunch or before school. It means giving up some of my own time, but it's much more effective than talking during class in front of everyone.

Sensitivity also means noticing if someone looks especially edgy, depressed, or angry and privately communicating your concern. As Donnie puts it:

 Sometimes a student will come in and they just don't have the same *glow*. I'll go over and say, "Is everything OK?" And sometimes they'll say, "No, Miss, I'm having problems at home" or "I'm having trouble with my boyfriend." If they tell me that, I try to respect that and give them some space. I'll go a little easier on them that day, like I won't call on them as much.

"The best advice I can give, to a young teacher, is to realize that students will probably forget most of what you say but not how it made them feel."

FIGURE 3.1   *Source:* www.cartoonstock.com. Reprinted with permission.

In addition, it's important to take students' concerns seriously if they choose to confide in you. From your adult vantage point, breaking up with a girlfriend, having to be home by 1:00 A.M. on a Saturday night, or not making the track team might not be sufficient cause for depression. But Christina emphasizes how important it is to acknowledge the legitimacy of students' concerns:

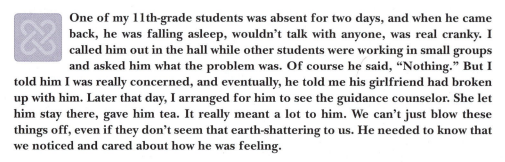

One of my 11th-grade students was absent for two days, and when he came back, he was falling asleep, wouldn't talk with anyone, was real cranky. I called him out in the hall while other students were working in small groups and asked him what the problem was. Of course he said, "Nothing." But I told him I was really concerned, and eventually, he told me his girlfriend had broken up with him. Later that day, I arranged for him to see the guidance counselor. She let him stay there, gave him tea. It really meant a lot to him. We can't just blow these things off, even if they don't seem that earth-shattering to us. He needed to know that we noticed and cared about how he was feeling.

Finally, be sensitive to anxiety or difficulty your students may be experiencing with course material or requirements. During a visit to Sandy's class after a severe blizzard that had closed school for several days, we watched students resume a lab activity they had begun before the "vacation." It required them to use pipettes, and several students expressed concern about having forgotten how to use them. Here is an excerpt from our field notes:

Sandy acknowledges their concerns: "I know that some of you are worried that you don't remember how to use the equipment. That's a valid concern, since it's been such a long time since you practiced. But don't worry. See if you remember, and if not, just call me over and I'll help you out." Later, when two students express confusion about the lab procedure, she comments: **"Your confusion is understandable, because this is the first time we're doing this procedure. Next time we do it you'll know what to do. Remember when we were learning to use the balance, and you were so confused? The first time is always a challenge."**

Establish and Enforce Clear Expectations for Behavior

Establishing and enforcing clear norms for behavior makes the classroom a safer, more predictable environment and communicates that you care about your students' well-being. With clear rules and routines, there is less likelihood of confusion, misunderstanding, and inconsistency—and more likelihood that teachers and students can engage in warm, relaxed interactions. As Christina puts it:

I feel like the more organized and the more structured the class is, the more I can show that I'm human, joke around, invite students to tell me things they would like to change. I can let my guard down, because they know what is expected.

Donna feels the same way. On the second day of school, she asks students to respond in writing to this question: "What does the word 'non-negotiable' mean to you?" Afterward, students volunteer their definitions, and Donna presents her non-negotiable rules for the classroom. It's evident that she has very clear expectations about how students are to behave, and that she works to establish herself as the classroom leader from the very beginning of school. Research has indicated how important this is for preventing inappropriate behavior.

Research has also demonstrated the *long-term benefits* to students of organized classrooms with clear norms to students. In one study (Catalano, Haggerty, Oesterle, Fleming, & Hawkins, 2004), elementary teachers from schools in high-risk neighborhoods were trained in the use of proactive classroom management techniques (e.g., establish consistent classroom expectations and routines at the beginning of the year; give clear, explicit instructions for behavior; recognize desirable student behavior and efforts to comply). Not surprisingly, the students of those teachers demonstrated a higher level of school bonding and fewer problem behaviors than did students in a control group. What is even more noteworthy is the fact that when those same students were followed into high school, their levels of school attachment, commitment, and academic achievement were higher than those in the control group, and school problems, violence, alcohol abuse, and risky sexual activity were reduced. (Establishing clear norms for behavior will be addressed more fully in Chapter 5.)

Be Fair

It seems obvious that caring teachers must strive for fairness. For example, issues of fairness often arise in relationship to evaluation and grading, so be explicit about how you're going to grade an assignment (e.g., use a rubric). Don't withhold information and then play "gotcha." If class participation counts when you're calculating report card grades, explain that too, and describe what constitutes participation.

Christina earnestly follows this advice. Because she counts participation as one-third of students' grades, she provides her classes with a weekly "participation check-sheet" that lists the behaviors she expects, and she spends considerable time explaining how it works. During one interview, she shared her reasoning:

> **Most teachers don't use participation as an actual portion of the grade; they use it as a tie-breaker (like if you're trying to decide between an A and a B). But I think it's one of the most important things. Participation is not just raising your hand and speaking out. It's also having your work done, being prepared for class, being engaged, staying on task. I know some kids are going to be more verbal and more confident, but everyone can make some contribution to class.**

In these instances, caring and fairness seem to go hand in hand. But it's not always so simple. Being fair generally involves "making judgments of students' conduct and academic performances without prejudice or partiality" (M. S. Katz, 1999, p. 61). In terms of classroom management, this translates into ensuring that rules apply to everyone, no matter what. On the other hand, being fair can also imply a recognition that people may need different, personalized treatment, and being caring certainly seems to demand that we acknowledge students' individuality. From this perspective, treating everyone the same is *unfair*. So what is a teacher to do?

Even experienced, masterful teachers who care deeply about students' well-being may have conflicting positions on this fundamental dilemma. Consider Sandy and Fred. Sandy observes:

> **You can't have community in the classroom unless everyone feels that they'll be treated fairly, whether they're the student congress president or not. You're better off having a class with very few rules that apply to everyone, rather than a lot of rules that apply to only some people.**

Sandy demonstrated this principle not too long ago when three of her students, including a boy classified as having an emotional disorder, didn't have their homework and asked for permission to turn it in the next day:

> **My answer was no. I don't accept late homework, and they know it. I want them to learn how to budget their time and to prepare. This was a 20-point homework assignment, due on Monday. I reminded them all week, and made a big point of it on Friday. Then they walk in on Monday without it. I said, "I believe you did it; your integrity is not in question. But it's not here." To my horror, Billy (the boy classified as emotionally disturbed) started to cry in front of the whole class. I got him out of the room and talked with him. I told him I understood that other things can interfere with doing homework, but the rule applies to everyone. I know this seems harsh, but I think this was a really significant event. It was important for Billy—and the rest of the class—to see that he has to meet the same expectations.**

From Sandy's perspective, having the rules apply to everyone is both fair *and* caring. But Fred takes a somewhat different position:

 I try to treat kids fairly in that my decision is always based on what is best for the kid. At times that means you treat everyone the same, and that's the right decision. Other times you may treat everyone differently, and that's the right decision. There's no recipe for being fair that we can all follow. We have to constantly examine our decisions and ask, "Is this in the best interest of the kid?"

I gain some things by not always treating everyone the same. I have more flexibility this way. I can say, "This kid is having a really hard time, and I'm not going to give him a zero for the day, no matter what the rule says." I'm just going to throw out that rule. And I've never had a kid say, "That's not fair." But I lose some things too—namely, the consistency that comes when everyone knows exactly what's going to happen. So you have people who push the envelope. I have to be more on guard; I have to watch for people who are trying to take advantage.

In sum, being fair is certainly an essential component of being caring, but it's not always obvious what this means in terms of actual practice. Teaching is messy and uncertain, and we often don't know what the right decisions are until after we've made them. What *is* certain, however, is that teachers need to engage in ongoing reflection about these complex moral issues. (We return to these issues in Chapter 12, when we discuss the issue of consistency.)

Use Humor

Sharing a laugh can strengthen the bond between teachers and students. During observations of our five teachers, we were struck by how often they use humor to create a sense of fun or to soften a reprimand. For example, when Donna's class was studying Greek and Roman mythology, a student asked why the gods all had beards. Without missing a beat, Donna responded: "No barbershops?" When she returned to school—exhausted—after chaperoning a class trip to Washington, D.C., Donna asked one of her students why he had his head down on the desk. He explained that he was tired. "Don't even go there," she warned. "My tired is more than your tired!" He smiled and got back to work. At the very end of the school year, when many students had already "checked out," Donna told students to take out a piece of paper and then added, "If you don't have paper, let me know, and I'll give you a piece." About 10 students raised their hands, and, with a look of exaggerated dismay, Donna asked, "What am I now? Office Max?"

A note of caution: When using humor, be careful to stay away from sarcasm that can cause humiliation and pain rather than laughter. Also be aware that light moments can sometimes deteriorate into a loss of order. As a student in one study explained, "They [the teachers] have to laugh with you instead of just sitting there, but still keep us in line" (Hullena & Hullena, 2010).

Welcome Students' Input

Allow students to voice their suggestions and opinions about lessons, assignments, or grouping decisions. Interestingly, all five teachers begin the school year by asking students to talk or write about their expectations for the class. As we saw in Chapter 1,

Sandy begins the school year by asking her students to write answers to four questions: (1) How do you learn best? (2) What do you expect to be excited about in chemistry? (3) What do you expect to be nervous about? and (4) What can I do to help? In similar fashion, Donna also solicits students' expectations. On the first day of school, she has students write a paragraph about why they are or are not happy to be in school. At the end of class, she assigns "mental homework" for the following day: to think about previous years in school, classrooms that made them feel good, and what they expect from their teacher and peers. On the second day of school, students work in small groups to discuss these topics and to come up with three ways they want to be treated.

Christina not only asks students to write about their expectations but also invites their continuing suggestions and feedback on the class:

> "I want you to know that I really welcome your input. I'm sure you have good ideas, and I'm interested in hearing your suggestions for things we can do. Also, if you think something didn't work very well, I welcome your criticism too. For example, you might say, 'I know that you were trying to have a good discussion today, but a lot of people weren't responding because. . . . ' That kind of feedback would be very helpful." Christina points out her school e-mail address and encourages students to use it.

There is an interesting postscript to our first-day observations of Christina's request for suggestions and criticism. Several months later, it became clear that a few students were disgruntled by the amount of work they had been assigned. Christina tells it this way:

> It was right after spring break, and there were a couple of kids who seemed upset and were complaining about work. So, wondering how widespread it was, I opened up a discussion. It was like opening Pandora's box. Out came all these complaints about how I was giving too much homework, and some of it was too difficult for them to do by themselves—they wanted partners. They kept saying it was like college work, and that they were only 15!
>
> I was floored at first, but after everyone had their say, I tried to address their concerns. We made some changes. I postponed some assignments and promised to give them in-class time to work in groups on some of them. I explained why I was giving them challenging work, and I made it clear that I am here every day to work with anybody who needs help. But I also told them that what was most upsetting to me was the fact that they hadn't come to me about all this sooner.
>
> Since the discussion, a lot of kids have been coming in for help, and things really seem to be better. But what I learned is that even if you invite kids to provide input, you still have to go back and check that it's working. You have to teach them that it's really okay to come to teachers and talk about these things. I just assumed my invitation was enough, but it wasn't.

Be a Real Person (as Well as a Teacher)

On the first day of school, Donnie takes a few minutes to explain how she got the name Donnie, that her husband is the principal of a nearby elementary school, and that they have a daughter who "is one year short of a quarter of a century." (When students look at her questioningly, she laughs and tells them, "Do your math!") Similarly, Donna uses the U.S. map posted on the wall to trace the moves her military family made when she was in eighth grade: from Tucson to Winston-Salem to New York to Chicago to Montana to Anchorage. ("Do you have any idea how hard it is to be stuck in a car with four brothers for that long?!") Within the first few minutes of the very first class meeting, both teachers have already communicated an important message: In addition to being teachers, they are real people with real lives outside of school.

Beginning teachers often puzzle over the extent to which they should share information about their personal lives. We remember having teachers who refused to reveal their first names—as if that would somehow blur the boundary between teacher and student and diminish their authority. On the other hand, there are teachers who are extremely open, sharing stories of a parent's alcoholism, their own poor test scores, and other extremely personal—and potentially embarrassing—information (Christensen, 2007).

As a new teacher, it's probably wise to find a happy medium between these two extremes and to share limited information (e.g., about vacations, cultural and athletic activities, hobbies, or pets). Once you gain experience and confidence, you can decide whether you want to share more information about your personal life. During a visit to Christina's classroom, for example, we watched as she introduced a writing assignment on identity. She began by distributing copies of her own identity essay. In it, she reflects on her Puerto Rican father, her "all-American" mother (unable to "recount all of her various nationalities"), her "Asian eyes" (with eyelids that "kept escaping" the blue eye shadow she tried to use), and the "curious ambiguity" of her skin. Four months later, near the end of the school year, Christina talked about her students' reactions to the essay:

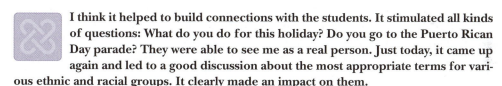

I think it helped to build connections with the students. It stimulated all kinds of questions: What do you do for this holiday? Do you go to the Puerto Rican Day parade? They were able to see me as a real person. Just today, it came up again and led to a good discussion about the most appropriate terms for various ethnic and racial groups. It clearly made an impact on them.

Before you start your first teaching job, be sure to review any online profiles you may have on social network sites. Make sure they don't reveal more than you would want your students (and their parents) to know about you. Also think *very* seriously before friending a student on Facebook and find out whether your school or district has a social-media policy regarding this issue. As of 2012, at least 40 school districts nationwide had such policies, and schools in New York City and Florida have disciplined teachers for Facebook activity (Matthews, 2012). In one of the New York cases, a teacher friended several female students and wrote comments including "this is sexy" under their photographs. Such behavior clearly oversteps boundaries. On the other hand, some teachers say that social media—in particular Facebook—can be a primary means of communicating with today's students for whom even e-mail is obsolete. Friending students also allows teachers to see whether anything on students' Facebook pages, such as sexual content, raises a red flag. If your district does allow teachers to friend students, be extremely careful: Manage your privacy settings so students cannot see personal information. You could also consider setting up a separate

Facebook page for your classroom, where you can friend your students and share professional posts. This keeps your personal Facebook page off limits to your students.

Finally, keep in mind that presenting yourself as a real person to your students doesn't mean that you should dress like them. Students, and also parents, tend to respect teachers who dress professionally. If you are coming straight from college, your clothes may be too casual for the classroom. Use other teachers as a model or ask the principal about expectations for professional dress. You should also learn about school policy or norms about piercings and tattoos.

Become Aware of Adolescent Culture

Positive relationships with students can be facilitated if you have what Robin Gordon (1997) calls "social insight"—knowledge of popular music, styles of dress, current movies, and other aspects of adolescent culture. Donna jokes about how she often incorporates vampires into her instruction. During one observation, for example, students were reviewing the components of narrative plot lines (e.g., exposition, rising action, climax). Donna provided an illustration: "I like to think about vampires. First the people have to figure out the problem: Who the vampire is. Then, once they figure out who the vampire is, they have to think about how to kill him—or marry him." Donna's comment was met with laughter and helped to reinforce her image as an "awesome" teacher who understands her students' out-of-school interests.

Teachers also need to be aware of the social media tools that are an integral part of students' lives and that drive much of their digital culture. Today's teenagers consider the Internet as a primary source of information and use social tools such as Facebook and YouTube to remain connected to the world around them. As phones have become smarter, faster, and cheaper, teens carry in their pockets the tools necessary to capture and share every aspect of their lives. When connected to the Internet, these devices allow students to build complex social networks of family, near friends (within their school or community), and far friends (located anywhere in the world). Within these networks, they communicate differently than older generations do. Texting is their primary mode of communication, followed by Facebook postings, and periodic phone calls. E-mail is reserved for parents, primarily because parents don't text.

When working with today's students, it is important to understand how digital technologies have fundamentally changed the way adolescents live and think to help guide them through the complexities of the digital world. A number of organizations are available on the web to help you learn more. A good starting point is the International Society for Technology in Education (www.iste.org) and the Partnership for 21st Century Learning (www.p21.org).

Promote Autonomy

Visiting kindergarten classes, we're always struck by how much more choice and control these young students have over their day than secondary students do. We see kindergartners making decisions about what they want to do and with whom they want to do it. Ironically, as students advance through the grades, becoming more capable of making decisions and more concerned about having autonomy, we offer fewer opportunities for choice and involvement in decision making (Nucci, 2006). At the junior high level, research has documented the decline in intrinsic motivation and interest in school that result from this mismatch between adolescents' increasing desire for greater autonomy and schools' increasing emphasis on teacher control (e.g., Eccles, Wigfield, & Schiefele, 1998).

Think about ways the students in your classes could make decisions about their own behavior and class events. For example, you might sometimes allow students to choose their own groups for cooperative learning activities. You might give students responsibility for creating assignments, constructing questions for class discussions and tests, leading class activities, and evaluating their own progress and behavior (Ridley & Walther, 1995). At the end of her poetry unit, Donna allows her students to choose the type of poem that they write. She sets the same standards for all the poems, but students can choose to create a sonnet, an epic, or other type of poem to demonstrate their mastery.

You might also assign "block homework assignments" that require students to develop their own time line for completion. For example, Sandy usually assigns a certain amount of reading and 25 to 30 problems that are due in a week or so. She recommends that students do four or five problems a night, but she does not require them to show her their work on a daily basis. She realizes that this means some students will wait until the last night to do all the problems:

High school teachers have to remember that students want to be treated like young adults, not like babies. It's important to give them some responsibility for their own behavior. They might make the wrong decisions and "fall and scrape their knees," but then they can see the consequences. I think they're more likely to take responsibility for their mistakes if teachers don't dictate everything.

Sharing decision making can be difficult for teachers. When you're feeling pressured to cover the curriculum and to maximize learning time, it's easier to make the decisions by yourself. For example, assigning topics for a term paper is faster than allowing students to decide on their own topic; giving students a set of instructions for a laboratory activity is simpler than allowing them to develop their own procedures. Involving students can be messy and time-consuming, and allowing students to make decisions about their own behavior means that they'll sometimes make the wrong decisions. Nonetheless, a "short-term investment of time" can lead to "a long-term gain in decision-making ability and self-esteem" (Dowd, 1997).

Be Inclusive

In recent years, *inclusive education* has been used to refer to the practice of placing students with disabilities in general education classrooms rather than segregating them in special classrooms or schools. As our teachers can attest, physical inclusion does not guarantee social inclusion, and they all work hard to enhance the acceptance of students with disabilities and to develop sensitivity and understanding among their nondisabled peers. (This topic will be discussed more fully in Chapter 6.) But the term *inclusive* can also be used more broadly, to describe classes in which differences related not only to disability, but also to race, class, ethnicity, gender, cultural and linguistic background, religion, and sexual orientation are acknowledged, understood, and respected.

This, of course, is easier said than done. Before we can create a classroom community that acknowledges and respects differences, we need to recognize that we are often afraid and suspicious of those differences. Sometimes we deny even *seeing* differences. It is not uncommon, for example, for our European American teacher education students to pride themselves on being "color-blind, that is, fair and impartial when it comes to judging people based on their race" (Nieto & Bode, 2008, p. 75). Yet, to deny cultural or racial differences is to deny an essential aspect of people's identity—and recognizing those differences does not make us racist. During one conversation, Fred spoke passionately about these issues:

> **So many times I hear teachers say things like, "I don't think of kids as Black or Hispanic or Asian—just as kids." But being Black or Hispanic or Asian is part of who those kids are—just like being Polish and Russian is part of who I am. . . . A part of the whole community-building thing is acknowledging that these differences exist. We're *not* all the same. . . . To build community we also need to face the fact that racism and bias are part of the real world. People don't want to admit it's there. But it's everywhere; it's part of all of us. The question is not "Are you a racist?" but "How much of a racist are you, and how can you become less so?"**

In addition to *acknowledging* differences, creating inclusive classrooms means learning about disabilities, or cultures, or races, or religions that we've never before encountered. For example, you can't acknowledge and respect behaviors that have cultural origins if you have no idea that the behaviors are rooted in culture. Teachers may be shocked when Southeast Asian students smile while being scolded if the teachers are unaware that the smiles are meant not as disrespect but as an admission of culpability and an effort to show that there is no grudge (Trueba, Cheng, & Ima, 1993). Similarly, teachers who are unaware that the culture of most American Indians tends to emphasize deliberate thought may become impatient when those students take longer to respond to questions (Nieto & Bode, 2008).

A particularly heated debate about students' use of Ebonics or Black English illustrates the problems that occur when teachers are unaware of the cultural origins of language. Ernie Smith (2002), an African American linguist, notes that during his years of schooling, teachers often equated the use of Ebonics with deficiency and used terms like "corrupt speech," "broken English," "verbal cripple," "linguistically handicapped," and "linguistically deprived" to describe the way he and his Black classmates spoke (pp. 17–18). Not surprisingly, this negative reaction to children's home language frequently leads to alienation from school. As Lisa Delpit argues in *The Skin That We Speak* (2002), "Language is one of the most intimate expressions of identity" so "to reject a person's language can only feel as if we are rejecting him" (p. 47). Rejection like this has no place in an inclusive classroom; instead, inclusive teachers honor students' home language while teaching them the importance of learning to speak Standard English—what Delpit (1995) calls the "language of the culture of power." In other words, our goal is to enable students to "code switch" according to the norms of the setting.

It's unrealistic to expect beginning teachers (or even experienced ones) to have familiarity with all of the cultures that might be represented in their extremely diverse classrooms. Certainly, developing this kind of "cultural literacy" takes time and effort. Some specific suggestions are listed in the Practical Tips box. Meanwhile, when you

PRACTICAL TIPS FOR

Developing Cultural Literacy

■ *Examine your own taken-for-granted beliefs, values, and assumptions and reflect on how they are influenced by your cultural, racial, and socioeconomic identity.* As we mentioned in Chapter 1, many European Americans consider their beliefs and values to be normal, correct, and universal, not realizing that these are products of their particular cultural background. Developing cultural literacy begins by examining one's own cultural norms. For example, a White middle-class worldview emphasizes individual achievement, independence, and competition. This is in stark contrast to the worldview of more collectivist cultures (e.g., Asian, Latino, and Native American) that avoid displays of individual accomplishment and, instead, stress cooperation, harmony, and working for the good of the group. One worldview is not necessarily better than the other—but the two are certainly different. Failing to appreciate and respect these differences can lead to misunderstanding and miscommunication.

■ *Explore students' family backgrounds.* Where did the student come from? Was it a rural or urban setting? Why did the family move? How long has the student been in this country? How many people are in the family? What are the lines of authority? What responsibilities does the student have at home? What are parents' beliefs with respect to involvement in the school and in their child's education? Do they consider teachers to be experts and therefore refrain from expressing differences of opinion? Is learning English considered a high priority?

■ *Explore students' educational background.* If students are new to this country, how much previous schooling have they had? What kinds of instructional strategies are they used to? In their former schools, was there an emphasis on large group instruction, memorization, and recitation? What were the expectations for appropriate behavior? Were students expected to be active or passive? independent or dependent? peer oriented or teacher oriented? cooperative or competitive?

■ *Be sensitive to cultural differences and how they may lead to miscommunication.* How do students think about time? Is punctuality expected or is time considered to be flexible? Do students nod their heads to be polite or to indicate understanding? Do students question or obey authority figures? Do students put their needs and desires before those of the group or vice versa? Are expressions of emotion and feelings emphasized or hidden?

■ *Use photographs to communicate without words.* Take pictures of the students engaged in various activities to take home to parents; display photographs around the room; invite students to bring in pictures of themselves and their families; use photographs for get-acquainted activities.

Sources: Kottler, 1994; Sileo & Prater, 1998; Weinstein, Tomlinson-Clarke, & Curran, 2004.

encounter behaviors that seem inappropriate and inexplicable, ask yourself whether these behaviors might, in fact, be culturally grounded. In addition, think about how you can use your students as a resource. Listen to Fred:

 If I have kids from other countries in my class, I'll ask about customs there, and how they compare with customs here. Not only do I learn something I didn't know before, but I can just see the "little lights go on." It's like, "Hey, here's someone who's interested in my experiences." We don't have to be intrusive about it, but it's important that classrooms be a place where we can learn about one another. I can use my classroom like a textbook.

Just as we must learn to acknowledge and respect racial and cultural diversity, we must also learn to create an accepting classroom environment for other, less visible kinds of differences. In recent years, countless newspaper articles have described the peer harassment faced by students who are lesbian, gay, bisexual, and transgender (LGBT). These reports also describe the detrimental effects of such harassment—high levels of depression and anxiety, decreased levels of self-esteem, increased risk for poor school performance and dropping out, physiological problems such as difficulty breathing and hypertension, and most alarming, dramatically higher suicide rates (Connolly, 2012). There were at least 10 suicides by gay teenagers in September and October of 2010 alone. One of these was Seth Walsh, a 13-year-old boy in California, who was taunted, menaced, and jostled in school by students who threatened "to get him" on his way home. He tried switching schools and then home schooling, but he was unable to escape the physical and verbal abuse of his peers, one of whom asked, "Why don't you hang yourself?" Given the climate of homophobia that is common to many U.S. schools, teachers must send a clear-cut message that students who are LGBT are valued members of the class, that their well-being is as important as those of their heterosexual peers, and that gay bullying is absolutely unacceptable.

Search for Students' Strengths

In *The Culturally Responsive Teacher* (2007), Villegas and Lucas tell the story of Belki Alvarez, an eight-year-old girl from the Dominican Republic. As the oldest child in the family, Belki was responsible for getting her brother and sister ready for school and caring for them until her parents came home from work. On weekends, she joined her mother at a community street fair, selling products prepared at home, negotiating prices with customers, and handling financial transactions. She also served as an English language translator for her parents. But Belki's teachers didn't see this competent, responsible child. They saw only a youngster lacking in language and math skills and made no effort to tap into her life experiences. In other words, they focused on her deficits rather than her strengths.

Searching for deficits makes a certain amount of sense. After all, if we can identify what students don't know or can't do, we can try to fix the problems. But responsible teaching also involves a search for strengths. In *Teaching to Change the World* (2007), Oakes and Lipton argue that when teachers and students have a caring relationship, they work together to find competence: "The student's search is his own discovery of what he knows and how he knows it. The teacher's search—an act of care and respect—is also discovering what the student knows and how he knows it" (pp. 266–267).

We thought of this perspective on caring during one meeting with the teachers, when Sandy talked about her conviction that "everyone needs their 15 minutes of fame":

> **Chemistry lends itself to a variety of talents—the math problems, the writing, the spatial relations, the mechanical ability. So I can give different people a chance to shine. Take Adam. He's really good at spatial relationships so I know that I can call on him to do diagrams.**
>
> **When we have student presentations, I always try to think who I want to call on so I can showcase kids' different strengths. For example, I told the class that I was going to randomly choose a lab group to present the lab to the rest of the class. Everyone had to think about how to teach this and to be prepared. It was a nice safe situation—a great opportunity to get these two quiet girls to shine. I knew they had done a good job on the lab. So I wrote their names 12 times and put the slips in a beaker, and had someone pull out a slip. Of course their presentation went very well. But it was important for the girls—and everyone else—to think it was a risky situation, that they had just gotten chosen by chance. When they got a great evaluation, they felt terrific.**

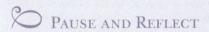

PAUSE AND REFLECT

At the beginning of this chapter, we stressed the fact that students are more likely to cooperate with teachers who are perceived to be caring. Because a big part of showing care is being a good listener, it's important to think about exactly what that means. Before reading the next section on communication skills, think about a time when someone *really listened well* to a problem you were relating. What kinds of behaviors did this person display? How did you know she or he was *really* listening?

Develop Communication Skills

Another way to show students that you care is by being a good listener. Sandy puts it this way:

> **How come there are only certain teachers in the school that kids will go to [when they have a problem]? After all, most kids have six teachers a day. It's all about listening. When you're a high school teacher, you have to listen seriously to problems that might not be problems to you, but they are to them. And that's a way of gaining their trust. A kid is not going to come to you and say, "I want to commit suicide" if three weeks earlier you said, "Oh grow up, you'll get over her."**

Being a good listener means being attentive, trying to understand students' feelings and concerns, asking appropriate questions, and helping students solve their own problems. In the following sections, we will examine each of these. As you read, keep in mind that as a teacher, you are required by law to report child abuse or neglect and sexual abuse or assault, so there may be times when you will need to go beyond merely listening. It's important to let your students know that if you do learn about any of these abuses, you will need to report the information to the appropriate child welfare agency.

ATTENDING AND ACKNOWLEDGING

Giving a student your complete, undivided attention is the first and most basic task in being helpful (Kottler & Kottler, 1993). It is rare that individuals are fully attentive to one another. Have you ever tried to talk with someone who was simultaneously organizing papers, posting notices on the bulletin board, or straightening rows of desks? Divided attention like this communicates that the person doesn't really have time for you and is not fully paying attention.

Attending and acknowledging involve both verbal and nonverbal behaviors. Even without saying a word, you can convey that you are totally tuned in by orienting your body toward the student, establishing eye contact, nodding, leaning forward, smiling, or frowning. In addition, you can use verbal cues. Thomas Gordon (2003) recommends using "acknowledgement responses" or "empathic grunting"—the little "uh-huhs" and phrases (e.g., "Oh," "I see," "Mmmmm") that communicate, "I'm really listening." When a student needs additional encouragement to talk more, you can use an explicit invitation, what Gordon calls a "door opener": "Tell me more." "Would you like to say more about that?" "Do you want to talk about it?" "Want to go on?"

ACTIVE LISTENING

Attending and acknowledging communicate that you are totally engaged, but they do not convey whether you really *understand*. Active listening takes the interaction one step further by having you reflect back what you think you heard. This feedback allows you to check out whether you're right or wrong. If you're right, the student knows that you have truly understood. If you're off target, the student can correct you, and the communication can continue. Examples of active listening appear in Table 3.1.

If you're new to active listening, you may find it useful to use the phrase, "You feel . . ." when you reflect back what you heard. Sometimes, novices feel stupid, as if they're simply parroting back what the person just said. As you gain more skill, however, you are able to *paraphrase* what you hear, and the interaction becomes far more subtle.

You can also use active listening to respond to the nonverbal messages contained in students' facial expressions and body language. For example, if you see that a student entering the room looks really angry, you might be able to ward off problems by recognizing that something is wrong. Here is a journal entry from a student teacher who did this without even knowing about active listening:

> *I was writing the "Do Now" on the board when all of a sudden I heard a loud crash behind me—the sound of a backpack crammed full of books thrown to the floor. I turned around, and there was John sulking in the seat directly behind me. I quickly finished writing the "Do Now" for the rest of the class to begin and went over to John. I squatted down and asked, "What's wrong? You seem really upset"—not knowing at the time this was a communication strategy called Active Listening. His immediate response was, "Nothing." I paused, trying to come up with something "teacher-y" to say, and in that pause of 10 seconds, John spoke! The problem was that he was mad at his parents. He had broken his book bag the day before, and since he had to use the same broken bag the next day, he was extremely embarrassed. We talked about his anger and he started to work once he had vented. [It was obvious that] he was glad I paid attention to him and his problem.*

(like spending time on Facebook), if they do their homework in a quiet place or in some place where they are constantly getting distracted. All of these factors play a role in making a decision about what to do.

Then, they need to figure out what their values and priorities are: Which activities are most important to them? Which demand the most time? Do they really need all of them to make them attractive to colleges? How would they feel about dropping out from some of them and what would the ramifications be? Finally, I try to help them figure out the alternatives—for example, cutting down on activities, cutting down on work, talking to their boss about changing their work schedule, changing where they do homework, eliminating time wasters.

In situations like this, I don't tell kids what to do (although it's always a temptation). Instead, I try to listen compassionately, understand the situation, and help them clarify exactly what's going on. Many of these students are in this situation because of expectations that their parent may have for them. I want them to realize that they have the tools to manage their dilemma. They're confused, and as an outside party who can think clearly, I can help them see alternatives they haven't thought of. But I'm always prepared for a call from the parents! Many times the parents are thankful that their son or daughter was able to come up with a plan that worked for them, but every so often I get a call where the parents are angry that their child gave something up. Nonetheless, my goal is to help my students make the best possible decision for themselves. If it is truly the student's solution, then you have empowered them and they will have the confidence to explain to their parents the choices that they have made.

Ask Students How They Feel about the Class Atmosphere

Teachers are often inaccurate in their assessment of class atmosphere or the relationships they have developed with students. For example, one recent study (Brekelmans, Mainhard, den Brok, & Wubbels, 2011) used the Questionnaire on Teacher Interaction (QTI) to examine the perceptions of approximately 6,000 secondary teachers and a group of their students regarding the teacher's "affiliation" and "control" (terms that are comparable to those used in Chapter 1: warmth/responsiveness and demandingness). The researchers found that relative to the reports of their students, 66% of the teachers overestimated their affiliation and 55% overestimated their control. On the other hand, 33% of the teachers underestimated their affiliation and 43% underestimated their control.

For this reason, it's a good idea to ask students how they feel about the classroom environment. A sample of items from the QTI appears in Table 3.2.

Be Careful about Touching

In recent years, the fear of being accused of sexual harassment and physical abuse has made teachers wary of showing students any physical affection. This is a particularly salient issue for males (King, 1998). Indeed, one of our male student teachers wrote this entry in his journal:

> *I had occasion to talk to a student who had a death in the family. She was pretty upset. After explaining that she needn't worry about her class work for that day, I tried my best to comfort her. It's funny, under any other circumstances I would have put an arm around a person in that state, but in this case, I wasn't sure if that would be right.*

> **TABLE 3.2 Items from the *Questionnaire on Teacher Interaction***
>
> This teacher acts as if she/he does not know what to do.*
> This teacher knows everything that goes on in the classroom.
> This teacher lets us boss her/him around.*
> This teacher realizes when we don't understand.
> This teacher is not sure what to do when we fool around.*
> This teacher is patient.
> This teacher is sarcastic.*
> This teacher helps us with our work.
> This teacher is friendly.
> We can influence this teacher.
> This teacher is someone we can depend on.
> This teacher puts us down.*
> This teacher has a sense of humor.
> If we have something to say, this teacher will listen.
>
> Items are scored 0, 1, 2, 3, and 4, with 0 representing "Never" and 4 representing "Always."
> Those with an asterisk are scored in reverse.

Source: Wubbels & Levy, 1993.

This student is not alone in his concern. A study of male teacher education students about to begin their teaching careers revealed a tension between their natural inclinations to be warm, caring, and affectionate to students and the fear that their behavior would be misconstrued as sexual (Hansen & Mulholland, 2005). Fortunately, the anxiety about showing physical affection decreased somewhat as the teachers became more experienced. The young male teachers also found other ways of expressing their affection—for example, by talking and listening with empathy.

Although our five teachers have all been told to avoid touching students, they do not want to forgo all physical contact. Fred notes:

 I have colleagues who say they'll never touch a kid at all. I understand, but I think you have to touch people if you're going to be a teacher. There have to be rules, of course. I would never be alone with a kid, because of the appearance of impropriety, but I'll hug kids. . . . It doesn't have to be any big demonstrative thing, but just touching somebody's hand or shoulder can mean a lot. If someone's getting antsy, I'll put my hand on their shoulder, and they'll settle down. If they're hurting, and they need a hug, I'll give them one. What kind of community is it if you can't give someone who's hurting a hug?

 PAUSE AND REFLECT

Where do you stand on the issue of touching students? Did your own teachers ever touch you in ways that felt nurturing, comfortable, and caring? Were you ever on the "receiving end" of physical contact by teachers that made you uneasy? What factors are responsible for the difference in your reactions?

It's important to point out that Fred has been in his district for many years and has a solid reputation. As a new teacher, you are in a very different situation. Speak with your colleagues about the policy in effect in your school; some schools actually direct teachers to "teach but don't touch." Even if there is no explicit prohibition against touching students, you need to be cautious so that your actions are not misconstrued. Give your hugs in front of others. Be alert for signs that students feel uneasy about touch. Donna gives high fives or fist bumps, noting that these are more comfortable for some of her eighth graders.

CONCLUDING COMMENTS

Alfie Kohn (1996) suggests that it would be helpful if we all reflected on "what makes school awful sometimes" (p. 114). Then we might be more inclined to make sure that those kinds of experiences and situations don't happen for students in our classrooms. Following his advice, we reminisced with our students about awful times we had experienced. A common theme was being humiliated by teachers. Here are two of our students' memories:

> *In second grade, my teacher constantly yelled at me and made me sit in the corner facing the wall. But the worst was when she drew a two-column chart on the board and labeled the two columns "Things we like about Elizabeth" and "Things we don't like about Elizabeth." She encouraged the kids in the class to contribute items for each side, but needless to say, the "don't like" column was a lot longer than the "like" column. This incident shaped my attitude toward myself and school for many years, and even now in college, it's still vivid and disturbing.*

> *As a high school junior, I took Algebra II and Trigonometry. Although I was a good student, the teacher and I did not hit it off for some reason. . . . Midyear, we had an exam on logarithms. I thought I understood it, but I made the same mistake reading the log charts for every problem and I failed the test. I came into class the next day thinking I had done OK on the test. The teacher held up my exam in front of the class and gloated that he had failed me. I hated going to that class for the rest of the year, and I hated that teacher for humiliating me.*

Because one of the reasons people choose teaching as a career is that they like working with young people, it's hard to fathom how teachers could treat a student like this (even if they had had a particularly bad day). Yet from our students' responses (and our own memories), it is clear that behavior like this is all too common. As you interact with students, think of all the ways you can show them caring and respect so that school (or at least your classroom) is a good place to be, not an awful one. And remember this lesson from Fred:

Every year, students enter school with a "special need"—a relationship with a calm, confident, and caring adult who is worthy of their trust. In my classes, building that kind of relationship begins each year the very first time I meet with students. I promise them that I will do all I can to help them make this the best year of their high school career. I work at memorizing the names and faces of each student by our third class together (and I tell them that if I fail to remember their name after that, they get a small treat). During that first week of school, my priority is turning *You* and *Me* into *Us*. In every interaction, I try to be intentional, so I can make this transition happen.

SUMMARY

This chapter began by discussing the key role that positive teacher-student relationships play in classroom management. The chapter then considered ways of showing students that you care about them.

Ways to Show Care and Respect

- Be welcoming.
- Learn about students' lives.
- Be sensitive to students' concerns.
- Establish and enforce clear expectations for behavior.
- Be fair.
- Use humor.
- Welcome students' input
- Be a real person (as well as a teacher).
- Become aware of adolescent culture.
- Promote autonomy.
- Be inclusive.
- Search for students' strengths.
- Develop communication skills:
    Attending and acknowledging
    Active listening
    Open-ended questioning
    Problem solving
- Ask students how they feel about the class atmosphere.
- Be careful about touching.

ACTIVITIES FOR SKILL BUILDING AND REFLECTION

In Class

1. Think about the teachers you had in junior and senior high school. Select one teacher who showed caring to students and one teacher who did not. Write a paragraph about each teacher, providing details and examples to illustrate what each teacher actually did. Share these in small groups.

2. In the following bits of conversation, students have confided in teachers about problems they are experiencing, and the teachers have responded in ways *not* suggested in this chapter. Provide a new response for each case, using the communication skills discussed in this chapter: acknowledging, active listening, asking open-ended questions, and problem solving.

    Student: My parents won't allow me to go visit my boyfriend at college for the weekend. They say they trust me, but then they don't show it!

    Teacher: Well, I'm sure they have your best interests at heart. You know, you really shouldn't gripe. After all, a lot of kids don't have parents who care about them. I see a lot of kids whose parents let them do anything they want. Maybe you think you'd like that, but I'm sure you wouldn't. . . .

Student: I can't stand my stepmother. She's always criticizing me and making me come home right after school to watch my sister, and making me feel really stupid.

Teacher: Oh, come on now, Cinderella. I'm sure it's not that bad.

Student: My parents want me to go to college, but I really want to join the Marines. What do you think I should do?

Teacher: Do what your folks say. Go to college. You can always join the Marines later.

On Your Own

1. Interview a few middle school or high school students about their definitions of caring teachers. Ask them to identify the ways in which teachers show caring to students.

2. Do some planning for the first week of school. First, think about how you will introduce yourselves to your students. What will you tell them about yourself? Second, plan a way to show students that you welcome their input. (Will you have students verbally share their suggestions and opinions about rules, lessons, assignments, or grouping? Write a letter to you? Answer specific questions?)

3. Visit a middle school or high school classroom that you have never been in before. Record your immediate thoughts when you walked into the room about how it feels to be a student in that room. Observe the class for a little while and jot down any ways that the teacher is communicating caring and respect for students.

For Your Portfolio

Document the ways in which you work (or will work) to establish positive relationships with students. Include artifacts such as welcoming letters to students, inventories or questionnaires you will administer to learn about their lives and/or their feelings about the subject you teach, and rubrics that clearly communicate your expectations for assignments.

FOR FURTHER READING

Building classroom relationships (2003). *Educational Leadership, 61*(1).
   This entire issue is devoted to issues such as winning students' hearts and minds, giving students what they need, personalizing schools, practicing democracy in high school, and building relationships with challenging children.

Marlowe, M. J., & Hayden, T. (2013). *Teaching children who are hard to reach: Relationship-driven classroom practice.* Thousand Oaks, CA: Corwin.
   This book focuses on how to build a relationship-driven classroom, develop a positive classroom climate, and strengthen classroom dynamics. Although the authors focus on teaching resistant students, the strategies will benefit all students.

Ridnouer, K. (2006). *Managing your classroom with heart: A guide for nurturing adolescent learners.* Alexandria, VA: ASCD.
   Written by a long-time teacher at a large and diverse urban school, this book is focused on how to create a learning community in your classroom. The author draws on her own experiences to illustrate how to teach with high expectations and a lot of heart.

Rodriguez, L. F. (2005). Yo, Mister! *Educational Leadership, 62*(7), 78–80.

    Rodriguez, a teacher in an alternative urban high school, shows how he tries to acknowledge students as people, legitimize their knowledge and experiences, and engage with them personally and intellectually.

Stipek, D. (2006). Relationships matter. *Educational Leadership, 64*(1), 46–49.

    When teachers must focus their energies on preparing students for high-stakes tests, they have less time to get to know students personally or make them feel valued, respected, and supported. Stipek reviews research on the importance of strong teacher-student relationships and provides suggestions for strategies.

CHAPTER 4

Fostering Positive Peer Relationships

In Chapter 3, we talked about Alfie Kohn's (1996) suggestion to reflect on "what makes school awful sometimes" and focused on how teacher humiliation can make school intolerable for students. But teachers are obviously not the only ones who shape the experience of school. Consider two more tales our students shared about "when school was awful":

> When I was a sophomore in high school, one of the girls would follow me around and torment me, call me names, and threaten to hurt me. . . . None of my teachers or any authority figure ever helped. I'm still curious why she hated me so much.

> The worst was in junior high. . . . I was made fun of by the other girls, girls with whom I had been friends the year before. . . . I was tormented for not having money or clothes and for having a conscience (and by that I mean not breaking the law or hurting other people's feelings). It was the first year I didn't like going to school.

Students, like all of us, have a fundamental need for a sense of belonging, trust, and safety. A large body of evidence indicates that the experience of an emotionally supportive classroom is related to better attitudes toward school; higher achievement; greater engagement, enjoyment, and motivation; and less violent behavior (Brackett, Reyes, Rivers, Elbertson, & Salovey, 2011). Although research has generally focused on teacher-student relationships, it is clear that peer relationships have a significant impact on the emotional well-being of students (Osterman, 2000). When students face taunting, rejection, bullying, and exclusion, it's difficult to concentrate on academic learning, and their lack of motivation, alienation, and poor academic performance are understandable.

A great deal has been written about ways to create classroom communities in which students feel connected and valued. But this doesn't happen by itself. No teacher can simply declare, "We are a community" and leave it at that. Communities develop only when teachers provide opportunities for students to learn about one another: to interact in respectful, supportive ways, and to share experiences. This chapter focuses on strategies for building community and positive peer relationships. As you read, recall the fact (discussed in Chapter 1) that, unlike most other social groups, students do not come together voluntarily and do not usually choose their peers. Keeping this in mind makes it easier to see why teachers must work deliberately to create a sense of community.

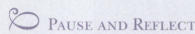

PAUSE AND REFLECT

Think about your years in elementary, middle, or high school. What were some of the ways that teachers worked to foster positive peer relationships and create a cohesive community?

BUILDING CARING RELATIONSHIPS AMONG STUDENTS

Much of the advice about building community focuses on elementary classrooms in which teachers generally work with the same group of children for the entire day and have more opportunity to build a sense of connectedness. The challenge of creating a safe, caring community is certainly more daunting when you teach three or four or five groups of students a day for 42 or 60 or even 84 minutes. What can secondary teachers possibly do in the limited amount of time—especially in this era of high-stakes testing and pressure for academic excellence? We posed this question to our five teachers. Some of their suggestions along with others from educational writers interested in students' social and emotional learning follow.

Model and Recognize Prosocial Behavior

Teachers frequently exhort students to treat one another with respect. Yet exhortation is unlikely to be effective unless teachers themselves are respectful. "Do as I say, not as I do" definitely does not work (Williams, 1993). Students resent teachers who tell them to be kind and to respect others and then treat students in demeaning ways. Moreover, in classrooms where teachers treat students with warmth, respect, and responsiveness, students themselves are more likely to engage in prosocial behavior toward their peers (Luckner & Pianta, 2011).

Teachers not only must be models of respectful behavior but also can discuss what respectful peer relationships would look like. In the following vignette, Donna describes how she talked about bullying with her students:

 I started off by talking about all the names I was called when I was in school— "all legs," "stupid," "poor," "the N word." But I didn't tell them I was talking about me. Then I asked, "Who *was* this person? How do you think this person felt? What happened to her?" Finally, I told them, "This happened to *me*."

They were shocked, and they had so many questions: "How did you come through it?" "How did you deal with it?" "Is this why you became a teacher?" Then we talked about bullying and how it affects everyone, how it makes you feel, what the overt and covert types of bullying are. You could feel the emotion in the classroom as they shared their experiences. That led to a discussion about respectful behavior and treating each other with kindness. What would that look like? When have you seen people act that way? I'm gratified to say that I've noticed changes in their behavior: they're opening doors for each other, not writing all over desks, not ripping each other's stuff.

In addition to modeling and discussing the kind of behavior we want from our students, teachers need to acknowledge students' prosocial behavior. We saw Donna do this on an uncomfortably warm afternoon when a student in her last period class mentioned that she wasn't feeling well. Donna advised her to drink a lot of water before she started walking home. Manuel, another student in the class, overheard the interchange and told the girl that he would buy her a bottle of water after school. Donna responded, "Manuel, thank you. I love it when I see you kids being kind to each other!" On another occasion, we watched Donna recognize how well students had worked together on a cooperative activity: "I want to compliment you guys. You worked very well together. You were encouraging each other, not putting each other down. You took turns writing. You corrected each other when you saw a mistake. I thank you for that. That was great work that I saw today." Later in the period, before students packed up to leave, Donna repeated how pleased she was that students had worked well together, telling them, "Awesome, awesome work in your groups today."

Provide Opportunities for Students to Get to Know One Another

On the first day of school, Christina distributes a handout entitled "Find Someone Who." Students must find one person in the class who fits each of the 36 descriptions (e.g., someone who "has read at least three Stephen King novels," someone who "has the same favorite television show as you do," someone who "is a procrastinator," and someone who "would rather work alone than in groups") and have the person sign his or her name next to the appropriate statement. Students are allowed to sign their names only once per sheet, even if more than one item applies.

"Find Someone Who" can be especially useful if you include items relating to race, cultural and linguistic background, and disability and solicit information in addition to a signature. Consider these examples from a "Diversity Treasure Hunt" (Sapon-Shevin, 2010):

Find someone who grew up with an older relative. What did he or she learn from this experience?

Find someone who has a parent or a grandparent who came to this country from another country. What customs or traditions has he or she learned from this person?

Find someone who has a person with a disability in his or her immediate or extended family. What did he or she learn from this experience?

To build community, we have to create opportunities for students to learn about one another and to discover the ways in which they are both different and similar. Numerous getting-acquainted activities such as the one Christina chose are available for teachers to use. Some of these are listed in the Practical Tips box.

 PRACTICAL TIPS FOR

Helping Your Students to Get Acquainted

- *Guess Who?* Have students write a brief autobiographical statement (family background, hobbies, extracurricular activities, etc.), which they do not sign. Collect the statements, read them aloud, and ask students to write the name of the individual they believe wrote each description. (You can participate too.) After all the descriptions have been read, reread them and ask the authors to identify themselves. Ask students to indicate how many classmates they correctly identified (Jones & Jones, 2010).

- *Two Truths and a Lie (or Two Facts and a Fiction).* Have students write down and then share three statements about themselves, two of which are true and one of which is a lie. For example, one of the authors (Carol) might write, "I once played the princess in Once Upon the Mattress, and one night during a performance I fell from the top of 15 mattresses and herniated a disk in my back"; "I won third prize in the All-Alaska Logging Championship for the rolling pin toss"; and "I trekked through Nepal on my honeymoon." Students guess which one is the lie, and then she tells the truth. (Carol didn't trek through Nepal; she backpacked through Colorado and Wyoming.) The activity can be done with the whole class or in small groups. In either case, because the activity allows students to select what to disclose about themselves, there is little chance of embarrassment. It also provides opportunities for students to discover common interests and experiences and to test assumptions and stereotypes. (No one looking at her today, for example, would ever guess that Carol had camped on her honeymoon!) (Sapon-Shevin, 2010).

- *Little-known Facts about Me.* This is a variation of the previous activity. Students write a statement about themselves that they think others won't know. The papers are folded, collected, put in a box, and shaken. Students take turns drawing a paper and reading the statement aloud. Everyone guesses who wrote the little-known fact (Sapon-Shevin, 2010).

- *Three Crucible Events.* Each student has to tell (not read) three stories of events that shaped the trajectory of his or her life. Students have five minutes to tell the stories and tie them all together in a culminating message (Schultz, 2012).

- *Lifelines.* Each student draws a line on a piece of paper and then marks 6 to 10 points representing important events in their lives that they are willing to share (e.g., the birth of a sibling, the death of a close family member, the time they starred in the school play, when they moved to this school). Students then get into pairs and share their life stories. Members of each pair could also introduce each other to the rest of the class, referring to points on the lifeline (Sapon-Shevin, 2010).

(continued on next page)

- *Your Inspiration.* Have students bring in pictures of people or things that inspire them and an accompanying quotation. Post them on a bulletin board (Schmollinger, Opaleski, Chapman, Jocius, & Bell, 2002).
- *What Are You Most Proud of Yourself For?* Have students write their individual responses to this question on paper in the shape of a footprint. Post these on a bulletin board in the shape of a path labeled "success" (Schmollinger, Opaleski, Chapman, Jocius, & Bell, 2002).
- *Cultural Artifact Sharing.* Students bring in something that represents their background (e.g., their family, religion, or ethnicity). They then share their object with the class and answer questions (Sapon-Shevin, 2010).
- *Who Is It?* The teacher or a student describes a member of the class, one detail at a time, starting from general descriptions that could fit many individuals (e.g., "I'm thinking of someone who is wearing a T-shirt") and then adding more specific, unique details. The other students guess who the mystery student is (Sapon-Shevin, 2010).
- *The Six-Word Memoir.* Students (and teachers) tell their life story in six words. These can be done in different colors, fonts, or positioning of the words and can be accompanied by an illustration (www.sixwordmemoirs.com).

It's important to note that one or two activities at the start of school are not sufficient to enable students to get to know one another, let alone to build community. Christina learned this lesson halfway through the school year:

Since my basic skills class only has 11 kids I figured that they had all gotten to know one another, especially since I had done getting-to-know-you activities at the beginning of school. But one day, when they were working in small groups, I found out that some kids didn't know other kids' names. I was astounded. The class was a combination of English language learners and native English speakers who were very low achieving, and I realized that these two groups of kids had never really gotten to know one another. Obviously, I should have done more team building throughout the year; once or twice at the beginning of school was just not enough.

Hold Class Meetings

During advisory or homeroom periods, middle school teachers can implement a type of class meeting called "Circle of Power and Respect" or "CPR" (Kriete, 2002). CPR is the middle school version of "morning meetings" with which many elementary teachers begin the day, and it contains the same four components. Sitting in a circle, students first **greet one another;** the greeting can be simple—a simple hello, a handshake, or a high-five. As students become more comfortable, the teacher can introduce variations (e.g., greeting one another in different languages). *Sharing* comes next; during this phase of CPR, a few students present news they wish to share, and others ask questions and comment. Sometimes teachers can generate a question for a "focused sharing" (e.g., "What's one accomplishment you feel proud of?" "If you could change one thing about school, what would you change and why?" "What person do you most

November 21, 2005

Good Morning, Everyone!

Today there will be an assembly program at
11:15 honoring Rosa Parks, who died last month.
Ms. Parks is known as the "mother of the civil
rights movement." In 1955, she changed the
course of American history by refusing to give up
her seat on a bus for a white man.

Write something you know about Rosa Parks
here:

FIGURE 4.1   An Example of a News and Announcements Chart

admire? Why?"). After sharing, the class engages in a *group activity* to build team
spirit and to encourage cooperation, participation, and inclusion. Group activities can
include games (e.g., Twenty Questions, Charades, Telephone), puzzles, and choral
readings of poems. Finally, students focus on a chart containing *news and announcements;* typically, the chart tells them about class and school events and presents an
"academic challenge" to develop and reinforce language, math, and other academic
skills. (See Figure 4.1.)

Ideally, CPR should be done at least three times a week at the beginning of the day,
although schedules do not always allow that. Implemented regularly, CPR allows middle school students to learn CARES—cooperation (rather than competition), assertion
(rather than aggression), responsibility (rather than apathy), empathy (rather than self-
absorption), and self-control (rather than lack of control). For detailed information
about this type of class meeting, see Kriete (2002).

Many high schools are also incorporating a homeroom or advisory period into
their daily schedules to allow opportunities for class meetings. These opportunities
for groups of students to meet regularly with mentors is part of the philosophy of the
Small Learning Communities movement, which focuses on establishing small communities, either in a stand-alone school or within a larger school (Cotton, 2001). Even
if your school schedule doesn't include regular time for class meetings, including
team-building activities into your classes can help build caring relationships among
students.

Two educators who emphasize the importance of class meetings are Jane Nelsen
and Lynn Lott. See Meet the Educators Box 4.1 for information on their ideas.

Use Cooperative Learning Groups

Research suggests that there are few opportunities for interaction among students
during the school day (Osterman, 2000). These findings are disturbing in light of
innumerable studies attesting to the power of cooperative learning to promote the
development of positive peer relations. More specifically, cooperative learning

BOX 4.1   MEET THE EDUCATORS

Meet Jane Nelsen and Lynn Lott

Jane Nelsen and Lynn Lott are therapists and educators who write, lecture, and conduct workshops for parents and teachers on Positive Discipline. Their work is grounded in the ideas of Alfred Adler (1870–1937) and Rudolf Dreikurs (1897–1972), two Viennese psychiatrists who advocated treating children respectfully and kindly, but firmly. Nelsen and Lott's collaboration began in 1988 with the book that is now entitled *Positive Discipline for Teenagers.* Since then, the Positive Discipline series has grown to include titles that address different age groups, settings (e.g., home, school, and child care), and types of families (e.g., single parents, blended families).

Some Major Ideas about Classroom Management

1. Methods of classroom management must be based on *caring and mutual respect* with the goal of creating a climate that is nurturing to self-esteem and academic performance.

2. Five criteria for effective positive discipline are (1) helps children feel a sense of connection, (2) is mutually respectful and encouraging, (3) is effective long term, (4) teaches important social and life skills, and (5) invites children to discover how capable they are.

3. *Class meetings* not only help to minimize discipline problems but also help students

develop social, academic, and life skills. A specific format provides structure: (1) express compliments and appreciations, (2) follow up on prior solutions to problems, (3) go through agenda items that students and teachers have written in a special notebook, and (4) make future plans.

4. To ensure that class meetings are effective, teachers need to take time to teach students eight skills: (1) form a circle, (2) practice compliments and appreciations, (3) respect differences, (4) use respectful communication skills, (5) focus on solutions, (6) practice role-playing and brainstorming, (7) use the agenda, and (8) understand the four reasons people do what they do.

Selected Books and Articles

Positive discipline in the classroom: Developing mutual respect, cooperation, and responsibility in your classroom (4th ed., Nelsen, Lott, & J. A. Glenn, New York: Three Rivers, 2013)

Positive discipline for teenagers (3rd ed., Nelsen & Lott, New York: Three Rivers, 2012)

Positive discipline: A teacher's A–Z guide: Hundreds of solutions for every possible classroom behavior problem (2nd ed., Nelsen, Escobar, Ortolano, Duffy, & Owen-Sohocki, New York: Three Rivers, 2001)

Website: www.positivediscipline.com

---

facilitates interaction and friendship among students who differ in terms of achievement, sex, cultural and linguistic background, and race; fosters the acceptance of students with disabilities; increases positive attitudes toward school; and promotes empathy (Good & Brophy, 2008).

David and Roger Johnson (1999), two prominent researchers in the field of cooperative learning, distinguish among three types of cooperative learning. In *formal cooperative learning,* teachers assign students to small heterogeneous groups that work together on carefully structured tasks; groups may stay together for one class period up to several weeks. Sandy, who frequently uses this type of cooperative learning, comments:

 Having students do cooperative group activities takes a lot longer than just getting up there and telling them the material. But I really believe that this is the best way. When they've worked through the material in a group, they really understand. And they're also learning the value of cooperating with one another.

In *informal cooperative learning,* students work together in temporary groups that might last from a few minutes to a whole period. For example, during a whole-class presentation, Donnie frequently tells her students to "turn to your neighbor and talk about how you'd tackle this problem." Finally, *cooperative base groups* are long-term, heterogeneous groups in which students support one another's academic progress and emotional well-being. Members of the base group can collect assignments for absent students and provide assistance when they return, tutor students who are having problems with the course material, check homework assignments, and provide study groups for tests. It's helpful to have base groups meet several times a week for 5 to 15 minutes. (See Chapter 11 for a more detailed discussion of cooperative learning.)

Teach Social-Emotional Skills

Consider the following scenario: An eighth-grade girl finds out that some of her peers have been spreading rumors about her. In response, does she corner them in a hallway and call them names, or does she realize she is angry and hurt, try to calm down, and decide to speak to them about how she is feeling? The answer depends on her "emotional competence"—the ability to understand and manage social-emotional situations (Elias & Schwab, 2006; Woolfolk, 2007). Individuals with emotional competence can identify and regulate their feelings, solve problems by generating alternative solutions and selecting the best action, show respect and empathy for others, and communicate effectively. Numerous programs are now available to foster skills such as these. Although the research on such programs does not always show consistent results, a recent, comprehensive review of more than 213 schoolwide social-emotional learning (SEL) programs found significant positive effects on students' social-emotional skills; attitudes about self, others, and school; prosocial behavior; and academic performance (Durlak, Weissberg, Dymnicki, Taylor, & Schellinger, 2011).

Being able to resolve conflicts constructively is a key social-emotional skill that is the focus of numerous programs. There is great diversity in approaches, but generally the programs fall into two categories: those that train the entire student body in conflict resolution strategies and those that train a particular cadre of students to mediate disputes among their peers (Johnson & Johnson, 2004). An example of a program that targets the entire student body is Johnson and Johnson's *Teaching Students to be Peacemakers* (2005). The program spans grades 1 through 12; each year all students learn increasingly sophisticated negotiation and mediation procedures.

Research conducted by Johnson and Johnson indicates that students trained in the peacemaker program are able to apply the negotiation and mediation procedures to a variety of conflicts—both in and out of the classroom. In addition, training results in fewer discipline problems that the teacher and the principal must manage (Johnson & Johnson, 2004).

In a peer mediation program, selected students guide disputants through the problem-solving process. The advantage of using peers rather than adults as mediators is that students can frame disputes in a way that is age appropriate. Generally working in pairs, mediators explain the ground rules for mediation and provide an opportunity for disputants to identify the problem from their differing perspectives, explain how they feel, brainstorm solutions, evaluate the advantages and disadvantages of each proposed solution, and select a course of action.

Obviously, peer mediation is not an option when the conflict involves drugs, alcohol, theft, or violence because these are criminal actions. But mediation *can* help to resolve disputes involving behavior such as gossiping, name calling, racial put-downs, and bullying, as well as conflicts over property (e.g., borrowing a book and losing it). Even then, mediation must be voluntary and confidential. In cases when school rules have been violated, mediation should not substitute for disciplinary action; rather, it can be offered as an opportunity to solve problems and "clear the air."

Curb Peer Harassment and Bullying

Efforts to promote prosocial behavior must be matched with intolerance for antisocial behaviors that might threaten the safe and caring community. Every day, students suffer name calling, teasing, ridicule, humiliation, social exclusion, ostracism, and even physical injury at the hands of their peers. When this peer harassment is repeated over time (rather than being infrequent or incidental); is intended to cause harm, discomfort, or fear; and involves an imbalance in strength or power, it becomes *bullying* (Hyman et al., 2006; Olweus, 2003). Boys bully other students more often than girls do, and their bullying tends to be physical. Girls typically use more subtle, "relational bullying," intended to harm victims socially rather than physically by giving them the "silent treatment," excluding or isolating them, gossiping, and spreading rumors.

The problem of peer harassment and bullying is pervasive (although frequency rates vary significantly, depending on the way bullying is measured). In one large-scale study of almost 40,000 high school students, 47 percent said that they had been "bullied, teased, or taunted in a way that seriously upset them," and 50 percent admitted that they had bullied (Josephson Institute, 2010). The primary targets include girls who are unattractive, unstylish, or physically mature, and boys who don't fit the "stereotypic male mold" (Shakeshaft et al., 1997). Especially at risk are adolescents with autism spectrum disorders who are often socially awkward and have trouble communicating and recognizing social cues. (See Chapter 6.) Ironically, high-functioning students who are included in general education classes are at greatest risk because their unusual behaviors stand out more and they are more exposed to bullies (Sterzing, Shattuck, Narendorf, Wagner, & Cooper, 2012).

Another particularly vulnerable group includes teens who are lesbian, gay, bisexual, and transgender (LGBT). A study of school climate found that 82 percent of LGBT students had been verbally harassed during the past year, 38 percent had been physically harassed, and 18 percent had been physically assaulted (Kosciw, Greytak, Bartkiewicz, Boesen, & Palmer, 2012). Some 30 percent of LGBT students had missed one class or one day of school in the past month because they felt unsafe. In addition, almost 85 percent of teens frequently heard students say "that's so gay" or "you're so gay" when "gay" means something bad or devalued.

Despite its prevalence, teachers, counselors, and administrators often think that bullying is not a problem in *their* schools. According to Kazdin and Rotella (2009), that's because they typically see only 4 percent of bullying incidents; in contrast, students witness an estimated 85 percent (Farrington & Tfoti, 2009). Unfortunately, even when teachers are aware of bullying, they do not always intervene, or they intervene in a minimal manner. A student in one study commented, "For name-calling, they'll [teachers] just say, 'I don't want to hear that,' and then that's it. They really don't do anything else. . . . I wish teachers would stop it right away; even if they hear only one thing" (Shakeshaft et al., 1997, p. 25).

One reason for the lack of intervention may be the perception that bullying is "quasi-acceptable" (Hoover & Oliver, 2008). Bullies can be popular, and their behavior is often dismissed as normal. In one study of 1,900 middle school students, the students who were identified as the most aggressive were also identified as the "coolest" (Preidt, 2013a). When the bullies are males, it is not uncommon for adults to comment that "boys will be boys." Indeed, almost one-third of teachers in the United States perceive bullying as "normative behavior" that victims must learn to resolve (Hyman et al., 2006). Finally, much peer harassment and bullying take place in hallways and in the lunchroom, places where teachers may feel they don't have jurisdiction.

Taking peer harassment seriously and intervening to stop it—wherever it occurs—is crucial if teachers are to build safer, more caring classrooms. You need to be alert to hurtful comments about race and ethnicity, body size, disabilities, sexual orientation, unfashionable or eccentric dress, use of languages other than English, and socioeconomic status. You need to make it clear that disrespectful speech and slurs—even when used in a joking manner—are absolutely unacceptable. These interventions can be short: "We don't talk like that here" or "That word hurts people."

Because much peer harassment and bullying occurs out of teachers' sight and hearing, it is important to teach students how to become "upstanders"—that is, to stand up for those being bullied. This is not an easy task:

> Upstanders are, by definition, exceptional. They go against the tide; they buck social norms. No widespread system of prevention can depend on the capacity of individual children for heroism and self-sacrifice. (Weissbourd & Jones, 2012, p. 27)

Rather than expecting individual students to fight against the tide, we need to create school and classroom cultures where caring and responsibility for others are the norm (Weissbourd & Jones). Students take their cues from other students, so it is essential to get students involved in framing and enforcing this norm. For example, in one school, students developed a "friend zone," a place where any isolated or threatened student can take refuge and get support. In another school, a group of students created a video that conveyed how vicious cyber-bullying can be. In still another school, a group of students posted on the walls of the cafeteria all the derogatory comments that students had posted on Facebook (minus names or identifying details). They called their display "the walls of shame."

We, the students of the _____ school district, agree to join together to stop bullying.

BY SIGNING THIS PLEDGE I AGREE TO:

- Treat others respectfully.
- Try to include those who are left out.
- Refuse to bully others.
- Refuse to watch, laugh, or join in when someone is being bullied.
- Tell an adult.
- Help those who are being bullied.

Signed by

_____

Date

_____

FIGURE 4.2   Anti-Bullying Pledge

Source: Harrison, 2005.

Another way to involve students is in the creation of an anti-bullying pledge (see Figure 4.2). Having students read it aloud before signing an individual copy, and periodically rating how well they have been doing, are ways to enhance the likelihood that the pledge will be more meaningful (Elias, 2011).

It's also important to help students understand what behaviors constitute peer harassment and bullying. (See Figure 4.3.) For example, teasing is the most frequent

"That's a good question, Godzilla. Class, is threatening to stomp on someone's house considered bullying?"

FIGURE 4.3   *Source:* www.cartoonstock.com. Reprinted with permission.

bullying behavior at all ages, but it can be difficult for students to draw the line between playful exchanges and hurtful harassment. During one discussion with Christina, she related a story that illustrated the pain that "friendly" teasing can cause.

This year I've got a freshman named Anita in one of my classes. Last year, I had her boyfriend, who's a junior. He's been in a lot of trouble; last year he was arrested. But he's been doing a really good job of turning his life around. Anyway, one day I heard kids teasing Anita about him. They'd ask if he was on house arrest, or if he was in jail again. She looked unhappy about it, but she didn't say anything to me. After class, I told her that I had heard what the kids were saying, and I asked how she felt about it. She indicated that she didn't like it, but she didn't want to make a "big deal." She said she didn't want to get them in trouble. I offered to talk to the other kids—without indicating that I had spoken with her. I told her I'd make it clear that she hadn't asked me to intervene. The next day, I took the kids aside—there were two boys specifically—and said I had overheard them saying these things to Anita, and that I didn't think it was appropriate. They said they were "only teasing." I told them, "But teasing can hurt." I said that from the expression on Anita's face, it was clear that she didn't think it was funny. They looked surprised—as if they just hadn't given it any thought before. They promised to stop it, and they did.

Whether an exchange represents teasing or friendly banter may have to do with the social level or popularity of the individuals involved (Hoover & Oliver, 2008). If a higher-status student mocks a lower-status student, the exchange is likely to be seen as an attack. Teasing someone of the same status is more likely to be interpreted as playful. Here are some other guidelines (adapted from Hoover & Oliver) about teasing to help your students understand what is and isn't appropriate:

- Ask whether teasing about a certain topic is hurtful and don't tease about it.
- Watch for body language that conveys that teasing bothers someone.
- Stand up for a student who is being teased.
- Speak up if teasing about a certain topic bothers you.
- Be careful about using humor, especially sarcasm.
- Avoid teasing someone you don't know well.
- Never tease people about sex, being a boy or girl, their bodies, or their family members.
- Refrain from teasing someone who seems to be having a bad day.
- Accept teasing that is meant in a friendly way.

To raise awareness, it's also useful to incorporate reflective activities into your curriculum whenever possible. Donna's discussion about bullying (described earlier) was followed by poetry writing:

I told them to choose a type of poetry that we had studied (sonnet, haiku, diamonte, etc.) and write a poem about the things we had been discussing: acceptance; bullying; kindness; open-mindedness. Their poems were beautifully written and very expressive. They could really relate to the topic.

Similarly, students in literature classes can read fiction that relates to the topic of harassment and bullying. In math classes, students can conduct surveys and analyze the results. In art classes, students can depict their feelings about name calling and put-downs.

One final note: Although we have urged teachers to be alert for bullying, it is impor-

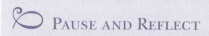

PAUSE AND REFLECT

As a student in elementary, middle, or high school, did you witness and/or experience incidents of bullying? Did your teachers intervene, and if so, were their interventions effective? Why or why not?

tant to recognize that teenagers and adults may see instances of interpersonal conflict very differently. Adults may label gossip, exclusion, name calling, ridicule, and humiliation as bullying, but teenagers themselves may refer to these as *drama*. Labeling a conflict as drama allows teens to downplay its significance and to "save face" rather than seeing themselves as bullies or victims. As Marwick and boyd (2011) assert: "Most teens do not recognize themselves in the 'bullying' rhetoric used by parents, teen advocates, and mental health professionals" (p. 23). In addition, unlike bullying, which by definition involves an imbalance in strength or power, drama can occur between individuals who possess equal status. And because drama is often an attempt to gain attention, it almost always takes place in front of an audience and involves social media such as Twitter and Facebook.

Be Alert for Instances of Cyber-Bullying

Peer harassment and bullying are no longer confined to school grounds because "cyber-bullies" use e-mail, cell phone text messages, instant messages, Web logs (blogs), and other social networking sites such as Facebook to pursue their victims. In a recent survey of more than 15,000 high school students, about 16% reported being cyber-bullied; girls were twice as likely to be targeted than boys (Preidt, 2013b). When eighth-grader Amanda Marcuson reported the fact that some of her classmates had stolen her makeup, she was immediately hounded by instant messages that began by calling her a tattletale and a liar and escalated to "increasingly ugly epithets" (Harmon, 2004). When 16-year-old Denise broke up with her boyfriend, he retaliated by posting her e-mail address and cell phone number on sex-oriented Web sites and blogs. For months, Denise was besieged with messages and calls that were embarrassing and frightening (Strom & Strom, 2005). And when a middle school student decided to do a survey on the top five "hated kids" in the sixth grade, he set up a website where students could vote (Lisante, 2005). Fortunately, the parents of one "winner" reported the survey to the principal, which prompted an in-school program on the damage that cyber-bullying can cause.

Online harassment is less visible to adults than "off-line" harassment, and they may have no sense of the nature or magnitude of the problem. In one study, researchers found that students engaged in bullying by text message because they easily could hide it from teachers (K. P. Allen, 2011). Said one student, "Texting has opened a whole new realm of bullying, because it's harder for the teachers to find out . . . because they don't know" (p. 111). At the same time, cyber-bullying can be vastly more humiliating to victims. Rumors, ridicule, embarrassing pictures, and hateful comments can be circulated among a huge number of peers with just a few clicks, and home no longer provides a safe haven from the taunting. Furthermore, adolescents may say things online they would never say in person, mainly because of the feeling of anonymity and the distance from the victim. As one student commented, "Over the Internet you don't really see their face or they don't see yours, and you don't have to look in their eyes and see they're hurt" (Leishman, 2002, cited in Shariff, 2004). Cyber-bullying also seems to have a particular appeal for girls, who prefer "relational aggression" rather than physical harassment and often try to avoid direct confrontation (Harmon, 2004).

See the Practical Tips box for some strategies for dealing with cyber-bullying.

 PRACTICAL TIPS FOR

Dealing with Cyber-Bullying

- Develop an explicit policy for acceptable in-school use of the Internet and include it in the school handbook (or your class rules). The policy should spell out what constitutes cyber-bullying and list consequences.
- Educate yourself about the technology tools your students use. Don't give students the opportunity to exploit your ignorance.
- Make sure that students are aware that bullying will be dealt with seriously.
- Ensure that parents/guardians who express cyber-bullying concerns are taken seriously.
- Explain to students that they:
    - Should never share personal information online, such as address, school, or phone numbers.
    - Should not post identity-revealing photos of themselves online or post photos of friends without their permission.
    - Should limit access to their online profiles (in Facebook or MySpace) to their friends and be cautious about accepting friend requests, especially from people they don't know.
    - Should not delete messages; they do not have to read them, but they should show them to an adult they trust. Messages can be used to take action against cyber-bullies.
    - Should not open a message from someone they don't know.
    - Should *never* reply to the message.
    - Can block the sender's message if they are being bullied through e-mail or instant messaging.
    - Can forward the messages to their Internet service provider.
    - Should tell an adult.
    - Should show the message to the police if it contains physical threats.
    - Should speak out against cyber-bullying.
    - Should never send messages when they are angry.
    - Should never send messages they wouldn't want others to see.
- Make parents aware that they can set age-appropriate filters on computers and other devices to prevent their children from accessing certain sites.
- Encourage parents to keep computers in a public room in the house.
- Invite members of the local police department to come to school to speak with parents and students about proper Internet use.
- Make sure ethics is included in any computer instruction given at your school.

Source: Adapted from Keith & Martin, 2005; Lisante, 2005; and the National Crime Prevention Council, 2009.

Be Alert for Student-to-Student Sexual Harassment

On the way out of your classroom, a boy pats a girl on her bottom. She gives him an annoyed look and tells him to "quit it." Another girl comes to you in tears because a boy in the class is spreading stories about

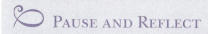

PAUSE AND REFLECT

Before going any further, think about the differences between flirting and sexual harassment. When and how do words or actions cross the line? How can you tell a line is being crossed?

what they did on a date last weekend. You hear two girls in your class laughing and teasing a boy about what a "stud" he is. Are these instances of sexual harassment? And should you do anything about them?

Sexual harassment is generally defined as *unwanted and unwelcome sexual attention.* This includes a wide range of behaviors:

> leering, pinching, grabbing, suggestive verbal comments, pressure for sexual activity, spreading sexual rumors, making sexual or sexist jokes, pulling at another student's clothing, cornering or brushing up against a student in a sexual way, insulting comments referring to students' sexual orientation, date rape, sexual graffiti about a student, or engaging in other actions of a sexual manner that might create a hostile learning environment. (Hyman, 1997, p. 318)

Sexual harassment is an all too common occurrence in U.S. middle and high schools. When almost 2,000 students in 7th to 12th grades were surveyed, 48 percent reported that they had been sexually harassed during the 2010–2011 school year (American Association of University Women, 2011). A significant part of the sexual harassment problem was "gender harassment"—students being targeted for not adhering to typical gender norms (e.g., boys who are called gay because they wear colorful clothes or girls who are labeled lesbian because they engage in sports). Verbal harassment (e.g., unwelcome sexual comments, jokes, epithets) was the most common, but physical harassment was also frequent as was sexual harassment by text, e-mail, Facebook, and other electronic means. It can sometimes be difficult for you—and your students—to distinguish between harmless flirting and sexual harassment. When you're faced with this situation, it's helpful to keep in mind the fact that whether harassment has occurred is truly in the "eye of the beholder." In other words, the determining factor is "how the person on the receiving end is affected by the behavior, not with what the other person means by the behavior" (Strauss with Espeland, 1992, p. 15). Kissing, touching, and flirting that the recipient likes or wants is not sexual harassment (although it may be inappropriate in school).

Our five teachers stress the importance of responding seriously when students complain that other students are making them feel "uncomfortable." Donnie tells about a first-year teacher in her school who failed to take action when a girl in his class complained that the boy sitting behind her kept touching her hair and "bothering" her:

> **Her complaint was vague (I think she didn't want to spell out what was happening), and so even though she kept asking to be moved, he [the teacher] didn't do anything. He just kept saying she should ignore the boy or tell him to stop. Finally, the girl's mother e-mailed [the teacher] with a copy to the**
principal and the superintendent, saying that repeated requests to be moved had been

ignored. It was a mess, but the teacher learned a good lesson: If kids are complaining that someone is bothering them, you have to take it seriously. People need to feel comfortable in your classroom and they need to feel that they can trust you to keep them safe.

Given the importance of the recipient's feelings in determining whether sexual harassment has occurred, people can be nervous about whether signs of affection and compliments will be misunderstood. You can suggest that students ask themselves a few simple questions to guide their behavior (Strauss with Espeland, 1992):

Would I want my comments or behavior to appear in the newspaper or on TV?

Is this something I would say or do if my mother or father, girlfriend or boyfriend, sister or brother were present?

Is this something I would want someone else to say or do to my mother or father, girlfriend or boyfriend, sister or brother?

Is there a difference in power between me and the other person (e.g., in size or social status)?

In recent years, an increasing number of districts have written and distributed sexual harassment policies for both students and school personnel. These generally define sexual harassment, outline the procedures to follow when a teacher learns about an incident of sexual harassment, and spell out the consequences. It's important that you obtain a copy of this policy and follow the specified procedures. Keep in mind that the Supreme Court has ruled that school districts can be found liable if they are "deliberately indifferent" to information about "severe, pervasive, and objectively offensive" harassment among students (Walsh, 1999).

A CAUTIONARY TALE

Building a caring classroom community is not an easy task, especially for secondary teachers who see students for such a limited amount of time. This lesson was brought home to us during a meeting in which Sandy ruefully described an incident that had just occurred in her classroom. We relate the incident here, not to discourage you, but to acknowledge the reality that building community is challenging work.

My kids were going over homework, and they were in groups of three. I picked the groups. In one group, I had a girl who happens to be an honors student and a boy who had to be convinced to take chemistry. They finished reviewing the homework pretty quickly. Another group was in need of assistance, so I suggested that they get help from the first group. Mitchell, one of the kids in the second group, called over to the girl—the honors student—to come and help them. So Ryan—the kid who had to be convinced to take chemistry—says, "Wait a minute. Why did you just ask her, not us? Do you think we're stupid?" Then he turns around to me and says, "See, Mrs. K., that's why I didn't want to take chemistry. Because all the smart kids know who they are and they know who's stupid. They think that kids who haven't done well in school could never do well in chemistry."

I'm standing there thinking, How do I get out of this one? What do I say? I had watched it all unfold in front of me. And 24 pairs of eyes are looking at me. Finally I said, "Well, I guess you certainly fooled them." I wish you could have seen it. Ryan's chest puffed up, and he says to Mitchell, "Lucy's not going to help you; I'm going to help you."

Here I thought that we had created a cohesive community, and then I find out there are all these little subgroups. The kids have these perceptions of one another, and they become barriers between them. Mitchell's perception was that Lucy would be best at explaining. Ryan's perception was that Mitchell thinks he's stupid. I'm always trying to demonstrate that people have multiple intelligences, multiple talents. I have them working in all these cooperative learning groups, and still, there are these barriers. But I'll just keep trying to knock them down.

CONCLUDING COMMENTS

As a content specialist eager to focus on academic instruction, you may be reluctant to put aside time to build respectful relationships among students—especially when there is so much pressure to cover the curriculum and prepare students for standardized tests. But teachers who care about students cannot stand by and hope for the best, and simple reminders to "be nice" are hardly sufficient. By establishing warm, respectful relationships with students (as described in Chapter 3), teachers *indirectly* influence behavior by providing a supportive context within which students can practice relationship skills (Gest & Rodkin, 2011). This indirect influence is not enough, however. Building community requires planning and implementing strategies deliberately designed to promote positive peer interactions. The result will not only be a more harmonious classroom but also increased motivation, academic engagement, and achievement (Watson & Battistich, 2006).

The fact that teachers play a critical role in making classrooms safe, inclusive, and nurturing has received increasing attention in recent years. But no one has captured this sentiment better than Haim Ginott, a teacher, child psychologist, and educator:

> I've come to a frightening conclusion that I am the decisive element in the classroom. It's my personal approach that creates the climate. It's my daily mood that makes the weather. As a teacher I possess a tremendous power to make a child's life miserable or joyous. I can be a tool of torture or an instrument of inspiration. I can humiliate or humor, hurt or heal. In all situations, it is my response that decides whether a crisis will be escalated or de-escalated and a child humanized or de-humanized (1972, 1993).

SUMMARY

Given the evidence that positive peer relationships have a significant impact on the emotional well-being of students, their attitudes toward school, and their academic performance, this chapter focused on ways to build a caring classroom community.

- Model and recognize prosocial behavior.
- Provide opportunities for students to get to know one another.

- Hold class meetings.
- Use cooperative learning groups.
- Teach social-emotional skills.
- Curb peer harassment and bullying.
- Be alert for instances of cyber-bullying.
- Be alert for student-to-student sexual harassment.

Content-area specialists are often reluctant to take time away from academic instruction to foster positive peer relationships. Remember that time you take to build community will pay off in terms of a harmonious, respectful classroom and increased motivation and achievement.

ACTIVITIES FOR SKILL BUILDING AND REFLECTION

In Class

1. Write a brief paragraph about your experiences in middle and high school. How widespread were teasing, bullying, name calling, put-downs, and rejection? Were you ever the victim of peer harassment? What did your teachers do (if anything) to put an end to these behaviors? Were their actions effective? Once everyone has finished writing, these recollections can be shared in small groups or as a class. (If students prefer to be anonymous, papers can be collected and randomly redistributed before being read.)

2. Given the current emphasis on high-stakes standardized testing and academic achievement, think about ways you can incorporate community building into your content area. In other words, how can you foster positive relationships among students while still meeting your academic objectives? How would you defend using class time to build community to parents or administrators who are most concerned about academic achievement? Share your ideas in small groups.

On Your Own

1. Interview a few middle or high school students about any teasing, name calling, bullying, and rejection that goes on in their school. Ask them about the ways teachers intervene (if at all) to put a stop to this kind of peer harassment. Does their school have any formal anti-bullying program?

2. Do some planning for the first week of school. Develop three introductory activities designed to help students become acquainted.

3. Visit a middle or high school classroom that you have never been in before. Record your immediate thoughts when you walked into the room about how it feels to be a student in that room. Observe the class for a little while and jot down any ways that the teacher is promoting positive peer relationships as well as your ongoing impressions about the tone of the classroom.

For Your Portfolio

Document the ways in which you work (or will work) to build positive relationships among students. Include artifacts such as lesson plans that incorporate cooperative learning, plans for holding class meetings and resolving conflicts, and getting-to-know-you activities.

FOR FURTHER READING

Hoover, J. H., & Oliver, R. O. (2008). *The bullying prevention handbook: A guide for principals, teachers, and counselors* (2nd ed.). Bloomington, IN: Solution Tree.

 The authors present an overview of bullying along with ideas for bullying intervention, anti-bullying educational campaigns, and working with families to prevent bullying.

Miller, C., & Lowen, C. (2012). *The essential guide to bullying: Prevention and intervention.* New York, NY: Alpha Books (Penguin Group, USA).

 This reader-friendly book discusses "21st century bullying" from teasing to cyber-bullying; examines the reasons why bullying happens; and offers strategies for prevention, identification, and intervention.

Sapon-Shevin, M. (2010). *Because we can change the world: A practical guide to building cooperative, inclusive classroom communities,* 2nd ed. Thousand Oaks, CA: Corwin.

 This book explores the many facets of community building and provides practical strategies for creating classrooms that support and nurture diversity.

Sherer, M. (Ed.). (2011). Promoting respectful schools. *Educational Leadership, 69*(1).

 This entire issue is devoted to the topic of creating respectful schools with articles on bullying, confronting racial tensions and hate language, creating a supportive school culture, and teaching students how to talk about controversial issues in civil ways.

ORGANIZATIONAL RESOURCES

The Anti-Defamation League (ADL), www.adl.org. Dedicated to combating anti-Semitism, hate crime, and bigotry through programs, services, and materials. (The *ADL Material Resource Catalog* contains a wealth of resources, including lesson plans, curriculum guides, and lists of children's books.)

Collaborative for Academic, Social, and Emotional Learning (CASEL), www.casel.org. Dedicated to the development of children's social and emotional competencies and the capacity of schools, parents, and communities to support that development. CASEL's mission is to establish integrated, evidence-based social and emotional learning (SEL) from preschool through high school.

GroundSpark, groundspark.org. Produces and distributes films and educational resources on issues ranging from environmental concerns to affordable housing to preventing prejudice. The Respect for All Project (RFAP), its landmark program, seeks to create safe, hate-free schools and communities. *Let's Get Real* is a film and curriculum guide on name calling and bullying in middle school.

The Southern Poverty Law Center, www.teachingtolerance.org. The Teaching Tolerance project provides ideas and free resources for building community, fighting bias, and celebrating diversity for teachers at all levels.

5 CHAPTER

Establishing Expectations for Behavior

Middle and high school teachers sometimes contend that their students know how to behave because they've been in school for many years. The argument goes like this:

My kids aren't babies. By middle or high school, students know the importance of coming to class on time, doing homework, respecting other people's property, and raising their hands to make a comment. Besides, there's so much material to cover, I can't waste time teaching rules to kids who should already know all this stuff.

This reasoning has a certain appeal, particularly for teachers who are enthusiastic about their content area and eager to get started. Yet it's important to recognize that although your students have general notions about appropriate school behavior, they do not know your specific expectations. Your students probably see five different teachers each day, and specific expectations vary from class to class. A student's first-period teacher may not mind if everyone is milling around the room when the bell rings, but the second-period teacher may insist that students be in their seats. In third period, the teacher wants students to put homework in the upper right-hand corner of their desks, but the fourth-period teacher has students drop homework in a basket at the front of the room.

What will *you* expect with regard to such basic classroom routines—and how will your students know what to do if you don't tell them? It's unfair to keep students guessing about the behaviors you expect. Not knowing the norms for appropriate behavior causes insecurity and misunderstandings, even among "school-smart" adolescents. In contrast, *clearly defined classroom rules and routines help to create an environment that is predictable and comprehensible.*

Making expectations clear and explicit is especially important if you are working with students who live in low-income communities (Payne, 2008). The actions and attitudes that allow students to thrive in their home environments may clash with schools' rules and expectations. For example, students might need to be able to fight back if they are physically challenged in their home community but can be suspended or expelled for such behavior at school. One way to handle these opposing expectations is to teach students that there are different sets of rules for home and school just as there are different rules for basketball and football.

Clear expectations for behavior have another major benefit. As Chapter 1 emphasized, classrooms are crowded, public, unpredictable places in which individuals engage in a variety of activities, often within the time constraints of a 42- or 45-minute period. *Clear rules and routines minimize confusion and prevent the loss of instructional time.* They enable you to carry out "housekeeping" tasks (e.g., taking attendance, distributing materials) smoothly and efficiently, almost automatically. They free you and your students to concentrate on the real tasks of teaching and learning.

This chapter describes research that demonstrates the importance of rules and routines. We then consider some principles to guide you in establishing norms for your own classrooms. We'll also learn how Donnie, Christina, Sandy, Donna, and Fred introduce rules and routines to their students and what they think about this central task of classroom management.

RESEARCH ON EFFECTIVE CLASSROOM MANAGEMENT

Prior to 1970, teacher preparation programs had little to offer beginning teachers concerned about order in the classroom. Teacher educators shared useful "tricks of the trade" (e.g., flick the lights on and off for quiet), stressed the importance of firmness and consistency, and warned prospective teachers not to smile until Christmas. But research identifying the behaviors of effective managers was unavailable, and it was simply not clear why some classrooms function smoothly and others are chaotic.

That situation began to change with the publication of Jacob Kounin's (1970) study of orderly and disorderly classrooms. In an effort to explain the differences, Kounin set out to compare teachers' methods of responding to misbehavior. To his surprise, he found that the reactions of good classroom managers were not substantially different from the reactions of poor classroom managers. What *did* differ were the strategies that teachers used to *prevent* misbehavior. Effective classroom managers constantly monitored students' behavior, and they kept lessons moving at a brisk pace so that students had little opportunity to become inattentive and disruptive.

Kounin's work led researchers to wonder how effective managers began the school year, and a series of studies was launched to investigate this topic. One project (Evertson & Emmer, 1982) conducted in urban junior high schools identified more and less effective classroom managers and compared what they did during the first three weeks of school. Striking differences were apparent—even on the very first day of school! Among the major differences was the way teachers handled rules and procedures. Although all of the teachers had expectations for behavior and they all took time to present or discuss these with students, the more effective managers *taught* the rules and procedures. For example, the more effective teachers were likely to distribute handouts stating their behavioral expectations or to have students copy them into their notebooks. These teachers were also clearer and much more explicit about behaviors that are likely to cause problems—namely, those that occur frequently and that may vary from teacher to teacher (e.g., call-outs, movement through the room, student–student interaction, hand raising). Interestingly, for behaviors that occur infrequently per period (e.g., tardiness, bringing materials) and are fairly straightforward, no differences between the two groups of teachers were apparent.

Subsequent research has confirmed the importance of explicitly teaching students your expectations for their behavior. In one study, researchers videotaped two experienced and two inexperienced junior high school teachers (two in math and two in science) as they met with their classes for the very first time (Brooks, 1985). The contrast between the experienced and inexperienced math teachers is especially vivid.

The experienced math teacher whom students and administrators perceived as being exceptionally clear and organized began her presentation of behavioral expectations by distributing a copy of class rules that students were to keep in their folders. She first discussed schoolwide policies but spent most of the time on classroom standards—how to enter the class, how to use materials, how to interact with the teacher and other students, what to do in the case of an emergency, and how to exit the class. In general, *she stated a rule, explained the rationale, provided an example of an appropriate behavior, and concluded with the consequences for noncompliance.* Interestingly, she rarely smiled during her presentation of rules and procedures (although she smiled a lot during her later introduction to the course). She spoke in a businesslike tone and continually scanned the classroom; no instances of disruption were observed during her presentation.

In contrast, the inexperienced math teacher was rambling and disorganized. Students were not given a copy of the rules, nor were they encouraged to write them down. Even as the teacher presented rules and procedures about talking in class, she tolerated students talking to each other. In addition, she repeatedly smiled during her presentation of the consequences for misbehavior, a nonverbal behavior that seems incompatible with a discussion of detention and calling home (and might have sent the message that she was not serious about imposing these consequences).

The inexperienced math teacher also provided few examples or rationales. In fact, she *never* used the experienced teacher's sequence of rule-rationale-example-consequence. Although many of the rules resembled those of the experienced math teacher, she presented rules that she could not enforce (wanting students to respect all teachers), and she omitted discussion of some fundamental rules (listening while the teacher is talking). Furthermore, the rules did not appear to be prioritized or organized in any way.

It's natural to feel sympathy for this inexperienced teacher. After all, most beginning teachers, particularly those being observed, are nervous on the first day of school. But it is precisely *because* of this nervousness that you must (1) think about your expectations ahead of time and (2) plan the way you will present them to your students. Let's look at each of these steps separately.

DEFINING EXPECTATIONS FOR BEHAVIOR

Before the first student enters your classroom, you need to decide on *expectations for their general conduct* (commonly referred to as *classroom rules*) and to identify the *behavioral routines or procedures* that you and your students will follow in specific situations. As we will see, rules and routines may vary from class to class, but no class can function smoothly without them.

Planning Rules for General Conduct

Effective classroom managers typically have four or five rules for students' general conduct (Akin-Little, Little, & Laniti, 2007). These describe the behaviors that are necessary if your classroom is to be a good place in which to live and work—for example, "come prepared," "follow directions," and "respect others." In Christina's class, expected behaviors are contained in a "newspaper" that she wrote and distributes on the first day of class. Here are some of her basic rules:

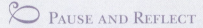 **PAUSE AND REFLECT**

We have distinguished between expectations for general conduct (*rules*) and the procedures that students will follow in specific situations (*routines*). To make sure that you grasp the distinction, consider the following expectations. Decide whether each one is a rule or a routine: (1) At the end of the period, students are to wait until you tell them class is over before beginning to pack up. (2) Students are to be prepared. (3) Students must listen respectfully when people are talking. (4) Students are to turn in homework at the beginning of class in the basket for their class period. (5) During small-group work, students may talk quietly with their group members. We will review this list later in the chapter.

- Respect every member of the class by using appropriate language, by paying attention when another person is speaking, and by raising [your] hand to speak.
- Complete all assignments on time and to the best of [your] ability.
- Come to class on time and be in [your] seat when the bell rings.

As you reflect on rules for your own classroom, keep in mind four guidelines, which are summarized in Table 5.1. First, *rules should be reasonable and necessary*. Think about the age and characteristics of the students you are teaching, and ask yourself what rules are appropriate for them. For example, it would be unreasonable to expect students to enter the classroom without greeting one another and chatting. Given adolescents' irresistible desire to interact, creating such a rule would only result in resentment, frustration, and subterfuge. It's far more sensible to establish a rule such as "talk quietly," which specifies *how* the talk is to occur.

TABLE 5.1 Four Guidelines for Planning Classroom Rules	
Guideline	Questions to Think About
1. Rules should be reasonable and necessary.	What rules are appropriate for this grade level? Is there a good reason for this rule?
2. Rules need to be clear and understandable.	Is the rule too abstract for students to comprehend? To what extent do I want my students to participate in the decision-making process?
3. Rules should be consistent with instructional goals and with what we know about how people learn.	Will this rule facilitate or hinder students' learning?
4. Classroom rules need to be consistent with school rules.	What are the school rules? Are particular behaviors required in the halls, cafeteria, during assemblies, etc.? What is school policy with respect to electronic devices such as cell phones?

Also ask yourself whether each rule is necessary. Is there a compelling reason for it? Will it make the classroom a more pleasant place to be? Will it increase students' opportunity to learn? Can you explain the rationale to students, and will they accept it? Sandy stresses the importance of this guideline when she comments:

Rules have to have reasons. For example, one of my rules is about coming to class on time. Students know they'll get detention if they're late—even once. At the beginning of the year, students think I'm unnecessarily strict about that. But I'm not trying to be mean. I want students there on time because I always start class when the bell rings, and if they're not there, they miss important material. After a while, they begin to realize there's a real reason for the rule. I hear them say to their friends, "I have to get to class on time because they'll have started."

It's easier to demonstrate that a rule is reasonable and necessary if it applies to *you* as well as your students. Although some rules may be intended only for students (e.g., raise your hand to speak), others are relevant for everyone (e.g., show respect for other people and their property). Sandy tells us, "If a rule is important for kids, it's important for you too. For example, I make sure that I get to class on time, and if I'm late, I owe them an explanation." Donna illustrates this idea when she discusses the rule about no gum in her classroom:

If you have gum, please get rid of it now, please. No one loves gum more than I do, but I don't chew it at school. I don't like to find gum under the desks or in the materials I buy for the classroom. I love gum, but too often I find it in the wrong places.

Second, *rules need to be clear and understandable.* Because rules are often stated in very general terms ("be polite"), they may be too abstract to have much meaning. When planning your rules, you need to think of specific examples to discuss with students. For example, one of Donnie's basic rules is "Be prepared." She makes sure that "preparation" is spelled out in precise, concrete behaviors: "Class preparation consists of having your homework, notebook, pen or pencil, and a covered textbook with you each day."

Some teachers believe that rules are more understandable and more meaningful when students are allowed to participate in the decision-making process. Participation, especially at higher grade levels, may increase students' willingness to "buy into" the rules, may make them more invested in seeing that rules are followed, and may help to prepare students for adult life. At the middle-school level, some teachers begin by asking students what their "hopes and dreams" are for that class (e.g., "What are your most important hopes and dreams for math this year? What would you really like to accomplish?"). Students then reflect on what they will need—from others as well as from themselves—to fulfill these hopes and dreams. Generating ideas for rules comes next.

Donna uses an approach like this. On the second day of school, she ends class by saying:

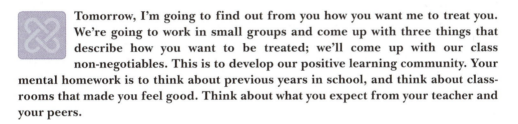

Tomorrow, I'm going to find out from you how you want me to treat you. We're going to work in small groups and come up with three things that describe how you want to be treated; we'll come up with our class non-negotiables. This is to develop our positive learning community. Your mental homework is to think about previous years in school, and think about classrooms that made you feel good. Think about what you expect from your teacher and your peers.

As a beginning teacher, you may feel more comfortable presenting rules you have developed yourself. In fact, despite their many years of experience, neither Donnie, Sandy, nor Fred allows students to create classroom rules. They do, however, discuss the rationales for the rules they have established, and they solicit examples from students. If you do decide to involve your students in developing a list of rules for your classroom, you need to think carefully ahead of time about the rules that are important to you and make sure those are on the final list. Also, be aware that this process might result in a different set of rules for each class period, and you will probably want to shape the students' lists so they can apply to all your classes.

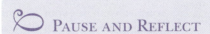 PAUSE AND REFLECT

Take a moment to reflect on the idea of having students generate the rules. Did any of your own secondary teachers ever use this approach? What do you see as the benefits? If you were to do this, what would you have to keep in mind, and what pitfalls might you need to plan for?

A third guideline to keep in mind when planning classroom expectations is that *rules should be consistent with instructional goals and with what we know about how people learn.* Chapter 1 discussed the principles underlying this book. One principle was that the need for order should not supersede the need for meaningful instruction. As you develop rules for your classroom, think about whether they will *facilitate or hinder the learning process.* For example, in the pursuit of order, some teachers prohibit talking during in-class assignments. Although such restrictions are necessary at times (e.g., during testing), it would be unfortunate if this became the status quo. Educational psychologists who study the ways children learn stress the importance of their interaction. For this reason, it seems sensible not to eliminate interaction but to spend time teaching students how to interact in ways that are appropriate. (We'll address this topic more fully in Chapter 11.)

Finally, *classroom rules need to be consistent with school rules.* The importance of this guideline can be illustrated by an excerpt from a student teacher's journal entry:

> *The first week of school I ejected a student from the room and told him he couldn't come back into the class until he had a note from his parents. Not only was the student back in class the next day without a note, but I was informed that (1) I was in violation of the school code when I ejected the student, and (2) only homeroom teachers communicate directly with the parents.*

Your school may hold an orientation meeting for new teachers during which school rules, policies, and procedures are explained. In particular, find out about behaviors that are expected during assemblies and in the cafeteria, library, and hallways. If there is a school handbook, be sure to get a copy and use it as a guide for establishing your own rules and routines.

You also need to know whether you are supposed to review the handbook with students. For example, Fred's students receive a booklet explaining the school's "Rules, Regulations, and Policies," and teachers go over it with their first-period classes. The handbook addresses topics such as lateness; absenteeism; smoking; substance abuse; leaving school grounds; bias incidents; use of cell phones, MP3 players, and other electronics; fighting and physical assault; and possession of weapons. After reviewing the handbook, students sign a statement indicating that they agree to abide by the rules. The statement is then returned to the main office.

Reviewing the handbook with his students allows Fred to explain how his classroom rules and routines jibe with those of the school:

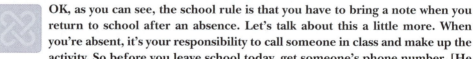 **OK, as you can see, the school rule is that you have to bring a note when you return to school after an absence. Let's talk about this a little more. When you're absent, it's your responsibility to call someone in class and make up the activity. So before you leave school today, get someone's phone number. [He smiles.] Try to get someone who is as smart or smarter than you. [The students laugh. He continues.] Now, about cutting. I can't teach you if you're not in my class. [He speaks slowly and with emphasis.] *If you cut my class, I take it personally.* Now I'm a human being. I realize there are times when you need to not be here; you have to go to the bathroom or the library. But you need to come and ask and get a pass. If you don't, that's a cut. *And I'm death on that one.* So don't cut.**

Planning Routines for Specific Situations

So many different activities occur in classrooms that trying to define behavior for specific situations can be daunting. For example, when students arrive at your classroom door, are they to go immediately to their seats, or may they congregate in small groups and socialize until you tell them to be seated? May they go to the storage cabinet and get the projects they've been working on, or should they wait for you to give out the projects one by one? When students are working at their seats, may they help one another or must they work individually? Because these seem to be such trivial, mundane issues, it is easy to underestimate their contribution to classroom order. But lessons can fall apart while you try to decide how to distribute paper, and students feel anxious if they're unsure whether answering a classmate's question during an in-class assignment is considered helping or cheating.

Researchers who observed the behavior of effective classroom managers grouped the routines they used into three categories (Leinhardt, Weidman, & Hammond, 1987). We have adapted their category system to provide you a way to think about routines for your own classroom.

CLASS-RUNNING ROUTINES

These are *nonacademic routines* that enable you to keep the classroom running smoothly. This category of routines includes *administrative duties* (taking attendance, recording tardiness, distributing school notices), *procedures for student movement* (entering the room at the beginning of the period; leaving the room at the end of the period; leaving the room to go to the nurse, the library, or lockers; participating in fire drills; moving around the room to sharpen pencils or get materials), and *housekeeping routines* (cleaning lab tables, watering plants, maintaining storage for materials used by everyone).

Without clear, specific class-running routines, these activities can consume a significant part of the school day. Research on the way time is used in fifth-grade classrooms has indicated that, on the average, these activities (transition, waiting, housekeeping) consume almost 20 percent of the time spent in the classroom—more than the amount of time spent in mathematics instruction (Rosenshine, 1980). This figure is undoubtedly higher in classrooms that are not well managed.

By defining how students are to behave in these specific situations, you can save precious minutes for instruction. You also enable students to carry out many of these routines without your direct supervision, freeing you to concentrate on instruction or other tasks. For example, Christina's students begin each class period by writing in their journals while Christina silently takes attendance. Students know that as soon as they enter the room, they are to get their journals, copy the journal topic from the board, and write silently for the allotted time. On the first day of school, Christina laid the groundwork for the smooth functioning of this activity. In the following vignette, we see her introduce the journals to her basic skills class.

Before we start going over what this class is going to be about, I want to give you your journals, which you will keep on a daily basis. . . . Write your name on the cover, then write English 3T, Block 2, then my name. [Points to her name on the board.] Open up your journals and write the date on the first page. I'm going to write a journal topic on the board, and I want you to copy it down, and then write a response to that topic. [Writes: *What do you expect from this class?*] When we do journals, you write until I say to stop writing, 5 to 10 minutes. Don't say you don't have anything to write about or that you can't think of anything else to say. If you run out of things to say about the topic I have given you, write about something else. OK, begin now.

Another important class-running routine involves what students are to do with electronic devices, such as cell phones and MP3 players. These devices are becoming ubiquitous on school campuses and, although students feel entitled to carry them, they can be extremely distracting. Unless your school has a specific policy forbidding their presence on campus, you will want to establish clear policies for your classroom. The most common classroom policy is to require that phones be turned off and put away while in class. (An exception, of course, is when you are having students use their phones for a class project or they are using the calculator function. For some ideas on instructional uses of cell phones, see Thomas & McGee, 2012.) Regarding MP3 players, some teachers allow their use during individual work only if the music is not so loud that other students can hear it.

Finally, it is essential to think about the routines you will establish for the use of computers in the classroom, library, or computer lab. Some specific suggestions are listed in the Practical Tips box.

PRACTICAL TIPS FOR

Using Computers in the Classroom

- Stress the importance of handling the computers with care.
- Set clear guidelines for using the computers (for example, remember to put your name on your work; save your work in your folder on the hard drive; leave the computer ready for the next person).
- If you have only a few computers, establish a set of guidelines for when and how long students can have access to the computers. Teach students how to transition from other activities to the computers and back.
- Have directions for frequently used computer operations (for example, opening programs, printing documents, inserting photos) next to each computer.
- Have students use headphones if programs have sound that will disturb others. (To prevent the spread of lice, have students bring their own headphones or clean the headphones every day.)
- Place a "help" sign or a symbol (such as a red flag) next to each computer, so students can signal when they need assistance.
- Teach a few students to be peer mentors or computer assistants who help those having problems.
- Determine a procedure for keeping track of students' computer use and progress. For example, have a computer log in which students sign in with name, date, time, and software program, URL, or project title. When they sign out, they can write a few sentences about what they've accomplished during their computer time.
- Teach students how to help each other without touching another student's computer.
- Have students keep a journal in which they record instructions on the use of software, as well as everyday procedures such as saving their work to a disk or the hard drive.
- Establish clear policies about acceptable use of the Internet (for example, which websites students can access). Discuss Internet safety issues, such as the dangers of sharing personal information online and cyber-bullying. Check to see whether your school has an Acceptable Use Policy (AUP) that you can present to students.
- If you use a computer lab, establish clear procedures for entering and leaving the lab (e.g., leave all backpacks and water bottles at the front of the room, stand at the computers while listening to teacher directions, and close all applications and push in chairs at the end of class).

LESSON-RUNNING ROUTINES

These routines directly support instruction *by specifying the behaviors that are necessary for teaching and learning to take place.* They allow lessons to proceed briskly and eliminate the need for students to ask questions such as "Do I have to use a pen?" "Should we number from 1 to 20?" and "What do I do if I'm finished?"

Lesson-running routines describe what items students are to have on hand when a lesson begins, how materials and equipment are to be distributed and collected, what type of paper or writing instrument is to be used, and what should be done with the paper (e.g., folded into eight boxes; numbered from 1 to 10 along the left margin; headed with name, date, and subject). In addition, lesson-running routines specify the behaviors that students are to engage in at the beginning of the lesson (e.g., have books open to the relevant page, silently sit and wait for instructions from the teacher) and what they are to do if they finish early or if they are unable to finish the assignment by the end of the time period.

Clear lesson-running routines are especially important in classroom situations that are potentially dangerous, such as woodworking, auto mechanics, and cooking. When Sandy introduces chemistry labs, for example, she is very careful to specify the special safety procedures:

 There are some special safety procedures for this lab. First, before working with the Bunsen burners, make certain that your hair is tied back. Second, make certain that your goggles are on. Third, I'll have a beaker on my desk where you can discard the metals. Everything else you can throw away in the sink.

Homework procedures can also be included among lesson-running routines because the pace and content of a lesson often depends on whether students have done their homework assignments. You need to establish routines for determining quickly which students have their homework and which do not as well as routines for checking and collecting assignments.

Also think about what routines will be followed when students are absent. How will you keep track of work for absent students? How will students learn what the day's assignments are? How will work get home to students who are absent? How many days will students have to complete work they missed?

INTERACTION ROUTINES

These routines refer to the *rules for talk*—talk between teachers and students and talk among students themselves. Interaction routines specify *when talk is permitted and how it is to occur.* For example, during whole-class discussions, students need to know what to do if they want to respond to a question or contribute a comment. All five of our teachers, like many others, usually require students to raise their hands and wait to be called on rather than letting them simply call out. In this way, the teachers can distribute opportunities to participate throughout the class and can ensure that a few overly eager individuals do not dominate the conversation. The teachers can also check on how well the class understands the lesson by calling on students who do not raise their hands.

Often it's hard to keep track of which students have had an opportunity to speak. To avoid this problem, Donnie sometimes creates a pattern for calling on students, one that is more subtle than simply going up and down rows:

> **I may start at the back corner of the room and call on students in a diagonal line. Or I might use the alphabetical list of students in my grade book, and alternate between students at the beginning of the list and those at the end.**
>
> **I try not to be obvious, but sometimes students figure out the pattern, and they'll say to me, "You missed so-and-so," or "I didn't get a question," so we'll go back and make sure that person has a turn.**

Another way to keep track of which individuals have had a turn is to use the "popsicle stick system." Many teachers use a container for each of their classes; each container has popsicle sticks labeled with students' names. To call on students, the teacher draws a stick from the container and then places the stick on the side until everyone has had a turn. Donna uses bowls containing papers with students' names on them. And as a variation to this system, she selects the first paper, and then each student she calls on draws a paper to select the next student to respond.

During some lessons, you may want students to respond chorally rather than individually. A simple signal can be used to indicate that the rules for talk have changed. For example, Donnie nods and extends her hands, palms up, in a gesture of invitation. Fred, with a background in music, literally conducts the group as if it were a chorus.

Sandy also suspends the normal rules for talk at times, but she adds words of caution for beginning teachers:

> **If I'm at the board, with my back turned to the class, and a student wants to ask a question, I don't mind if he or she just calls out, "Mrs. K., I don't understand. . . . " Or sometimes, during a whole-class discussion, someone will ask a question, and I'll ask other kids to help out. They'll turn to one another and start asking and answering questions as if I weren't even there. I can just stand aside and watch. It's great to see this kind of student–student interaction. But beginning teachers need to be careful about this. If things start to get unruly, I can just say, "Hey guys, use hands," and things settle right down, but I've seen situations like this get out of hand for beginning teachers.**

Interaction routines also include *procedures that students and teachers use to gain each other's attention.* For example, if students are busy working, and you need to give additional instructions, how will you signal that you want their attention? When Donna needs her students' attention, she counts down from five, expecting that they will be silent by the time she gets to one. You may decide to flick the lights, hold up your arm, or say, "Excuse me," the way Donnie does. If you are busy working with a small group or an individual, and students need your assistance, how will they communicate that to you? Will they be allowed to call out your name or leave their seats and approach you?

Finally, you need to think about the rules that will govern *talk among students.* When 20 to 30 students sit so close to one another, it's only natural for them to talk. You must decide when it's all right for students to talk about the latest video they watched (e.g., before the bell rings) and when their talk must be about academic work (e.g., during cooperative learning activities). You also need to think about times when students may talk quietly (e.g., during in-class assignments), and when you need to have absolute silence (e.g., when you're giving instruction or during a test). At Donna's school, all teachers are working on enforcing a numbering system to remind students of the voice level appropriate for talk in the classroom. Level four is an outside voice, three is a presentation voice, two is an inside voice, one is whispering, and zero is no talking. When students are working together in class, she expects them to use level two or one.

Table 5.2 summarizes the three types of routines we have just discussed.

TABLE 5.2 Summary of Classroom Routines

Class-Running Routines: Nonacademic routines that enable the classroom to run smoothly

Administrative routines
    Taking attendance
    Recording tardiness
    Distributing school notices

Routines for student movement
    Entering the room at the beginning of the period
    Leaving the room at the end of the period
    Going to the restroom
    Going to the nurse
    Going to the library
    Participating in fire drills
    Sharpening pencils
    Using computers or other equipment
    Getting materials

Housekeeping routines
    Cleaning chalkboards or whiteboards
    Watering plants
    Storing personal items (bookbags, cellphones, MP3 players)
    Maintaining common storage area

Lesson-Running Routines: Routines that directly support instruction by specifying the behaviors that are necessary for teaching and learning to take place

    What to bring to class
    Collecting homework
    Recording who has done homework
    Returning homework
    Distributing materials
    Preparing paper for assignment (heading, margins, type of writing instrument)
    Collecting in-class assignments
    Indicating what to do when assignments have been completed

Interaction Routines: Routines that specify when talk is permitted and how it is to occur.

Talk between teacher and students
    When whole-class lessons are in progress
    When the teacher is working with a small group
    When the teacher needs the class's attention
    When the students need teacher's attention

Talk among students
    During independent assignments
    Before the bell rings
    During transitions
    During loudspeaker announcements
    During cooperative learning activities
    During peer conferencing
    During the time a visitor is speaking with the teacher

As we wrap up our discussion of planning for rules and routines, let's go back to the first Pause and Reflect box that asked you to identify whether each expectation was a rule or routine. Example (1), students waiting for you to indicate that class is over before they begin to pack up, is a class-running routine. This is a nonacademic routine that allows the class to run smoothly. Example (2), students are to be prepared, is a rule. As discussed earlier, Donnie uses this rule and explains to her students what they need to bring to class each day to be prepared. Example (3), listen respectfully when people are talking, is also a rule that allows the students and the teacher to hear each other more clearly. Having students turn in homework in the basket for their class period, Example (4), is a lesson-running routine that streamlines homework collection and allows more time for learning. Finally, Example (5), students talking quietly during small-group work, is an interaction routine. It specifies one of the times when student–student talk is acceptable.

THE FIRST FEW DAYS OF SCHOOL: TEACHING STUDENTS ABOUT EXPECTATIONS

To minimize confusion, you need to teach students the rules for general conduct, defining terms clearly, providing examples, and discussing rationales. As we indicated earlier in this chapter, Evertson and Emmer's (1982) research indicates that this is crucial for behaviors that are likely to occur frequently and when the appropriate behavior may be ambiguous (e.g., talking during an independent assignment). You also need to teach the routines you want students to follow for specific situations. Such thoroughness is particularly important in new situations, such as science laboratories, wood shop, keyboarding, or ceramics studio, where students have had little prior experience. (See Meet the Educators Box 5.1 for information on Harry and Rosemary Wong who have written about the importance of teaching rules and routines during the first few days of school.)

Let's see what this looks like in action. On the morning of the first day of school, Donnie begins by introducing herself to her students and asking them to introduce themselves. Afterward, she introduces the topic of "ground rules." Note that she also provides information on topics that are sure to be on students' minds—homework, notebooks, grading, and extra help:

> **Today our main concern is to talk about how we're going to operate in here, what I expect of you in terms of behavior and what the consequences might be for some kinds of behavior. I want to discuss my ground rules or codes of behavior. I'll pass these out, and we'll discuss them. If you have any questions or problems, let me know. [She distributes a packet of handouts.] It looks like an awful lot, but it's not really. A lot will be familiar; I'm sure it will be similar to other teachers'.**
>
> **OK, let's look at the first page. Here we have my ground rules. The first item on the page deals with general class procedures. I expect you to be in your seat when the bell rings. [She says this slowly and firmly. Her tone is serious but pleasant.] Today several people were tardy. I can understand that. I recognize that today is the first day and you're running around, maybe lost. [She smiles.] But I anticipate that there will be no late arrivals after this. I'll talk about what happens for tardiness in a few minutes.**

Donnie continues to elaborate on the printed statements, answering questions and inviting comments. She reviews the ground rules for notebooks, homework, extra help, paper headings, and participation and goes on to explain the grading system. She then goes over an assignment sheet that students may use to record assignments and due dates and elaborates on a checklist she will use to evaluate notebooks.

BOX 5.1 MEET THE EDUCATORS

Harry and Rosemary Wong

Harry Wong, a popular educational speaker and consultant, taught middle school and high school science, garnering numerous teaching awards. Rosemary taught kindergarten through grade 8. The couple now have their own publishing company (Harry K. Wong Publications, Inc.), of which Rosemary is CEO. Together they wrote *The First Days of School,* which has sold more than 3 million copies, making it the best-selling book ever published in education. The Wongs have also produced the DVD series, *The Effective Teacher,* winner of the Telly Award for best educational video of the past 20 years and awarded the first place Gold Award in the International Film and Video Festival.

Some Major Ideas about Classroom Management

- What you do on the first days of school will determine your success or failure for the rest of the school year.
- Effective teachers introduce rules (i.e., expectations of appropriate student behavior), procedures, and routines on the very first day of school and continue to teach them the first week of school.
- The number one problem in the classroom is not discipline; it is the lack of procedures and routines.

- A procedure is a method or process for how things are to be done in a classroom. When the procedure becomes automatic, it is a routine.
- Effective teachers have procedures for taking roll, exchanging papers, sharpening pencils, entering the classroom, starting class, leaving the classroom, and so on.
- The three steps to teaching procedures are (1) explain clearly, (2) rehearse (until class procedures become class routines), and (3) reteach when necessary and reinforce (give specific praise).

Selected Books and Articles:

The first days of school: How to be an effective teacher (Wong & Wong, Mountain View, CA: Harry K. Wong Publications, 2009)

Monthly columns by the Wongs can be found at http://teachers.net/wong. Some examples are listed here:

- "Structure Will Motivate Students" (December 2012)
- "You Can Teach Classroom Management" (November 2011)
- "The Success of a Culture of Consistency" (May 2010)

Website: www.effectiveteaching.com

As this example illustrates, teaching students the rules for conduct doesn't have to be unpleasant or oppressive. In fact, some teachers don't even use the word rules. Sandy, for example, prefers to talk about "chemistry classroom guidelines," but like Donnie, she makes sure her expectations for behavior are explicit. Sandy defines terms ("Late means not being in the room when the bell rings."), provides examples wherever necessary, and stresses the reasons for each guideline. She explains why it's important for textbooks to be covered ("so they don't get chemicals on them"); why she has a "disclaimer" in her guidelines reserving the right to give unannounced quizzes ("That's there in case I see you're not doing the reading. But I really don't like to do this; I want kids to do well on tests."); why hats cannot be worn in class (for safety reasons); why she insists on promptness ("I start when the bell rings."); and why she lets them leave when the bell rings—even if she's in the middle of a sentence ("I will not keep you, because you'd be late to the next class and that's not fair to you or to the next teacher. But don't pack up books before the bell rings.").

In addition to going over her own class rules, Sandy also reviews the school's academic integrity policy. With an extremely serious demeanor, she explains the distinction between cooperating and cheating ("the ultimate disrespectful behavior"). She talks about the numerous behaviors that constitute cheating (e.g., giving or receiving test information, using "unauthorized written aids" or information from electronic devices during tests, claiming sole credit for work completed with other students, copying work that was supposed to be done independently, and fabricating laboratory data). She also gives students strategies for resisting peer pressure to cheat: "If someone asks you what was on the test, just tell them, "Oh, you know Mrs. K! You have to know everything!" Sandy also spends a lot of time talking about plagiarism. She tells students that "Plagiarism is like someone behind you reaching into your backpack and taking your cell phone. Ideas belong to people, just like cell phones."

Like Sandy, Christina also talks about "guidelines" for behavior. On the first day of school she distributes a newspaper that she creates for each class she teaches. (See Figure 5.1.)

Here's a page of information about this course. See the letter from the editor. That's me; I'm the editor. Read that silently, please. [She gives students a few minutes to read the letter.] There are a couple of things I want to point out.

Let's look at the objectives for this class. [She goes over the objectives, clarifying terms and talking about some of the activities they'll be doing to fulfill the objectives.] OK, let's look at the "Guidelines for Student Conduct." [She goes through the list commenting on some of the bulleted points.] We're all working together to make this a positive, comfortable class. I can't do it by myself. There are 29 of you and only one of me. So you have to contribute to the environment—being nice to each other, not using put-downs, using appropriate language. You won't hear me using inappropriate language, so I don't expect you to use it either; I'm very strict about that. . . . If you need to use the restroom, come to class first, put your books away, and let me know you're here. Then you can take the pass and go. That way if you're 10 or 20 seconds late, I'll know where you are.

Let me point out the penalty box: You get one warning for disruptive behavior and then you're removed from the classroom. Take a minute to look over the grading policy. . . . OK, to make sure that we're all on the same page about rules and procedures, read this paper and then sign it. [She gives out the "Dear Student and Parent/ Guardian" page.] Your first homework assignment is to take this home and get your parents to sign it too.

In contrast to Donnie, Sandy, and Christina, Donna introduces rules and routines in a less formal way. Throughout her first week of school, she weaves the oral presentation of her classroom rules and procedures into her introductory lessons. She states her most important rules (no bullying and no gum) on the first day and fills in the rest over

ENGLISH 10 R

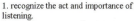

Fall Semester   *Mrs. C. Vreeland*

A Letter from the Editor:

Dear Students,

Welcome to tenth grade English. I hope you had a pleasant summer and are ready for some exciting educational experiences. I am looking forward to working with you this semester.

I have been working hard to plan this course for you and I think you will learn a great deal and have some fun this semester. In order to make this class successful, I must ask for your cooperation. I will ask for your input frequently, and if you have any ideas you may feel free to share them at any time.

Please raise any questions or comments at an appropriate time during class or check my schedule on the classroom door to reach me during the school day. In addition, you can reach me through school e-mail. However, please note that I can not guarantee immediate response to your e-mail. Therefore, questions or comments that require immediate attention (i.e.homework concerns) should be addressed before you leave school.

Please read the rest of this introductory handout carefully and share it with your parents, as it will provide you with an overview of the course. You will learn about rules, procedures, grading policies, and course objectives; all of which will be helpful to you throughout the semester.

I wish you much success this semester and I know that you will achieve your goals if you approach this class with enthusiasm and dedication.

Sincerely,

Mrs. C. Vreeland

Guidelines for Student Conduct

The student will be responsible to:

- create a positive, comfortable learning environment in the classroom and on electronic classroom forums.
- respect every member of the class by using appropriate language, by paying attention when another person is speaking, and by raising his/her hand to speak.
- complete all assignments on time and to the best of his/her ability.
- obtain and complete make-up work on time — two days for each day absent.
- listen to and follow all directions given by the teacher, asking for clarification if he/she does not understand the directions. (NOTE: Refusal to follow directions constitutes interference with the educational process and will result in disciplinary action.)
- come to class on time and be in his/her seat when the bell rings.
- bring his/her textbook, notebook, a writing implement, a pen AND pencil, and any other required materials (as assigned by the teacher) to class each day.
- leave ALL food, drink and outerwear in his/her locker, and leave cell phones at home.
- LEARN and THINK independently as well as cooperatively.

Penalty Box

Students who do not listen to directions or obtain make-up work will not receive credit for missed assignments. Late work will be marked down ten points for each day late.

Students who are not in their seats when the bell rings will be marked late (six lates equal loss of credit).

Students who disrupt the learning of others or refuse to follow directions given by the teacher will lose participation credit. If disruption or refusal persists, students will be removed from the classroom. Appropriate disciplinary action will follow.

Objectives

After successfully completing this course, students will be able to:

1. recognize the act and importance of listening.
2. organize, prepare and present a spoken presentation clearly and expressively.
3. collaborate by sharing ideas, examples and insights productively and respectfully.
4. recognize that reading has many purposes and demonstrate an ability to choose an approach appropriate to the text and purpose.
5. experience and respond to print and non-print media.
6. use research skills to access, interpret and apply information from a variety of print and non-print sources.
7. compose a variety of written responses for different purposes and audiences.
8. use a variety of technologies as a tool for learning.
9. use their language arts skills for decision making, negotiating and problem solving.
10. develop a better understanding of themselves, of others, and of the world through literature and through language.

Grading Policy

Marking period grades are comprised of a major assessment mark and a minor assessment mark, each counting for 50% of the marking period grade. The average of the two marking period grades will count as 80% of the course grade. The final exam will count as 20% of the course grade.

Major Assessments include activities covering large blocks of material such as long-term projects and tests. Minor Assessments include classwork, homework, quizzes, group activities and class participation.

FIGURE 5.1   Christina's Introductory Newspaper

the course of the week. Each day, she reviews the rules and procedures she presented on the previous day. On Friday of the first week, students write the rules and procedures in their own words. These are put in the students' individual folders for them to reference the rest of the year.

Fred is even more informal. As we saw earlier, when Fred reviews the school handbook with his first-period class of sophomores, he uses the school rules as a jumping-off point for a presentation of his class rules. But he distributes no handouts, nor does he post rules, and he interjects a degree of humor:

[Fred finishes reviewing the handbook and has students sign the page acknowledging receipt and agreement. He then continues with his own rules for the class.] Do you know what an acronym is? It's letters that form a word and each letter stands for a word. PITA is an acronym. And it's the main rule we have in here: *Don't be a PITA.* What's a PITA, Suzanne? [She shakes her head.] You don't know? [He looks around to see if anyone else knows. There's silence.] A PITA is a . . . pain . . . in . . . the . . . neck! [There's some laughter as the class catches on.] I want you to inscribe PITA across your forehead. Don't forget: *Don't be a PITA.* Now, I have one rule for me, too: *I must make you laugh once every day.* If I don't, I go home in a suicidal mood. [Students laugh.] OK, let's talk about what you'll be learning in U.S. History I.

With his seniors, Fred prefers an even less systematic approach. On the first day of class, he introduces himself, takes attendance, and immediately launches into a description of the course. During the period, he explicitly teaches his students routines for specific situations that arise (e.g., how to pass in papers), but he does not teach rules for general conduct. Instead, he monitors the class carefully and immediately informs students about behavior he finds unacceptable. The rest of them carefully watch his interactions with individual students—and they quickly learn what he expects. When Fred asks one student to take off his baseball cap, for example, another hears and takes off his own hat. To a student wearing sunglasses, Fred asks, "Is there is a medical reason for those glasses?" and the student immediately removes them.

As you can see, Fred communicates expectations for conduct to older students primarily by providing clear, immediate feedback when behavior is unacceptable. He recognizes that one reason this approach works for him is the reputation he has established during his years at the high school. Reflecting on this reputation, Fred's student teacher observes:

 PAUSE AND REFLECT

You have seen how each of our five teachers set up rules and routines in her or his classroom. Which teacher has an outlook most like yours? Is there a particular style that resonates with you, or will you borrow ideas from some or all of them? As you develop your own management style, keep in mind the ways these teachers approach their classrooms and use their thoughts to grow your own ideas.

Everyone knows that he plays the "dumb old man," but that he's not. He has this incredible relationship with the kids; he knew everyone's name within two days. He works them hard, but he projects warmth, and the kids know he really cares. I've never seen a kid give him lip. One look is enough.

CONCLUDING COMMENTS

Donnie, Christina, Sandy, Donna, and Fred all have well-defined expectations for student behavior, and they make these expectations absolutely clear. Nonetheless, the five teachers have somewhat different expectations, and they introduce rules and routines in different ways. These differences reflect their beliefs about what works best for their own particular students in their own particular contexts. Donnie, Christina, and Sandy teach rules and routines in a systematic, explicit fashion; they all spend considerable time explaining what they expect; and they distribute written copies of the rules for students to keep in their notebooks. Christina goes further: She requires her students to sign a statement that they have read and understood the information about student conduct, penalties, grading policies, and expected class procedures and to obtain their parents' signatures as well. Donna is somewhat more informal. She spends time each day during the first week of school discussing rules and illustrating procedures and then has students write them at the end of the week. Fred is the most informal. With his sophomores, he explicitly teaches rules, but he neither posts them nor distributes copies. With his seniors, he teaches specific routines but relies primarily on monitoring and feedback to communicate what he expects in terms of general conduct.

As a beginning teacher, you would be wise to adopt a deliberate, thorough approach to teaching rules and routines. If you have your own classroom, it is also a good idea to post your rules in the classroom—for example, on a front bulletin board—so your expectations are clear to your students. Once you've gained experience—and a reputation—you might try a less formal approach with your older students. Also keep in mind that rules and routines are not invented, polished, and fully developed in a single year. Instead, they will evolve over time, products of your experience and creative efforts.

One final note from our own teaching experience: On the first day of school, at the beginning of fifth period, one of us (Ingrid) distributed copies of her classroom rules. An audible groan went through the classroom, and the students noted that this was how every previous class that day had started! Although we have emphasized the importance of establishing behavioral expectations early in the year, rules and routines should not be the most salient aspect of the first days of the school year. As you plan the first few days, make sure that you balance teaching the rules and routines with a variety of learning activities that students will find meaningful, enjoyable, and memorable. We want our students to understand that they will learn more in our classes than simply how to behave.

SUMMARY

This chapter discussed two important functions of rules and routines in the classroom: (1) to provide a structure and predictability that help students to feel more comfortable and (2) to reduce the complexity of classroom life, allowing you and your students to concentrate on teaching and learning. It then outlined two broad categories of behavioral expectations—rules for general conduct and routines for specific situations—and emphasized the need to teach these explicitly.

Decide on Rules for General Conduct That Are

- Reasonable and necessary.
- Clear and understandable.
- Consistent with instructional goals and with what we know about how people learn.
- Consistent with school rules.

Plan Routines for Specific Situations

- Class-running routines
    - Administrative routines
    - Routines for student movement
    - Housekeeping routines
- Lesson-running routines
    - Use and distribution of materials
    - Assignment procedures
    - Early completion procedures
- Interaction routines
    - When and how talking is permitted
    - How teachers and students get each other's attention

Teach Rules and Routines Explicitly

- Define terms.
- Discuss rationales.
- Provide examples.

Remember that developing good rules and routines is only the first step. For rules and routines to be effective, you must actively teach them to your students. Time spent on rules and routines at the beginning of school will pay off in increased instructional time throughout the year.

ACTIVITIES FOR SKILL BUILDING AND REFLECTION

In Class

1. Working together in small groups, develop a set of rules for general conduct. About five rules should be sufficient. For each rule, list a rationale and examples that you will discuss with students to make the rules more meaningful. Think about which rules are most important to you and why.

2. In a small group, refer to Table 5.2, which lists the areas for which you will need specific behavioral routines. First, share your ideas about the actual routines you might use in each category (e.g., what kind of routine can you establish for taking attendance in an efficient way?). Then think about which routines need to be taught on the first day. In other words, decide on priorities so that you can teach routines when it is most appropriate (and most likely to be remembered).

On Your Own

If you are teaching, student teaching, or observing in another teacher's classroom, keep a reflective journal on developing and teaching rules and routines. Using the routines listed in Table 5.2, note which ones cause the most problems, the nature of the problems, and how you might respond to them. Also note which routines work particularly well.

For Your Portfolio

Write a brief statement on the rules that will guide behavior in your classroom. Will you develop and distribute them yourself? If so, what rules will you create? Will you generate rules with students? If so, how will you do this? Describe the specific approach you will take.

FOR FURTHER READING

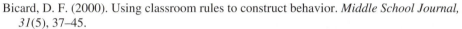

Bicard, D. F. (2000). Using classroom rules to construct behavior. *Middle School Journal, 31*(5), 37–45.

> Arguing that "rules are one of the most cost effective forms of classroom management available to teachers," Bicard reviews the characteristics of positive, negative, and vague rules and discusses the keys to developing and implementing positive rules in classrooms. The article also discusses what to do when students violate rules.

Brady, K., Forton, M. B., Porter, D., & Wood, C. (2003). *Rules in school.* Greenfield, MA: Northeast Foundation for Children.

> One of the Strategies for Teachers Series, this book provides practical suggestions for involving K through 8 students in generating classroom rules that grow out of their hopes and dreams. Chapter 6 focuses specifically on middle school (grades 6 through 8) and includes a discussion of logical consequences to ensure accountability.

Byrne, R. (2012, November 19). Free web tools make classroom management fun. See The Digital Shift retrieved from www.thedigitalshift.com/2012/11/ebooks/classroom-management-made-fun/.

> This article reviews three web-based tools that allow teachers to record attendance and behavior, and to allow students and parents to view their records.

Marzano, R. J., with Marzano, J. S., & Pickering, D. J. (2003). *Classroom management that works: Research-based strategies for every teacher.* Alexandria, VA: Association for Supervision and Curriculum Development.

> Chapter 2 focuses on rules and procedures. The authors first discuss research confirming the importance of classroom norms. They then outline a series of "action steps" that teachers can take to identify appropriate rules and procedures and to involve students in their design.

Knowing Your Students and Their Special Needs

Getting your class lists at the beginning of the school year always brings a sense of anticipation, excitement, and curiosity: What are these students like? What do they know? How do they think? What strengths do they bring? What struggles do they face? Where do they come from? Over the first few weeks and months of school, you begin to formulate answers to those questions. Gradually, you gain an understanding of *who your students are.* This understanding allows you to tailor your teaching to their specific needs and to find ways to build connections. And *knowing your students is essential if you are to build an inclusive, caring environment for learning.*

Knowing your students means recognizing and appreciating the ways each is a unique individual as well as understanding the common characteristics of adolescence. Undoubtedly, your class will be composed of students with a wide range of abilities, social skills, and emotional maturity. In addition, your class will probably include students with "special needs." Although this term is generally used to refer to those with disabilities, students who are learning English as a second language also have special needs. Likewise, young people who are growing up in impoverished, unstable, or abusive circumstances can have physical, emotional, or psychological problems that must be addressed.

This chapter begins by looking at some of the common developmental characteristics of middle and high school students and considering the implications for classroom management. Then we discuss strategies for supporting students who are English language learners (ELLs). Next, we examine ways to help students with disabilities and attention-deficit/hyperactivity disorder (ADHD), the most commonly diagnosed behavior disorder among children in the United States (Coles, 2000). We then consider the needs of students who are troubled—namely, those who suffer from the problems associated with substance abuse, child abuse and neglect, and eating disorders. Finally, we discuss approaches to working with students who are poor or homeless.

THE DEVELOPING ADOLESCENT

The middle school and high school years are marked by tumultuous physical, emotional, and social changes. During this period, adolescents can become confused, moody, short tempered, and rebellious. They can alternate between confidence and high expectations on one hand and insecurity and anxiety on the other; indeed, middle-graders suffer from the lowest self-esteem of any age group (Charles & Charles, 2004). Adolescents increasingly turn to their peer group, trying hard to "fit in," and become extremely concerned about appearance, clothes, and body image. Recent research has also found that adolescents who were told peers were observing them while they were completing a driving simulation took more risks than those who were told they were alone (Albert, Chein, & Steinberg, 2013).

According to Erik Erikson (1963), the major developmental task of adolescence (starting at age 13) is the development of identity. Young people must find the answer to the question, "Who am I?" or experience "role confusion" or "identity diffusion." As they work to forge an identity and "keep themselves together," adolescents experiment with different roles and temporarily "overidentify" with the "heroes of cliques and crowds" (Erikson, p. 262). During this phase, they can be "remarkably clannish," excluding all those who are different. Erikson cautions adults to understand (although not to condone) this intolerance as a "defense against a sense of identity confusion" (p. 262).

During early adolescence (middle school and the freshman year of high school), teens might also begin to question norms and social conventions (e.g., no running in the hallways) that they readily accepted at an earlier age (Nucci, 2006). Viewing norms as the arbitrary dictates of those in power, early adolescents are more likely to violate school conventions. Fortunately, by middle adolescence (about 15, or the sophomore year), most U.S. adolescents have moved on to the next stage of reasoning about social conventions, recognizing that they are necessary for ensuring orderly interaction among members of a society.

At the same time, changes are also occurring in the way adolescents view matters of personal prerogative and privacy. Domains in which convention touches on personal expression (hair, dress), personal associations (friends), or personal safety (sexuality) become "zones of dispute" over which adolescents want autonomy and control (Nucci, 2006, p. 725).

Together, the negation of convention and the extension of what is considered personal (and therefore off limits to interfering adults) make the period of early adolescence a difficult time for parents and teachers trying to guide students' behavior.

Implications for Classroom Management

Because middle-graders tend to "push the limits," it is helpful to distinguish between norms that are absolutely necessary to create a safe, secure environment and those that are really only a minor threat. As Larry Nucci (2006) argues:

> To put it another way, it is important for teachers to realize that there are times when it makes more sense to say "yes" in response to student noncompliance than it is to simply say "no" in an effort to maintain consistency for its own sake. For example, marking a student tardy for being next to his seat rather than sitting in it as the bell rings may make the adult feel powerful, but it does little to enhance the student's appreciation of the norm of promptness. (pp. 725–726)

Nucci reminds us that this phase will pass and that teachers (and students) will benefit from patience: "Firm and fair enforcement of rules with a dash of humor will work better than rigid requirements for compliance" (p. 726).

Unfortunately, middle schools do not generally adopt this more sensitive, understanding approach. In fact, a number of educators have commented on the mismatch between schools and young adolescents around these issues. Despite the increased maturity of adolescents and their need to obtain more autonomy, middle schools and junior high schools emphasize heightened teacher control and discipline and offer fewer opportunities for student involvement in decision making, choice, and independence (Eccles, Wigfield, & Schiefele, 1998). Moreover, just when students face the task of constructing a firm sense of self, they move from an environment where they were the most mature and highest status students to being the babies in a large, impersonal middle school (Woolfolk, 2007). They go from close connection with one teacher to more impersonal relationships with many teachers. They go into a more competitive environment with lots of social comparison just at a time when they are very self-conscious and their self-concepts are particularly fragile. Not surprisingly, middle-school students often show decreased motivation and interest in school (Nucci, 2006).

Obviously, all students can thrive when teachers are fair, encouraging, and willing to listen and when they provide opportunities for independence along with needed support. But the "developmental peculiarities" of adolescents (such as the struggle for identity, insecurity, fragile self-concept, self-consciousness, and concern about fitting in) make this even more critical (Emmer & Gerwels, 2006, p. 412). At this stage, it is essential not to put students down, not to embarrass them in front of their peers, and to show a sense of humor. Teachers who are sensitive to the emotional stresses that characterize this stage and treat adolescents with respect and understanding strengthen their attachment to school. This has far-reaching implications: Attachment to school significantly decreases the likelihood that students will become involved in dangerous behavior such as smoking, drinking, marijuana use, or violence (Emmer & Gerwels).

ENGLISH LANGUAGE LEARNERS (ELLs)

During the past two decades, the number of school-age children who speak a language other than English at home has increased significantly. Federal legislation provides funding and encouragement for programs to assist ELLs; however, there are no federally mandated programs, so laws vary from state to state. Despite the variability, state laws generally call for the identification and assessment of ELLs and describe options for providing special services. One option is a *bilingual education program,* which teaches students in their native language as well as in English, thus allowing them to learn academic subjects while they're learning English.

When ELLs come from many different language backgrounds, bilingual education programs are impractical. In this case, schools typically place students in regular English-only classrooms and pull them out for instruction from a specially trained teacher in *English as a second language.* Because the focus is on learning English, students with different native languages can be in the same room.

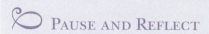 **PAUSE AND REFLECT**

Bilingual education programs are extremely controversial, and in some states, laws have been passed restricting bilingual education and substituting programs that stress the use of English. Even the parents of some ELLs oppose bilingual education, contending that it hinders children's learning of English. At the same time, scholars in bilingual education stress the importance of receiving instruction in a child's first language to build on his or her existing literacy skills. What do *you* think about this issue?

In general education, English-only classrooms, ELLs will undoubtedly have problems if they are expected to "sink or swim," and if teachers are unwilling to make any modifications for these students. ELLs might be able to function admirably, however, if you implement some of the environmental supports used in "sheltered instruction" or "specially designed academic instruction in English" (SDAIE). Listen to what Donna has to say about her ways to work with ELLs:

> **Almost all of the kids in my fifth-period class are ELLs. I have students from French-controlled areas of Africa, Vietnam, Arabic countries, Mexico, and South America. They've all passed a language proficiency test, but they still need a lot of support. I try to make the environment very nonthreatening. I tell them about my own African ancestry and ask them about their countries of origin. I put them up front and close to me so we can easily work one-on-one; I use a lot of visuals; I go at a slower pace; and I ask a lot of questions requiring a verbal response. Sometimes I have them tell a neighbor the answer, which they really like. I also let the kids speak in their first language to explain things to other students who are confused. I hear a lot of "Ohs," that indicate they "got it." Overall, I try to make the language friendly enough so they feel comfortable and so I can be confident that they understand the key concepts.**

A comprehensive model of SDAIE includes five components (Diaz-Rico & Weed, 2009). First—and critical—is the *teacher's attitude;* unless the teacher is open and willing to learn from students, SDAIE cannot be successful. The second component is *content,* meaning that lessons must have both subject matter and language objectives, and lessons must be planned and implemented with language in mind. Third is an emphasis on *comprehensibility;* lessons must include explicit strategies that aid in students' understanding (e.g., modeling, frequent comprehension checks, adjustment in use of language). Fourth, *connections* refers to the importance of connecting curriculum to students' background and experiences. The final component is *interaction:* Students in a sheltered English classroom have frequent opportunities to work together, to clarify concepts in their native language, and to represent learning in a variety of ways. Having a number of ELLs in your class will add to the cultural richness and global understanding of your students. It could also be a source of stress, especially for new teachers. Questions are likely to arise about how to meet the needs of your ELLs while not shortchanging the rest of the class; however, incorporating some sheltered English strategies into your teaching and following the suggestions listed in the Practical Tips box should benefit *everyone.*

 PRACTICAL TIPS FOR

Helping English Language Learners

- Provide a safe, welcoming environment for language risk taking. Be aware of your own biases toward cultures different from yours.
- Take time to learn about the discourse patterns of cultures besides your own so you don't misinterpret students' words, gestures, or actions. (See Chapter 12 for some examples of discourse patterns.)
- Communicate the expectation that all students can succeed and show students that you are eager to help them.
- Increase time and opportunities for meaningful talk; small-group or whole-class discussions provide opportunities to practice language skills.
- Find ways for students to participate in group activities, giving them roles that depend less on language use (e.g., have them draw pictures or serve as timekeepers).
- Encourage speaking English while honoring students' first language and culture. Allow students to use their native language at appropriate times (e.g., when they need to process new material with another speaker of their language or need to construct meaning from a reading selection).
- Encourage students to tell about their culture. Listen carefully and ask questions. View ethnic and linguistic diversity within a classroom not as a problem but as an asset from which both teachers and students can profit.
- Build on and utilize students' background knowledge and personal interests.
- Encourage students to write about topics of their choice and for real-world purposes.
- Encourage parents to develop and maintain their primary language at home.
- Learn some second language and use it yourself with students.
- Emphasize collaborative over individual work.
- Emphasize doing rather than telling.
- Speak a bit more slowly and enunciate clearly with your mouth in direct view of the students.
- Use gestures and body language to accompany your verbal messages to students.
- Make the language of the text comprehensible by interpreting it in simple, everyday language.
- Offer periodic summaries.
- Paraphrase questions and statements to allow for different levels of proficiency. Use synonyms to clarify the meaning of unknown words.
- Control vocabulary and sentence structure (e.g., if you use idioms such as "It's raining cats and dogs," explain what they mean).

(continued on next page)

- Ask questions that require different degrees of English proficiency in responding (e.g., nonverbal signals to communicate agreement or disagreement, yes-no, single-word, or short answers).

- When students respond to your questions, focus on the content rather than on the form of the response.

- Use objects, videos, pictures, or movement to increase comprehensibility and provide a context for learning.

- Apply SDAIE strategies across the curriculum. Often known as "sheltered instruction," SDAIE focuses on core curriculum content and uses a rich variety of techniques and materials such as artifacts, visuals, video, storyboarding, movement, role-plays, and collaborative learning.

- Think aloud and model a variety of reading comprehension strategies (e.g., making connections, predicting, inferring).

- Use a variety of reading supports such as text tours and picture walks (to preview material), graphic organizers (story maps, character analyses), and text signposts (chapter headings, bold print).

- Use a variety of writing supports, such as group composing, graphic organizers, and drawing-based texts.

Sources: Cary, 2007; Henning, 2008; Romero, Mercado, & Vazquez-Faria, 1987.

STUDENTS WITH DISABILITIES AND ADHD

Matthew is a student in Sandy's last-period class who has been identified as emotionally disturbed. Although he's very quiet, he erupts angrily when provoked and is prone to violent outbursts. Sandy says that you can tell something is boiling just beneath the surface. She makes sure to place him in groups with students who are cooperative and supportive; even so, he frequently gets tense and frustrated with group members who he thinks are "wasting his time." According to Sandy, "Matthew is really bright, and when students are quibbling over something he thinks is silly (like how to write down an answer), he'll get a funny look on his face and turn his back on the other group members. It's almost as if he's trying to block out whatever's bothering him. When I see that look, I know to get over there and intervene." Sandy has carefully reviewed Matthew's individualized education program (IEP), but the close communication with his case manager and the school psychologist has allowed her to gain a deeper understanding of Matthew's behavior. As she puts it, "Matthew's having a successful year in chemistry—and that's due to the fact that many people are helping *me* to help *him*."

Matthew's presence in Sandy's classroom is a direct result of the Individuals with Disabilities Education Act (reauthorized as IDEA 2004, and also referred to as the *Individuals with Disabilities Education Improvement Act,* or *IDEIA*), the federal legislation mandating a "free appropriate public education" for all students with disabilities. According to the IDEA, *disability* is defined as mental retardation, a hearing impairment including deafness, a speech or language impairment, a visual impairment including blindness, serious emotional disturbance, an orthopedic impairment, autism, traumatic brain injury, other health impairment (e.g., limited strength or vitality due to chronic or acute health problems such as asthma or diabetes), a specific learning disability, deafness-blindness, or multiple disabilities.

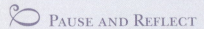

Pause and Reflect

What do you think about the inclusion of students with disabilities in the general education classroom? Do your views depend on the type of disability (e.g., physical, emotional, cognitive)? What are your specific concerns, if any, about teaching in inclusive classrooms?

In the next section of the chapter, we summarize the characteristics of students with learning disabilities, hearing loss, emotional and behavior disorders, autism spectrum disorders, and ADHD and suggest some strategies for effectively working with these students. We then discuss a variety of general strategies that could be useful as you work to achieve a classroom that is truly inclusive.

Learning Disabilities

More students are identified as having "specific learning disabilities" than any other type of disability, yet, it is difficult to get a satisfactory definition of learning disabilities (LD) because students diagnosed with it are a heterogeneous group. The IDEA defines learning disabilities as a "disorder in one or more of the basic psychological processes involved in understanding or in using language, spoken or written," which results in learning problems that are not explained by some other disability (such as mental retardation). Common problems include trouble reading; not understanding what is read; confusing similar letters and words; difficulty with fine motor activities (including handwriting); trouble understanding and following directions; and lack of organizational skills.

Many schools make a diagnosis of LD when there is a severe discrepancy between intellectual ability and academic performance. Another approach is to use a student's *response-to-intervention (RTI)*. Small-group, intensive instruction in the needed academic areas is provided to these students early. If this early intervention fails to benefit the student, then he or she could qualify as having a specific LD.

Reviews of research indicate that three teaching strategies are particularly powerful in promoting the academic success of students with LD (Vaughn, Gersten, & Chard, 2000). First, teachers need to match tasks to the student's abilities and skills, sequencing examples and problems to allow high levels of student success. Second, small-group instruction with no more than six students appears to be especially beneficial. Finally, students with LD need to learn self-questioning strategies (i.e., to ask themselves questions while reading or working on an academic task). Teachers can model this by thinking aloud about text being read or mathematics problems to be solved. These instructional practices are hardly revolutionary; unfortunately, they are too rarely implemented in classrooms (Vaughn, Gersten, & Chard).

Hearing Loss

IDEA defines a hearing loss as "an impairment in hearing, whether permanent or fluctuating, that adversely affects a child's educational performance." A student with hearing loss in the moderate to severe range most likely has difficulty hearing at conversational levels, and speech must be loud to be understood. Many of these individuals wear hearing aids. A student with a great degree of hearing loss could have a cochlear implant, a surgically implanted device that transmits electrical impulses to stimulate the hearing nerve within the inner ear.

Some students benefit greatly from hearing aids and cochlear implants, but amplification does not restore hearing like eyeglasses can give a person perfect sight. For example, hearing devices amplify *all* the sounds coming to a student, so it is often difficult for him or her to filter out unnecessary noise in a classroom (i.e., the student might have difficulty hearing a teacher's voice when their classmates are talking to each other). An FM system, which utilizes radio frequencies to transmit sound, is often used in classrooms to provide for communication needs beyond what the hearing device can offer. With this system, one speaker (typically the classroom teacher) wears a microphone connected to a small unit that clips onto clothes. The sound from the microphone is transmitted by FM radio frequency directly into a receiver attached to the student's hearing aid or cochlear implant. This allows the student to hear the teacher's voice directly in his or her ear. (Remember to turn off the microphone when talking privately to another student!) The Practical Tips box provides suggestions for helping students with hearing loss in your classroom.

 ## PRACTICAL TIPS FOR

Helping Students with Hearing Loss

- Teach students to be their own advocate when it comes to telling you whether they can hear what they need to in the classroom. Develop a hand signal—such as pointing to their ear—that they can use to tell you they missed something or would like you to repeat information.
- Have the students be in charge of the hearing equipment. Students can be taught to change their own hearing aid batteries (although it is advisable always to have extra batteries on hand), charge their FM system, and remind the teacher when to use and turn off the FM.
- Use visual aids to assist in the learning process (such as overheads, charts, outlines, etc.).
- Seat a child with hearing loss close to the teacher, although it is preferable to have other students seated in front of them so that they might watch those students and pick up signals from them.
- Obtain students' attention prior to speaking to them and/or giving them directions.
- Reduce distractions or background noise as much as possible. Simple things such as closing the classroom door and having carpet or tennis balls on the legs of chairs can help tremendously.
- If a student with hearing loss does not understand what you have said, make sure you are enunciating properly or try rephrasing your statement. Talking louder does not help a student with hearing loss as much as speaking more clearly and precisely.
- Frequently check for understanding of information.
- Maintain eye contact when speaking with the student with hearing loss because many students depend on lip reading or facial cues to understand spoken language.
- Learn some sign language for enhanced communication options. Often students with hearing loss will know a few signs themselves and those signs can be used for all students in the classroom.

Other students with hearing loss might rely on sign language to communicate. If these students are included in the general education classroom, they will normally be assigned an educational interpreter or translator who remains with the student throughout the school day. This person can be a sign language interpreter who interprets spoken language into sign language or a language facilitator who aids communication between the student with hearing loss and others in the educational setting. If a student in your classroom has been assigned an educational interpreter or translator, you will need to work with that person to decide where he or she can sit in the classroom so that the student can see both you and the interpreter at all times. When speaking with a student who uses sign language, you should always speak directly to the student and maintain eye contact, even though the interpreter might be "voicing" the student's thoughts. You might also want to learn a few basic signs, and teach them to the students in your class so that communication with this student can be enhanced.

Emotional and Behavioral Disorders

When teachers are asked to talk about "problem students," they tend to speak about those who are disruptive, aggressive, and defiant and whose behaviors interfere with others—students whose behavioral disorders are *externalizing* (Vaughn, Bos, & Schumm, 2003). Such students have a *conduct disorder (CD)* characterized by a "repetitive and persistent pattern of behavior in which the basic rights of others or major age-appropriate societal norms or rules are violated" (American Psychiatric Association, 2013). It's easy to identify students who display this type of behavior, but what do you do about it?

First, it's essential to be *proactive.* Too often, teachers react only to the student's negative behaviors, but students with CD must be taught how to behave more appropriately. This means monitoring students' behavior closely so that you can prompt, recognize, and reward acceptable behaviors (i.e., "catch 'em being good") and anticipate and head off unacceptable behavior. Second, students with CD can benefit from *direct teaching of appropriate social behavior* with rewards provided for the display of these behaviors as well as a response-cost procedure in which points (or tokens) are lost for inappropriate behavior (Ostrander, 2004). Third, *exploring the intent or purpose of the unacceptable behavior* can reveal what a student needs in order to behave more appropriately and to learn, such as getting help with a difficult or frustrating assignment. Some additional suggestions are listed in the Practical Tips box. (Also refer to the section on defiance in Chapter 12 and the section on de-escalating potentially explosive situations in Chapter 13.)

Donna used these strategies with a low-achieving student who was angry and aggressive. After looking into her background, Donna found out the girl was living with her mother and the mother's boyfriend, a sister and her sister's two children (from two different fathers). Her home life was unstable and unsupportive. Donna was able to arrange for the student to become her "teacher's aide," a prestigious position contingent on the girl's appropriate behavior in class. As Donna comments, "This one-on-one time allowed us to establish a really trusting relationship, and although she was ostensibly there to help me, I used the time to tutor her and to reinforce basic skills." With this emotional and academic support, the girl was able to go to high school and graduate on time—the first high school graduate in her family.

PRACTICAL TIPS FOR

Helping Students with Conduct Disorder

- Make sure your classroom environment is organized, predictable, and structured.
- Plan and implement activities to promote a sense of community (see Chapter 3).
- Actively work on establishing positive relationships; provide consistent, positive attention and decrease negative comments.
- Closely monitor behavior and acknowledge and reward positive behavior.
- Directly teach social skills (e.g., anger management).
- Provide structured choices ("Would you prefer to do your math or your writing first?" "Do you want to do this alone or work in a group?").
- Have a plan for removing the student if she or he becomes disruptive.
- Learn to anticipate and de-escalate problem situations (see Chapter 13).
- Use self-management approaches (see Chapter 12) such as self-monitoring, self-evaluation, and self-instruction.
- Develop and implement contingency contracts (see Chapter 12).
- Make sure that instruction is appropriate for the student's level of ability because frustration and academic failure can exacerbate the student's emotional/behavioral problems.

Children and adolescents with emotional disturbance might also show a pattern of *internalizing* behaviors, such as shyness, withdrawal, anxiety, and depression (Vaughn, Bos, & Schumm, 2003). Consider the following journal entry written by a student teacher:

> *I'm really worried about one of my kids. She's unbelievably shy and withdrawn. It took me a long time to even notice her. She never participates in class discussions, never raises her hand, and never volunteers for anything. When I call on her, she looks down and doesn't answer, or her answer is so soft that I can't hear her. The other kids aren't mean to her—they act like she doesn't even exist—and that's sort of the way I feel too!*

Such students who act sad, reserved, withdrawn, or irritable, could actually be suffering from depression. It is important to consult a school counselor or psychologist if you are concerned that a youngster is depressed (Schlozman, 2001). Journals, drawings, or essays that suggest suicidal or homicidal thoughts certainly warrant a formal referral. In addition, teachers need to understand that depressed students often feel as though they have little to contribute. To counter these feelings, you need to communicate respect and confidence in the student's abilities, minimize the possibility of embarrassment (e.g., by calling on depressed students to answer questions that have no clearly correct answer), and encourage them to assist younger or less able students. Most importantly, you need to forge a connection with the depressed student. Adults who suffered from depression when they were younger frequently remember a specific teacher as key to their recovery (Schlozman).

Autism Spectrum Disorders (ASDs)

Marked impairments in the development of social interaction and communication skills characterize ASDs. The Centers for Disease Control and Prevention (2012) report that the prevalence of ASDs has increased rapidly since 2000 and now affects approximately 1 child in every 88. ASDs are almost five times more common among boys (1 in 54) than among girls (1 in 252).

It is important to note that ASDs can range from mild to severe. Some students might have little or no verbal language; others can perform at high academic levels. Until recently, these high-performing individuals were often diagnosed with Asperger syndrome, but that term is now used less frequently and is being replaced by ASD-Level 1 (mild).

Children with an ASD display a lack of responsiveness and unawareness of social situations; for example, they might make little or no eye contact, exhibit a lack of interest in sharing enjoyable activities with other people, and have difficulty understanding nonverbal social cues and the subtleties of language such as irony and humor (National Dissemination Center, 2010). Those who do have spoken language could use it idiosyncratically (e.g., repeating sentences said to them, a condition known as *echolalia*). Finally, individuals with an ASD often exhibit restricted, repetitive patterns of behavior (e.g., body rocking or hand flapping; inflexible adherence to routines or rituals) and have a consuming preoccupation with specific topics (e.g., train schedules). Hypersensitivity to sensory input such as noise, lights, and touch is also common.

Although there are no cures for ASDs, educational interventions can be effective in bringing about improvements. For example, see the Practical Tips box for suggestions on helping students with ASDs.

Because an ASD is generally evident by age three, it is unusual for teachers in middle and high school to have a student who has not already been identified and provided support. But it does happen. Donna describes this situation:

 John acted really strange in class. He would blurt out things with no relationship to the topic and that were sometimes offensive. He would tap on his desk all the time and drive people crazy. Everything on his desk had to be neat and ordered. He wouldn't make eye contact and just didn't seem to know how to make friends. I found out that he had a long history of detentions and referrals to the office, and he had been in a whole bunch of schools. From the third week of school, I had the psychologist and the school social worker come in to watch him, and we met with his father, who just didn't know how to help him. It took all year, but John was finally diagnosed with autism. It was hard to believe that no one had ever picked it up. Getting him the help he needed was probably my proudest moment in teaching. Now he's in high school, and he's thriving. He plays multiple instruments and is in band; it turns out that when he was tapping on his desk, he was actually tapping out notes!

PRACTICAL TIPS FOR

Helping Students with Autism Spectrum Disorders

- Use clear, unambiguous language. Avoid humor, irony, and idiomatic expressions such as "It's raining cats and dogs." Explicitly teach common similes and metaphors.
- Provide warning of any impending change of routine or switch of activity.
- Explicitly teach social rules or skills, such as turn taking and social distance.
- Explicitly teach how feelings are expressed and communicated and how, therefore, they can be recognized.
- Protect the student from teasing and provide peers some insight into the needs of students with ASDs.
- Establish a "home base," a safe area in which a student can calm down, away from the overstimulation of the classroom (e.g., a counselor's office, a resource room, the nurse's office). Home base should not be used for time-out or punishment.
- Use "priming" to familiarize students with academic material prior to its use in school. Priming can reduce the stress associated with new tasks and increase success. A typical priming session lasts 10 to 15 minutes and is held in a quiet space the evening or morning before the materials are to be used.
- Provide opportunities for students to share their strengths (e.g., by linking work to the student's particular interests)
- Modify the environment:
    Seat the student in an area free of distraction.
    Keep the student's space free of unnecessary materials.
    Use checklists to help the student be organized.
    Provide opportunities for the student to move around.
- Modify instruction:
    Focus the student's attention before any communication, such as by using his or her name or using some prearranged signal.
    Provide clear, simple instructions, one at a time.
    Because fine motor skills can make handwriting difficult, let the student type or record responses.
    Because verbal information can be difficult to process, use visual supports whenever possible.
    Color code assignments.
    Provide the student a skeletal outline of the main ideas of a topic.
    Schedule short, frequent conferences with the student to check for comprehension.
    Break assignments into short tasks.
    Allow the student to use a computer or calculator.
    Use simple charts to record progress and regularly praise or provide more tangible rewards to mark good performance.

Source: Myles, Gagnon, Moyer, & Trautman, 2004; D. Chamblis (personal communication, October 2012).

Attention-Deficit/Hyperactivity Disorder (ADHD)

Although teachers often find working with students who have ADHD particularly challenging, this condition is *not* included in IDEA's definition of children with disabilities. However, students could be able to receive special services under another disability category such as "other health impairments" as well as Section 504 of the Rehabilitation Act of 1973, which defines a person with a disability as any person who has a physical or mental impairment substantially limiting a major life activity such as learning.

No diagnostic test for ADHD is currently available, but students frequently exhibit inattention, distractibility, difficulty in organizing tasks and activities, fidgeting, excessive physical movement, and impulsivity. Keep in mind that any one of the behaviors can be normal, but when an individual frequently displays a large number of these behaviors at a developmentally inappropriate age, the possibility of ADHD should be considered.

Approximately 8 percent of school-age children in the United States is estimated to have ADHD with far more boys than girls affected (Centers for Disease Control and Prevention, 2005; Pastor & Reuben, 2008). Students with ADHD often have difficulties in school. They might be underproductive or disorganized, fail to complete their work, or even lose it. They might also have problems with memory, language, visual perception, and fine motor control, which interfere with academic achievement. Indeed, as many as 35 percent of children and adolescents with ADHD might have learning disabilities compared with 3 percent of all children (Wodrich, 2000). Finally—and not surprisingly—individuals with ADHD might have problems meeting behavioral expectations and getting along with their peers.

To help students with ADHD, your classroom needs to be predictable, secure, and structured. Behavioral expectations must be clear, and consequences must be fair and consistent. The Practical Tips box offers some more specific suggestions.

 PRACTICAL TIPS FOR

Helping Students with ADHD

- Provide structure, routine, predictability, and consistency.
- Make sure that behavioral expectations are clear.
- Seat these students close to you among attentive, well-focused students.
- Make frequent eye contact.
- Make sure these students' desks are free of distractions; provide cardboard dividers to block out distractions.
- Provide a quiet work area or a "private office" to which these students can move for better concentration.
- Provide headphones to block out noise during seatwork or other times that require concentration.
- Provide opportunities to move around in legitimate ways (e.g., exercise breaks, doing errands).
- Use physical contact (e.g., a hand on a shoulder) to focus attention.
- Develop private signals to help focus attention.
- Ease transitions by providing cues and warnings.

(continued on next page)

- Use positive reinforcement and behavior modification techniques.
- Modify assignments:
    Cut the written workload.
    Break the assignment into manageable parts.
- Limit the amount of homework.
- Allow additional time on assignments or tests.
- Assist with organization (e.g., assignment pads; checklists; color coded notebooks for different subjects; accordion folders for loose papers).
- Try to give these students at least one task each day that they can do successfully.
- Try to call on these students when they are paying attention; use their first names before calling on them.
- Provide extra sets of books to keep at home so that these students are not overwhelmed after an absence and to prevent problems caused by forgetting books.
- Provide access to a computer along with keyboard and word processing instruction; do not remove access to the computer as a penalty.
- DO NOT PUNISH; DO NOT ASSUME STUDENTS ARE LAZY; DO NOT GIVE UP.

Sources: Adapted from CHADD, 1993; Rief, 1993.

General Strategies for Helping Students with Disabilities and ADHD

Implementing inclusion on the secondary level is especially challenging because content-area teachers generally feel pressure to "cover the curriculum"—pressure that has been heightened in this age of high-stakes testing. Teachers also expect students to have independent study skills and to possess the prior knowledge required to master new material, something that might not be

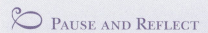 **PAUSE AND REFLECT**

In recent years, dramatic increases in the number of children who have been diagnosed and treated for ADHD have stirred debate not only about the possibility of overdiagnosis but also even whether the disorder really exists. Skeptics criticize teachers for wanting to suppress children's natural enthusiasm and energy, parents for failing to provide appropriate guidance and discipline, and physicians for overmedicating. What do you think about this?

true of students with disabilities (Mastropieri & Scruggs, 2001). Nonetheless, research indicates that inclusion on the secondary level can be successful in terms of academic and social outcomes (Mastropieri & Scruggs; Wallace, Anderson, Bartholomay, & Hupp, 2002). The following section of the chapter delineates some of the ways to enhance the likelihood of such success.

BECOME FAMILIAR WITH THE STUDENT'S IEP OR 504 PLAN

The IDEA requires that an individualized education program (IEP) be developed for each student with a disability. IEPs are developed by a team composed of a representative of the local education agency (e.g., an administrator who can commit school district resources), one of the student's general education teachers, the special education teacher who will have primary responsibility for implementing the IEP, parents or guardians, a person who can interpret the instructional implications of the evaluation results, the student (when appropriate), and other individuals at the discretion of the parent or school.

Similarly, a student who is eligible for special services under Section 504 of the Rehabilitation Act will have a "504 plan" outlining the accommodations and services needed to ensure that the student receives an appropriate education. Like the IEP, a 504 plan is developed by a team, although its composition is not specified by law.

Unfortunately, at the middle- and high-school levels, general education teachers often do not participate in the IEP or 504 process; sometimes they do not even know which students in their classrooms have been identified as having special needs (Schumm & Vaughn, 1992). Moreover, obtaining access to students' IEPs and 504s is not always easy. Policies and procedures vary from school to school. Sandy reports that by the second day of school, her mailbox is filled with the IEPs and 504s of students in her classes, and she has to sign a form indicating that she's received them. In contrast, Christina never gets copies; instead, a special educator or the school nurse shows her the documents. However they're told, our teachers emphasize the fact that implementation is their responsibility. As Sandy comments: "Teachers need to realize that 504s and IEPs are not optional. You can't ignore them. And if no one shows you any IEPs or 504s (as sometimes happens), it's your responsibility to track them down and read them."

It's also important to reexamine IEPs every marking period and make sure that you are monitoring the progress of students with disabilities. In this regard, it's helpful to keep a folder of relevant work samples to document progress (Vaughn, Bos, & Schumm, 2003).

CREATE AN ACCEPTING CLIMATE

Secondary teachers often display a less positive attitude toward inclusion than their elementary-level counterparts (Scruggs & Mastropieri, 1996). This is unfortunate because the success of inclusion largely depends on a teacher's ability and willingness to create a positive atmosphere that is accepting of individual differences (Mastropieri & Scruggs, 2001). You can promote a positive climate by making clear that all students are accepted, valued members of the class; establishing norms that emphasize belonging and respect; and implementing group activities that foster interaction between students with disabilities and their nondisabled peers (Soodak & McCarthy, 2006). Students with special needs can display significant social deficiencies and have difficulty establishing friendships (Meadan & Monda-Amaya, 2008); in this case, you can help students find common interests regardless of their abilities or special needs (Grandin, 2007). If social interaction is fostered through commonalities, students might be more likely to accept each other as equal members of the classroom community. (Refer back to Chapters 3 and 4 for additional ideas to create an accepting classroom climate.)

COORDINATE AND COLLABORATE WITH SPECIAL EDUCATION TEACHERS AND PARAPROFESSIONALS

In addition to following your students' IEPs and 504 plans, communicating regularly with special services personnel is important. For example, you can ask a special educator for suggestions about enhancing the learning of your students; you might also ask the special educator to demonstrate lessons or to come in and help you instruct students with special needs. You should also inform the special education teacher if you are concerned about a student's progress.

When approaching special services personnel, bring specific information about the student and about the interventions and accommodations you've already tried. Complaints like "He's driving me crazy," "She constantly demands attention," or "He just can't hack it in my class" are not helpful. The more detailed your information can be, the more likely you are to receive assistance. Here are some of our teachers' suggestions about the types of information to bring:

- An overall description of the student (both strengths and weaknesses).
- A detailed description of any inappropriate behavior the student exhibits:

  When does the student exhibit the behavior?
  How frequently does the student exhibit the behavior?
  What antecedent events set off the behavior?
  What is the duration of the behavior?
  What is the reaction of other students in the class?

- If the student is having academic problems, a detailed description of her or his academic difficulties (with work samples to support your description).
- Efforts on your part to correct or deal with the problem.
- How you'd like to be helped or what type of help you believe the student needs.

Just as inclusion in the general education classroom has become more widespread, so too has the practice of having content specialists co-teach with special educators. *Co-teaching* is defined as two or more people sharing responsibility for planning, teaching, and evaluating some or all of the students in a class (Villa, Thousand, & Nevin, 2008). Co-teaching, also known as *collaborative teaching* or *cooperative teaching,* can take a variety of forms (Dieker, 2001). For example, in the "lead and support" model, one teacher takes responsibility for instruction while the other offers assistance and support to individuals or small groups. In *parallel teaching,* teachers jointly plan instruction, but each delivers it to half the class, and in *team teaching,* both teachers share the planning and instruction of students.

Although co-teaching can be very effective, it also poses challenges for both parties. Some of these difficulties stem from inadequate school support (e.g., lack of common preparation time), personality conflicts, and a lack of clarity about roles and responsibilities in co-taught classrooms (Murray, 2004). None of our five teachers works in a co-teaching arrangement, but they have seen situations that are less than ideal. Christina comments:

> **Regular ed teachers sometimes have a problem working with special ed teachers; they are very "territorial" and treat the special educator like an aide. They don't do collaborative planning; they just say, "Here's what we're doing."**
>
> **But sometimes the problem is the other way around. You have a regular ed teacher who really wants to collaborate with the special ed teacher, but the special ed teacher wants to sit in the back of the room and only help a couple of kids.**

To avoid these problems, discussing the roles that each teacher will have in the general education classroom is essential. The Practical Tips box lists strategies for co-teaching at the secondary level.

PRACTICAL TIPS FOR

Co-teaching in Secondary Classrooms

- *Begin slowly.* Discuss your respective understandings of co-teaching; examine various models.
- *Involve an administrator.* Discuss the types of administrative support that are needed (especially with respect to common planning time). Find out whether such support will be forthcoming.
- *Get to know your partner.* Discuss your expectations with respect to roles and responsibilities regarding:

    Planning whole-class instruction.
    Planning modifications for individual students.
    Conducting instruction.
    Grading.
    Contacting parents.
    Providing discipline.
- *Create a workable schedule.* Decide how often co-teaching will occur (daily, a few times a week, for a specific unit). Decide on the model that will be used. Think about how to ensure that both teachers are actively involved and that neither feels over- or underutilized. Arrange for common planning time.

Source: Adapted from Murawski & Dieker, 2004.

Like co-teaching, using paraprofessionals or teaching assistants has become an increasingly popular method for supporting students with disabilities in general education classrooms. In fact, in many schools, having a paraprofessional accompany a student with disabilities to class is the "primary or exclusive" way in which inclusion is accomplished (Giangreco & Doyle, 2002, p. 2). Paraprofessionals can play a valuable, vital role in inclusive classrooms, but too often, they become the student's actual instructor, and the teacher becomes the delegator (Giangreco & Doyle). This creates a situation in which those who are least qualified to teach are responsible for instructing the students who present the most complex challenges.

If you have paraprofessionals in your classes, it is critical that you remain engaged with the students who have disabilities and not turn their education over to someone who might be uncomfortable and unknowledgeable about the subject matter. You also need to discuss explicitly what your respective roles and responsibilities will be with respect to instruction and behavior management. Paraprofessionals can provide support by carrying out a variety of noninstructional activities (e.g., preparing materials, taking attendance) as well as instructional tasks (e.g., assisting students during independent work, providing additional practice opportunities to reinforce previously taught material), but they should not have primary responsibility for a student's learning. It is also desirable to have paraprofessionals interact with *all* students, not just those with disabilities.

EXAMINE YOUR CLASSROOM ENVIRONMENT
FOR POSSIBLE MISMATCH

It's important to remember that problems do not always reside exclusively within a student. Sometimes problems are the result of a discrepancy between a student's needs and the classroom environment. A student teacher shared this account of a mismatch:

Jason is an autistic student who has a full-time aide. While Jason is very intelligent and capable of completing assignments, he is often frustrated and agitated in class. The other students, including the teacher, often make inappropriate comments about his outbursts and seem to lack patience with him. And his aide doesn't try to educate them about his condition. Jason's teacher has placed him with a group of students who are not easily distracted, to prevent Jason's occasional outbursts from disturbing the group. However, the students in Jason's group rarely include him in their discussions and often completely ignore him. It's not surprising that Jason reacts by getting agitated.

As this story illustrates, we sometimes think of a student as disabled when actually the problem is the result of a *disabling situation* (Gearheart, Weishahn, & Gearheart, 1992). Before concluding that "the entire problem is the kid," examine your classroom situation and reflect on ways the environment might be contributing to the student's difficulties. Here are some questions that our teachers ask themselves:

- Where is the student sitting? Is the seat near a source of distraction? Is it too far from the teacher?

- Is sitting in groups too difficult for the student to handle? Should I move the student to a pair or to individual seating?

- What type of academic work am I providing? Are assignments too mechanical? Too dry? Too long? Do they require too much independence? Do I ever allow choice?

- How do I speak with the student? How do I praise the student? *Do* I praise the student?

- What rules and routines have I set up? Are they contrary to the student's ability to comply? Am I expecting quiet behavior too long? Am I setting the student up for failure?

- Am I allowing an appropriate amount of time for completing assignments? For transitions?

REFLECT ON THE APPROPRIATENESS
OF YOUR EXPECTATIONS

Sometimes in our efforts to be understanding and sympathetic, we lower our expectations so much that we teach students to accept less from themselves as well. We water down curriculum; we forgive inappropriate behavior; we place students in safe environments where they will never be asked to do things we are sure they can't do. And when, in fact, they cannot do them, when they behave inappropriately, and when they do not learn, our beliefs seem justified.

Last year, one of Sandy's classes included a student who had a brain tumor that caused permanent motor skill damage; an aide attended classes with him. As Sandy recounted:

 I never lowered one standard nor did I lower my expectations for this wonderful young man. He had to do what everyone else in the class had to do but we had to be creative in some situations. Every year I give a major lab in which students must develop a plan and perform a series of experiments in order to identify an unknown solution. This young man obviously could not safely handle chemicals in the laboratory. I did not excuse him from the lab nor did I substitute a different activity (as his IEP suggested), but rather he developed a plan on his own and I became his hands the day of the lab. He told me step by step what he wanted me to do and I followed his instructions exactly.

I have to admit that while he was instructing me through his plan I really thought that he was on the wrong track. I couldn't see the direction in which he was heading because it certainly wasn't the way that I would have approached the unknowns. It wasn't until the end that I was able to see how this unique plan was going to result in a successful identification. He successfully identified his unknown in his own unique manner. Needless to say he was beaming! Having students like this young man in your classroom makes you grow as a teacher as you strive to help them reach their potential.

USE PEER TUTORING, PEER ASSISTANCE, AND COOPERATIVE LEARNING

Successful inclusion programs use peers effectively. Students can serve as *tutors* on academic tasks, *buddies* who assist with difficult activities, or *advocates* who "watch out" for the welfare of those with special needs (Gearheart, Weishahn, & Gearheart, 1992). For example, peer buddies is a structured program of peer support in which a nondisabled high school student is paired with a student with disabilities for at least one period each day. The buddies support their partners in a variety of ways and of settings. Buddies can accompany them to a school pep rally, introduce them to other general education students during lunch, help them complete a lab project in a science class, or teach them to set tables at a restaurant serving as a job training site. (See Table 6.1 for additional ways that peers can provide supports.) Copeland and her colleagues (2002) found that general and special educators involved in a peer buddies program reported both academic and social benefits; in particular, students who received support from peers seemed more independent, more self-confident, and more willing to participate in everyday high school activities.

Research has also demonstrated that cooperative learning can promote positive social relationships between students with disabilities and their peers. The use of cooperative learning can help to minimize the problem of students with special needs being isolated and rejected *socially* even though they are included *physically* in the regular classroom. (See Chapter 11 for guidance on implementing successful small-group work.)

TABLE 6.1 Ways That Peers Can Support Classmates with Disabilities

- Teach classroom routines (e.g., where to put homework, what to do when they first get to class).
- Read a test and record answers.
- Read or record selections from a textbook, paraphrasing as needed.
- Take notes during a teacher lecture and spend time discussing the notes and answering questions at the end of the period.
- Help a classmate fulfill an assigned role during cooperative learning activities.
- Facilitate conversation with other general education students during free time.
- Keep track of assignments when students are absent.
- Provide tutoring in a specific skill.
- Provide assistance with organization (e.g., recording assignments, finding the relevant place in the textbook, organizing notebooks).

Note: Although peers can support classmates with disabilities, it is important to make sure that every student has an opportunity to be the tutor or supporter; in other words, students with disabilities should not always be relegated to the position of "helpee."

Source: Adapted from Copeland, et al., 2002.

STUDENTS WHO ARE TROUBLED

During one meeting, the teachers talked about how they try to be alert to problems their students might be experiencing. Sandy told us how she tries to distinguish between problems that warrant immediate action and those that do not, and how she collects additional information:

 I watch for changes in students' behavior. If I see anything that looks like drug abuse, I report it immediately. If it doesn't seem like a drug problem, I generally approach the student and ask what's going on. If the kid seems depressed, I'll say something like, "Hey, you seem a little down today. Are you having a problem? Do you want to talk?" We all have bad days, and adolescents have wide swings of mood; it's the nature of the beast. A day or two of strange behavior doesn't necessarily mean there's a big problem. Adolescents aren't very good at masking their emotions, and most of the time they're upset because they had a fight with their mother, or the dog had to be put to sleep, or their boyfriend or girlfriend broke up with them. But if a kid is acting weird or seems depressed for longer than a few days, I check with other teachers to find out if they're seeing anything unusual too. If they've also noticed problems, I go to the principal or the vice principal; often they know if something is going on at home. If there appears to be a real problem, I'll report it.

As Sandy's comments illustrate, *you need to be alert to the indicators of potential problems.* As an adult immersed in adolescent culture, you will probably develop a good idea of what typical teenage behavior is like. This allows you to detect deviations or changes in a student's behavior that might signal the presence of a problem.

Learn to ask yourself a series of questions when you notice atypical behavior (Kottler & Kottler, 1993):

- What is unusual about this student's behavior?
- Is there a pattern to what I have observed?
- What additional information do I need to make an informed judgment?
- Whom might I contact to collect this background information?
- What are the risks of waiting longer to figure out what is going on?
- Does this student seem to be in any imminent danger?
- Whom can I consult about this case?

Substance Abuse

Substance abuse touches middle and secondary classrooms in two ways—when students are the children of alcoholics or addicts (COAs) and when students themselves abuse drugs and alcohol. We consider the problems of COAs first.

According to a counselor in Fred's district, COAs can exhibit a wide variety of behaviors:

Some children become perfectionists and peacemakers. They want to prevent situations that might evoke their parents' anger because their parents' responses are so unpredictable. It's as if they think to themselves, "I'm not going to disturb anything; I'm not going to do anything wrong; I'll try and keep the peace, so that no one will be angry." Some children become class clowns; maybe they've found that making people laugh breaks the tension, or maybe they're seeking attention. Others become very angry; they may begin to lie, or steal, or cheat. Some become sad and melancholy; everything about them says, "Nurture me." We see a whole spectrum of reactions—and it's the same spectrum of behaviors that we see in kids from violent homes.

It's important to understand that for COAs, family life revolves around the addiction. Rules are arbitrary and irrational; boundaries between parents and children are blurred; and life is marked by unpredictability and inconsistency.

It is frustrating to realize that you do not have the power to change a student's home life. Instead, you must concentrate on what you *are* able to do during the time the student is in your classroom. Many of the strategies are not different from those we have espoused for all students. (See the Practical Tips box.) For example, it is essential that you establish clear, consistent rules and work to create a climate of trust and caring.

A second way that substance abuse can affect middle- and high-school classrooms is when students themselves abuse drugs and alcohol. To a large extent, counselors rely on teachers to refer students who might be having problems with alcohol and other drugs or who might be at risk for such problems. But teachers can be particularly reluctant to make referrals about suspected drug use. Several different reasons for this reluctance emerged during conversations with teachers and counselors. First, some teachers think drug use is just not all that serious. According to a counselor in Fred's school, "Some teachers have a tendency to minimize the situation—especially if it

PRACTICAL TIPS FOR

Helping Children of Alcoholics/Addicts

- *Be observant.* Watch your students not just for academic or behavior problems but also for the more subtle signs of addiction and emotional distress. Remember that COAs can be overachieving, cooperative, and quiet as well as disruptive and angry.
- *Set boundaries that are enforced consistently.* When chaos exists at home, some sense of order is crucial at school.
- *Be flexible.* Although it is necessary to set boundaries, classroom rules that are too rigid and unyielding could invite students to act out.
- *Make addiction a focus of discussion.* Find a way to deal with this subject. Incorporate addiction into literacy instruction, science, social studies, and so on.
- *Make it clear that you are available.* Communicate that you are eager and open to talk. Reach out to the troubled student in a gentle, caring way. "I notice you are having some difficulty. I just want you to know that I care about you. Call me any time you are ready to talk. And if you would rather speak to someone else, let me find you someone you can trust."
- *Develop a referral network.* Find out what services are available to help and refer the student for appropriate professional care.
- *Accept what you can do little about.* You can't make people stop drinking or taking drugs.

Source: Adapted from Powell, Zehm, & Kottler, 1995.

involves alcohol or pot. They just don't consider pot to be a 'real' drug. They think, 'Oh, all kids do this; it's not that big a deal.'"

In addition, the counselor in Fred's school speculates that some teachers feel it's not their role to get involved; others want to play the role of confidante:

Sometimes, teachers are overwhelmed by all the responsibilities of teaching. They feel like they have more than enough to do without getting involved in students' personal problems. . . . But other times, teachers don't refer because they want to try to help the kid themselves. You know, a lot of teachers really like the role of mediator, caretaker, trusted confidante. They like the fact that a student is confiding in them about a problem, and sometimes they make a pact of confidentiality with the student: "You can tell me your secret. I won't tell anybody." But if the kid is in serious trouble, that can be a problem. First of all, [teachers] don't really have the training to help the way a counselor could. Second, they might be sending a message to the kid that it's not okay to go to a counselor or a mental health professional—and that's not a message we want to send. . . . Third, they could actually be serving as a "professional enabler"— they're allowing the kid to continue behavior that could be self-destructive. . . . What you've got to do is say to the kid, "I care too much about you to allow this to continue. We've got to get help for you."

Another reason for teachers' reluctance to refer is the belief that they are "turning kids in" when they would rather "give the kid a break" (Newsam, 1992). Sandy herself comments on this attitude:

 Some teachers are afraid to report suspected drug use because they don't want to create a hassle for the kid. They don't want to get the kid in trouble. They may also be afraid that reporting kids will ruin their relationship with students. But I haven't found that to be the case. Sometimes, the kid will come back and say, "Why did you do that?" But I say, "This is too big for us. We need more help." Sometimes, I'll even have kids come to tell me about a problem with a friend. They know I'll find help. *That's what they want.*

Finally, teachers could be reluctant to report suspected drug use because they are unsure about the indicators. A counselor in Sandy's district is very sensitive to this problem:

Teachers tell me, "I have no idea what substance abuse looks like. It wasn't a part of my training. I wouldn't know when to refer a student." I tell them, that's okay. You can't tell substance abuse just by looking. There has to be a chemical screening. But you can see changes in behavior. You know enough about kids to know when somebody's behavior has changed, or if their behavior is different from all the other kids. You don't need to know the student is using; you just need to suspect that there may be drug use or a problem related to drug use.

What are the behaviors that might lead you to suspect drug use and to make a referral? Many schools use a checklist that asks about academic performance (e.g., drop in grades), school attendance, social problems, physical symptoms (e.g., sleeping in class), disruptive behavior, and behaviors that are atypical for a particular individual. Find out whether your school has such a checklist and, if it does, keep it handy so you can stay alert to the possibility that students are using drugs or living with addiction in their families.

It's important to distinguish between situations in which a pattern of behavior problems suggests possible *drug use outside of school* and situations in which a student appears to be *under the influence of drugs during school, at school functions,* or *on school property.* When you see students who might be "under the influence," you cannot wait to fill out a behavior checklist; you need to alert the appropriate personnel as soon as you possibly can. Fred shares this experience:

 A few years ago, I had this really bright kid in my first-period class. . . . But he got into drugs. I remember one day in particular when he came into class high. I didn't realize it at first, because he just sat down quietly and everything seemed okay. But then he got up to sharpen his pencil, and I could see that he was walking funny. He was actually leaning to one side. It looked like he was going to fall over. . . . I gave the rest of the class an assignment and asked him to come with me out into the hall. I tried to be really discreet; I didn't want everyone watching and talking about him. I planned to call the assistant principal, but the principal happened to be walking by just at that minute, so he took him to the nurse.

Make sure you know to whom you're supposed to refer students who appear to be under the influence of drugs. In Fred's and Christina's schools, teachers call an administrator who comes to the classroom and accompanies the student to the nurse. In Sandy's school, teachers send students to the nurse who then contacts the student assistance counselor. In Donnie's school, teachers call a security guard. Donna e-mails the principal, vice-principal, counselor, and nurse.

Because you cannot be sure that a student is using drugs just by looking, it's important not to be accusatory when you talk with the student. Sandy describes how she usually handles this situation:

> **If I see a kid with his head down on the desk, I'll go over and ask real quietly, "Do you need to see the nurse?" Usually they'll say, "No, I'm just tired," or "No, I'm bored." I'll tell them, "But this is chemistry! This is supposed to be fun." Usually, the head stays up after that. But if the head goes back down, I'll say, "I think you need to see the nurse. You don't seem to be feeling well." I'm not confrontational, and I try to show the kid that I'm acting out of concern. Sometimes I'm wrong, and it turns out that the kid just stayed up until 4:00 A.M. doing a term paper. That's fine. It's better to err on the side of caution.**

Making a referral can be difficult, but you need to remember that turning away and remaining silent can send the message that you condone the behavior—or that you don't care enough to do anything.

If you suspect that a student has drugs or alcohol in school (e.g., in a purse or backpack), it's important to bring that person to the appropriate school official rather than undertake a search by yourself. In a landmark case (*New Jersey v. T.L.O.,* 1985), the U.S. Supreme Court ruled that a school official may properly conduct a search of a student "when there are reasonable grounds for suspecting that the search will turn up evidence that the student has violated or is violating either the law or the rules of the school" (Fischer, Schimmel, & Kelly, 1999). In other words, students in school have fewer protections than are normally afforded to citizens under the stricter "probable cause" standard (Stefkovich & Miller, 1998). Nonetheless, searching a student's belongings is best left to an administrator who is aware of the subtleties of the law. (We will discuss this further in Chapter 12.)

One final note: It's important for teachers to keep up with the latest "fashions" in substance abuse. For example, while writing this chapter, we became aware of the "cinnamon challenge," in which students dare one another to swallow a tablespoon of cinnamon in under 60 seconds. Doing so causes individuals to gasp, spit, and choke, and can cause injury to mouths, throats, and lungs (Sifferlin, 2012).

Abuse and Neglect

During one conversation with Donnie, she emphasized the difficulty of detecting abuse and neglect among older students:

> **At the high school level, abuse and neglect are not as obvious as they are at the elementary level. Kids cover up more. But it's clear that a lot of them live in situations that are really awful. Teachers have to watch really carefully and listen to all the conversations that you're not supposed to hear. That way you can learn about what's going on in kids' lives and in the community.**

As Donnie points out, abuse of adolescents is often well hidden. Furthermore, adolescents just don't seem as vulnerable as younger children: They could have as much strength or weight as adults; they seem able to run away from abusive situations; and they appear to have more access to potential help outside the family. For these reasons, it's easy to think that abuse and neglect are not problems at the high school level. But adolescents still need protection. During one meeting, Christina recalled a girl who had worn a short-sleeved shirt in December when temperatures were in the 20s:

> It was as if she was saying, "Please look at my arm." I did—and saw she had bruises all over it. As a new teacher, I was a little nervous about handling this the right way, so I went to consult with a more experienced teacher. We spoke with one of the school counselors, who took the student to the nurse.

It's also important to realize that girls are not the only victims of abuse. Consider this tale shared by Donnie:

> A number of years ago, I had a 16-year-old football player in my class. I noticed that he seemed really quiet, which was unusual for him. I asked him to come see me after school. When he came in, I said, "You don't seem yourself. Is everything OK?" To my amazement, he started to cry. It turned out he had been seduced by a 35-year-old woman living next door. Obviously, she didn't tie him down, but having sex with a minor constitutes sexual abuse. It was the last thing I expected. I figured he had broken up with his girlfriend, or he was having a problem on the football team. I was really hit between the eyes, and I was furious. I kept thinking, "How could she do that? He's just a kid." I had difficulty thinking straight. I thought, "Now what do I do?" I was the first person he had told. It was after school, and the psychologist was gone, the counselor was gone. But I convinced him to go with me to the principal. The office took over from there.

All states have laws requiring educators to report suspected abuse to the state's "child protective service." Although definitions of abuse vary, states generally include nonaccidental injury, neglect, sexual abuse, and emotional maltreatment. It is essential that you become familiar with the indicators of these problems, including physical indicators such as bruises, burns, fractures, and unattended medical problems as well as behavioral indicators such as aggressiveness or withdrawal; inappropriately adult or infantile behaviors; and constant falling asleep in class.

Teachers are often reluctant to file a report unless they have absolute proof of abuse. They worry about invading the family's privacy and causing unnecessary embarrassment to everyone involved. Nonetheless, it's important to keep in mind that *no state requires the reporter to have absolute proof before reporting.* What most states do require is "reason to believe" or "reasonable cause to believe or suspect" that abuse has occurred (Fischer, Schimmel, & Kelly, 1999). If you are uncertain whether abuse is occurring but have reasonable cause, you should err in favor of the student and file a report. Waiting for proof can be dangerous; it can also be illegal. If a child is later harmed and it becomes clear that you failed to report suspected abuse, both you and your school district could be subject to both civil and criminal liability. Also keep in mind that every state provides immunity from any civil suit or criminal prosecution that might result from reporting suspected child abuse or neglect—as long as you have acted "in good faith" (Fischer, Schimmel, & Kelly).

It's essential that you learn about the reporting procedures in your state *before* you face a situation of suspected child abuse. Some states explicitly name the school personnel who are required to file the report. Other states have more general provisions that require reporting by "any person" who works with children; this would clearly include teachers, nurses, therapists, and counselors (Fischer, Schimmel, & Kelly, 1999). The form and content of reports required also vary among states. Most states require an oral report followed by a more detailed written report, and some states also have a 24-hour, toll-free hot line. Generally, you should be prepared to provide the student's name and address; the nature and extent of injury or condition observed; and your own name and address (Fischer, Schimmel, & Kelly).

The variation among states underscores the importance of becoming familiar with the procedures and resources in your own school. The best way to do this is to speak with people who can provide guidance and direction—experienced teachers, the principal, the school nurse, and the counselors.

Eating Disorders

During a visit to one of Fred's honors classes in late April, we were shocked by the emaciated appearance of one of his female students, Sara. Her eyes and cheeks were sunken in, and her arms looked like twigs. We couldn't take our eyes off her. After class, Fred shared the story:

This kid is a straight A student. . . . Everything she does is perfect. I don't think she's ever gotten less than 100 on any test or assignment I've given. And she's a fantastic soccer player. . . . To me, it looks like she couldn't even kick the ball. But I know that she practices every day, and she runs too.

A couple of Sara's friends have come to talk with me after school—they're worried about her too. They say that she insists she's fat and that she hardly eats. She seems to be particularly obsessed about not eating anything with fat in it—no pizza, no cheese, no cakes or cookies, and of course no meat of any kind. Apparently, all they ever see her eat is bagels and lettuce!

I've talked with Sara—I've told her that I'm really worried about her, but she insists that she's fine and that everyone's overreacting. I've also reported the situation to the school psychologist and the student assistance counselor, and I know that they've called Sara's parents. I even called her parents myself. But her parents don't acknowledge that there's a problem. . . .

Sara seems to suffer from anorexia nervosa, an eating disorder that generally begins during adolescence and primarily afflicts White females, although it's increasing among Black females and does occur among males (Brodey, 2005; Gonet, 1994). Anorexic adolescents literally starve themselves; even so, they continue to feel fat and can actually perceive that they are becoming heavier. Sara's involvement in running and soccer is also typical; in an attempt to lose weight more quickly, anorexics can combine excessive physical exercise with dieting.

Another eating disorder is bulimia nervosa, in which individuals starve themselves, then binge (often on high-calorie or high-sugar foods), and finally purge themselves (by inducing vomiting). Individuals with bulimia can be underweight, overweight, or average, but they share an intense fear of gaining weight. They can also feel that they have lost control over their lives; thus, they seek to control their eating and their weight (Gonet, 1994).

Of the two eating disorders, bulimia is more common, but anorexia is more severe and can actually be fatal. Both are long-term illnesses that require treatment; they will not go away by themselves. This means that you need to be alert to the signs of eating disorders and report your concern to the appropriate person in your school. Too often, teachers overlook eating disorders because concern about weight is a "normal pathology" in our society. Furthermore, the young women who most frequently suffer from eating disorders are often high-achieving, compliant, perfectionist students who cause no problems in class.

STUDENTS LIVING IN POVERTY

Children and adolescents living in poverty obviously face enormous challenges. They are far less likely than those from middle-class backgrounds to have access to adequate physical, dental, and mental health care. They can suffer from physical, emotional, and psychological problems, experience developmental delays, exhibit academic and behavioral difficulties, and be at risk for school failure. Living arrangements for homeless children are varied and far from adequate: Some double up with other family members or friends; others live in shelters, emergency foster care, abandoned buildings, vehicles, or motels; still others are on the street (National Coalition of Homeless Children and Youth, 2007).

School can be a haven for children living in poverty. But what can you possibly do? First, *effective teachers are wary of claims about a "culture of poverty" whose members have shared (often negative) traits.* From this perspective, those who are poor are a homogeneous group with characteristics that differ starkly from those who are middle class. These characteristics include *language patterns* (casual rather than formal*), values* (money is to be spent rather than saved*), worldviews* (a focus on the present rather than the future*), ways to interact with others* (physically rather than verbally), and *daily life* (noisy and chaotic rather than quiet and orderly). The idea of a culture of poverty has become popular among administrators and teachers, and numerous professional development workshops on this topic are offered throughout the country (e.g., Payne, 2005). Although these are intended to help teachers better educate poor children, some critics dispute the existence of a culture of poverty and contend that there is no research evidence to support this notion (e.g., Bomer, Dworin, May, & Semingson, 2008). They argue that traits such as those listed previously are undoubtedly true of *some* poor individuals (and some who are not poor!), but they do not define all poor people. Moreover, these critics warn that this characterization of poor people can lead teachers to engage in deficit thinking, a tendency to attribute school failure to internal deficiencies such as lack of motivation rather than to external factors such as inadequate funding to schools that serve poor students. Teachers who engage in deficit thinking are likely to overlook or dismiss the strengths of poor students, to "blame the victim," and to adopt negative stereotypes.

Second, *effective teachers of poor or homeless students are "bearers of hope"* (Landsman, 2006). They believe in the ability of all their students to learn even if they're wearing dirty clothes or come to school hungry. They examine and monitor their assumptions. On one hand, they are careful not to assume that poor students will be unable to meet class expectations; on the other hand, they don't assume that students will be able to complete assignments in a comfortable, quiet room at a desk stocked with all needed materials. They do not lower their expectations in terms of class participation and work, but they show flexibility and compassion (e.g., by extending a due date). They try to give their students as much choice and control over assignments as possible so that they can feel they have a say in their education.

Third, *effective teachers of poor or homeless adolescents work especially hard to build a supportive, trusting relationship.* They listen respectfully and respond empathically, using active listening skills to keep the lines of communication open. (See Chapter 3.) They are alert to opportunities to provide assistance. Donnie tells us, "Some of my students come early or hang around after school. They pretend that they need extra help, but they really don't. It's just that it's better than going home. And I always provide snacks or breakfast bars for them." Sandy also tries to help students in need:

 I remember one girl who was around the age of my daughter. I had noticed that the winter coat she was wearing had a broken zipper. I waited until she was alone with me after school and was getting ready to leave my classroom. It was very cold outside and I said to her, "You are just like my daughter Jennifer. She always manages to break the zippers on her jackets on the coldest day of the year! It's a good thing she has an older cousin so I always have an extra coat around for her. She's already on her second coat this winter." I told her that I had an extra jacket in my office and wanted her to try it on and see if it fit her. Of course, it did. After that I would bring in clothes (just a few pieces at a time) and just hand her the bag when we were alone. I would just say something like "Jennifer's cousin gave her too many," or "I have some extras," or "I thought that you might like these." I then gradually added some women's and men's clothing to the bag. I always tried to make it seem as if Jennifer was receiving clothes from other people and that it was no big deal. Of course, it was all a lie (Jennifer does not have an older female cousin), but you do what you have to do to help someone maintain their dignity.

Some specific strategies for helping children who are poor or homeless are listed in the Practical Tips box.

 PRACTICAL TIPS FOR

Helping Students Who Are Poor

Provide basic "survival" assistance:

- Keep granola bars and other healthful snacks on hand.
- If students live where things are stolen, allow them to leave school materials in school.
- Keep basic toiletries in your room for students who don't have access to personal hygiene items.
- Have extra school supplies on hand.

(continued on next page)

Be sensitive when disciplining:

- Think about whether students are purposefully misbehaving or whether they are behaving in ways that are acceptable in their home culture. Explain that their behavior might be all right at home but not at school, and explain why.
- Don't penalize students who are asleep without talking to them first; maybe they have no bed or quiet place to sleep.
- If students laugh when disciplined, recognize that this might be a way to save face. Teach other behaviors that are more appropriate.
- If students make inappropriate or vulgar comments, have them generate (or teach them) other phrases that are more acceptable for school and can be used to say the same thing.
- If students are physically aggressive, tell students that aggression is not an option in school. Have them generate (or teach them) more appropriate options.

Encourage academic achievement:

- Examine what and how you're teaching. Do you assume that students living in poverty will not be going to college anyway, so it's okay if they're getting a watered-down curriculum?
- Give students as much choice and control over their assignments as possible so that they feel that they have a say in their education.
- Include topics that are familiar and relevant.
- Teach ways to keep materials organized.
- Help students to set goals and to keep track of progress.
- Use rubrics that show levels of performance so students can begin to critique their own assignments.
- Maintain realistically high expectations.

Provide special help for students who frequently change schools:

- Assign a buddy who can show them the ropes.
- Explicitly welcome them to class.
- Have a special lunch with them.
- If you know they will be leaving, create a "memory book" for them to take.
- Coordinate with the homeless education liaison in your school.

Sources: Grossman, 2004; Landsman, 2006; Payne, 2005.

CONCLUDING COMMENTS

We strongly believe that teachers are responsible for all the students in their classes, including typical adolescents, English language learners, students with disabilities and ADHD, and students who are troubled or living in poverty. By keeping in mind the principles of effective classroom management, working to create an accepting climate for all students, and utilizing the strategies presented in this chapter, you can enhance the school experience for all your students.

Keep in mind, however, that there might be students whose problems are so great that you really cannot help a whole lot. As Fred reminds us,

There's failure in this business. Some problems transcend the classroom, and there's only so much an individual teacher or the school can do. Sometimes you just have to say, "I tried. Now I need to let go."

"Letting go" means recognizing that you might not be able to change a student's life; it *doesn't* mean abandoning your responsibility for making that student's time in school as productive and meaningful as possible. A counselor at Fred's school believes that, to some extent, teachers need to treat troubled students "like everyone else":

> *Sometimes teachers think, "These kids are going through a hard time; I'll give them a break." But out of this sense of caring, they give kids breaks they shouldn't get. Kids need to be held accountable. They have to learn to live in the real world where you can't hide behind your problems. You have to learn to cope, and you* mustn't *learn "I don't have to cope." I'm not saying that we shouldn't give them some leeway if their problems are really great; obviously, we need to be flexible and supportive. But they still need to be responsible for their current behavior. If we always bail kids out, we're enabling. That's not helpful—and it's even dangerous.*

When students have serious problems, it's more important than ever to create a classroom that is safe, orderly, and humane. You might not be able to change youngsters' relationships with their families, but you can still work to establish positive teacher–student relationships. You might not be able to provide students control over unstable, chaotic home lives, but you can allow them opportunities to make decisions and have some control over their time in school. You might not be able to do anything about the violence that permeates the neighborhoods in which they live, but you can structure classroom situations to foster cooperation and group cohesiveness. In Fred's words, "You can show them you care enough about them not to let them slough off. You can still keep teaching."

SUMMARY

Building a caring, inclusive classroom begins with knowing who your students are. Today's classrooms contain students at various stages in their physical and emotional development and from a wide range of cultural and linguistic backgrounds. Many are learning English as a second language. Students with disabilities are frequently educated alongside their nondisabled peers. Increasingly large numbers of young people are growing up in circumstances that put them at risk for physical, emotional, and psychological problems.

The Developing Adolescent

Students in middle and high school are
- Developing their identity.
- Changing their thinking about and reaction to societal norms.
- Changing their views of personal prerogative and privacy.

Developmentally aware teachers:

- Help students find and develop areas of competence.
- Give students opportunities to make decisions.
- Affirm students' growing sense of self.

English Language Learners

- Provide a safe environment for language risk taking.
- Avoid idioms and complex sentences.
- Ask questions that allow for different levels of proficiency in responding.
- Encourage English speaking while honoring students' first language.
- Offer periodic summaries and paraphrases.
- Emphasize collaborative more than individual work.
- Emphasize process over product.
- Apply SDAIE strategies across the curriculum.
- Encourage students to write about topics of their choice and for real-world purposes.

Students with Disabilities and ADHD

- A diagnosis of LD is made when there is a "severe discrepancy" between intellectual ability and academic performance or when the student fails to respond to early, intense intervention.
- Students could have hearing loss in the moderate to severe range and might benefit greatly from hearing aids and cochlear implants, but amplification does not restore perfect hearing. Additional modifications and support are necessary if students are to obtain optimal hearing in the classroom.
- Emotional/behavioral disorders can be externalizing (e.g., conduct disorder) or internalizing (e.g., depression).
- Autism spectrum disorders are characterized by marked impairments in the development of social interaction and communication skills.
- ADHD is characterized by inattention, hyperactivity, and impulsivity. ADHD is not included as a disability in the IDEA; however, individuals might receive services under Section 504 of the Rehabilitation Act of 1973.

Ways to Help Students with Disabilities and ADHD

- Become familiar with students' IEPs or 504 plans.
- Create an accepting climate.
- Coordinate and collaborate with special education teachers and paraprofessionals.
- Examine your classroom environment for possible mismatch.
- Reflect on the appropriateness of your expectations.
- Use peer tutoring, peer assistance, and cooperative learning.

Students Who Are Troubled

- Substance abuse:
  - Students might be children of alcoholics/addicts (COAs) and/or be abusing drugs and alcohol themselves.
  - Teachers must be watchful for students who might be abusing drugs and alcohol and refer these students to a counselor or other appropriate persons.
  - Distinguish between situations in which drugs are being used outside of school and situations in which students are under the influence during school.
- Abuse and neglect:
  - Educators are required to report suspected abuse and neglect to the state's child protective service.
  - No state requires the reporter to have absolute proof before reporting.
  - Most states require "reason to believe" or "reasonable cause to believe or suspect."

- Eating disorders:
  - Students who suffer from eating disorders are often high achieving, compliant, and perfectionist.

Students Living in Poverty

- Be wary of claims about a "culture of poverty" whose members have shared (often negative) traits.
- Strive to be a "bearer of hope."
- Work hard to build a trusting relationship.

Sometimes the problems that students bring to school can be overwhelming, especially for beginning teachers who are still learning the basics. And in fact, there can be students whose problems are so great that you just cannot help. Nonetheless, you can still try to create a classroom environment that is safe, orderly, and humane. You can show students you care by holding them accountable for their behavior and by continuing to teach.

ACTIVITIES FOR SKILL BUILDING AND REFLECTION

In Class

1. In a small group, read the following scenario and discuss the questions that follow.

   Joanne Wilson's second-period English class has 28 students. One has been identified with learning disabilities, and he struggles with the novels the class is reading as well as the writing assignments. In addition, two students are recent immigrants with very limited English. Another student has ADHD, and although he is supposed to be on medication, he sometimes skips a dose; on days like that, he "bounces off the walls" and accomplishes very little in terms of academic work. Ms. Wilson is very concerned about these students' academic progress, and she doesn't know where to turn. An in-class support (ICS) teacher provides some assistance two days a week, but they have no planning time, so she functions more like an aide than a real teacher. Ms. Wilson is also painfully aware of the fact that the class is not a cohesive community; although there is no obvious disrespect, the other students generally ignore those with special needs and are reluctant to work with them in cooperative groups.

   Questions
   a. What strategies could Ms. Wilson use to help create a more inclusive, more accepting climate?
   b. For each student with special needs (i.e., the student with LD, the two ELLs, and the student with ADHD), think of one strategy that Ms. Wilson could use to enhance his or her academic progress.
   c. What types of help could Ms. Wilson ask for from the ICS teacher?

2. Working together in a small group, imagine that you are a general education teacher working in a co-teaching arrangement with a special education teacher. Generate a list of issues that you would want to discuss before beginning to teach together. In particular, consider what expectations you have with respect to planning and delivering instruction and with respect to classroom management. Then assume the role of the special education teacher and repeat the process.

On Your Own

1. In the school where you are observing or teaching, interview the principal or the director of special services to learn about the district's policies and procedures for supporting students with disabilities. Are any students with severe disabilities being educated in the general education classroom? If so, what special supports are being provided to those individuals? Interview a teacher about his or her attitudes toward including a student with special needs who previously would have been educated in a special education classroom or sent to a special school.

2. In the school where you are observing or teaching, interview the principal or an ESL teacher about the district's policies and programs for supporting ELLs. How many languages are represented in the school? Interview a teacher in an English-only classroom who has ELLs in his or her classroom. How does the teacher provide supports for them?

3. In the school where you are observing or teaching, interview a counselor or the director of special services to determine the policies for reporting drug abuse. Get copies of the referral forms that are used.

For Your Portfolio

Reporting suspected abuse and neglect varies from state to state. Find out the policies used in your state. Also find out whether your school has particular policies and procedures you are to follow. In particular, get answers to the following questions and compile your findings into a set of guidelines that you keep in your portfolio.

Who is required to report abuse and neglect?
When should you report child abuse? (When you have reasonable cause to suspect? Reasonable cause to believe?)
To what state agency do you report?
What information must be included in the report?
Do you have to give your name when reporting?

FOR FURTHER READING

Cary, S. (2007). *Working with second language learners: Answers to teachers' top ten questions,* 2nd ed. Portsmouth, NH: Heinemann.

    This book addresses teachers' "top ten" questions chosen with four criteria in mind: veracity (meaning that they were asked by real teachers teaching real kids), frequency, relevancy, and difficulty (they needed to be challenging). Questions addressed include: How do I assess a student's English? How do I find useful information on a student's cultural background? How do I make my spoken language more understandable? How do I get my reluctant speakers to speak English?

Gorski, P. (2008). The myth of the "culture of poverty." *Educational Leadership, 65*(7), 32–36.

    In this reader-friendly, provocative article, Paul Gorski refutes "common and dangerous myths about poverty." Chief among them, he argues, is the "culture of poverty"—the idea that "poor people share more or less monolithic and predictable beliefs, values, and behaviors." Gorski looks at some of the stereotypes held about poor people and concludes that teachers must consider how their class biases affect their interactions with students.

Hallowell, E. (2012). Ferrari engines, bicycle brakes. *Educational Leadership, 70*(2), 36–38.

    The author is a psychiatrist who has both ADHD and dyslexia. He provides some advice to educators about how to help students with ADHD succeed in the classroom.

Irwin, C. (2007). *Monochrome days: A firsthand account of one teenager's experience with depression.* New York: Oxford University Press.

    The author has battled depression since the eighth grade, and this book recounts her dawning recognition of her condition, the treatment she has undergone, and the importance of supportive family, friends, and teachers. Although the book is aimed at teenagers suffering from depression, it's a useful resource for teachers who want to learn more about the impact of depression. Each chapter concludes with useful information, such as symptoms of depression, treatment options, and how to find help.

Kline, F. M., & Silver, L. B. (Eds.) (2004). *The educator's guide to mental health issues in the classroom.* Baltimore: Paul H. Brookes.

    This book is dedicated to "general education classroom teachers who are charged with serving ALL students!" It is designed to serve as a reference for educators who work with students who have mental health issues and who need to collaborate with mental health workers. Chapters address biologically based disorders (e.g., ADHD), biologically based and/or psychologically based disorders (e.g., substance abuse), and behavioral disorders (e.g., oppositional defiant disorder).

Sherer, M. (Ed.). (May 2013). Faces of poverty. *Educational Leadership, 70*(8).

    This entire issue is devoted to articles on the effects of poverty and ways to help students growing up in impoverished conditions.

Snell, M. E., & Janney, R. (2000). *Social relationships and peer support.* Baltimore: Paul H. Brookes.

    This book is part of a series of reader-friendly teacher guides to inclusive practices. This one focuses on ways to facilitate positive peer relationships in an inclusive classroom. Topics include creating a positive atmosphere, establishing peer support programs, teaching social skills, and building friendship groups.

Soodak, L. C., & McCarthy, M. R. (2006). Classroom management in inclusive settings. In C. M. Evertson & C. S. Weinstein (Eds.) *Handbook of classroom management: Research, practice, and contemporary issues.* Mahwah, NJ: Lawrence Erlbaum.

    This chapter reviews research-based practices that promote positive academic, social, and behavioral outcomes for students in inclusive classrooms. Practices include teacher-directed strategies (such as building classroom community and establishing programs that foster acceptance and friendship), peer-mediated strategies (such as cooperative learning and peer tutoring), and self-directed strategies (such as self-monitoring). The authors stress the role of teachers in creating classrooms in which all students have increased access to the general education curriculum.

Villa, R. A., Thousand, J. S., & Nevin, A. I. (2008) *A guide to co-teaching: Practical tips for facilitating student learning,* 2nd ed. Thousand Oaks, CA: Corwin Press.

    This book highlights the benefits and challenges of co-teaching and addresses both the No Child Left Behind requirement that all students have access to highly qualified teachers and the IDEA requirement that students with disabilities have access to the general education curriculum. The following four types of co-teaching models are described in detail: supportive, parallel, complementary, and team teaching.

ORGANIZATIONAL RESOURCES

Autism Society of America (ASA), www.autism-society.org. ASA exists to improve the lives of all affected by autism by increasing public awareness about the day-to-day issues faced by people on the autism spectrum, advocating for appropriate services for individuals, and providing the latest information regarding treatment, education, research, and advocacy. Their website includes links to resources and local referrals.

Center on Addiction and the Family (COAF), www.coaf.org. COAF works to promote the healing of families affected by substance abuse. Its website includes information on the impact of substance abuse and how to work with children and families.

Children and Adults with Attention-Deficit/Hyperactivity Disorder (CHADD), www.chadd. org. This is a nonprofit organization serving children and adults with ADHD. It runs the National Resource Center on ADHD, a national clearinghouse for evidence-based information about ADHD.

The Council for Exceptional Children (CEC), www.cec.sped.org. CEC is the largest international professional organization dedicated to improving educational outcomes for students with disabilities and those who are gifted.

Center for Research on Education, Diversity, and Excellence (CREDE), www.crede.org. A federally funded research and development center, CREDE focuses on improving the education of students whose ability to reach their potential is challenged by language or cultural barriers, race, geographic location, or poverty. It offers a wide range of multimedia products.

Learning Disabilities Association of America (LDA), www.ldanatl.org. LDA is the largest nonprofit volunteer organization advocating for individuals with learning disabilities. Its website includes links to information for teachers and parents.

National Center for Homeless Education, www.serve.org/nche. This organization serves as a clearinghouse for information and resources on the educational rights of homeless children and youth.

National Eating Disorders Association, www.nationaleatingdisorders.org. This organization is devoted to the prevention of eating disorders, improved access to quality treatment, and increased research funding to better understand and treat eating disorders. It operates a toll-free helpline and provides resources for students, teachers, and families.

Working with Families

"I had no idea his mother lost her job and his father hasn't been around for a month. No wonder he's been so belligerent!"

"Her grandmother has been so good about making sure she's doing her homework. She's really working with me on this."

"His father has offered to chaperone the eighth-grade cookout and to organize the softball game! It will be terrific to have him along!

Comments such as these can be heard in teachers' rooms all across the country. They reflect some of the benefits that accrue when teachers and families establish positive, productive relationships. A growing body of evidence shows that family involvement in schooling is linked to students' academic achievement (Anderson & Minke, 2007; Jeynes, 2007). But family-school relationships also have definite payoffs in terms of classroom management.

First, *knowing about a student's home situation provides insight into the student's classroom behavior.* Listen to Donnie:

> **It was the very first day of school—when everyone is still being really good— but this one girl was really loud and hyperactive. It was clear that everyone disliked her. She seemed completely unable to control herself. I checked into her home situation as soon as I had a free period. I found out that her mother had kicked her out of the house; she said she couldn't handle all the kids. The girl had tried to commit suicide, but now she was really trying to get her act together. She had**

gotten a part-time job, and she was living with an aunt. This girl had really been thrown out into the world, and school is her haven. Actually, when I think about what she's facing, I'm really impressed by how well she's doing.

As Donnie's example illustrates, it's easier to understand why Johnny sits with his head down on his desk if you're aware that he spent the night in a homeless shelter; Carla's apathy makes sense if you know that her mother is going through chemotherapy; and Jana's anxiety about getting all As is understandable if you appreciate how much her parents pressure her to succeed. Furthermore, such insights can help you decide what course of action to take when you're dealing with a student's problems. You're better able to judge whether a suggestion that a parent proofread term papers is inappropriate because the parent can't read or whether a note home will lead to benefits or to beatings.

Second, *when families understand what you are trying to achieve, they can provide valuable support and assistance.* Most parents want their children to succeed in school and will do what they can to help. But they can't work in a vacuum. They need to know what you are trying to achieve and how you expect students to behave in your classroom. Familiarizing parents with your curriculum, routines, and policies minimizes confusion, misinterpretations, and conflict. For this reason, Christina requires parents to sign an acknowledgment form at the beginning of the course to indicate that they have read and understood the "newspaper" she sends home describing course objectives, policies, and procedures.

Third, *families can help to develop and implement strategies to change students' behavior.* Working together, parents and teachers can bring about improvements in students' behavior that would be impossible working alone. Fred shares this example:

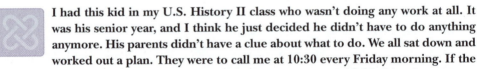

I had this kid in my U.S. History II class who wasn't doing any work at all. It was his senior year, and I think he just decided he didn't have to do anything anymore. His parents didn't have a clue about what to do. We all sat down and worked out a plan. They were to call me at 10:30 every Friday morning. If the report on their son was good, he got the car keys, got to go out with his friends, got to go to the ball game. If the report was bad, the weekend did not exist. We told him, "We really care about you and if this is what we have to do to get you through senior year, then so be it." The kid tested the plan once, and there was no weekend for him. After that, he really started to perform and ended up with a B for the year. Plus, there was an additional payoff. His parents were able to give him all kinds of good strokes because he started taking responsibility.

Fourth, *parent volunteers can provide needed assistance in the classroom and the school.* Because schools are almost always short staffed, parents can provide an extra pair of hands: They can work in libraries, computer centers, and homework programs; greet visitors in the front office; accompany students on field trips; make phone calls to other parents; and join with school personnel to create, manage, and deliver special programs. They can also enrich the curriculum by sharing information about their hobbies, careers, travels, and ethnic backgrounds.

Finally, *involving families pays long-term dividends for both the school and families.* Parents actually feel more satisfied with the quality of their children's education when they perceive that teachers welcome their involvement, invite them to participate, and offer strategies for helping with their children's learning (Patrikakou & Weissberg, 2000). And teacher invitations to parents cause parents to become more involved both at school *and* at home (Green, Walker, Hoover-Dempsey, & Sandler, 2007). Donna notes:

When we have parent involvement, we see everything get better: grades, behavior, etc. Parent involvement falls off at middle school, but this is when it's most important. Middle school is when parents need to stay close, and know who their children are hanging around with and who their teachers are. This is when we need to bring the parents back into school.

Despite the obvious benefits of close communication and collaboration, parents and teachers are often at odds with one another. Sometimes the relationship is detached and distant; sometimes it's distrustful and adversarial. What causes this adversarial relationship and what can teachers do to avoid it? In this chapter, we examine teacher reluctance to involve parents and parent reluctance to become involved. We then turn to our teachers and to the literature on parent involvement to suggest ways that teachers can reach out to families to foster more positive relationships.

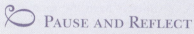

PAUSE AND REFLECT

Before reading on, think of three possible answers to each of the following questions:

- Why would teachers sometimes be reluctant to involve parents in their students' schooling?
- Why would parents sometimes be reluctant to become involved?

CHALLENGES TO FAMILY-TEACHER COOPERATION

Teacher Reluctance to Involve Families in Schooling

Although most beginning teachers recognize the importance of parent involvement, a lack of confidence could make them reluctant to reach out to their students' families. Beginning teachers simply do not feel equipped with the knowledge of and skills for *how* to involve parents. They also are not sure how to work with families that they perceive as being different based on culture, values, and language (Walker & Hoover-Dempsey, 2008). Indeed, during their preparation to become teachers, most have received little training in family-involvement practices (Graue & Brown, 2003) and have had limited opportunities to interact with families during their fieldwork and student teaching (Walker & Dotger, 2012). Although some teacher educators are attempting to help preservice teachers become more comfortable in interacting with parents by having them participate in simulated parent-teacher conferences and then reflect on the experience (Dotger, 2010), this still remains the exception rather than the norm.

Even when teachers know how to effectively involve families, they might be disinclined to do so because of the *extra time and energy that are required.* Teaching is physically and emotionally exhausting, and reaching out to parents is sometimes viewed as one more burdensome task. For example, telephoning 30 parents and talking for 10 minutes to each requires a five-hour commitment—and that presumes that the parents are available when you first call and you don't have to spend additional time calling again. And that's for just one class! Because this is in addition to the normal workload, it's understandable that teachers wonder whether the extra time required is worth the trouble. For new teachers, the task of reaching out to parents can seem even more onerous. As Christina admits, "I'm always preparing materials and lessons, grading, or commenting on student papers. It takes time to be creative and effective—and that means there's less time for parent contact than I would like."

In addition, *teachers' perceptions of families* undoubtedly contribute to the reluctance to seek increased parental involvement. Many teachers recognize that time is often a scarce commodity for parents, limited by work responsibilities, household chores, and care for other family members. These teachers question whether it is fair to ask already burdened parents to spend time working with their teenage children on academic activities or assisting with behavior problems. As Sandy told us:

 Some parents are just overwhelmed. One poor, single mother I know just doesn't have the time or energy to become more involved. She's worried about keeping her job and making ends meet. Her plate is just too full; she can't handle anything else. It's not that she doesn't care. But the fact that her kid is not doing his homework is just not her highest priority right now. Knowing this is important. Once you know you're not going to get parent involvement, you can figure out another approach.

Another reason for teachers' reluctance to involve parents is *the worry that parents might not understand their role in the classroom.* Some parent volunteers intervene when they shouldn't (e.g., imposing their own punishments for inappropriate behavior instead of consulting the teacher); they could instruct students in ways that contradict what the teacher has demonstrated; or they could violate confidentiality by sharing student records and relating sensitive information. When situations such as these occur, teachers might wonder whether parent volunteers are more a hindrance than a help.

Teachers could also be reluctant to involve parents because of the *authority and autonomy they enjoy within their classrooms.* Teachers are often exposed to criticism. Parents might blame them for children's problems or question their professional competence. It's not surprising that teachers sometimes become guarded and protective of their "turf," especially if they lack confidence in their skills and expertise. Indeed, research has shown that teachers with higher levels of "teacher efficacy" (teachers' beliefs that they can teach and that their students can learn) are more likely to reach out to parents (Hoover-Dempsey, Walker, Reed, & Jones, 2002).

Finally, teachers might be *uncertain how to effectively and respectfully interact* with the variety of families in which their students are being raised, families that are often very different than the teachers' families. (See Figure 7.1.) Student families can include single-parent households, blended families, or same-sex couples. In some cases, their students are being raised in "kinship care" by grandparents, aunts, uncles, brothers, or sisters. In other cases, their students are living with foster families or in homeless shelters, and some older students are emancipated minors living on their own. With a surge in immigration from Central and Latin America, the Middle East, Southeast Asia and the Pacific, and Russia and Eastern Europe, many students come

" I want you to write on the blackboard 100 times :
' I will not make fun of a classmate just because
he comes from a two-parent family.' "

FIGURE 7.1   www.cartoonstock.com. Reprinted with permission.

from homes where a language other than English is spoken, and their families are unfamiliar with schools in the United States.

Parent Reluctance to Become Involved in Schooling

It is well recognized that family involvement in schools declines as students move from elementary to middle school and that by high school, it has practically disappeared (Rioux & Berla, 1993). Part of the decline could be due to the fact that, compared to elementary teachers, secondary teachers use fewer strategies to involve families (Pelco & Ries, 1999). Donnie offers an additional explanation for the decline:

 Once kids leave elementary school, parents seem to feel it's time to cut the cord. They think the kids need to be on their own more, and that school should be the kids' responsibility. Also, they feel they can't help anymore because they don't know the content. They tell me, "I don't know algebra or geometry" or "I don't understand these new ways of teaching math." They're scared off by the content and feel they can't offer assistance.

There are also more general reasons why families across the grade levels might resist involvement. Clearly, the demands of work compete for parents' time and energy, especially in low-income households, which are more likely to have two parents who work full-time, parents who have two or more jobs, parents who have to work evenings and nights, and parents who have jobs with inflexible or unpredictable hours.

In addition, some adults have *unhappy, even traumatic, memories* of their own experiences as students. According to Sara Lawrence-Lightfoot (2003), parents' encounters with school are shaped by their own autobiographical stories—"their own childhood histories, their own insecurities, and their own primal fears" (p. xxii). These "ghosts" from the past could make parents nervous about or even hostile to schools and teachers and less than eager to return for conferences or open houses.

Other families might *feel guilty* when their teenage children have difficulties in school. They can become defensive and uncooperative when teachers try to discuss their youngster's problem or be too embarrassed to disclose troubles they are having at home. Rather than deal with the child's problem, these families might try to deny what is occurring and to avoid communication with the teacher.

Still other families could be *unnerved and intimidated by schools*. This is particularly so when parents are poor, uneducated, or have limited proficiency in English. Some find teachers and administrators unresponsive to their requests (Gutman & McLoyd, 2000); others might even fear teachers, viewing them as authority figures who must not be questioned (Lindeman, 2001). Consider the story of Sylvia, a parent involved in an Immigrant Parent Leadership class at a high school in Virginia. Sylvia emigrated from Guatemala as a child and attended U.S. schools from fourth grade on. She speaks English well and is committed to helping her stepdaughter who recently arrived from Guatemala. According to Sylvia, "One of my stepdaughter's teachers thought someone else did her homework. But the reason she is doing so well is that I am working with her at home." When the leader of the class advised her to call the teacher and clear up the misunderstanding, Sylvia was amazed: "You mean I can talk to the teacher? I felt I would be insulting her if I did" (Sobel & Kugler, 2007, p. 62).

Finally, some families *do not view participation at school as part of their parental roles* (Hoover-Dempsey & Sandler, 1997). They might believe that schooling should be left to the professionals or that they are showing their support for teachers by not interfering. Immigrant families might not even realize that parental involvement is expected and valued: "In most countries outside the United States, the unspoken norm is that it's the teacher's job to educate a student and that participation from parents shows disrespect for the teacher's expertise" (Sobel & Kugler, 2007, p. 63). Asian American families, for example, generally hold high expectations for their children's academic success; nonetheless, they tend to view educational matters as the province of the school (Fuller & Olsen, 1998). Similarly, Latinos typically perceive their role as ensuring their children's attendance; instilling respect for the teacher; encouraging good behavior in school; meeting their obligations to provide clothing, food, and shelter; and socializing children to their family responsibilities (Chrispeels & Rivero, 2000; Trumbull, Rothstein-Fisch, Greenfield, & Quiroz, 2001). Parental presence at school is *not* a key component of this role.

A good example of how both the demands of work and parents' role definition can affect involvement comes from a study of the Padillas, an immigrant, migrant family whose children were all very successful in school (Lopez, 2001). Their parental involvement, however, took the form of exposing their children to their hard work in the fields and teaching them that without an education, they might end up in the same situation. Here is an excerpt from one interview:

Interviewer: Now I want to know if you or your wife are involved in the schools in one way or another? For example, like volunteers or in the Parent's Committee.

Mr. Padilla: No sir. . . .

Interviewer: Hmmm. Haven't you gone to a parents' meeting or something like that?

Mr. Padilla: No. Not really. It's just that we're always busy with work. We rarely go to the school.

Interviewer: Not even to a conference with the teachers?

Mr. Padilla: Well, maybe once in a while. But it's really difficult. There's a lot of work.

Interviewer: So how are you involved in your children's education?

Mr. Padilla: Well, I have shown them what work is and how hard it is. So they know that if they don't focus in their studies, that is the type of work they'll end up doing. I've opened their eyes to that reality. (Lopez, p. 427)

If the Padillas' "involvement" were defined by participation in bake sales and back-to-school nights, they would appear to be uninvolved in their children's education. Yet they were *highly* involved in fostering their children's positive attitudes toward school. Clearly, we need to be cautious about assuming that parents who do not attend school events are unconcerned and uncaring. Teachers who equate parent involvement with presence at school are likely to overlook or underestimate the involvement that occurs at home (Anderson & Minke, 2007; Lee & Bowen, 2006; Loera, Rueda, & Nakamoto, 2011).

These aspects of parental reluctance make communication and collaboration with families more complicated than ever. Nonetheless, research has found that one of the best predictors of parental involvement is the perception that the teacher values and invites such involvement (Walker, Ice, & Hoover-Dempsey, 2011). In other words, the teacher's attitudes and behavior are what make the difference. For this reason, you must not only understand the challenges to parent involvement but must also be aware of the ways that families and schools can work together. (Note that in this chapter, when we refer to "parents," we are referring to all the various types of caregivers noted earlier that your students might have in their lives, not only birth parents.)

FOSTERING COLLABORATION BETWEEN FAMILIES AND SCHOOLS

Joyce Epstein and her colleagues at Johns Hopkins University have studied comprehensive parent involvement programs and have identified six different types of family-school collaboration. These are listed in Box 7.1, Meet the Educator. The first four of Epstein's categories provide a framework for our discussion. For more information on the last two categories—including families as participants in school decision making and collaborating with the community—see Epstein and colleagues, 2002; Chapter 6 is specifically devoted to "Strengthening Partnership Programs in Middle and High Schools."

Helping Families to Fulfill Their Basic Obligations

This category refers to the family's responsibility to provide for children's health and safety, to supervise and guide them at each age level, and to build positive home conditions that support school learning and behavior (Epstein & Dauber, 1991). Schools can assist families in carrying out these basic obligations by providing workshops

BOX 7.1   MEET THE EDUCATOR

Joyce Epstein

Joyce Epstein is professor of sociology at Johns Hopkins University and director of the Center on School, Family, and Community Partnerships. She began research on parent involvement in elementary schools in 1981 and then extended her inquiries to middle schools and high schools. In 1996, Epstein and her colleagues established the National Network of Partnership Schools, which assists schools, districts, and states to use research-based approaches to develop programs of family involvement and community connections and to meet the requirements of No Child Left Behind for parent involvement. The Network now includes more than 1,200 schools located in 21 states.

Some Major Ideas about Family, School, and Community Partnerships

1. Well-designed programs of school, family, and community partnerships benefit students, families, and schools.

2. There are six types of involvement for comprehensive partnership programs:
   - Type 1: Parenting—Help all families establish home environments to support children as students.
   - Type 2: Communicating—Design effective forms of school-to-home and home-to-school communication about school programs and students' progress.
   - Type 3: Volunteering—Recruit and organize parent help and support.
   - Type 4: Learning at Home—Provide information and ideas to families about how to help students at home with homework and other curriculum-related activities, decisions, and planning.
   - Type 5: Decision Making—Include parents in school decisions, developing parent leaders and representatives.
   - Type 6: Collaborating with the Community—Identify and integrate resources and services from the community to strengthen school programs, family practices, and student learning and development.

3. To create a lasting, comprehensive partnership program, each school needs an action team for partnerships (ATP) to assess present practices and needs, develop options for action, implement selected activities, evaluate next steps, and coordinate practices.

Selected Books and Articles

Multicultural partnerships: Involve all families (Hutchins, Greenfeld, Epstein, Sanders, & Galindo. Larchmont, NY: Eye on Education, 2012).

School, family, and community partnerships: Preparing educators and improving schools (Epstein. Boulder, CO: Westview Press, 2011).

Family reading night (Hutchins, Greenfeld, & Epstein. Larchmont, NY: Eye on Education, 2008).

Website: www.partnershipschools.org

on parenting skills, establishing parent support groups, holding programs on teenage problems (e.g., drug and alcohol abuse, eating disorders), and referring families to community and state agencies when necessary.

Asking teachers to assume responsibilities for the education of *families,* in addition to the education of *students,* can seem onerous and unfair. Not surprisingly, some teachers hesitate to become "social workers," a role for which they are untrained. Others feel resentment and anger toward parents who do not provide adequate home environments. Although these attitudes are understandable, you need to remember that your students' home environments shape their chances for school success. As the number of distressed families grows, assisting families to carry out their basic obligations becomes increasingly critical.

What can you, as a teacher, realistically do to assist families in carrying out their basic obligations? Although you will probably not be directly involved in planning parent education workshops or leading support groups, you can play an important, *indirect* role. You can let families know about available materials, motivate and encourage them to attend programs, bring transportation problems to the attention of appropriate school personnel, and help families to arrange car pools (Greenwood & Hickman, 1991).

In Sandy's and Fred's districts, parent support groups enable families to get together to share concerns and to discuss topics such as communicating with adolescents, discipline, resisting peer pressure, and home–school cooperation. A similar program, the Parent Involvement Corps (PIC), was established at Donnie's school some years ago. Designed for parents of ninth-grade students, the program was intended to welcome parents to school, to help them feel comfortable there, to teach parenting skills, and to inform parents of their rights. Donna's district includes an office of Family and Community Outreach that coordinates district and community resources for families. If such programs exist in your school or district, you can make sure families are aware of them; if you see a family with special needs, you can alert school personnel involved in these programs about the situation.

In addition to playing this indirect assistance role, at times it might be appropriate to work *directly* with families. Fred reports that he often needs to provide parents some perspective on "this unique creature called 'teenager'": "They haven't had 150 kids, and it's often a revelation for them to learn that they're not the only parents having problems." Similarly, Sandy tells us that many of her interactions with parents involve helping them to communicate more effectively with their teenage children:

 Many times, I find that my discussions with parents begin with the problems their children are having in chemistry class, but move on to more general problems. You start talking about grades, and the next thing you know you're talking about curfews and dating. Many of the parents have no control over their 15- and 16-year-olds. They'll say to me, "I just don't know what to do. He or she is the same way at home. I'm at a loss." I acknowledge their frustration and the difficulty of working with teenagers. (It helps that I have teenagers too!) I tell them, "You're not alone. Many 15- and 16-year-olds behave this way, and many parents feel this way." I try to provide some perspective and give them some tips about communication. I try to encourage them to set some limits. I find that a lot of parents don't like to set limits; they don't want confrontations with their kids, and they need encouragement to monitor what their kids are doing.

Sometimes I encounter overbearing parents who put too much pressure on their kids. Their expectations are unrealistic. Ninety-five on a test is not good enough; they want their child to have the highest test grade in the class. I tell them, "Wait a minute, we both want what's best for your child; we want him to work to his utmost ability, but utmost ability is not perfection on every test." I remember one situation, where a girl in my class was putting out very little effort. She got a 79 on the first test, which was far below her ability. After I spoke with her, she started working a lot harder, and her grade on the next test was 89. I told her how proud I was of her, and said something like, "Your parents must have been delighted." She got this funny look on her face, and I knew something was wrong. I found out that they had made only one comment: "Why wasn't it an A?" They didn't give her any praise at all. I decided I needed to speak with them about the situation. I told them, "Look, your daughter went from doing no work and getting a 79 to working hard and getting an 89, and you didn't even acknowledge the improvement. She's going to figure out that she might as well do no work and get 79s, since working hard and getting 89s doesn't get her any approval." Parents like this need to understand the importance of acknowledging improvement, instead of holding out for the perfect grade.

As you reflect on how to help families with parenting responsibilites, keep in mind that there are cultural differences in beliefs about child-rearing, and these differences can lead to cultural clashes between home and school—with students caught in the middle. Parents from collectivistic cultures, for example, might emphasize respect, obedience, helpfulness, and responsibility to the family while teachers from individualistic cultures stress individual achievement, independence, and self-expression (Trumbull, Rothstein-Fisch, Greenfield, & Quiroz, 2001). A counselor at Sandy's school, provides additional examples of cultural clashes:

> I see so many students who are caught between two cultures. At home, they're expected to follow a set of traditional values, but at school they really want to be American teenagers. It's so hard. We hold dances, but we have kids who are going to have arranged marriages. An Indian father wouldn't let his daughter go to Project Graduation [a boat trip the school organizes after graduation so that students will be in a safe, confined space without alcohol or drugs]. He said she couldn't stay out all night. An Iranian girl couldn't go to the prom; her father didn't believe in it. An Asian girl who just got 1,400 on her SATs has to spend the summer taking review courses for college achievement tests. Her parents stress the need to achieve, while mainstream American culture stresses the importance of being well rounded.

If you have students whose families have recently immigrated to this country, you might also help them to understand the expectations and norms of U.S. secondary schools. For example, teachers and administrators at Jericho High School on Long Island, New York, made a concerted effort to reach out to Asian parents who appeared reluctant to attend school events such as orchestra concerts because they viewed such events as unrelated to students' college aspirations. The goal of the project was to convey the message that parental involvement in all aspects of school life (not just worrying about test scores and college admission) is critical to help students become emotionally well adjusted and socially successful. As a result of these efforts, more Asian parents are attending school events and becoming part of the school community (Hu, 2008).

When families express values and goals that differ from those of the school, it is all too easy to dismiss them as "out of touch," "narrow minded," or just plain "wrong." But attitudes like this only increase parents' resentment and suspicion. Awareness and respect are the keys to reaching cross-cultural understanding.

Communicating with Families

Epstein's second category of family-school involvement refers to the school's obligation *to communicate about school programs and students' progress.* Communications include electronic communication (e-mail and websites), phone calls, report cards and progress reports, and open houses and parent-teacher conferences. This is certainly the most commonly accepted way to work with parents, and there is no doubt that these communications are essential. The crucial question, however, is not only whether these communications occur but also *when they occur, whether they are being understood, and whether they lead to feelings of trust and respect or alienation and resentment.*

All of our teachers stress the importance of communicating with parents in a way that promotes a feeling of partnership. Donna comments:

> **I'll say, "Please drop by anytime; my door is always open." I try to get them on my side as much as possible. They need to know that their kids are doing good things.**

Fred echoes Donna's message:

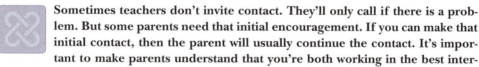

> **Sometimes teachers don't invite contact. They'll only call if there is a problem. But some parents need that initial encouragement. If you can make that initial contact, then the parent will usually continue the contact. It's important to make parents understand that you're both working in the best interests of the kid. When you make that clear, even the most irate parent turns into a pussycat. I tell them, "Listen, everything I do is designed to be the best for your kid. But if you're concerned about something, let me know. Feel free to call." I tell my parents: "We need to work together as a team. And your kids need to know we're working together."**

It is clear that Donnie, Sandy, Christina, Donna, and Fred are able to establish productive partnerships with families, and the next few sections of this chapter describe some of the ways they do this. In addition, the Practical Tips box lists some suggestions for communicating with parents who are particularly difficult to reach.

PRACTICAL TIPS FOR

Reaching "Hard-to-Reach" Parents

Step 1: Try to figure out why parents are hard to reach. Ask yourself (or someone in the school or community who would know):

- Do parents speak English?
- Do parents come from cultures that do not identify parent involvement as a priority? Do they come from cultures that believe schooling should be left to the educators?
- Do parents have work schedules that conflict with conferences?
- Do parents live far from the school? Do they have transportation?
- Do parents have other children who would require child care during parent-teacher meetings?
- Do parents know where the school is?
- Are the parents homeless (and therefore have no good address for receiving written communications from school)?

Step 2: Develop outreach strategies to address the underlying issue. For example:

- Make sure that parents receive messages in their native language.
- Make sure that written communications are easy to read, warm, and friendly.
- Figure out how to get messages to parents who are homeless.
- Schedule conferences at flexible times to accommodate parents with conflicting work schedules.
- Provide child care for meetings, conferences, and events.
- See whether neighbors or friends can be used as a liaison.
- Determine whether meetings can be held in a more convenient, more familiar, more neutral location.
- Arrange for home visits (with appropriate security).
- Make it clear that you value the language, culture, knowledge, and expertise of parents and family members.

Source: Adapted from Swap, 1993.

ELECTRONIC COMMUNICATION

In recent years, more and more teachers have begun using e-mail, social media, and other online tools to facilitate communication with parents. Teachers can utilize text-messaging tools that allow them to easily send multiple messages from their computers without revealing their phone numbers (Lepi, 2013). A class website can list assignments and due dates, the subject for the week, dates of quizzes and tests, news about current and upcoming events, and requests for supplies or assistance. The website can also provide links to related sites that might help students to complete assignments. As an alternative to a class website, many schools have adopted student information management systems, which allow staff members to track attendance and tardiness, record grades and standardized test results, and generate reports, among other features. These systems typically provide parents web-based access to their child's records. To address inequitable access to technology, some school district personnel are teaching parents how to use digital tools to communicate with teachers and access information about their students' performance (Fleming, 2012).

As one example of a management system, Sandy uses ParentConnect, software that allows parents and guardians to visit a password-protected, read-only site to view their children's grades in her online grade book. (Note that parents have access for their child only.) Having grades online makes it easier for parents to track their children's academic progress, but teachers can't assume that all parents have Internet access (or that they use it even if they have it). As Sandy emphasizes, "Teachers still have to take responsibility for calling parents if their kid is not doing well in class."

Students' grades are the most frequent topic of e-mails from parents (B. Thompson, 2008), so convenient access to this information is clearly important to parents. In fact, one study documented an increase in overall parental involvement at a school in Israel that used an automated system to notify parents of academic or attendance problems (Telem & Pinto, 2006). Because they received early notification of problems and could respond quickly, parents also came to view the school personnel as more professional.

Like many teachers, Sandy and Christina communicate with parents and students via e-mail, and they have a few words of caution. First, keep in mind that many parents do not have or use e-mail as frequently as a teacher might hope. As of December 2012, 35 percent of American homes did not have broadband Internet access (Brenner & Rainie, 2012). Second, e-mail seems to encourage sloppiness and inaccuracy, so be sure to edit your e-mails for misspellings or grammatical errors. Third, be careful about using e-mail to discuss sensitive issues or problems. E-mail doesn't allow you to convey your message in a calm, quiet tone of voice or to "soften" it with smiles, gestures, or body language; nor can you see or hear parents' reactions. For this reason, e-mail is more likely to lead to misinterpretations than face-to-face interactions or even phone calls. Furthermore, e-mail can also be made very public with a simple touch of a few computer keys (intentional or not). You need to keep this in mind as you compose e-mail messages to parents and to save sensitive or personal issues for phone calls or face-to-face interactions.

On the positive side, written messages (whether e-mail or snail mail) enable you to choose your words carefully and deliberately, an advantage you might not have when you're interacting with parents in "real time." So, don't fire off an e-mail in anger. Wait until you've calmed down and think carefully about what you want to say. Also be prepared for the fact that parents will not always follow this advice and will e-mail you when they are angry or upset about something. In these cases, try not to let the tone detract from dealing with the issue.

PHONE CALLS

Given the hectic lives that people lead, one of the main problems about telephone calls is making the connection! At the beginning of the school year, all five of our teachers find out when and how to contact the families of their students. Some businesses have strict policies about employees' receiving phone messages, and a call during work hours could result in a reprimand. Some parents work at night, and a call in the morning will interrupt much-needed sleep; others might not have a phone at all, and you'll need to send a note home asking them to call you. (Donnie and Sandy both send notes home in plain, white envelopes—without the school's return address. This way there is less chance that a wary teenager will remove the letter from the pile of mail before the parent ever sees it.) All of our teachers also let parents know when they can receive telephone calls during the school day. Donnie even gives parents her home phone number; she says that no parent has ever abused the information.

To get the information she needs, Sandy has her students fill out a card with their parents' home and work numbers on the first day of school. She also asks students to indicate whether their parents are permitted to get telephone calls at work. In addition, when Sandy has to call a parent, she'll often make a "precall," asking when it would be a convenient time to call and reassuring the parent that there's no earth-shattering problem. She's especially careful about checking the school personnel records to see which parent should be contacted:

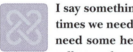 **A majority of my students come from divorced homes. If the parents are not sharing joint custody, you cannot talk to the noncustodial parent. If the parents are sharing custody, then the record tells which parent the student is residing with, and I call that parent. Sometimes, the records will indicate if calls are to be made to both parents or if written communications are to be done in duplicate for both parents.**

Before calling a parent about an academic or behavior problem, Sandy always gives her students notice:

I say something like, "I know you want to be treated like an adult, but sometimes we need to work together with mom or dad to ensure your success. We need some help here. We can't solve this alone." I never use the telephone call as a threat or punishment. And I always wait 24 hours before calling. That way, the student can tell the parent that the call is coming (or that the 75 they said they got on the test was really a 55!). When I talk with parents, I'm really careful about how I phrase things, so that I don't promote a negative reaction. Instead of saying, "Your son is disrupting the class," I'll say something like "We have to help your son control his behavior so that he can learn some chemistry." If the kid is disrespectful, I'll say, "I'm calling you about this because I know you wouldn't approve of this. I know you'd want to hear." In this way, you're conveying the idea that the parent will be supportive of you and that you don't think the kid comes from a family that would approve of such behavior.

During one meeting, we asked the teachers to share some of the ideas they have for ensuring that telephone contacts with parents are productive. Their responses are listed in the Practical Tips box.

A few additional words of caution are in order. Although it's important to contact parents about serious problems, frequent phone calls about minor misbehaviors can be annoying. Furthermore, the practice can convey the message to both parents and children that the school can't deal with problems that arise; it's like saying, "Wait 'til your parents find out!"

PRACTICAL TIPS FOR

Making Productive Telephone Contacts with Parents

- When the office receives a telephone call for you from a parent and you're in class, have the staff member ask when would be a good time to call back.
- Even if a call comes during your free period, have the office take the message and say you'll call back. That gives you time to shift gears and prepare for the call. You can check your record book so that you are familiar with the student's progress.
- If a parent is calling with a complaint, try very hard not to get defensive. Listen and try to understand the parent's frustration. Respond by expressing your concern and assuring the parent that you are really committed to finding a solution.
- If a parent calls to complain that a child is upset about something ("He says you're picking on him" or "She says you're embarrassing her in front of the class"), acknowledge the student's perception. Convey your regret that the student has that perception. For example: "Gee, I'm really sorry that she has that perception. What specifically has she said, so that I can figure out what's going on? Help me to understand because I don't want her to feel that way." Don't start out defensively: "I don't pick on kids."
- For chronic callers (parents who call three times a week), make it clear that it's important for you and the student to work the problem out. Explain that the frequent calls are embarrassing the student.
- If the telephone call is difficult, and there's a danger of your becoming defensive, have another person in the room to help monitor your tone of voice. He or she can tap you on the shoulder or make a face if you begin to get hostile or defensive.
- If a parent is out of control, suggest that you talk again at a later time so that you both have a chance to calm down.
- If parents ask you to call every week with a report on their child's progress, suggest that they call you instead. (After all, you could have 150 students to think about, but they have only one!) Designate a day and time for them to call (e.g., on Fridays, during your prep period).
- To help keep the conversation productive, keep in mind the mnemonic, LAFF, don't CRY:
     Listen, empathize and communicate respect.
     Ask questions and ask permission to take notes.
     Focus on the issues.
     Find a first step.
  DON'T
     Criticize people who aren't present.
     React hastily and promise something you can't deliver.
     Yakety-yak-yak.

Source: McNaughton & Vostal, 2010.

It's also important to emphasize that phone calls should not be reserved for problems. As Donnie reminds us:

> Teachers shouldn't just call when there's something bad. It's really important to call parents to give good news, to say "Your kid is really doing well," to tell them about something terrific that happened. Sometimes, when I do that, the student will come in the next day and say, "You called my house! And you didn't say anything *bad* about me!" And I'll tell them, "I had nothing bad to say!" I'll also let parents know what's coming up, the things that are going on. If you do that, then you've laid the foundation for a good relationship, and parents are more open later on. If you do have to call about a problem, they're less likely to be hostile or defensive.

REPORT CARDS

Report cards have been the traditional way to communicate with families about a child's progress in school. Unfortunately, they're often not very informative. What exactly does it mean when a student receives a C in Spanish? Is she having problems with vocabulary, with comprehension, or with conversation? Is another student's D in mathematics due to difficulties with problem solving, or is it merely a result of careless computational errors? Because many high schools use computerized report cards, it is not always possible for the teacher to elaborate on grades with a personalized narrative. Donnie tells us:

> On our report cards, you can pick from nine little statements, like "the student is disruptive," "comes late," "is doing well," "is working at or above grade level," "has missed tests." But you're only allowed to check two! And they're so impersonal, I'm not sure that they really communicate much of anything.

Another common problem with report cards is timeliness. If you rely solely on report cards to communicate with parents about a student's progress, two months might pass from the time a problem first appears until parents learn about it. To avoid this problem, some schools require teachers to send out progress reports midway through each marking period. Specific policies vary from district to district. Sandy explains what happens at her high school:

> Progress reports have to be sent out mid-marking period for all seventh- and eighth-graders. In grades 9 through 12, we only have to send home a progress report if a student is in danger of receiving a D or an F for the marking period, but I send them out for other reasons too, like attendance or behavior or for commendable progress. I also tell students that I'm sending a progress report home, and I show it to them. I believe that they have the right to know.
>
> Sometimes, showing students the progress reports encourages them to clean up their act. For example, Edward had a 75 average because he had two assignments missing. When I told him I was sending home a progress report, he asked me to just report the 75 average and leave off the part about the two missing assignments. He said his mother "would kill" him if she found out he wasn't doing his homework consistently. He promised he'd never miss another assignment. I decided he was serious, and so I agreed, but I told him that if she asked, I'd have to tell her. He never missed another assignment.

Although Sandy is conscientious about sending home progress reports, she also believes that any serious problem should be dealt with sooner:

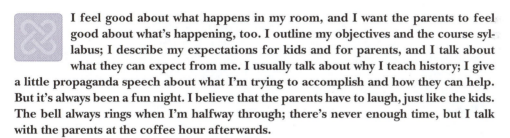

> Teachers should not rely on progress reports to tell parents about serious problems. Teachers need to contact parents if a problem develops. All of my students' parents know if their child has a D or an F before progress reports. I send progress reports because I have to, but my parents already know. Relying on progress reports is not very smart, since probably 50 percent of the kids take them out of the mail before their parents ever see them!

BACK-TO-SCHOOL NIGHT

For many parents, open house or back-to-school night is the first opportunity to meet you and to see the classroom. It's also the first opportunity *you* have to show parents all the great things you've been doing and to tell them about the plans you have for the future. As Fred says,

> I feel good about what happens in my room, and I want the parents to feel good about what's happening, too. I outline my objectives and the course syllabus; I describe my expectations for kids and for parents, and I talk about what they can expect from me. I usually talk about why I teach history; I give a little propaganda speech about what I'm trying to accomplish and how they can help. But it's always been a fun night. I believe that the parents have to laugh, just like the kids. The bell always rings when I'm halfway through; there's never enough time, but I talk with the parents at the coffee hour afterwards.

If you don't feel quite as enthusiastic as Fred, don't feel bad. Even teachers as experienced as Sandy sometimes feel nervous about back-to-school night. In fact, she tells us: "I hate back-to-school night! The one good thing is that I always get so nervous that I talk really fast and finish early. That leaves plenty of time for people to ask questions."

As these comments suggest, back-to-school night usually involves a brief presentation to groups of parents who move from room to room, following their children's schedules. This is not always the case, however. In Christina's school, for example, teachers remain in their assigned rooms for 90 minutes while parents visit teachers in any order they wish to have brief, individual conferences. Because the time with each parent is so limited, Christina's goals are simply to attach a face to a name, to give parents a general sense of their children's progress, and to invite them to set up a longer conference. She also displays current class projects so parents can look them over while they are waiting to see her.

Regardless of the format your school uses, keep in mind that first impressions *do* matter, so you need to think carefully about how you will orchestrate this event. The Practical Tips box contains some guidelines that emerged during discussions with Sandy, Fred, Donnie, Donna, and Christina. (Obviously, some of them apply only if you are giving group presentations.)

As a final comment about back-to-school night, it's important not to take low attendance personally. As noted earlier in this chapter, parents might have work schedules that prevent them from attending; they might feel just as nervous as you about the

PRACTICAL TIPS FOR

Back-to-School Night

- To increase attendance, consider sending e-mail invitations to the parents of your students, indicating that you are looking forward to meeting them. If you maintain a class website, include a prominent announcement about the night.
- Make sure your classroom looks especially attractive and neat. Display the books and materials that are used in your courses as well as student projects from this year or previous years.
- Greet people at the door, introduce yourself, and find out who they are. *Do not assume that the student's last name is the same as the parents' last name or that both parents have the same last name.*
- Make sure your presentation is succinct and well organized. Parents want to hear about your goals, plans, and philosophy as well as the curriculum and policies about homework and absences. Create a PowerPoint presentation that incorporates photos of your students involved in class activities. (Be sure to find out if you have to obtain parents' permission before photographing students.)
- Provide a hand-out with a statement of goals, class schedules, homework policies, and so on, for parents to take home. You can also e-mail this handout to parents who weren't able to attend back-to-school night.
- If parents raise issues that are unique to their child, let them know in a sensitive way that the purpose of open house is to describe the general program. Indicate that you're more than happy to discuss their concerns during a private conference. You might want to have a sign-up sheet available for this purpose.
- Listen carefully to parents' questions. Provide an opportunity for parents to talk about *their* goals and expectations for their children in the coming school year. This can begin the two-way communication that is so crucial for family-school collaboration.
- Provide a sign-up sheet for parents who are able to participate in classroom activities (e.g., as a guest speaker or chaperone on field trips).
- If refreshments are being served after the class meetings, go down and join in conversations with parents. Clustering with the other teachers separates you from parents and conveys the idea that there is a professional barrier.
- RELAX AND HAVE FUN MEETING YOUR STUDENTS' PARENTS!

evening and decide not to come; or, if they have children of various ages, they could be at the back-to-school night of a younger sibling. Relax and enjoy meeting the parents who are there, and send follow-up e-mails to parents who didn't attend.

PARENT-TEACHER CONFERENCES

Schools generally schedule one or two formal parent-teacher conferences during the school year. Interestingly, these meetings are often a source of frustration to both teachers and parents. Parents resent the formality of the situation (Lindle, 1989) and find the limited conference period frustrating. As one mother puts it, "Ten minutes is ridiculous, especially when other parents are waiting right outside the door. I need time to tell the teacher about how my child is at home, too" (Lindle, p. 14).

Teachers, too, are sometimes unhappy with these formal conferences. They agree with parents that the brief time allotted often precludes meaningful exchange. Furthermore, teachers complain about the lack of attendance: "The parents you *don't* need to see show up, but the ones you desperately *want* to talk with don't come." Interestingly, Donnie doesn't mind that the parents of good students come to parent conferences:

 If there's a real problem, I've already contacted the parents by the time parent conferences come along. We've already met. So I think it's nice to see the ones whose kids are doing well. It's nice to be able to give positive reports. And parents want reassurance that all is going well.

Before a conference, it's important to prepare carefully. For example, Donna puts together a packet that includes samples of the student's work, grades, records of attendance and tardiness, and any records of detentions or referrals.

Conferences can be tense—especially if you're meeting with family members for the first time—so our five teachers begin by trying to put parents at ease. They suggest leading with something positive: "You son is a delight to have in class" or "Your daughter appears to be really interested in the topics we've been studying." You should be aware, however, that immigrant Latino parents (and others from collectivistic cultures) could be uncomfortable hearing extended praise of their children because praise singles a person out from the group (Trumbull, Rothstein-Fisch, Greenfield, & Quiroz, 2001).

Next, problems or weaknesses can be broached—not as character flaws ("she's lazy") but as problems that need to be solved ("She's having difficulty getting her assignments in on time. What can we do about this?"). Donnie puts it this way:

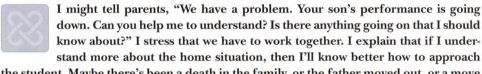 I might tell parents, "We have a problem. Your son's performance is going down. Can you help me to understand? Is there anything going on that I should know about?" I stress that we have to work together. I explain that if I understand more about the home situation, then I'll know better how to approach the student. Maybe there's been a death in the family, or the father moved out, or a move is imminent. All this helps me to be more effective.

Sandy also tries to enlist parents' assistance in dealing with problems; however, she cautions teachers not to make demands that are impossible for parents to carry out:

 Don't say things like, "You have to get your child to participate more in class." Be reasonable. If you're talking about a 17-year-old senior, what are the chances that a parent can do that? On the other hand, you can say, "Joanne is very quiet in class. Is this her normal behavior?"

Although they try to provide substantive information to parents, our teachers emphasize the need *to listen.* All five teachers always allow time for parents to ask questions and to express their concerns, and they solicit parents' suggestions. A conference should be a two-way conversation, not a monologue. *It's also critical not to assume that poor parents, uneducated parents, or parents with limited English proficiency have nothing of value to offer.* One immigrant mother expressed her frustration this way: "Whenever I go to school, they want to tell me what to do at home. They want to tell me how to raise my kid. They never ask what I think. They never ask me anything" (Finders & Lewis, 1994, p. 53).

Kottler (1994) stresses the importance of encouraging families whose first language is not English to help you understand their children's educational and cultural background. For example, you might ask about past educational experiences, whether their son or daughter is experiencing any cultural conflicts, what their educational goals for their child are, whether English is used at home, and whether there are any special needs or customs that you need to consider. If you are meeting with parents who are using an interpreter, keep in mind that your conversation is with the parents, not the interpreter. You should speak to and make eye contact with the parents. Speak no more than two or three sentences at a time, and then pause for the interpreter to speak.

You also need to be sensitive to cultural differences in communication styles. Cultures shape the nature of verbal interaction, providing norms for who can initiate conversation, whether it's all right to interrupt, and how long to pause between a question and its answer (Swap, 1993). If these norms are not shared, parents could feel uncomfortable. In addition, you need to recognize that different cultures hold different views about appropriate classroom behavior. For example, a European American teacher might encourage students to participate actively in classroom discussions, to voice their opinions, and to ask questions. In contrast, some Latino and Asian American parents might expect their children to be quiet and obedient and not to contradict the teacher or ask questions (Scarcella, 1990). It's also important to understand that Latino immigrant parents might be primarily interested in the child's social and moral development:

> [B]eing a respectful contributor to group well-being rather than focusing on one's own achievement is highly valued. So when immigrant Latino parents come for a parent–teacher conference, their first question is likely to be, *"Como se porta mi hijo/hija?"* ("How is my son/daughter behaving?") A teacher may find it difficult to stifle her consternation after hearing the same question from 25 or 30 sets of parents, believing that all the parents care about is their child's behavior when the teacher's goal is to discuss the child's academic progress. (Rothstein-Fisch & Trumbull, 2008, pp. 14–15)

Finally, our teachers stress the importance of not closing doors to further communication. If a conference is not going well, you might suggest another meeting, perhaps with the department supervisor or a guidance counselor on hand to mediate the discussion.

Some schools have started to use three-way conferences that include the teacher, the parent or guardian, and the student (Bailey & Guskey, 2001). First, all participants, beginning with the student, share their perceptions of the strengths demonstrated in her or his work. They then discuss two areas on which the student needs to work, outline goals for the future, and agree on the types of support that each party will provide. Finally, the teacher answers questions and summarizes agreements.

Research indicates that the three-way conference has distinct advantages over the traditional parent-teacher conference. One study, for example, compared traditional parent-teacher conferences with conferences that included students as participants ("family-school conferences") (Minke & Anderson, 2003). Families chosen to participate in the project had children with mild learning or behavior problems. Two primary findings with respect to traditional conferences emerged. First, both teachers and parents agreed that conferences are important opportunities for an exchange of information; second, both groups approached conferences with trepidation. Parents used words such as *worried, nervous, overwhelmed, angry,* and *apprehensive* to describe their emotions, and teachers described their feelings of "exhaustion and relief" when conference days were over (p. 59). In contrast, both parents and teachers felt that the family-school conference model increased trust and communication and provided effective opportunities to learn about one another and the child. Adults were particularly impressed by students' "unexpectedly mature behavior" and their "honest, insightful comments about their own learning" (p. 60). Indeed, "Teachers often noted that the child was the first one to bring up 'bad news,' which teachers saw as relieving them of a worrisome burden and greatly reducing parental defensiveness" (p. 60). Evidence also suggested that family-school conferences could be conducted in the same 15 to 20 minutes usually allotted to the routine, two-party conferences. It should be noted, however, that such three-way conferences require training and careful preparation. (See Bailey and Guskey, 2001, for practical strategies and suggestions.)

PAUSE AND REFLECT

We have already noted that family involvement in school drops off in middle and high school. Before reading the next section, think about the types of family involvement that could benefit your classroom and students and the ways that you could encourage and nurture this involvement.

Family Involvement in School

At the high school level, most family involvement in school consists of attendance at student performances, athletic events, or other programs. Family involvement can also take place "behind-the-scenes"; for example, parents could engage in fund-raising activities, interview prospective teachers and administrators, prepare breakfast on "Teacher Appreciation Day," participate on committees developing discipline and attendance policies, and chaperone social events.

Participation in classroom activities is far less common, but involving even a few parents can provide considerable support and enrich the curriculum. When Fred's classes study religions, for example, parents of different faiths come in to explain their religious beliefs; in his law and politics class, parents who are lawyers sometimes share their expertise; and survivors of Nazi concentration camps might visit his history classes. In Sandy's chemistry classes, parents speak on scientific or environmental issues, and parents who are faculty members at a nearby university have set up tours of the chemistry labs there. Donnie holds a "mini-career day" when successful former students share their career experiences and communicate the message, "You can do this too." In Christina's journalism classes, parents, friends of parents, former students, and local contacts speak about their careers as journalists.

If you decide to invite parents to participate in your classroom, you need to think carefully about how to recruit them. Sometimes parents don't volunteer simply because they're not sure what would be expected or how they could contribute.

Back-to-school night offers a good opportunity to make a direct, in-person appeal and to explain the various ways parents can assist. If you do invite parents to make a presentation in your classroom, make sure you are clear about whether they will need to repeat the presentation in multiple classes. An engineer friend was surprised to learn that she would need to repeat her presentation in all three of the physics classes that one of us taught!

Another way to involve parents is in helping you get resources for your classroom. Perhaps one of your students' parents works in a laboratory and can arrange to donate surplus equipment to your science classroom. Or perhaps a parent who works in a bookstore can arrange to have slightly damaged books donated to your literature classroom. (These types of donations to a school typically qualify as a charitable contribution at tax time.) You can use e-mail or a class website to distribute a "wish list" of resources for your classroom as another way to invite parental involvement.

If you're teaching in a district where there has been little parent involvement in school, you will need to make special efforts to change the situation. At Donnie's high school, a committee has been established to consider ways to make the school more "parent friendly." As a result of the committee's efforts, teams of teachers have visited neighborhood churches on Sunday mornings to invite parents to the high school. As Donnie puts it,

Parents were complaining that they don't feel welcome. Well, the point of these trips is to say, "We want you to visit. This is your school; come in and see what's going on. If you can, volunteer, work in the library, help kids with homework. We welcome you."

Donnie's sentiment is echoed in research that found that increasing cultural programming in a school encouraged more American Indian parents to get involved (Powers, 2006) and that inviting Latino parents to become active in school government increased involvement of Latino families (Marschall, 2006).

PARENTS OF STUDENTS WITH SPECIAL NEEDS

According to the Individuals with Disabilities Education Act (IDEA), parents of children with disabilities have a legal mandate to participate in planning their children's Individualized Education Program (IEP). Given the fact that inclusion is now widespread, you are likely to have contact with parents of children with disabilities and, it is hoped, to be involved in the annual IEP meetings (at which a teacher must be present). But Sandy, who has an emotionally disturbed student in her class this year, cautions teachers not to wait for the formal, mandated meetings or even for the regularly scheduled parent conferences:

Anytime I have a student with an IEP, I go to the case manager right away and say, "Tell me about this kid." Then I ask them to set up a time for us to meet with the parents, usually in the first week and a half of school. This shows parents that you're aware of the IEP; it gives them a sense of relief and

confidence. They know that the IEP isn't just a piece of paper, that the teacher is already thinking about how to modify the course for the student. It starts you off on the right track, establishes the right tone.

At our initial meeting, we talk a lot about the IEP. You've got to remember that IEPs are open to interpretation, and that needs to be discussed. For example, an IEP may say that the student can have more time for tests. What does that mean? Is that an indefinite amount of time? Ten minutes? What?

I also want parents to educate me about their kid. This year, with an emotionally disturbed boy, it was important for me to know what sets him off. What will be stressful for him that might result in an outburst? Every kid is different, and I don't like surprises if I can avoid them. Sometimes it's as simple as "don't pair him with another male."

To help educate you about a student with special needs, you could invite the student's family to create a portfolio of information about their child (Gregg, Rugg, & Souto-Manning, 2011) and share it with you at a meeting. This portfolio would contain information about the student's out-of-school behavior; interests, hopes, and dreams; and how family members support her or him at home.

In addition to scheduling a meeting early in the year, Sandy keeps in close contact with parents throughout the year. Sometimes parents want a weekly report, and she is happy to comply; however, she asks them to take the responsibility for calling or e-mailing: "With so many kids, it's just too hard for me to remember."

Family Involvement in Learning Activities at Home

Epstein's fourth type of involvement refers to the ways families can assist their children's learning at home. At the secondary level, this type of involvement often creates considerable anxiety for parents. As Donnie mentioned earlier, some parents are scared off by the subject matter. Donna notes that parents sometimes ask to attend class with their son or daughter: "They may come in and say, 'My child is having trouble in class; can I watch your lesson so I can help him at home?'"

Parents aren't the only ones who wonder how they can help with their teenagers' homework assignments. Some teachers also question whether parents can really be useful. In contrast, our five teachers believe that parents can play an extremely important role. Although they might not be familiar with the subject matter, parents can still help by monitoring their children's schoolwork, providing support and encouragement, and setting limits. Fred tells us:

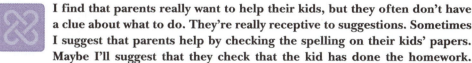 I find that parents really want to help their kids, but they often don't have a clue about what to do. They're really receptive to suggestions. Sometimes I suggest that parents help by checking the spelling on their kids' papers. Maybe I'll suggest that they check that the kid has done the homework. Maybe I'll explain the requirements for a research paper and suggest they check to see that the requirements are met. I'll suggest they ask to see the papers the kid brings home. A lot of times kids put their papers in the garbage and never show them to their parents.

A review of research on parent involvement in homework (Patall, Cooper, & Robinson, 2008) reinforces our teachers' beliefs. The review concluded that of all the various types of parent involvement, setting rules about when and where homework should be done can have the most beneficial effect on students' achievement. Moreover, this type of involvement does not require years of higher education. A survey of middle-school students' homework practices (Xu and Corno, 2003) found that family members were especially helpful in arranging the environment (e.g., finding a quiet area, creating space for the child to work, turning off the television) and assisting children in controlling their emotions (e.g., calming a frustrated child, providing encouragement when a child is upset). The homework helper's educational level was unrelated to effective homework assistance

It is important to recognize that this view of the parental role can conflict with some families' beliefs about the importance of independence and self-sufficiency. For example, a mother in one study explains why she stays out of her daughter's schooling:

It's her education, not mine. I've had to teach her to take care of herself. I work nights, so she's had to get up and get herself ready for school. I'm not going to be there all the time. She's gotta do it. She's a tough cookie. . . . She's almost an adult, and I get the impression that they want me to walk her through her work. And it's not that I don't care either. I really do. I think it's important, but I don't think it's my place. (Finders & Lewis, 1994, p. 52)

Clearly, this mother is concerned for her child's well-being, but she sees independence as critical if her daughter is to survive and succeed.

> **PAUSE AND REFLECT**
>
> Homework is a controversial subject. For example, in *The End of Homework: How Homework Disrupts Families, Overburdens Children, and Limits Learning,* Etta Kralovec and John Buell (2000) argue that homework actually promotes discrimination. Children who are able to get support and assistance from their families (the "haves") can surge ahead, but those who come from families who are unable to help them (the "have-nots") fall further and further behind. What do you think about this issue?

CONCLUDING COMMENTS

This chapter has described different ways that teachers can reach out to families. Our suggestions vary considerably in terms of how common they are and how much time and energy they demand. As you get to know your students and their family situations, you will be able to decide which practices are most appropriate and most feasible. Of course, you need to be realistic: As a beginning teacher, you might have to delay major efforts to facilitate communication and collaboration with families. Nonetheless, remember that family involvement can be key to students' success and that extending specific invitations to participate has been shown to have a powerful impact on family involvement at home and in school (Deslandes & Bertrand, 2005).

This is an age of many single parents; of parents who work long hours or more than one job; of same-sex parents; of grandparents, aunts, and neighbors who care for children; and of increasing numbers of families whose cultural backgrounds differ from that of most teachers. Family-school collaboration has never been more difficult—but it has never been more important.

SUMMARY

This chapter began by discussing the benefits of working closely with families. It then outlined the challenges to family-teacher cooperation and stressed that teachers' attitudes and practices significantly affect parents' involvement in their children's schooling. Finally, the chapter presented strategies for overcoming the challenges and fostering collaboration between families and schools.

Benefits of Working Closely with Families

- Knowing about a student's home situation provides insight into the student's classroom behavior.
- When families understand what you are trying to achieve, they can provide valuable support and assistance.
- Families can help to develop and implement strategies for changing behavior.
- Parent volunteers can provide assistance in the classroom and school.

Challenges to Family-Teacher Cooperation

- Teachers are sometimes reluctant to involve families in schooling because of:
    The extra time and energy required.
    Their perceptions that families are too overburdened or that they lack the skills needed.
    The level of authority and autonomy teachers enjoy within their classrooms.
    Uncertainty about how to effectively and respectfully interact with the variety of families in which their students are being raised.
- Parents are sometimes reluctant to become involved in schooling because they:
    Are overburdened by the demands of work.
    Have unhappy memories of school.
    Believe schooling should be left to the experts.
    Feel guilty if their children are having problems.
    Find schools intimidating and threatening places.
    Do not see involvement in school as part of their parental role.

Fostering Collaboration between Families and Schools

- Schools can assist families in carrying out their basic obligations by providing parent education, establishing parent support groups, and referring families to community and state agencies.
- Teachers need to communicate about school programs and students' progress through websites and e-mails, phone calls, report cards, progress reports, and face-to-face interactions (e.g., back-to-school night, parent conferences).
- Family members can serve as volunteers in classrooms and schools.
- Families can assist their children at home on learning activities:
    Supervising homework.
    Providing encouragement and support.
    Setting limits.

As a beginning teacher, you have to decide what you can realistically accomplish with respect to communication and collaboration with parents. Nonetheless, you need to remember that family involvement is critical to students' success. In this age of single parents, parents who work long hours, different family structures, and students who come from diverse cultural backgrounds, meaningful family-school collaboration has never been more challenging, but it has never been more essential.

ACTIVITIES FOR SKILL BUILDING
AND REFLECTION

In Class

1. Read the following e-mail, which is from a teacher to her students' parents, inviting them to the upcoming Open House. First, individually correct all the mechanical errors in the teacher's writing. Second, in small groups, compare your corrections and then discuss how you would feel as a parent if you received the uncorrected version of the e-mail.

    Dear Parent's:

    I hope UR as excited as I am about our upcoming Open House!! I am so looking forward to meeting you and describing my plans for class this year. My students have been busy helping me to decorate my classroom and I have put up some of there work on the walls for you to see. I will also have some of my planned activity's for you to try out and I will be happy to answer any question's you may have about my class. Your always welcome in my classroom, and I can't wait for the Open House next week.

2. Working in small groups, read the following vignettes (one per group) and do the following:
    - Discuss the information provided in the vignette.
    - List other information you might like to get and how you might get it.
    - List possible ways you might address the issue aside from talking to the parent/guardian/ family. What might some underlying issues be?
    - Think about what you will do to prepare for the conference.
    - Decide how you will structure the meeting so that you can state your information in a productive way without being defensive.
    - Role-play the conversation that you might have with the family member about this issue.

Vignette 1

You have stressed that research scientists work in teams, and you use a lot of cooperative learning activities in your seventh-grade general science class. Although students sit in rows, their seats are assigned so that they can quickly turn their desks around to form four-person "research groups" that are heterogeneous in terms of race, ethnicity, gender, and achievement level. At parent conferences, the father of a Pakistani girl in your class requests that you place his daughter in an all-girl group. As he explains, his culture frowns upon girls and boys sitting together, and he was extremely unhappy when he learned about his daughter's seat assignment and the composition of her research team.

Vignette 2

Last week you conducted a parent conference with Mrs. Lewis, Joey's mother. During the conference, you described his disruptive behaviors and what you've done to deal with them. You also explained that he is in danger of failing your class because he rarely does homework and has gotten poor grades on most quizzes and tests. Mrs. Lewis seemed to accept and understand the information; however, the next day, an irate *Mr.* Lewis called. He told you that he had never seen his wife so upset and that he wants another conference as soon as possible to get to the bottom of the problem. He also intimated that the problem might be due to a personality conflict between you and his son. Although the phone call caught you off guard, you scheduled the conference for two days later.

Vignette 3

You have a student in your 10th-grade class who is failing to complete her homework. She is an academically competent student in class; she does most of her classwork and is friendly and easygoing. You have asked the student repeatedly to do her homework, yet she comes in almost daily with little or none of it complete. When you ask her why she has not done the work, she answers by saying, "I don't know." You have sent two letters home and left one phone message for her family. Her mother shows up unexpectedly at the end of a school day, demands to speak with you, and tells you that her daughter is complaining that you are picking on her and do not like her.

Vignette 4

Paul is an African American student in your sixth-grade class. You know his mother is very active in the PTA and is quite involved in school and district politics. Unfortunately, Paul is not doing well in class. He is an excellent reader and writer and is quite intelligent, but you have documented his lack of class work, and you have anecdotal notes referring to his negative comments about the types of assignments you assign the class. He is getting more and more disengaged and disrespectful to you. You feel well prepared for the parent conference because you have very thorough records and notes. When Paul's parents come to the conference, you carefully lay out your case. His father responds by explaining that in their home, they encourage their children to question what they are taught and not to believe information just because it is presented in class. He explains that many students of color disengage from school because they are not represented in the Eurocentric curriculum. Paul's mother then suggests that as a European American teacher, you need to learn about the history and culture of the students that you teach in order to fully engage them. She even goes on to suggest that you should listen to Paul's criticisms of your assignments and use that as a way to examine and evaluate what is essentially a biased curriculum.

On Your Own

1. In getting ready for the school year, you have decided to send a letter to the family of each student in your classes. The point of the letter is to introduce yourself, describe the curriculum, highlight a few upcoming projects, and explain your expectations in terms of homework, behavior, and attendance.

   Select a subject that you might actually teach (e.g., American history, Algebra I, Spanish, Home Economics I, world literature, physical education, etc.), and write such a letter. As you write, think about the need to create a warm tone, to be clear and organized, to avoid educational jargon, and to stimulate interest about school.

2. Anita is extremely "forgetful" about doing homework assignments. She has received innumerable zeros and regularly has to stay for detention to make up the work. You have called her mother to report on this behavior and to ask for assistance, but her mother does not want to get involved. As she puts it, "I've got all I can do to handle her at home. What she does with school work is your responsibility!"

   Interview two experienced teachers about what they would do in a case such as this, and then formulate your own course of action based on what you learn.

For Your Portfolio

Demonstrate your capacity to communicate with families by including two or three artifacts (e.g., newsletters, requests for parental help with homework, invitations to class events, student award certificates, check sheets to be used at parent conferences).

FOR FURTHER READING

Allen, J. B. (2007). *Creating welcoming schools: A practical guide to home-school partnerships with diverse families.* New York: Teachers College Press.

  This book contains many practical strategies for engaging families in schools, learning about diverse cultures, and building partnerships between school and home.

Lawrence-Lightfoot, S. (2003). *The essential conversation: What parents and teachers can learn from each other.* New York: Ballantine Books.

  According to Lawrence-Lightfoot, "beneath the polite surface of parent-teacher conferences . . . burns a cauldron of fiery feelings." For parents, there is no more dreaded moment; for teachers, these meetings engender feelings of uncertainty, defensiveness, and exposure. This book focuses on the experiences of 10 exemplary teachers in an effort to understand how parents and teachers "negotiate the treacherous and tender terrain" between them.

Marsh, M. M., & Turner-Vorbeck, T. (Eds.) (2011). *(Mis)Understanding families: Learning from real families in our schools.* New York: Teachers College Press.

  The chapters in this text examine how teachers and school personnel can effectively and inclusively identify, address, and meet the needs of the diverse forms of families represented in today's classrooms.

Padak, N., & Rasinski, T.V. (2010). Welcoming schools: Small changes that can make a big difference. *The Reading Teacher, 64*(4), 294–297.

  This article presents a number of small strategies to make your school and classroom more welcoming to your students' families.

Pushor, D. (2011). Looking out, looking in. *Educational Leadership, 69*(1), 65–68.

  This article presents ideas for a partnership approach that respects the strengths and knowledge of students' families.

Sanchez, C., Plata, V., Grosso, L., & Leird, B. (2010). Encouraging Spanish-speaking families' involvement through dichos. *Journal of Latinos and Education, 9*(3), 239–248.

  This article explores the use of *dichos,* or popular sayings in the Spanish language, as tools that have the potential to enhance school-home communication. Given their prevalence in everyday oral discourse for the transmission of values and beliefs, *dichos* should facilitate communication with Latino Spanish-speaking families.

Scherer, M. (Ed.). (2011). *Educational Leadership, 68*(8).

  This theme issue on schools, families, and communities includes several articles about how and why to join forces with families and communities.

ORGANIZATIONAL RESOURCES

The Family Involvement Network of Educators (FINE), www.hfrp.org. The goal of FINE is to bring together thousands of stakeholders committed to promoting strong partnerships among schools, families, and communities. It provides information about family involvement, including teaching tools, training materials, and research reports. Members can receive a free subscription to the FINE e-mail newsletter, which regularly highlights new resources for strengthening, family, school, and community partnerships.

The National Network of Partnership Schools (NNPS), www.partnershipschools.org. NNPS provides information on implementing comprehensive, goal-oriented programs of school, family, and community partnerships. It also provides interactive homework assignments (TIPS) and the collections of "Promising Partnership Practices" on its website.

The National Parent Teacher Association (PTA), www.pta.org. PTA provides a set of standards for family-community-school partnerships. Teachers, schools, and parents can use these standards to assess their own efforts. Additionally, the website provides materials for parents on how to help their children learn and how they can join their local PTA.

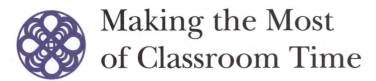
Making the Most of Classroom Time

On the first day of school, the academic year seems to stretch out endlessly. If you're a beginning teacher, you might wonder how you'll ever fill all the hours of school that lie ahead—especially if you're not even certain what you're going to do *tomorrow*. And yet, as the days go by, you could begin to think that there's never enough time to accomplish all you need to do. With assemblies, fire drills, announcements over the intercom, standardized testing, snow days, holidays, and clerical tasks, the hours available for instruction seem far fewer than they did at the beginning of the school year.

Indeed, by the end of the year, you might view time as a precious resource—not something that has to be filled (or killed) but something that must be conserved and used wisely.

This chapter discusses issues of time and time management. Guiding the chapter is the premise that the wise use of time will maximize opportunities for learning and minimize opportunities for disruption. First, we look at the amount of school time that is actually available for teaching and

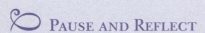

PAUSE AND REFLECT

Keeping in mind that the average student spends 1,170 hours per year in school (180 days × 6.5 hours per day), estimate either the number of hours or the percentage of time that students are actually involved in productive learning (i.e., they are engaging in meaningful, appropriate academic tasks). Then read on to see what researchers have calculated and find out whether you are on target.

learning. Then we consider strategies for using classroom time efficiently, focusing on three complementary approaches: maintaining activity flow, minimizing transition time, and holding students accountable. Finally, we examine block scheduling, which replaces the traditional 42- or 50-minute period with fewer, longer classes of 80 to 90 minutes.

HOW MUCH TIME IS THERE, ANYWAY?

Although this seems to be a straightforward question, the answer is not so simple. In fact, the answer depends on the *type* of time you're talking about. Most states mandate a school year of approximately 180 days. Let's suppose that you're teaching in a high school that has divided each of these days into 42-minute periods. This amounts to 126 hours of *mandated time* for each of your classes. But students are absent, and special assembly programs are scheduled, snowstorms cause delayed openings, and parent conferences require early closings. Factors such as these immediately reduce the time you have for teaching, so the *time available for instruction* can be substantially less than mandated time. Listen to the reflections of a student teacher who has learned to deal with the constant interruptions and cancellations:

> *"Well, at least you're learning to be flexible!" If I heard that once, I heard it a million times. I believe every teacher that I've had contact with this semester has made this statement to me. A record snowfall, proficiency testing, marine biology field trips, half-day inservice days, pep rallies, assemblies. . . . The actual time I have had a full class of students . . . for more than two consecutive days is minimal. Nowhere is the realization that I must be flexible more evident than in my lesson plans. When I began student teaching, my lesson plans were printed and clipped into a binder (and labeled "Monday," "Tuesday," etc.). A short time later I began calling each day "Day One," "Day Two," "Day Three," and so on. About halfway through my student teaching experience, I began printing each of my activities on separate pages, which I could arrange as needed. I only finalized the lesson on the district's template as I became absolutely sure that they would not be disrupted. I have continued to use this practice with great success and have actually started one of my cooperating teachers on the same method.*

Even when school is in session, students are present, and you have your class for the full 42 minutes, some portion of the available class time must be spent in noninstructional activities. This means that only part of the 42-minute period actually constitutes *instructional time*. In *A Place Called School* (1984, 2004), John Goodlad reports that the senior high school teachers he studied generally spent about 76 percent of available class time on instruction, 20 percent on routines, and 1.3 percent on behavior control; the remaining 2.2 percent was spent on socializing. Interestingly, the figures varied by subject area: Foreign language classes ranked first in terms of time spent on instruction; English classes ranked last. School-to-school differences were also apparent with instructional time varying from 68 percent to 84 percent.

Even within a school and a subject area, there can be considerable variation from teacher to teacher. In some classes, settling in at the beginning of the period, taking attendance, distributing materials, collecting homework, and reprimanding misbehaving students consume an inordinate amount of time. Karweit (1989) describes a "one-hour" math class, for example, in which the first 10 minutes were typically used to collect lunch money, and the last 10 were used to line up the students for lunch—leaving only 40 minutes for actual instruction. In a more recent study, Fisher (2009) found that students in one suburban high school spent an average of nine minutes per class per day waiting while the teacher was taking attendance, talking with a student about missed work, trying to find something, or trying to get equipment to work. And students were *not* engaged in school-related tasks while waiting.

Such situations aren't unusual in the classrooms of teachers who lack efficient strategies for carrying out routine, noninstructional tasks. Consider the difficulties encountered by one hypothetical beginning teacher, Ms. Diaz, as she attempted to check homework at the beginning of math class (adapted from Leinhardt & Greeno, 1986). She had two goals: to identify who had done the homework and to correct it orally. She began by asking, "Who did their homework?" In response, students did one of three things: They held up their completed work, called out that they didn't have it, or walked over to the teacher and told her whether they had done it or not. Ms. Diaz then talked about the importance of homework and marked the results of this check on a posted sheet of paper.

Next, Ms. Diaz chose students to give the correct answers to the homework problems, first asking Britanny to call out the answers to the first 10 problems. After a pause, Britanny volunteered the answer to the first problem; her answer was incorrect. Ms. Diaz corrected her answer and asked Britanny for the answer to the second problem; after another pause, she volunteered another incorrect answer. Ms. Diaz realized that Britanny had not done her homework and was trying to do the problems in her head. Ms. Diaz then began to call on other students for answers to the homework problems while the rest of the class checked their work. After each answer was given, Ms. Diaz either confirmed that it was correct or provided a corrected verbal answer. However, because each answer was a fairly complicated algebraic expression, students spent quite a bit of time asking each other whether their answers were correct. Ms. Diaz's entire homework check took six minutes—and it was clear that she was never certain which students had done their homework, and students were uncertain whether their answers were correct.

In contrast, consider a homework check conducted by Ms. Clift, a successful, experienced (hypothetical) teacher. She first gave a cue, "Okay, let's check homework set 43," and then began to call the students' names. Students responded "yes" or "no," and in 30 seconds—with a minimum of fuss—Ms. Clift was able to determine who had completed the assignment.

The next goal was to correct the work; Ms. Clift switched her interactive whiteboard to a screen that listed the correct answers to the homework. Students checked their own papers, using colored pens, and then passed their graded homework sheets to the front of each row, where Ms. Clift collected them for later review. This entire process required two minutes.

Ms. Clift's homework check is not presented as a model to be copied in your classroom; indeed, her procedure might not be appropriate for your particular class. The important point is that she has established a routine that enables her to check homework efficiently, almost automatically, but Ms. Diaz does not yet have a workable strategy. Although the difference in the time used by the two teachers is only about four minutes, it is probably symptomatic of the ways they manage class time in general.

Even when teachers are actually teaching, students are not necessarily paying attention. We must consider still another type of time—*engaged time* or time-on-task. Let's suppose that while you're teaching, some of your students choose to text about last Saturday night's party, do their homework for the next period, comb their hair, or stare out the window. In this case, the amount of time you are devoting to instruction is more than the amount of time students are directly engaged in learning. This is not an atypical situation. Research documents the fact that students tend to be "on-task" about 70 percent of the time (Rosenshine, 1980). Again, there are sizable variations from class to class. A study of 30 middle and high school science teachers (McGarity & Butts, 1984) found that some classes had an engagement rate of 54 percent (i.e., the average student was attentive about one-half of the time), and in other classes, the engagement rate was 75 percent.

To a large extent, variations such as these reflect teachers' ability to manage classroom events and to get students involved in learning activities. But other factors also come into play—students' attitudes toward school and subject matter, time of day, and day of week. (Some teachers even insist that attention falls off when there is a full moon!) Many teachers note that students are more likely to be off-task before a school vacation or long weekend. Donna speculates that this could reflect her students' anxiety about being in a chaotic home situation for several days: "For some of my students, school may be the only place where they have a consistent routine and where they feel appreciated and supported."

Substantial differences in engagement also occur from activity to activity. In one study, for example, high school students reported higher engagement (defined as interest, concentration, and enjoyment) during group-work and individual work than while listening to lectures or watching videos (Shernoff, Csikszentmihalyi, Schneider, & Shernoff, 2003). It seems clear that instructional strategies requiring students to be active are more engaging than those in which students are passive. Students also reported more engagement when they perceived the task at hand to be relevant and appropriately challenging—which brings us to a final type of time.

This last type of time is the *amount that students spend on meaningful and appropriate work.* We sometimes get so caught up in trying to increase students' time-on-task that we overlook the tasks themselves. We once saw students in a ninth-grade general science class spend 15 minutes coloring a worksheet that showed diagrams of flower parts. The students seemed absorbed; indeed, an observer coding time-on-task would have recorded a high engagement rate. But what was the purpose of the activity? In first grade, coloring can be useful for developing children's fine motor skills, but it is difficult to imagine why it would be worthwhile in high school. Coloring flower parts is not science, and in this case, one-third of the science period was allocated to a nonscientific activity. It also makes no sense to have students spend time working on tasks they don't understand and are unable to complete successfully.

This chapter began by asking, "How much time is there, anyway?" Figure 8.1 depicts the answer to this question. The bar at the far left shows the number of hours that a typical 42-minute class would meet in the typical mandated school year—126 (180 days × 42 minutes). For the sake of argument, let's assume that student absences

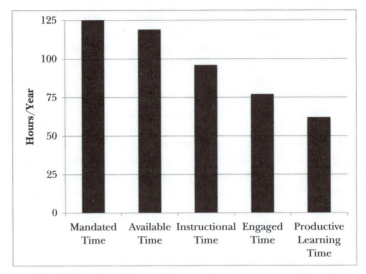

FIGURE 8.1   How Much Time Is There, Anyway?

and assembly programs reduce this figure by 10 days, or 7 hours (10 days × 42 minutes). Thus, the second bar indicates that available time is 119 hours. To be consistent with Goodlad's (1984) findings on the use of available class time, let's also assume that clerical and administrative tasks consume 20 percent of each class, leaving only 34 minutes each day for actual instruction. This yields 96 hours (bar 3). If students pay attention 80 percent of that time (an optimistic estimate), engaged time is 77 hours (bar 4). And assuming that students work on meaningful, appropriate tasks for 80 percent of the time they are engaged, we see that productive learning time is only 62 hours—*about one-half of the "mandated" school time for this typical secondary class* (bar 5).

Obviously, these figures are estimates. As we have stressed, there are substantial variations from subject to subject, school to school, and classroom to classroom. Nonetheless, the graph illustrates the fundamental point: *The hours available for learning are far more limited than they initially appear.*

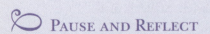

PAUSE AND REFLECT

Most teachers are surprised when they see how little time is actually spent in productive learning. What are some practices that erode the amount of time? What are some practices that you could use to maximize the opportunity for productive learning? Keep both of these in mind as you read the next section of the chapter.

INCREASING OPPORTUNITY TO LEARN

Over the years, time has been a popular topic for reform-minded educators. In 1983, for example, the National Commission on Excellence in Education declared that we were "a nation at risk" because of "a rising tide of mediocrity" in our educational system. The report advocated a variety of reforms, including recommendations to extend the school day to seven hours and to lengthen the school year to 200 or 220 days.

A decade later, the National Education Commission on Time and Learning (1994) also argued the need for more time. The commission characterized teachers and students as "prisoners of time" and paraphrased Oliver Hazard Perry's dispatch from the War of 1812: "We have met the enemy and they are [h]ours" (p. 1).

More recently, an education task force reached the same conclusions about the need for more time. In a report entitled *Getting Smarter, Becoming Fairer* (Brown, Rocha, & Sharkey, 2005), the task force observed that "the allocation and use of time today is still tied to an agrarian economy . . . , where children were needed to help in the fields during the after-school hours and summer months" (p. 15) and asserted that "abruptly thrusting American children out of the classroom door in the middle of the afternoon is a wasted opportunity" (p. 18). The task force's first recommendation was to increase the amount of time that students spend in school by lengthening the school day and, in the case of low-performing schools, the school year.

It appears that the recommendation to expand learning time is finally beginning to gain acceptance. Just over 1,000 U.S. schools now operate on expanded schedules, an increase of 53 percent over 2009 (Edwards, 2012). Indeed, as we were working on this chapter, five states (Colorado, Connecticut, Massachussetts, New York, and Tennessee) announced that they were instituting pilot programs that add up to 300 hours to the school calendar.

Nevertheless, the 6.5-hour, 180-day school year is still the norm in the United States. For this reason, it is critical for teachers to manage the limited time available with skill and efficiency. The next sections of this chapter discusses three strategies for increasing students' productive learning time: *maintaining activity flow, minimizing transition time, and holding students accountable.* (See Table 8.1 for a summary.) Of course, these strategies not only maximize time for learning but also help to create and maintain classroom order.

TABLE 8.1 Increasing Students' Learning Time

- *Maintain activity flow*
    Avoid flip-flopping.
    Avoid "stimulus-bounded events" (being pulled away from the ongoing activity by an event or object that doesn't really need attention).
    Avoid overdwelling and fragmentation.
- *Minimize transition time*
    Have clear beginnings and endings: Bring the first activity to a halt, announce the transition, monitor the transition, make sure everyone is attentive, and begin the second activity.
    Prepare students for upcoming transitions.
    Establish clear routines.
- *Hold students accountable*
    Communicate assignments and requirements clearly.
    Monitor students' progress.
    Coordinate with special services to schedule pullouts to minimize disruption.
    Establish routines for collecting and checking classwork and homework.
    Maintain good records.

Maintaining Activity Flow

Tom Good and Jere Brophy (2008) observe that "four things can happen" when students must wait with nothing to do, and "three of them are bad: (1) Students may remain interested and attentive; (2) they may become bored or fatigued, losing the ability to concentrate; (3) they may become distracted or start daydreaming; or (4) they may actively misbehave" (p. 79). Given the three-to-one odds that waiting will result in undesirable behavior and a loss of valuable learning opportunities, it's essential for teachers to learn how to maintain the flow of classroom activities.

Once again, we turn for guidance to the work of Jacob Kounin (1970) who investigated differences in teachers' ability to initiate and maintain activity flow in classrooms. He then looked for relationships between activity flow and students' engagement and misbehavior.

Kounin's research identified many differences in the ways teachers orchestrated classroom activities. In some classrooms, activities flowed smoothly and briskly, but in others, activities were "jerky" and slow. Kounin even developed a special vocabulary to describe the problems he observed. For instance, he found that some ineffective managers would terminate an activity, start another, and then return to the first activity. Kounin called this *flip-flopping.* The following situation illustrates it: A foreign language teacher finishes reviewing homework with the class and tells students to turn to the next chapter in their textbook. She then stops and says, "Wait a minute. How many got all the homework exercises right? . . . Very good. . . . Okay, now let's talk about the imperfect tense."

Kounin also observed *stimulus-bounded events,* situations in which teachers are "pulled away" from the ongoing activity by a stimulus (an event or an object) that really doesn't need attention. Kounin describes the case of a teacher who is explaining a math problem at the board when she notices that a student is leaning on his left elbow as he works the problem. She leaves the board, instructs him to sit up straight, comments on his improved posture, and then returns to the board. Contrast this to how Donna reacts when an office aide shows up with a note: Donna takes the note without interrupting what she is doing and deals with it during the next logical break in her lesson.

Sometimes, teachers slow down the pace of activity by *overdwelling*—continuing to explain when students already understand or preaching at length about appropriate behavior. Another type of slowdown occurs when a teacher breaks an activity into components even though the activity could be performed as a single unit—what Kounin called *fragmentation.* Consider a science teacher making a transition from a laboratory task to work in another part of the classroom: "All right, everyone, please stand next to your lab stations. Make sure all of your lab equipment is washed and put away." The teacher moves to each lab station to check. "OK, good . . . now go back to your desks and sit down quietly." After all the students are seated, the teacher stands at the front of the room waiting until all students are silent. "Now, take out your textbook and turn to page 65. You are to work on problems 1–10 in your class notebook, so take out your notebook as well. There should be nothing on your desks but your textbook and notebook."

Flip-flops, stimulus-boundedness, overdwelling, fragmentation—all are threats to the flow of classroom activities. Not only do they result in lost learning time but they can also have a significant impact on students' behavior. When activities proceed smoothly and briskly, students are *more involved in work and less apt to misbehave.* Indeed, as Kounin concluded four decades ago, *activity flow plays a greater role in classroom order than the specific techniques that teachers use to handle misbehavior.*

During one visit to Sandy's classroom, we watched the skillful way she maintained the flow of activity in her class. It was the end of October, and students were in the middle of a very intriguing lab that involved the production of silver. As you read the vignette, note how Sandy ensures that there will be no "down time" by preparing the board for the homework review before class begins, by starting class promptly, by having students put homework problems on the board during the lab activity, and by ensuring that students will have something to do if they finish the lab before others.

11:21 Sandy writes the numbers 4 through 11 on the chalkboard, evenly spacing them across the entire width.

11:22 She positions herself by the classroom door to greet students as they enter the room.

11:23 The bell rings. Sandy moves from the door to the front of the room. "Hats off, please. We have a lot to do today. First, we have to finish the lab. Second, I want to review the chemical equation sheet you did. You'll put the final balanced equations on the board. And third, you'll learn to solve problems associated with the balanced equations. So let's get going."

11:24 The students move to lab tables, get their equipment, and begin working. While students are doing the lab, Sandy moves around the room, assisting, questioning, and monitoring. The atmosphere is very relaxed. Sandy smiles, laughs, and jokes with students about the silver they're producing. While she circulates, she also notes which students are just about finished with the lab and selects them to put the homework problems on the board: "Joe, are you finished? You have all your data? Okay, put number 4 up. Kim, you're finished? Please put number 5 on the board." They leave their lab tables, get their homework, and put their assigned problems on the board. By the time the lab is over, numbers 4 through 11 are up on the chalkboard.

11:33 Sandy notices that students are nearing the end of the lab. She tells them: "When you're finished, take your seats so I know you're finished." Students begin to move back to their seats; they take out their homework and begin to compare their answers to the work on the chalkboard.

11:37 The equipment is all put away, the lab tables have been cleaned, and the class is all seated.

11:38 Sandy introduces the problems on the chalkboard: "OK, let's turn to the equations on the board. Let me preface this by saying that you should not panic if you're having trouble writing formulas. You don't have to be able to write formulas until December. But what you do need to know now is how to balance the equations. All right, let's look at the first one." She turns to the first problem written on the board and begins the review.

12:00 All the problems have been discussed, and Sandy moves to the third activity. "Now I want you to listen very carefully. Do not take notes. I know this

> sounds strange, but I want you to be able to watch and listen and think. I'm going to show you a new type of problem." She writes a chemical equation on the board and challenges them to think about it. The students are stuck. Sandy lets them ponder the problem; she asks some easier questions to help them get started, and suggests they use paper if they want to. She walks around the room to see how they're doing, commenting on their efforts, encouraging them to consult with one another.

12:07 The bell rings. Students are still involved in trying to solve the problems. Sandy tells the class, "Think about this tonight, and come back with your ideas tomorrow."

Later, Sandy reflected on the day's lesson and talked about her very deliberate attempts to maintain the flow of activities:

> Some people would regard this as obsessive. Many teachers have kids finish the lab, sit down, and then put all the problems on the board. But what do you do when students are sitting there and others are putting things on the board? Even during labs, if they have to boil something for 10 minutes, I'll give them a problem to do. Kids can't just sit and watch something boil for 10 minutes. That's when they'll start squirting water bottles. There's so much to accomplish and so little time.

Minimizing Transition Time

From the perspective of time management, transitions between activities can be very problematic. An analysis by Gump (1982, 1987) helps us to understand the reasons. First, Gump observes, there could be difficulty "closing out" the first activity—especially if students are deeply engaged. (Ironically, the very involvement that teachers strive to achieve makes it more difficult to get students to switch activities!) Second, transitions are more loosely structured than activities themselves. Because there's usually more leeway in terms of socializing and moving around the room, there is also more opportunity for disruption. In fact, in a study of 50 classes taught by student teachers, there was almost twice as much disruption during transitions (e.g., hitting, yelling, obscene gestures) as during nontransition time (Arlin, 1979).

Third, students sometimes "save up" problems or tensions and deal with them during the transition time. They might seek out the teacher to complain about a grade, ask for permission to retrieve a book from a locker, or dump out the contents of their bookbags in search of a lost homework assignment. Although these behaviors are legitimate—and help to protect the adjacent activities from disturbance—they also make transitions more difficult to manage. Finally, there could be delays in getting students started on the second activity. Students might have difficulty settling down, or teachers could be held up because they are dealing with individual students' concerns or are busy assembling needed materials.

Gump's analysis suggests that teachers can reduce the potential for chaos by *preparing students for upcoming transitions, by establishing efficient transition routines,* and *by clearly defining the boundaries of lessons* (Ross, 1985). These guidelines are especially important for students with attention-deficit/hyperactivity disorder

(ADHD) and those with autism, who might have particular difficulty with transitions and changes in routine (McIntosh, Herman, Sanford, McGraw, & Florence, 2004).

ADVANCE PREPARATION

Transitions are far more chaotic when teachers fail to warn students about the imminent change of activity. This is illustrated in the following scenario observed by Arlin (1979):

> The lesson was still continuing when the bell would ring. Not having reached any closure, the teacher, with some degree of desperation, would say something like "OK, you can go," and pupils would charge out of the room, often knocking each other over. (Sometimes, pupils did not even wait for the signal from the teacher.) The teacher might then remember an announcement and interject to the dispersing mob, "Don't forget to bring back money for the trip!" (p. 50)

In contrast, our five teachers are very diligent "clock watchers." They take care to monitor time and to inform students when the class period is drawing to a close. They make sure that students are quiet and ready to leave and that they leave the room in an orderly fashion.

This is not as easy as it sounds, even for the four very experienced teachers. During one visit to Donnie's class, we watched both teacher and students get caught up in the lesson and lose track of time. When the bell rang, one girl actually blurted out, "Dang! That went fast!" Donnie laughingly agreed, broke off the lesson, and gave the homework assignment. Fortunately, she had taught her students early in the year that *she*, not the bell, dismissed them, so students stayed seated and attentive until she was finished.

In addition to warning students about the end of the period, it's also helpful to prepare them for changes in class activities during the period. In the following example, we see Fred explain to students what they will be doing that day and remind them periodically about how much time is left before they will be changing activities.

 The bell rings. Fred tells his students to take out paper and pencil while he distributes an article from *Newsweek* magazine regarding human rights and China. "While I meet with people one by one to go over grades, you will read and take notes on this article. You'll have about 12 minutes. At the end of that time, we will discuss these questions: What is the problem we're trying to solve between China and the United States? And is this just a case of Western arrogance? Take good notes—I'm going to collect them—and I will ask you to give an oral presentation of your views."

As students settle down to read, Fred gets out his grade book and sits at his desk. He quietly signals for individuals to come up to discuss their marking quarter grades. A few minutes later, he checks his watch. "Ladies and gentlemen, you have about seven more minutes to finish reading and taking notes."

Later, he issues another warning about the time: "About two more minutes, so you should be finishing up." At the end of 12 minutes, he gets up from his desk. "Okay, you've had enough time now to read the article and take some notes. At the bottom of the paper, please summarize in 25 words or less what the basic problem is between China and the United States."

THE USE OF TRANSITION ROUTINES

In Chapter 5, we talked about the importance of having clear, specific routines in order to keep the classroom running smoothly. At no time is the use of routines more important than during transitions. Well-established routines provide a structure to transitions that helps to prevent confusion and lost time.

In Christina's class, the routine for entering the room is very clear. Her students come in, take their seats, take out their journals, and begin writing on the journal topic posted on the board. According to Christina, using the journal achieves a number of objectives:

 Using this routine allows me to have students engaged in a meaningful activity while I'm taking attendance, checking homework, etc. The journal is a timed writing exercise that encourages fluency in writing. I make it clear that students are not allowed to stop writing until I signal that time is up. . . . Also, the journal entries are often related to the literature we're studying so they help to introduce or extend the reading. And having a daily journal assignment creates a nice, quiet atmosphere in which I can give instructions for the next activity.

Similarly, when Donna's students enter the classroom, they pick up their individual folders, take their seats, and do their "Daily Oral Language Assignment" while she takes roll. She stresses that this is not busywork that is disconnected from the lesson; rather, it assesses students' understanding of material covered the day before or provides a "kickoff" for the current lesson.

In many classrooms, the transition routines are *implicit,* and students are expected to figure out what to do by picking up on subtle cues. This might be fine for the majority of students, but those with ADHD, autism, or other disorders could have trouble and end up getting reprimanded. If you have students with such disorders in your classes, it is essential (and only fair) to spend time teaching them how to make efficient, orderly transitions. McIntosh and his colleagues (2004) suggest that you teach routines explicitly, provide "precorrections" and positive reinforcement, and actively supervise. These techniques are described more fully in the Practical Tips box.

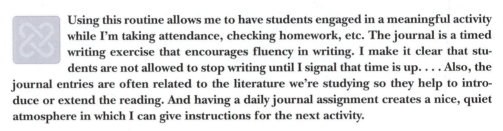

PRACTICAL TIPS FOR

Teaching Transitions

- Think about the transitions that occur during the period, such as the following.
    Entering and leaving the classroom.
    Putting materials away and preparing for the next task.
    Cleaning up a work area.
    Moving from group to independent work.
    Turning in homework.
    Choosing partners for small-group activities.
- Explicitly teach the expected transition behavior.

(continued on next page)

Model the behavior using both correct and incorrect examples.

Provide opportunities for students to practice.

Provide feedback.

Reteach if needed.

■ Provide precorrections (reminders of the expected behavior *before* the transition begins).

■ Provide positive reinforcement for efficient, orderly transitions.

Give specific praise or special privileges and activities.

Use tangible rewards if necessary.

■ Actively supervise the transition.

Scan the room, looking for both appropriate and inappropriate behavior.

Walk around the room, using proximity to encourage students to engage in the appropriate behavior.

Interact with students during the transition, providing reminders and specific praise.

Source: McIntosh, Herman, Sanford, McGraw, & Florence, 2004.

CLEAR BEGINNINGS AND ENDINGS

Transitions proceed more smoothly if teachers bring the first activity to a halt, announce the transition, allow time to make sure that everyone is attentive, and then begin the second activity (Arlin, 1979). In other words, smooth transitions are characterized by well-defined boundaries.

In the following vignette, we see Christina implement a transition with well-defined boundaries. Watch the way she prepares her students for the transition from small-group work to a whole-class activity.

 Students are seated in clusters of four or five, working on the poetry lessons they are creating for the rest of the class. Christina is circulating. She checks the clock and then moves to the front of the room. "May I have your attention please? We are ready to move to the next part of the lesson. Please listen carefully to all of my instructions and do not move until I tell you to. First, you will have one member of your group hand in your assignment. This person will check to make sure each person's name is on the paper. Then you will return to your regular seats, take out your notebooks and textbooks and open your books to page 295. Also, have a pen out and on your desk. When you are settled, please begin reading the brief introduction on page 295. Are there any questions? Good. You may move now."

Later, when we commented on how quickly and efficiently her students had made the transition, Christina observed that it was sometimes difficult to get students to wait patiently for instructions:

 What I mean is, if the transition will require a series of movements, they want to move as soon as you give them the first direction. If you allow them to do this, they won't hear the rest of the directions. The transition time will actually be longer, since you'll have to spend time repeating everything. I've learned to tell them, "Don't move until I'm finished."

Sometimes, in an effort to maintain activity flow, teachers rush into instructions and activities without checking that students are "with them." Arlin (1979) writes: "Several times I noticed over 15 children continuing the previous activity while the teacher was giving directions for the new activity" (p. 50). Needless to say, those teachers then became exasperated when students asked questions about what to do. On the other hand, Gump (1982) warns that waiting *too* long can cause a loss of momentum: "Waiting for absolute and universal attention can sometimes lead to unnecessarily extended transition times" (p. 112). Gump reminds us that by keeping the instructional program going, teachers can often "pull in" students whose attention has momentarily wandered.

Holding Students Accountable

Walter Doyle (1983) has commented that students tend to take assignments seriously only if they are held accountable for them. Your own school experiences probably testify to the truth of this statement. Even as adults, it takes a good deal of self-discipline and maturity to put your best effort into work that no one will ever see. And secondary students are *adolescents*. Unless they know that they will have to account for their performance, it is unlikely that they'll make the best use of class time.

Furthermore, students are *unable* to make good use of their time if they are confused about what they're supposed to be doing. Teachers sometimes tell students to "get to work" and are immediately bombarded by questions: "Can I use pen?" "Do I have to write down the questions or can I just put the answers?" "Do we have to show all our work?" "Can I work at the lab table?" When this happens, precious class time has to be spent clarifying the original instructions.

To help students use their time wisely, teachers must *communicate assignments and requirements clearly and monitor students' progress* (Emmer & Evertson, 2013). Before students begin to work, for example, you should explain what they'll be doing and why, how to get help, what to do with completed work, what to do when they're finished, and how long they'll be spending on the task. You also need to make sure that students are familiar with your work standards—for example, what type of paper to use, whether they should use pencil or pen, how to number the page, whether or not erasures are allowed, and what it means to "show all their work." Once you've given your instructions, have students explain what they will be doing in their own words and give them a chance to ask questions. Asking, "Does everyone understand?" rarely yields useful information.

In addition to providing explicit directions for in-class activities, teachers need to *communicate homework assignments in a clear, organized manner*. This is particularly important if you are working with students who have difficulty remembering what they are supposed to do. Sandy has devised a routine for assigning homework that she first developed to help students with learning disabilities. She soon realized, however, that the routine was helpful for everyone:

> **When I first write a homework assignment on the board, I write it really big in the middle of the board and tell students to copy it down now. Then I move it to the left-hand corner of the board where it remains until the due date. Periodically, I remind students about it. I'm also really clear about the numbers of the problems that students have to do. For example, if the assignment is to do**

numbers 1 through 5, and then 7, 9, 11, and 13 through 16, I'll write out 1, 2, 3, 4, and 5, because some kids (especially my learning disabled students) don't see the difference between the comma and the dash.

Christina is also very diligent about writing out assignments and directions, especially for big projects. Sometimes she provides a printed hand-out with detailed instructions. Other times, she'll have students copy the directions from the board. During one meeting, she explained why she gives such explicit directions:

> Not only does this help to alleviate the number of questions I need to answer—over and over again—it also makes students accountable for the details of the assignment. They can't say, "You didn't tell us we needed five sources" if they've copied it down from the board, or "You didn't say to use textual evidence to support our answers" if the written hand-out states this requirement. I've also learned that doing this is useful for meeting with parents because you have every assignment documented. I save all my hand-outs and files with the directions. This way, I can prove I stated the requirements to students (and to parents on the rare occasions when I'm questioned). And I also save myself from rewriting directions when I'm using an assignment again.

Once you've given directions for an assignment and your class gets to work, it's important to *monitor how students are doing by circulating around the room*. This practice enables you to track students' progress, to identify and help with problems, and to verify that assignments are matched to students' ability. Circulating also helps to ensure that students are using their time well.

Observations of our five teachers revealed that they rarely sit down unless they're working with a small group.

> Donnie's class is working with rulers and protractors to discover the properties of parallelograms. As students work, Donnie continually circulates. She keeps up a steady stream of comments, questions, and praise: "Very good, Veronica." "Everybody finished with that first question?" "Answer the questions as you go, so you'll have all the answers when you finish." "Anyone need help?" "What does consecutive mean, José?" "Is there anyone who's having problems with the protractor?"

After class, Donnie talked about the fact that she is constantly on the move:

> I don't see how a person can teach math and sit down. I just wouldn't feel comfortable sitting down. You have to write on the board, you have to guide students through the problems, you have to see they're on the right track. By walking around the room, I can catch mistakes. I can ask, "What were you doing here? Explain your reasoning." I can talk them through the problem. I have to be up and moving when I'm teaching.

In addition, it's essential to monitor whether students are regularly completing assignments. This requires you to *establish routines for collecting and checking classwork and homework.* For example, at the beginning of class, Donnie has students take out their homework and put it on their tables. While they review the assignment, she circulates around the room and notes in her grade book who has done the homework. The whole procedure takes just a few minutes and there's no loss of instructional time because the class is simultaneously going over the homework problems.

Sandy uses a different system. She has a folder for each class that she keeps on the front table. Homework assignments are to be placed in the folder at the very beginning of class. She gives a "last call for homework," and then closes the folder. Sometime during the period, Sandy checks the papers to see if any assignments are missing. This allows her to verify immediately that she does not have an assignment from a particular student and to find out what happened. As she puts it, "This way I can avoid the situation where a student says, 'But I *did* do the homework. You must have lost it.'"

It's especially important to *keep track of students' progress on long-term homework assignments.* By establishing intermediate checkpoints, you can help students develop a "plan of attack." For example, if they are writing a research paper, you can set due dates on which they have to submit each stage of the assignment (e.g., the topic; preliminary notes; a list of references; the first draft; the final draft). This not only allows you to monitor students' progress but also helps to lessen the anxiety that adolescents sometimes feel when faced with a large assignment.

Fred tells an ironic story that points out the value of this approach:

Last year, my students did a long research paper. I had them turn in each piece to show me how they were coming along—a working outline, a bibliography, their notes, a rough draft, and then the final copy. I used a point system. The first four parts of the assignment were worth 10 points each; the final copy was worth 60 points.

This year, I decided it was babyish to do this, so I didn't do it. I told my classes, "I'm going to treat you like adults," and they said, "Great. We can do it." Well, they didn't get their papers in. They told me, "We messed up. We let it go, we procrastinated." They asked me to do what I had done last year! I trusted them to be mature, and they said, "We're not."

Finally, you need to *maintain records of what students are accomplishing.* In some districts, teachers can develop their own system for recording students' progress; others require teachers to follow a prescribed format. For example, Donnie's grade book has to reflect her weekly lessons plans and the "quarterly topic plans" she has to submit four times a year; following the district's objectives for her courses, these plans describe what she will be teaching day by day. For each marking period, Donnie must have two grades per week for homework and at least one test grade per objective. If five objectives are to be covered during a particular marking period, then Donnie would have to have at least five test grades.

In contrast, Fred is allowed to develop his own recordkeeping system. Nonetheless, like Donnie, he is careful to keep up-to-date records of students' progress. He explained his recordkeeping system to students at the very beginning of the year:

I want to take a minute or two to discuss grades with you. I keep your grades on the computer. What I use is homework, classwork, projects, tests, and quizzes. Each in-class assignment is about four points. A big exam would be worth about five in-class assignments—about 20 points. The total point value for the marking period is 120–130 points. . . . It's important to me that everyone in here passes this class and does well. If you need me to get on your case, so you'll do okay in here, let me know. Remember, the grades are yours. You can see them at any time.

Checking or grading all the work that students do each day is an arduous, time-consuming task. As Donna noted:

I recall my first couple of years of teaching. I graded everything. I think each quarter the students had about 50 graded assignments in my grade book. It was a nightmare and unnecessary. About year four, I realized I didn't need to grade every little thing. I also discovered the power of rubrics and how students could use them to gauge the quality of their own work. Using rubrics allows me more one-on-one time with students who need additional help in a specific area rather than spending time worrying about "little grades." And, most students perform just as well on the end-of-unit quizzes as the students who were obsessively graded.

We asked our teachers how they handle the paperwork. Their ideas are listed in the Practical Tips box.

PRACTICAL TIPS FOR

Handling Paperwork

- Check that students do in-class assignments and routine homework, but don't spend a lot of time reading and grading these. Develop a simple system for keeping track of students' routine assignments (e.g., four points for full credit; 3.5 points for an almost-completed assignment, etc.).
- Review homework every day, but have students check their own work. In your grade book, enter a check (as opposed to a grade) to show who has done the assignment. Have students grade one homework assignment each week that you record in your grade book. Collect one homework assignment each week to grade yourself.
- For the first few assignments, read *everything* really carefully. For example, review lab reports with a fine-tooth comb. That way, students come to see that you have really high expectations and that they have to be clear and thorough. Then, later, you can skim the first few pages (objectives, procedures, materials) and spend the bulk of your time on the data section.
- Refuse to grade papers that contain more than three technical errors (spelling, punctuation, etc.). (Fred tells his students, "I have 100 of these to grade; it's not fair for me to sit here and correct your spelling mistakes. I'm not here to proofread. . . . Have someone who's good at this proofread your papers before you turn them in.")
- Instruct students in proper editing, revision, and response procedures so they can provide feedback to one another. (For example, Christina provides a detailed response on the first draft of the first section of a long research paper. Then students use a checklist with marking instructions to provide feedback to one another on the second and third sections of the paper.)

(continued on next page)

- On tests, create "structured essay" questions. Construct your own answer to the essay. (Know what the essay is "supposed to say.") Look for key words when grading.
- Use detailed rubrics to provide feedback without having to write the same comments over and over again.
- Think of "time-spent-grading" as part of your lesson plans. Carefully plan activities and due dates to allow you enough time to grade assignments. (For example, after Christina collects research papers, she plans for students to be primarily engaged in classwork assignments that she can monitor without collecting very much paperwork. This allows her to spend the majority of her grading time on the research papers.)

THE USE OF BLOCK SCHEDULING

Many secondary schools have moved to block scheduling in an effort to maximize time for learning, to encourage the use of varied instructional strategies, and to allow teachers and students to explore topics in depth. There are two common scheduling configurations. On the 4 × 4 *block schedule,* four 80- or 90-minute instructional blocks are scheduled each day instead of the traditional six or seven. Because classes meet every day, a course that would normally last a year is completed in one semester or 90 days, and students take only four courses at a time. The *A-B, or alternating day, schedule* also offers four extended periods each day, but classes meet every other day for the entire school year. This means that students still take six or seven courses at one time.

Although one 80- or 90-minute block does not actually provide more contact time with students than two 42- or 50-minute periods, advocates of block scheduling contend that the extended class provides more *usable instructional time* (Fleming, Olenn, Schoenstein, & Eineder, 1997). Because classes meet half as many times, the time spent in routine tasks at the beginning of the period (e.g., taking attendance, getting students settled in, distributing materials) and at the end (e.g., talking about homework, getting packed up) is also halved. More importantly, instructional time is less fragmented.

At this point, research examining the effects of block scheduling on achievement is inconsistent with some studies showing academic gains (e.g., Lewis, Dugan, Winokur, & Cobb, 2005; Nichols, 2005), some showing no difference (e.g., Bottge, Gugerty, Serlin, & Moon, 2003), and some actually finding negative effects (e.g., Gruber & Onwuegbuzie, 2001). On the other hand, block scheduling *does* seem to lead to a more relaxed school climate and a decline in discipline problems—possibly because it cuts down on hallway traffic (Shortt & Thayer, 1998/99; Zepeda & Mayers, 2006). On the 4 × 4 schedule, teachers have an additional benefit: They generally teach only *three* classes a day instead of four or five, so they are responsible for approximately 75–90 students at a time rather than 125 or 150. Undoubtedly, this makes developing more attentive, caring relationships with students easier.

Unfortunately, block scheduling does not always result in the type of innovative, varied instruction that proponents envision (Queen, 2000). Richard Elmore (2002), an expert on school restructuring, reports that he once asked a high school social studies teacher what he thought of block scheduling. The teacher replied that it was the best thing that had ever happened in his teaching career. When Elmore asked why, the teacher explained: "Now we can show the whole movie." As this anecdote suggests, changing the *structure* of time doesn't always change the *use* of time. For example, in a study of 48 extended classes (Bush and Johnstone, 2000), teachers in algebra, biology, English, and U.S. history spent the majority of time doing traditional, teacher-centered instruction. One high school senior observed that having an 80-minute class can *"simply create more time for students to daydream, scribble in their notebooks or catch up on sleep"* (Shanley, 1999).

Although Christina recognizes the truth of this comment, she is an enthusiastic advocate of her school's 4 × 4 block schedule. During visits to her classroom, we observed the way she uses a variety of instructional formats—whole-group presentation, small-group work, student-led discussion, writing, student presentations—to maintain students' engagement and promote active participation. She might also include a variety of the content areas that comprise "English class." In the following excerpt, we see a class in which students write individually in their journals, work on reading strategy development in small groups, learn the format for a reference or "works cited" page in a mini-lesson, and act out a play they have been reading:

11:35 **Students enter, take their seats, read the journal entry written on the board, and begin to write on the day's topic: "Write about how your life would have been changed if one day in your past had come out differently. What actually happened that day?" While students write, Christina silently takes attendance.**

11:50 **Christina gives the agenda for the class: "First you're going to meet in your groups to practice making inferences. Then we'll have a mini-lesson on creating a works-cited page. On Wednesday, you'll be giving your speeches. I'll collect all the written components before you give your speeches, so I want to review what you'll need to turn in. Finally, we'll finish reading *Antigone*."**

11:52 **Students get into their small groups to practice making inferences. Christina circulates and assists.**

12:18 **Christina announces that the groups have two more minutes to work.**

12:20 **Students move the chairs back into rows and return to their regular seats. Christina tells them to take out their notebooks and turn to the section on doing research, stating that she wants to explain how to do the "works-cited" page for their research papers. While she reviews the required format with examples on the board, students are very attentive, taking notes and asking questions.**

12:40 **"Okay, guys, let's form the Greek Theater so we can finish reading *Antigone*." Students get into a new configuration, roughly a circle, with the "chorus" at one end and an opening for the entrance to the "stage." "We left off on page 337. Chorus, take your places." Christina reads the stage directions, and students begin acting out *Antigone,* ending with the queen's death. A boy reads the last speech of the play.**

12:58 **"All right, everyone, move your desks back to where they belong and listen to what you're going to do next." After students are back in their regular seats, Christina announces the final activity of the period: "Open your journals and open your book. You have four minutes. Write about the last speech you just heard. What does it mean? Why is it important? Do you agree with it?"**

1:02 **Students finish their journal entries. The bell rings.**

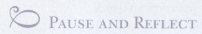

PAUSE AND REFLECT

Would you prefer to teach on a block schedule or a traditional schedule? What are your reasons? Do you think the difference in the length of the period would make a difference in your instruction?

CONCLUDING COMMENTS

Tracy Kidder's book, *Among Schoolchildren* (1989), describes one year in the life of Chris Zajac, an elementary teacher who's feisty, demanding, blunt, fair, funny, and hard working. At the very end of the book, Kidder describes Chris' thoughts on the last day of school. Although she is convinced that she belongs "among schoolchildren," Chris laments the fact that she hadn't been able to help all her students—at least not enough:

> Again this year, some had needed more help than she could provide. There were many problems that she hadn't solved. But it wasn't for lack of trying. She hadn't given up. She had run out of time. (p. 331)

Like Chris, we all run out of time. The end of the year comes much too quickly, and some students' needs are much too great. Hopefully, the concepts and guidelines presented in this chapter will help you to make good use of the limited time you have.

SUMMARY

This chapter described time as a "precious resource." First, it considered the amount of school time that is actually available for teaching and learning. Then it described three strategies for increasing students' academic learning time: maintaining activity flow, minimizing transition time, and holding students accountable. The last section of the chapter examined the use of block scheduling.

Types of Time

- *Mandated time:* The time the state requires school to be in session.
- *Available time:* The mandated time minus the time lost to absences, special events, half-days.
- *Instructional time:* The time that is actually used for instruction.
- *Engaged time:* The time a student spends working attentively on academic tasks.
- *Productive learning time:* The proportion of engaged time in which students are doing work that is meaningful and appropriate.

How to Increase Hours for Learning

- Maintain activity flow by avoiding:
    Flip-flopping.
    Stimulus-bounded events.
    Overdwelling.
    Fragmentation.
- Minimize transition time by:
    Defining boundaries to lessons.
    Preparing students for transitions.
    Establishing routines.
- Hold students accountable by:
    Communicating assignments and requirements clearly.
    Monitoring students' progress.
    Establishing routines for collecting and checking classwork and homework.
    Maintaining good records.

Block Scheduling

- Types of block scheduling
    4 × 4 block schedule: Four 80- or 90-minute instructional blocks scheduled each day for one semester or 90 days; students take four classes at a time.
    A-B, or alternating day, schedule: Instructional periods of 80 or 90 minutes for classes that meet every other day for the entire school year; students take six or seven courses at a time.
- Advantages
    More usable instructional time.
    Less fragmented instructional time.
    More relaxed school climate.
    Decreased hallway traffic.
    Opportunities for the use of varied instructional strategies.
- Problems
    Doesn't always result in the innovative, varied instruction that proponents envision.

By using time wisely, you can maximize opportunities for learning and minimize occasions for disruption in your classroom. Think about how much time is being spent on meaningful and appropriate work in your room and how much is being eaten up by business and clerical tasks. Be aware that the number of hours available for instruction are much fewer than they first appear.

ACTIVITIES FOR SKILL BUILDING AND REFLECTION

In Class

Read the following vignette and identify the factors that threaten the activity flow of the lesson. Once you have identified the problems, rewrite the vignette so that activity flow is maintained *or* explain how you would avoid the problems if you were the teacher.

Mrs. P. waits while her sophomore "A" level students take out the 10 mixed number addition problems she had them do for homework last night. Ryan raises his hand. "I brought the wrong book by mistake, Mrs. P. My locker is right across the hall. Can I get my math book?"

"Be quick, Ryan. We have 10 problems to go over, and the period is only 50 minutes long." Ryan leaves, and Mrs. P. turns back to the class. "OK, this is what I want you to do. Switch papers with your neighbor." She waits while students figure out who will be partners with whom. She scans the room, trying to make sure that everyone has a partner. "OK, now write your name at the bottom of the page, on the right-hand side, to show that you're the checker. When I collect these papers, I want to know who the checkers were, so I can see who did a really accurate, responsible job of checking." She circulates while students write their names at the bottom of the page. "Ariadis, I said the right-hand side." Ariadis erases her name and rewrites it on the right side. "OK, now let's go over the answers. If your neighbor didn't get the right answer, put a circle around the problem and try to figure out what they did wrong so you can explain it to them. OK, number one, what's the right answer?" A student in the rear of the class raises his hand. "Noah?"

"I don't have a partner, Mrs. P. Can I go to the bathroom?"

"Ryan will be right back, and then you'll have a partner. Just wait until we finish going over the homework." Ryan returns. "Take a seat near Noah, Ryan, and exchange homework papers with him."

Ryan looks sheepishly at Mrs. P. "It's not in my book, Mrs. P. I must have left it on my desk last night. I was working on it pretty late."

"Class, go over the answers to problems 1 and 2 with your neighbors. See if you agree, and if you did the problems the same way. Ryan, step outside."

Noah waves his hand again. "Mrs. P., can I please go to the bathroom now?"

"Yes, Noah. Fill out a pass, and I'll sign it. Just get back quickly." Noah leaves for the restroom. Leaving the door open so she can keep an eye on the other students, Mrs. P. follows Ryan out of class. "You haven't had your homework done three times in the last two weeks, Ryan. What's the problem?"

"Well, Mrs. P., my mother's been. . . . " The office intercom phone buzzes.

"Want me to get that, Mrs. P.?" a student calls from the class.

"Yes, tell them I'll be right there."

"They said to just tell you that Noah has to go to the office if he's not doing anything right now."

"Go take your seat, Ryan. I'll talk to you after class." Mrs. P. moves to the front of the room again. "I'm sorry, class, let's begin again. Did you all do numbers 1 and 2?" The class murmurs assent. "OK, number 3. Let's start with problem 3. Abby?"

Abby gives the correct answer. Mrs. P. gets responses and explanations for three more homework problems. As the class reviews the homework, she wanders up and down the rows. As she passes Tanya's desk, she notices a pink slip of paper. "Class, I almost forgot to collect the slips for the Academic Fair. This fair is a chance for us to show how much progress we've made this year in math. How many of you remembered to fill out the slip, describing the project you're going to do?" Students proceed to hunt through their backpacks and flip through their math books. Those who find their pink slips give them to Mrs. P. She reminds the others to return them tomorrow. "OK, let's get back to problem. . . . 6, no, 7. We were on 7, right? Shakia." Shakia begins to respond. Then Noah returns. A student in a seat by the door reminds Mrs. P. that Noah has to go to the office. "Noah, go to Mr. Wilkins's office."

"Why, Mrs. P.? All I did was go to the john."

"I don't know, Noah. Just go and make it quick. We're trying to have a class." Noah leaves, and Mrs. P. turns to the class. "Pass your papers to the front. I'll check the rest for you and give you credit for your homework. We need to move on to subtraction with fractions. Who can think of a real-life problem where you would need to subtract fractions? Kayla?"

"Can I go to the nurse, Mrs. P.? I don't feel good."

On Your Own

1. While you are visiting a class, carefully observe the way the teacher uses the time. Keep an accurate record for a complete period, noting how much of the available time is actually used for *instructional purposes.*

2. Observe a class that is on a block schedule. How is the extended time used? What instructional strategies are used (e.g., lecture, cooperative learning, discussion, simulations)? How long does each instructional strategy last? Does the teacher make use of the entire period? Do students seem able to sustain attention and involvement?

For Your Portfolio

Develop a transition routine for each of the following situations. Remember, your goal is to use time wisely.

1. Beginning the class each day.
2. Taking attendance.
3. Checking homework.
4. Collecting papers.
5. Returning papers.
6. Moving from the whole group into small groups.
7. Ending class each day.
8. Leaving class at the end of the period.

FOR FURTHER READING

Gabrieli, C., & Goldstein, W. (2008). *Time to learn: How a new school schedule is making smarter kids, happier parents, and safer neighborhoods.* San Francisco, CA: Jossey-Bass.

  Using common sense, experience, hard data, and personal observation, the authors of this book argue that the current school day is obsolete and out of step with the reality of working families without a stay-at-home parent.

Intrator, S. M. (2004). The engaged classroom. *Educational Leadership, 62*(1), 20–24.

  Sam Intrator, a college professor, spent 130 days shadowing students in a diverse California high school to understand the "experiential terrain of students' class time." In this article, he describes the different types of time that students experience: slow time, lost time, fake time, worry time, play time, and engaged time.

Shernoff, D. J., Csikszentmihalyi, M., Schneider, B., & Shernoff, E. S. (2003). Student engagement in high school classrooms from the perspective of flow theory. *School Psychology Quarterly, 18*(2), 158–176.

This study investigated how 526 high school students spent their time in school and the conditions under which they reported being engaged. Participants experienced higher engagement when the perceived challenge of the task and their own skills were high and in balance, when instruction was relevant, and when the learning environment was under their control.

Smith, B. (2000). Quantity matters: Annual instructional time in an urban school system. *Educational Administration Quarterly, 36*(5), 652–682.

The official time policy of the Chicago public elementary schools is to provide students with 300 minutes of instruction per day for 180 school days per year. This adds up to 900 hours of instruction annually. But based on classroom observation records, field notes, teacher interviews, school calendars, and other documents, this report concludes that nearly half of Chicago students could be receiving only 40 percent to 50 percent of the recommended hours.

ORGANIZATIONAL RESOURCES

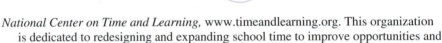

National Center on Time and Learning, www.timeandlearning.org. This organization is dedicated to redesigning and expanding school time to improve opportunities and outcomes for all students.

PART III

Organizing and Managing Instruction

Educators sometimes talk about classroom management and instruction as though the two were completely distinct and separate aspects of teaching. From this perspective, management and instruction occur in chronological sequence. First you establish rules, routines, and consequences; build positive relationships with students; and promote community. Then you begin to teach.

In contrast, we see these two tasks as being closely entwined—even inseparable. Consider the following scenarios:

> *Mr. Carson is checking on his eighth-grade students' understanding of metaphors and similes. He addresses his questions to the students sitting in the front-center of the classroom and calls only on volunteers. The result is that 6 of his 28 students are involved in the review, 2 have their heads down on their desks, 3 are looking at their cell phones, 5 are fiddling with materials in their desks or backpacks, and the rest are staring off into space. With obvious annoyance, Mr. Carson reprimands those who are not participating.*

> *Ms. Guerraro has divided her algebra class into small groups to graph the following equation: $y = 2x + 3$. She has told them to work together to select the x values, compute the y values, and plot the points, to make sure that they all understand the process, and to check to see that they all get the same line. In one group, students are all working independently, choosing their own x values. In another group, students are arguing over which values to select, and comments like, "That's stupid" are audible. In still another group, one boy has taken over and is simply telling the other group members which values to select. Meanwhile, Ms. Guerraro is grading papers at her desk. She occasionally looks up, scans the room, and tells students to get to work.*

In each of these situations, the students' lack of engagement and their inappropriate behaviors might have been avoided had the teachers understood the relationship between good instruction and classroom management. As we pointed out in Chapter 1, to avoid disorder problems, teachers not only must foster positive relationships and use good preventive management strategies but also must implement well-paced, organized, and engaging instruction.

In this section, we consider ways to plan and implement instruction to promote students' involvement and learning. Chapter 9 argues that teachers are responsible for stimulating students' motivation to learn and offers a variety of motivational strategies drawn from research, theory, and the practice of our five teachers. Chapters 10 and 11 examine four types of instruction that regularly arise in secondary classrooms: independent work (also known as *seatwork*), recitations, discussions, and small-group work (including cooperative learning). For each of these, we describe the unique managerial challenges that teachers need to be aware of and suggest ways to structure the instruction to increase the probability of success. As always, we draw on the experiences of our five teachers.

Enhancing Students' Motivation to Learn

Sitting in the teachers' room of a large suburban high school, we overheard a conversation among members of the social studies department. One ninth-grade teacher was complaining loudly about his third-period class: "These kids don't care about school. I'm not going to waste my time trying to get them motivated. If they can't be responsible for their own learning by now, it's just too bad." As we reflected on the teacher's statement, it seemed that he was suggesting that motivation is entirely the student's responsibility; to be successful in school, students must arrive motivated, just as they must arrive with notebooks and pens. The statement also suggests that motivation is a stable characteristic like eye color. From this perspective, some individuals come to school wanting to learn, and some don't. This can be a comforting point of view: If motivation is an innate or unchangeable characteristic, then we don't have to spend time and energy figuring out ways to motivate students.

On the other hand, some educators argue that motivation is an acquired disposition that is amenable to change. It can also be situation specific, varying with the nature of the particular activity. Thus, students in world language classes can be enthusiastic about role-playing a visit to a restaurant but can appear bored and uninterested when it's time to conjugate verbs.

According to this latter perspective, teachers are responsible for stimulating students' engagement in learning activities. It can be gratifying (and a lot easier) when students come to school already excited about learning; however, when this is not the case, teachers must redouble their efforts to create a classroom context that fosters students' involvement and interest. This year, for example, one of Fred's classes has a large proportion of students who, according to him, are "just marking time." During one conversation, Fred shared both his frustration and his determination:

 These kids are a constant struggle—the toughest kind of kids to work with. They're not dumb; they're not bad; they're just not intrinsically motivated when it comes to school. And they're used to taking it easy; for the last three years of high school, they've found that passive resistance works. They're so passive that teachers just leave them alone. But I refuse to give up on them. I look them in the face and say, "Tell me you want to stay home and be a slug and I'll leave you alone." And nobody's told me that. Actually, I think they're finally getting resigned to the fact that they can't coast in my class. And they can't even be mad at me, because they know that I'm on their side.

As Fred's comment indicates, stimulating students' motivation is easier said than done, especially when dealing with adolescents. The downturn in motivation during the transition years from elementary to secondary school is well documented (Anderman & Mueller, 2010)—and it is often dismaying to beginning teachers, particularly those who are passionate about their subject fields. Consider this entry taken from the journal of a student teacher in English:

I began my student teaching with all of these grand ideas about how I was going to enlighten students to the beauty of literature and unlock all the insight and talent that had been buried. . . . I gave serious, complicated lectures and multitudes of homework assignments, sure that my students would all be grateful when they witnessed the emergence of their intellectual prowess. Somewhere in the middle of the third week, however, the truth came rearing its ugly head: Most of my students did not, and probably never would, approach literature with [as much] enthusiasm [as they feel for] a new video game.

To assist teachers who find themselves in this all too familiar situation, this chapter focuses on ways to enhance students' motivation. We begin by reflecting on what is realistic and appropriate with respect to motivating secondary students. We then examine the factors that give rise to motivation. Finally, we consider a variety of motivational strategies drawn from research, theory, and the practice of our five teachers.

 PAUSE AND REFLECT

Think of a time when you were extremely motivated to learn. It might have been the preparation for your driver's license test or the winter you learned to ski. Why were you motivated to learn? What supported you in your learning? What made it a successful experience? Try to relate your experiences to what you will be doing every day in your classroom.

MOTIVATION: WHAT IS REALISTIC?
WHAT IS APPROPRIATE?

Many of the teacher education students with whom we've worked believe that teachers motivate students *by making learning fun.* In fact, they frequently mention the ability to design activities that are enjoyable and entertaining as one of the defining characteristics of the "good teacher." Yet as Jere Brophy (2010) reminds us, "Schools are not day camps or recreational centers" (p. xi), and teachers are not counselors or recreational directors. Given compulsory attendance, required curricula, class sizes that inhibit individualization, and the specter of high-stakes standardized testing, trying to ensure that learning is always fun is unreasonable and unrealistic. Bill Ayers (2010), a professor of education who has taught preschool through graduate school, is even more blunt. Characterizing the idea that good teachers make learning fun as one of the common myths that plague teaching, Ayers writes:

> Fun is distracting, amusing, diverting. Clowns are fun. Jokes can be fun. Learning can be engaging, engrossing, amazing, disorienting, involving, and often deeply pleasurable. If it's delightful, joyful, or festive, even better. But it doesn't need to be fun. (p. 24)

On the first day of school, Donna tells her middle-school students,

I'm not going to kid you—I'm hard. I have high expectations for you and myself. But I promise that I will be here for you. You won't always like what we do in this class; it isn't camp! This is a place of learning, and it isn't always what you like. But I love it when I see former students and they say, "Man, you were hard, but you taught me how to write, how to edit, and to enjoy this author. My freshman high school English class is easy in comparison to yours!"

Probably all of us can remember situations in which we were motivated to accomplish an academic task that was not fun but that nonetheless seemed worthwhile and meaningful. The example that immediately comes to our minds is learning a foreign language. Neither of us has ever been very good at languages, and we were anxious and self-conscious whenever we had to speak in language class. We found conversation and oral exercises painful; role-plays were excruciating. Yet one of us took three years of French in high school and two more in college, and the other one took three semesters of Spanish well after finishing college. Both of us were determined to communicate as fluently as possible when we visited foreign countries.

Brophy (2010) refers to this kind of drive as *motivation to learn*—the "tendency to find academic activities meaningful and worthwhile and to try to get the intended learning benefits from them" (p. 11). He distinguishes motivation to learn from *intrinsic motivation,* in which individuals pursue academic activities because they find them pleasurable. At times, of course, you might be able to capitalize on students' intrinsic interests so that they will perceive learning activities as fun. But it's unlikely that this will always be the case. For this reason, teachers need to consider ways to develop and maintain students' motivation to learn.

An Expectancy × Value Framework

It is helpful to think about stimulating motivation to learn in terms of an expectancy × value (or expectancy-times-value model) (Brophy, 2010; Wigfield & Eccles, 2000). This model posits that motivation depends on *students' expectation of success* and *the value they place on the task* (or the rewards that it might bring—such as being able to speak fluent French). The two factors work together like a multiplication equation (expectancy × value): If either one is missing (i.e., zero), there will be no motivation.

The expectancy × value model suggests that you have two major responsibilities with respect to motivation. *First, you need to ensure that students can perform the task at hand successfully if they expend the effort.* This means creating assignments that are well suited to students' achievement levels. This can also mean helping students to recognize their ability to perform successfully. Consider the case of Helpless Hannah (Stipek, 2002). During math class, she frequently sits at her desk doing nothing. If the teacher urges Hannah to try one of the problems she is supposed to be doing, she claims she can't. When the teacher walks her through a problem step by step, Hannah answers most of the questions correctly, but she insists that she was only guessing. Hannah considers herself incompetent, and she interprets her teacher's frustration as proof of her incompetence. Her behavior is a classic example of "learned helplessness" (Stipek, p. 2).

Fortunately, extreme cases such as Hannah's are uncommon (Stipek, 2002). But we've probably all encountered situations in which anticipation of failure has led to avoidance or paralysis. A lengthy term paper assignment is overwhelming, so we procrastinate until it's too late to do it really well. Calculus is daunting, so we take general mathematics instead. If failure is inevitable, there's no point in trying. And if we rarely try, we rarely succeed.

A second responsibility of teachers is to help students recognize the value of the academic work at hand. For example, Satisfied Santos (Stipek, 2002) is the class clown. He earns grades of C+ and B– although he's clearly capable of earning As. At home, Santos spends hours at his computer, reads every book he can find on space, loves science fiction, and has even written a short novel. But he displays little interest in schoolwork. If assignments coincide with his personal interests, he exerts effort; otherwise, he simply sees no point in doing them.

To help students like Santos, you need to enhance the value of class activities. For example, because Santos likes to interact with his peers, you might use small-group activities in class. To allow him to demonstrate his interests, Santos's English teacher might invite him to share excerpts from the novel he has written. His biology teacher might ask him to explain the science in his favorite science-fiction novel. Another strategy is to communicate the value of the *rewards* that successful completion or mastery will bring. For example, Santos might see little value in learning history but still recognize that a passing grade is required if he wishes to continue his study of science in college.

In accordance with the expectancy × value model, Brophy (2010) has reviewed relevant theory and research and derived a set of strategies that teachers can use to enhance students' motivation. The following sections of this chapter are based on Brophy's work. (See Table 9.1.) We begin with strategies that focus on the first variable in the model—students' expectations of success.

TABLE 9.1 Brophy's Strategies for Enhancing Motivation to Learn

Strategies for Increasing Expectations of Success
- Provide opportunities for success.
- Teach students to set reasonable goals and to assess their own performance.
- Help students recognize the relationship between effort and outcome.
- Provide informative feedback.
- Provide special motivational support to discouraged students.

Strategies for Increasing Perceived Value
- Relate lessons to students' own lives.
- Provide opportunities for choice.
- Model interest in learning and express enthusiasm for the material.
- Include novelty/variety elements.
- Provide opportunities for students to respond actively.
- Allow students to create finished products.
- Provide opportunities for students to interact with peers.
- Provide extrinsic rewards.

Source: Brophy, 2010.

As you read, keep in mind *that none of these strategies will be very effective if you have not worked to create and sustain a safe, caring classroom environment* (Chapters 3 and 4). Before students can become motivated, they must feel safe from humiliation, understand that it's all right to take risks and make mistakes, and know that they are accepted, respected members of the class (Ryan & Patrick, 2001). In fact, Brophy considers a supportive environment to be an "essential precondition" for the successful use of motivational strategies (Good & Brophy, 2008, p. 148).

 PAUSE AND REFLECT

Now that you have read about the expectancy × value model, reflect on its implications for teachers. How would you use this model to motivate a disinterested student in a topic in your content area?

INCREASING EXPECTATIONS OF SUCCESS

Provide Opportunities for Success

If tasks appear too difficult, students might be afraid to tackle them. You might have to modify assignments for different students; make open-ended assignments so that a variety of responses can be acceptable; provide additional instruction; divide lengthy projects into shorter, more "doable" parts; or allow extra time. Fred calls this the "slanty rope theory" of classwork: "If we set a rope across a room at four feet, some kids can get over it and some can't. But if we slant the rope, then everyone can find their way over at some point." According to Fred, "Success is a better motivator than anything else I know. If I can get kids to feel success, then maybe I'll be able to get through to them."

When Christina teaches her students to write research papers, she tries to guarantee success by breaking the assignment into small sections—taking notes, constructing a bibliography, creating an outline, writing the introductory paragraph, using parenthetical documentation—and having students turn in each part before writing the final paper. This not only makes the task seem less overwhelming but also enables Christina to correct mistakes and set students on the right course before it's too late.

Sometimes, it's necessary to go back and reteach material rather than simply plowing ahead. For example, during one class period when Donnie was explaining how to construct and bisect congruent angles, it became apparent that most students were lost. As they labored over their papers, frustrated comments began to come from all corners of the room: "I can't do it; you told me not to change the compass, but I had to"; "I need an eraser"; "Huh?"; "How do you do this?"; "I don't get this." Circulating around the room, Donnie tried to help individuals who were having trouble. Finally, she moved to the front and center of the room and addressed the class: "Okay, let's start again. I see a lot of people are out in left field." She began to explain the procedure again, very slowly. After every step, she asked, "Does everyone have this?" before moving on to the next step. Students began to respond more positively: "Yeah"; "Uh-huh"; "Okay, we got it." One girl, who had been having particular difficulty, called out, "C'mere, Miss Collins, I wanna show you what I got." Donnie checked her work; it was correct. The girl turned to her neighbor and announced loudly, "You see, all I needed was a little help. Sometimes I gotta work step by step. I got it. I got it."

Sometimes providing opportunities for success requires differentiated assignments for students of varying achievement levels. Listen to Donna:

> One of the biggest changes I've made this year is greater use of differentiated instruction. I assign students to three small groups based on past performance. The students who have a stronger grasp of a specific standard will have something to read, interpret, and respond to in writing. Sometimes the material is the same or each student in the group has his or her own article. These students check each other's work and make suggestions to their peers; at times, they use a rubric to grade each other's responses. This group is more independent, and I monitor from a distance. I want them to discuss openly without my assistance, but I'm nearby if they need me. I also encourage them to use the resources in the room or each other to answer any questions they may have.
>
> Students in the middle group will all read the same article, and their responses will be more formulaic, so that they build the basic concepts of grammar, vocabulary, and cohesive sentence structure. They too have a rubric to follow, and I expect them to assist each other. The lower group usually works directly with me so that I can guide them through the task, modeling the expected outcomes.
>
> By differentiating instruction I can challenge the higher-level students. I'm not asking them to wait for the rest of the class to catch up to them anymore. And I have time to work with the struggling students. What's interesting is that I've noticed that each time I've used differentiated instruction, I have a few more students in the higher-ability groups, as students meet the challenges I set.

Another way to enhance the probability of success is to vary instructional approaches so that students with different strengths have equal access to instruction. One such approach is based on Howard Gardner's (1993, 1995) theory of "multiple intelligences" (MI). According to Gardner, people have at least eight types of intelligences. (These are listed in Table 9.2.) Schools have traditionally emphasized the

TABLE 9.2 Gardner's Multiple Intelligences	
Type of Intelligence	Description
Linguistic	Capacity to use language to express and appreciate complex meanings; sensitivity to the sounds, rhythms, and meanings of words
Logical-mathematical	Capacity to reason and recognize logical and numerical patterns; to calculate, quantify, and consider propositions and hypotheses
Spatial	Capacity to perceive the visual world accurately; to think in three-dimensional ways; to navigate oneself through space; to produce and understand graphic information
Musical	Sensitivity to pitch, melody, rhythm, and tone; to produce and appreciate different forms of musical expression
Bodily-kinesthetic	Capacity to use the body and to handle objects skillfully
Interpersonal	Capacity to understand and interact effectively with others; to discern accurately the moods and emotions of others
Intrapersonal	Capacity to understand oneself; perceptiveness about one's own moods, emotions, desires, motivations
Naturalist	Capacity to understand nature and to observe patterns; sensitivity to features of the natural world

Sources: Arends, 2008; Campbell, Campbell, & Dickinson, 1999.

development of linguistic and logical-mathematical intelligences (and have favored those who are relatively strong in these), whereas they have neglected and under-valued the other intelligences. Although Gardner does not advocate one "right way" to implement a multiple intelligences education, he does recommend that teachers approach topics in a variety of ways to reach more students and to enable more to experience "what it is like to be an expert" (1995, p. 208). Although the theory of multiple intelligences has its share of critics (Klein, 1997; Peariso, 2008), varying instructional approaches can allow all students to experience success.

One other consideration regarding student success is important to mention here. Keep in mind that the process of learning something new often involves temporary failure and possibly some frustration (Alfi, Assor, & Katz, 2004). It's important that you allow your students to experience temporary failure in the safety of your class-room so that they can develop needed coping skills and a sense of mastery that will contribute to their motivation to continue learning.

Teach Students to Set Reasonable Goals and to Assess Their Own Performance

To help your students set reasonable goals, it is important that you first help them dis-tinguish between *learning,* or *mastery,* goals and *performance* goals. When students adopt learning goals, they focus on acquiring knowledge or skills. In contrast, when students adopt performance goals, their focus is on preserving their self-perception and public reputation as competent (Brophy, 2010).

Teachers play an important role in determining whether the overall tone of the classroom focuses on learning or performance. In a study of some 1,000 third- through eighth-grade students (Corpus, McClintic-Gilbert, & Hayenga, 2009), the researchers found that a schoolwide focus on mastery goals was positively related to students' intrinsic motivation. Moreover, a review of recent research concluded that in classrooms with a focus on mastery, students reported higher levels of competence and self-esteem as compared to classrooms with a performance focus (Rolland, 2012). This review also found that positive student-teacher relationships supported students in developing mastery goals. Another study (Walker & Greene, 2009) found that high school students who reported a sense of belonging in the classroom were more likely to adopt mastery goals and to expend effort in learning.

Some students might be very focused on not appearing stupid or not failing rather than on learning. Other students think anything less than 100 on a test is a failure, whereas others are content with a barely passing grade. You might have to help students set goals that are reasonable and obtainable and keep their focus on learning goals.

At the very beginning of each course, Christina has students set the goals they hope to reach. (See Figure 9.1.) Then, based on these goals, students decide the criteria

Goals

Your individual goals should represent what you wish to accomplish in this course. Choose goals that are directly relevant to your expectations for the course. For example, it is valid to say that you want to be a millionaire, but that goal is not specifically relevant to English class. Choose a more specific shorter-term goal.

Once you have chosen your goals, explain your reasons for selecting them in the space provided. Then list two ways that you think you can reach these goals.

Goal 1:	Reason for selection of this goal:
Two things you can do to help you reach this goal:	
Goal 2:	Reason for selection of this goal:
Two things you can do to help you reach this goal:	
Goal 3:	Reason for selection of this goal:
Two things you can do to help you reach this goal:	
Goal 4:	Reason for selection of this goal:
Two things you can do to help you reach this goal:	
Goal 5:	Reason for selection of this goal:
Two things you can do to help you reach this goal:	

FIGURE 9.1   Christina's Goal-Setting Handout

they will use to evaluate their work. They have to include four specific items that Christina requires and eight more that they devise for themselves. Throughout the marking period, students keep their work in a "collection folder" from which they then select work representing their progress in meeting the goals they set. For each selection, students also complete a "reflection sheet" that asks them to explain which goals and criteria the piece represents. The selected work, along with its reflection sheet, is moved into a portfolio that both they and Christina assess.

Christina also gives her students a rubric that details how each major project will be scored and requires students to score their work before turning it in: "This way, students are aware of the score they will be receiving, and they can make a choice about whether they're happy with that or want to do more." Interestingly, Christina finds that students' self-evaluations are usually within a few points of her own assessments of their work.

We observed another example of helping students set goals when one of Fred's students turned in an appalling essay at the beginning of the year. Not only was it short, superficial, and vague but also both the handwriting and spelling were atrocious. When Fred investigated, he found out that the student had a learning disability; nonetheless, he told the student in no uncertain terms that his performance was inadequate: "Look, you can't write, you can't even print, and you can't spell. But you're not stupid. So what are you going to do to get better? Let's set some goals." With the assistance of the resource room teacher, they devised a plan for the student to learn keyboarding and to use word processing software with a spelling checker. When the next writing assignment was due, the student came to Fred complaining that it was too hard. Fred was sympathetic and supportive—but adamant that the student complete it. He did, and although it was far from adequate, it was a definite improvement over the first assignment. Reflecting on the student's problems, Fred comments:

 We can all feel sorry for him, but he can't go around like this; he has to be pushed to overcome his deficits. People have allowed him to stay a baby, but it's time for him to grow up. There are ways he can improve. My job is to teach him to set some reasonable goals and then work to achieve them.

Help Students Recognize the Relationship between Effort and Outcome

Like Helpless Hannah, some youngsters proclaim defeat before they've even attempted a task. When they don't do well on an assignment, they attribute their failure to lack of ability, not realizing that achievement is often a function of effort. Donna observes that "middle school students are impatient. They want the answer immediately, and they always want to be right. They consider being wrong a personal indictment, so they don't want to take risks (at least openly)." To counteract this tendency, Donna frequently stresses the relationship between achievement and effort. She explicitly teaches and reinforces critical thinking skills so that students will be able to comprehend and evaluate what they are reading. During one lesson on inference, for example, she emphasized that "smart people are not the people who say they're smart. Smart people are the people who work hard and practice critical thinking."

Other students might be overconfident—even cocky—and think they can do well without exerting much effort. In either situation, you have to make the relationship between effort and outcome explicit. Whenever possible, point out students' improvement and help them to see the role of effort. At the beginning of one class, Donna told her students, "One thing that I'm very proud of is that you're making the effort to apply what you have learned in this class to your other classes. I hear from other teachers that you are writing much higher quality sentences, your spelling has improved, and you're using correct punctuation."

The relationship between effort and outcome became painfully clear to a student in Sandy's class who refused to take notes during class. When Sandy first noticed that he wasn't taking notes, she told him to take out his notebook and open it. He did, murmuring, "I'll open my notebook, but you can't force me to take notes." Later, he told Sandy he didn't need to take notes like the other kids because he had a good memory. She explained that her years of experience had shown her that taking notes in chemistry was absolutely necessary; she suggested he keep his notebook out and open "just in case." When the first test was given, the boy's grade was 40 percent. Sandy told him: "I know it's not because you're unable to do the work. So what do you think? What conclusion do you draw from this?" The boy responded, "I guess I gotta take notes."

Provide Informative Feedback

Sometimes turning in work to a teacher is like dropping it down a black hole. Assignments pile up in huge mounds on the teacher's desk, and students know that their papers will never be returned—graded or ungraded. From a student's perspective, it's infuriating to work hard on an assignment, turn it in, and then receive no feedback from the teacher. But a lack of academic feedback is not simply infuriating. It is also detrimental to students' motivation and achievement:

> One particularly important teaching activity is providing academic feedback to students (letting them know whether their answers are right or wrong, or giving them the right answer). Academic feedback should be provided as often as possible to students. When more frequent feedback is offered, students pay attention more and learn more. Academic feedback was more strongly and consistently related to achievement than any of the other teaching behaviors. (Fisher et al., 1980, p. 27)

If you circulate while students are working on assignments, you can provide them immediate feedback about their performance. You can catch errors, assist with problems, and affirm correct, thoughtful work. In the following vignette, we see Sandy help two girls having problems pouring a solution into a funnel. Only a clear, colorless solution was supposed to come out into the beaker, but the solution was yellow and had particles of the solid in it.

Sandy: **Why did this happen?**
Tanya: **Because I poured too fast and too much.**
Sandy: **Right. [She calls all the students over to see the problem that the two girls had.] So what happened?**
  Lisa: **The yellow stuff got over the filter paper, behind the fold.**
Sandy: **Okay, so what can you do?**
Tanya: **Pour it back in, but we're going to lose some.**

Sandy: [To the other students] Can they pour it back in?
Student: Yeah.
Sandy: Sure. It was good you washed the beaker.

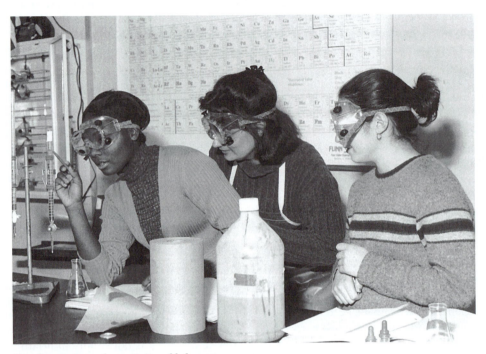

Sandy monitors the activity of lab groups.

Sometimes you're unable to monitor work while it's being done. In this case, you need to check assignments once they've been submitted and return them to students as soon as possible. You might also decide to allow your students to check their own work. Donnie believes this has numerous educational benefits:

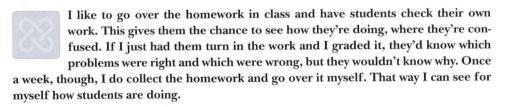

I like to go over the homework in class and have students check their own work. This gives them the chance to see how they're doing, where they're confused. If I just had them turn in the work and I graded it, they'd know which problems were right and which were wrong, but they wouldn't know why. Once a week, though, I do collect the homework and go over it myself. That way I can see for myself how students are doing.

As an English teacher, Christina finds that having students evaluate their own work and that of their peers is not only educational but also allows them to receive feedback more quickly:

I used to think it was an easy way out to have students grade their own papers or do peer editing, but experienced teachers told me it wasn't so, and I've come to agree. I couldn't have a writing-based classroom if I had to give all the feedback myself. My students write many drafts of their papers, and I simply cannot read them all quickly enough. . . . So I teach them to self- and peer-evaluate before revising. . . . They learn a lot when they do peer editing, and they can get instant feedback.

Whether you correct work while it's being done, at home over a cup of coffee, or together with your students, the important point is that students *need to know how they are progressing*. It's also important to give feedback in terms of *absolute standards or students' own past performance rather than peers' performance* (Brophy, 2010). Thus, instead of saying, "Congratulations! You received the sixth highest grade in the class," you should say, "Congratulations! You went from a 79 on your last quiz to an 87 on this quiz." Similarly, you can point out strengths and weaknesses and add a note of encouragement for further effort ("You've demonstrated a firm grasp of the perspectives of the slaveholders and the abolitionists but not the slaves themselves. Check the chapter again, and add a paragraph to round out your presentation").

Provide Special Motivational Support to Discouraged Students

For students with limited ability or learning disabilities, school might be a constant struggle to keep up with classmates and to maintain a sense of enthusiasm and motivation. Such students not only require instructional assistance (e.g., individualized activities, extra academic help, well-structured assignments, extra time) but also need special encouragement and motivational support. For example, Donnie constantly exhorts students not to get discouraged if they're having trouble and reminds them that people work and learn at different paces. Often she pairs low-achieving students with those she knows will be patient and helpful and encourages peer assistance and peer tutoring. Similarly, Sandy frequently reassures her students that they're in this together:

> So many of my students are afraid of taking chemistry, and they find it harder than any subject they've taken. I spend the first five or six weeks of school reassuring them—"You're not alone, there's support, I'm here to help you, we'll do this slowly and systematically. . . . You don't have to learn it in three or four days; it may be a long haul but that's OK." If I can get them to trust me, and I believe they can do it, then eventually they develop more confidence and a sense of well-being.

Sandy also makes sure that she expresses concern and surprise when students don't do well on a test or assignment. She'll ask, "What happened here?" or "What's the problem?" so that students know she's not writing them off:

> Too many times teachers will say "good job" to the person who's gotten the A, but nothing to the kid who got the D or F. But if you don't ask what happened, they think you expected it. Sometimes what you don't say is more powerful than what you do say.

Donna notes this about many poor performing students:

> By the time they reach me, those students who never mastered what they need to succeed in my class have amassed a variety of off-task strategies to avoid schoolwork. My job as a teacher is to know the difference between students who are simply being off task and those who genuinely don't have prerequisite skills and are afraid to be found out.

Christina finds that students who have failed the standardized test required for high school graduation are particularly discouraged and anxious. Like Sandy, she makes it clear that she expects them to pass the next time around; at the very least, they will improve their scores. She cheers them on as they take numerous practice tests and analyze their performances. Then she has them think of one thing they will do differently when they take the test again. Responses vary—"I won't fall asleep"; "I'm going to read *all* the answer choices before I choose one"; "I'm going to figure out what kind of text I'm reading and mark it up"—but simply having a plan seems to help students to be more optimistic. Christina also gives her students a "care package" the day before the exam with granola bars and other healthful snacks (in case they don't have the makings for a good breakfast) and a page of test-taking tips, which encourages them to go to bed early and remember to set the alarm clock!

Unfortunately, teachers sometimes develop counterproductive behavior patterns that communicate low expectations and reinforce students' perceptions of themselves as failures. Table 9.3 lists some of the behaviors that have been identified.

As Brophy (2010) points out, some of these differences are due to the behavior of the students. For example, if students' contributions to discussions are irrelevant or incorrect, it is difficult for teachers to accept and use their ideas. Moreover, the boundary between *appropriate differentiated instruction* and *inappropriate differential treatment* is often fuzzy. Asking low achievers easier, nonanalytic questions might make instructional sense. Nonetheless, it's important to monitor the extent to which you engage in these behaviors and to reflect on the messages you are sending to your low-achieving or learning disabled students. If you find that you are engaging in many of the behaviors listed in Table 9.3, you might be "merely going through the motions of instructing low achievers, without seriously working to help them achieve their potential" (Brophy, 2010, p. 109).

Research on gender bias in the classroom has revealed that teachers also communicate low expectations to their female students by displaying some of the behaviors listed in Table 9.3 (Sadker, Sadker, & Zittleman, 2009). Again, it's important that you monitor your interactions with female and male students to make sure you aren't sending an unintended message to your female students.

INCREASING THE PERCEIVED VALUE OF THE TASK

Recall that when we asked the students in the classes of our five teachers "why kids behave in some classes and not others," they stressed the importance of teaching in a way that is stimulating. As one student wrote, "Not everything can be fun. . . , but there are ways teachers can make [material] more interesting and more challenging." (See Chapter 1.) This student intuitively understands that motivation to learn depends

TABLE 9.3 Ways That Teachers Can Communicate Low Expectations

- Waiting less time for low achievers than for others to answer a question before giving the answer or calling on someone else.
- Giving answers to low achievers or calling on someone else rather than helping the students to improve their responses by giving clues or rephrasing questions.
- Rewarding inappropriate behaviors or incorrect answers.
- Criticizing low achievers more often for failure than other students.
- Praising low achievers for success less often than others.
- Failing to give feedback following responses of low achievers.
- Interacting less frequently with low achievers than with others.
- Calling on low achievers less often than on others to respond to questions or asking them only easy questions.
- Seating low achievers farther away from the teacher than other students.
- Demanding less from low achievers than they are capable of learning.
- Giving high achievers but not low achievers the benefit of the doubt in grading tests or assignments.
- Being less friendly in interactions with low achievers in comparison with others; showing less attention and responsiveness; making less eye contact.
- Providing briefer and less informative answers to their questions than to those of others.
- Showing less acceptance and use of low achievers' ideas than those of others.
- Limiting low achievers to low-level, repetitive curriculum with an emphasis on drill and practice tasks.

Source: Brophy, 2010.

not only on success expectations but also on students' perceptions of the value of the task or the rewards that successful completion or mastery will bring. Remember Satisfied Santos? Seeing no value in his course assignments, he invests little effort in them although he knows he could be successful. Because students like Santos are unlikely to respond to their teachers' exhortations to work harder, the challenge is to find ways to convince them that the work has (1) *intrinsic value* (doing it will provide enjoyment), (2) *utility value* (doing it will advance their personal goals), or (3) *attainment value* (doing it will affirm their self-concept or fulfill their needs for achievement, understanding, skill mastery, and prestige) (Anderman & Anderman, 2010; Brophy, 2010). Let's consider some of the strategies that teachers can use to enhance the perception of value.

Relate Lessons to Students' Own Lives

A study of the motivational strategies of first-year teachers demonstrated that students are more engaged in classrooms in which teachers provide reasons for doing tasks and relate lessons to students' personal experiences (Newby, 1991). Unfortunately, *the study also found that first-year teachers use these "relevance strategies" only occasionally.*

As we mentioned in Chapter 3, one important aspect of building positive relationships is learning about students' lives. The more you can learn about your students' interests, the more you can tailor your lessons to further engage them. One study (Walkington, 2012) investigated the impact of algebra word problems that incorporated scenarios that matched students' interests (e.g., sports, music, games). Students' performance on these personalized problems was better than on the standard problems, and this improved performance carried over into future units in the algebra class. Although this study is not meant to suggest that you should write personalized assignments for each of your students, incorporating their interests into assignments can pay off in both motivation and performance.

While you might not be able to determine the individual interests of all your students, you can be assured that as adolescents, they are all concerned with issues of identity, connectedness, and power (Phillips, 2013; also see Chapter 6). And, as good filmmakers and authors demonstrate, if you develop lessons and activities with which your students can connect emotionally, they will be more motivated to engage. Incorporating their fundamental concerns into literature and history is relatively easy; you can select readings that deal with characters figuring out their identity and their future directions or develop units about repression or struggles for equality. But you can forge emotional connections even in science, math, and art. Science units can focus on personal choices related to reducing carbon footprints, math units can overtly address math anxiety, and art assignments can ask students to represent their concerns.

When students are not from the dominant culture, teachers must make a special effort to relate academic content to referents from the students' own culture. This practice not only helps to bridge the gap between the two cultures but also allows the study of cultural referents in their own right (Ladson-Billings, 1994). Two English teachers in a large multicultural, urban school in California provide a compelling example (Morrell & Duncan-Andrade, 2002, 2004). Reasoning that hip-hop music could be used "as a bridge linking the seemingly vast span between the streets and the world of academics" (2002, p. 89), the teachers used hip-hop to develop the critical and analytical skills of their underachieving 12th-grade students. First, the teachers paired famous poems with rap songs. They then divided their class into small groups and assigned one pair of texts to each group. Students were to interpret their poem and song and analyze the links between them. This curriculum unit illustrates the power of what Gloria Ladson-Billings calls *culturally relevant teaching.*

Our teachers are well aware of the need to relate academic tasks to youngsters' lives. When Donnie teaches percents, for example, she has students do a project entitled "Buying Your First Car." Students work in small groups to determine how much a car they select will actually cost—a task that involves knowing and using interest formulas, calculating depreciation, learning about base prices and shipping fees, and figuring out whether monthly payments will fit in their budgets. Donna continually relates her lessons to her students' interests, sprinkling her teaching with references to current movies and books. In one lesson, she noted that "linking verbs are like the eHarmony or match.com of language; they connect things." In another lesson, she illustrated the five parts of a plot line with the *Twilight* book series. When Fred's students study the Bill of Rights, they debate whether wearing a T-shirt with an obscene slogan is protected free speech. Reflecting on the need for relevance, Fred comments:

You don't have to do it every day, but little bits and pieces help. Teachers always have to ask, "So what? What does this material have to do with me?" My brother always said, "If it doesn't make me richer or poorer then don't bother me with it." My brother was not a good student. So whenever I teach anything, I use "my brother Bob test." I ask myself, "So what? How will it make my kids richer or poorer in some way?"

Provide Opportunities for Choice

One of most obvious ways to ensure that learning activities connect to individuals' personal interests is to provide opportunities for choice. Moreover, research has shown that when students experience a sense of autonomy and self-determination, they are more likely to be intrinsically motivated (Ryan & Deci, 2000) and to "bond" with school (Roeser, Eccles, & Sameroff, 2000). These opportunities are especially critical in middle schools where students typically face more teacher controls than elementary school and grades are used as extrinsic rewards (Urdan & Schoenfelder, 2006). During the transition to middle school, teachers can help students develop self-reliance and challenge-seeking behaviors by allowing them some autonomy in the classroom. Although mandated curricula and high-stakes standardized testing thwart opportunities for choice, there are usually alternative ways for students to accomplish requirements. Think about whether students might (1) participate in the design of the academic tasks, (2) decide how the task is to be completed, and/or (3) decide when the task is to be completed (Stipek, 2002).

In one study, researchers asked 36 teachers about the types of instructional choices they gave to their students (Flowerday & Schraw, 2000). Although types of choices varied as a function of content areas and grade levels, all teachers agreed on six main types of choice: (1) topics of study (for research papers, in-class projects, and presentations), (2) reading materials (type of genre, choice of authors), (3) methods of assessment (exam versus final project), (4) activities (book report or diorama), (5) social arrangements (whether to work in pairs or small groups, choice of group members), and (6) procedural choices (when to take tests, what order to study prescribed topics, and when assignments were due). Teachers also expressed the belief that choice has a positive effect on students' motivation by increasing their sense of ownership and self-determination, interest, and enthusiasm.

Despite this belief, teachers tended to use choice as a *reward* for effort and good behavior rather than as a *strategy for fostering* effort and good behavior. Thus, teachers were most likely to give choices to students who were already self-regulated. It's easy to understand why teachers would provide choice to students who have previously shown that they are responsible, motivated, and well behaved. (It certainly seems safer!) But if we think of choice as a motivational strategy rather than a reward, we can see that it might be useful to motivate students like Satisfied Santos. These beliefs about motivation were confirmed by another study that investigated the effect of allowing students to choose the type of homework assignments to complete (Patall, Cooper, & Wynn, 2010). Students who were given a choice of homework assignments reported higher motivation to do homework, felt more competent regarding the homework, and performed better on the unit test compared with those for which they did not have a choice.

There are many ways to build choice into the curriculum. To prepare for the state's high school graduation test, Christina's students have to complete various writing tasks, such as a persuasive letter or essay on a controversial topic, a cause/effect essay, and a problem/solution essay, but students often choose their own topics for all of these. When Fred's classes report on a historical figure, they are instructed to choose the figure who seems most like them (or whom they'd like to be). Donnie encourages students to "put their heads together" in small groups to identify the homework problems that caused the most difficulty; those are the ones they then review. Donna allows her students to choose the country to study in her unit on Asian culture. Instead of writing a typical research paper, students design books that highlight their topics and what they learned. And all of our teachers sometimes allow students to choose their own groups for collaborative work.

Model Interest in Learning and Express Enthusiasm for the Material

To help keep your students interested in learning, it's important that you model an interest in it. You can talk with your students about classes you are taking, books you are reading, or other ways that you continue to learn. When we were teaching in precollege classrooms, we both made a point to share with our students things that we learned on vacation trips or what we were doing to prepare for these trips, such as learning a foreign language or learning to scuba dive. Middle and secondary teachers are typically passionate about their content area, so you can also make sure your students know what you are doing to stay current in your field.

Research has shown that when teachers model an interest in learning, their students perceive that their classroom is focused on mastering the content rather than merely earning grades (Urdan & Schoenfelder, 2006). Christina often refers to her love of reading and the fact that she writes poetry. When Donnie gives students complex problems that involve a number of skills and steps, she tells them, "I love problems like this! This is so much fun!" In similar fashion, Sandy frequently exclaims, "This is my favorite part of chemistry," a statement that usually causes students to roll their eyes and respond, "Oh, Mrs. K., *everything* is your favorite part!" When Fred is about to introduce a difficult concept, he announces: "Now please listen to this. Most Americans don't understand this at all; they don't have a clue. But it's really important, and I want you to understand it." When Donna introduced a unit on Asian cultures (a vehicle for learning to write a research paper), she commented, "What's going to be fun is that we're going to start by looking at western astrology. It's going to be really interesting to see how much your astrological sign is like you."

Include Novelty/Variety Elements

During a visit to Donnie's class, we watched as she introduced the "challenge problem of the day." Donnie distributed a photocopy of a dollar bill and told students to figure out how many $1 bills would be needed to make one mile if they were lined up end to end. The enthusiasm generated by the copies of the dollar was palpable. Fred also used money during one observation to make a point about choosing a more difficult but more ethical course of action. He moved up an aisle and dropped a $5 bill on an empty chair. Turning to the girl sitting in the next seat, he commented, "You could just stick that in your pocket, walk out the door, and go to McDonald's, right? Take the money and run. That would certainly be possible, but would it be right?"

In Christina's basic skills class, we watched as students read and discussed *The Martian Chronicles* by Ray Bradbury. Then Christina explained how they were to create small illustrations of key incidents in the story, which would then be assembled in sequential order on large pieces of butcher paper and mounted in the library.

As she assigned the incidents, it was clear that incorporating this art activity not only reinforced students' understanding of the story but also generated a great deal of enthusiasm. Similarly, when Donna's students did presentations on Greek and Roman mythology, they used PowerPoint, Prezi, or other presentation software rather than simply giving oral reports. These eighth-graders were obviously proud and excited about their visually striking presentations, and those of us in the audience were definitely more attentive.

Provide Opportunities for Students to Respond Actively

So often the teacher talks and moves while students sit passively and listen. In contrast, our teachers structure lessons so that students must be actively involved. When one of Fred's classes studies the judicial system, students engage in a mock trial. In Christina's classes, where many students voice an entrenched dislike of poetry, Christina works hard to have students experience poetry in a way that is memorable and personal. She divides the class into groups to design a poetry lesson that requires each student in the class (1) to write a poem that uses a particular literary device (e.g., allusion, metaphor, simile, irony, alliteration, consonance) and (2) to study a poem. Instructing the groups to use as a model someone like Mr. Keating (the Robin Williams character) from *Dead Poets Society,* Christina encourages students to design lessons that "appeal to the senses," that "are like games or sports with a lot of poetry added in," and that require students "to get up and move around." One group, for example, designed an impossible scavenger hunt for the class to attempt and then explained how the hunt related to Poe's poem "El Dorado."

Another simple way to engage students is to ask a question and have students respond with thumbs up or thumbs down or by holding up colored cards that correspond to answer choices. You could also have students solve math, chemistry, or physics problems on small dry-erase marker boards, individually or in pairs, while you circulate to monitor their work. If students are working on a more involved task (biography, lab report, analysis of a poem), you could have them write a summary on dry-erase marker boards, arrange these boards around the room, and have students do a "gallery walk" to view other students' works while they take notes for a summary that they can turn in.

Allow Students to Create Finished Products

Too much school time is devoted to exercises, drills, and practice. Students practice writing but rarely write. They practice reading skills but rarely read. They practice mathematical procedures but rarely do real mathematics. Yet creating a finished product gives meaning and purpose to assignments and increases students' motivation to learn.

After a fierce winter blizzard that closed school for seven days and left administrators trying to figure out how to make up the lost time, Fred's students wrote letters to state legislators offering various proposals. Because the task was *real,* the letters had to be suitable for mailing; motivation was far greater than it would have been if the task had been a workbook exercise on writing business letters. Similarly, Sandy's labs are not simply exercises in following a prescribed set of steps leading to a foregone conclusion. They are real investigations into real problems.

Fred's students compose letters to state legislators.

As an introduction to a multigenre project, Christina's students wrote children's books. First, a parenting-class teacher spoke with the students about writing for young children (e.g., how many characters would be appropriate, whether fantasy themes or something closer to children's own experiences would be most suitable, the importance of using simple vocabulary). Then students wrote their books and engaged in peer editing and revision. They read one another's books and chose six from each class. These were sent to the art classes where they were illustrated and bound. Drama classes also got involved: They chose four of the books to act out to first-graders who came to the high school.

Provide Opportunities for Students to Interact with Peers

All five teachers firmly believe that motivation (and learning) are enhanced if students are allowed to work with one another. They provide numerous opportunities for peer interaction (a topic that will be explored further in Chapter 11).

Sometimes, groups are carefully planned; at other times, they are formed more casually. For example, one day we saw Donnie shuffle a deck of cards (admitting that she never learned how to do this really well) and then walk around the room, asking each student to pick a card. She then told students to get up and find the person or persons with the same number or face card that they had. Once students had found their partners, she proceeded to explain the group task.

Provide Extrinsic Rewards

Some effective managers find it useful to provide students rewards for engaging in the behaviors that support learning (such as paying attention and participating) and for academic achievement. The use of rewards in classrooms is based on the psychological principle of *positive reinforcement:* Behavior that is rewarded is strengthened and is therefore likely to be repeated. Although rewards do not increase the perceived value of the behavior or the task, they link performance of the behavior or successful completion of the task to attractive, desirable consequences.

Rewards can be divided into three categories: social, activity, and tangible. *Social rewards* are verbal and nonverbal indications that you recognize and appreciate students' behavior or achievements. A pat on the back, a smile, and a thumbs-up signal are commonly used social rewards that are low in cost and readily available.

Praise can also function as a social reward. To be effective, however, praise must be *specific and sincere.* Instead of "Good paper," you can try something like this: "Your paper shows a firm grasp of the distinction between metaphor and similes." Instead of "You were great this morning," try, "The way you came into the room, took off your baseball caps, and immediately got out your notebooks was terrific." Being specific will make your praise more informative; it will also help you to avoid using the same tired, old phrases week after week that quickly lose any impact (e.g., "good job"). If praise is to serve as a reinforcer, it also needs to be *contingent on the behavior you are trying to strengthen.* In other words, it should be given only when that behavior occurs so that students understand exactly what evoked the praise.

Donnie distributes a lab worksheet that asks students to draw a parallelogram and then work through five activities to discover the figure's properties. She stresses that students should write down their observations after each activity and then draw some final conclusions. As students work on the problems, she circulates through the room. When she sees Shaneika's paper, she tells her: "Shaneika, you are really following directions. You're writing the answers as you go along."

In addition to pats on the back and verbal praise, some teachers institute more formal ways to recognize accomplishment, improvement, or cooperation. For example, they could display student work, provide award certificates, nominate students for school awards given at the end of the year, or select "Students of the Week." Whichever approach you use, be careful that this strategy of public recognition doesn't backfire by causing students embarrassment. As noted in Chapter 3, Sandy observed that secondary students generally do not want to stand out from their peers. Moreover, individual public recognition can be upsetting to students whose cultures value collective over individual achievement (Trumbull, Rothstein-Fisch, Greenfield, & Quiroz, 2001).

In addition to social rewards, teachers sometimes use *special activities* as rewards for good behavior or achievement. In middle and high school, watching a video, listening to music, having free time, or having a night of no homework can be very reinforcing. One way to determine which activities should be used as rewards is to listen carefully to students' requests. If they ask you for the opportunity to listen to music or have a popcorn party, you can be confident that those activities will be reinforcing (at least for those particular students). It's also helpful to observe what activities students engage in when they have free time (e.g., do they read magazines? talk with friends? draw?). Donna noted:

 Rewards work if they are something students value. A math teacher here presents a math problem of the week. Students who solved it correctly got "front of the line" lunch passes. This worked for the first few weeks, but now they don't care anymore about the passes. Teachers brainstormed some ideas and selected some new rewards such as helping another teacher or getting a homework pass. The challenge is discovering what they value, and one of the best ways is through discussion with the kids.

Finally, teachers can use *tangible, material rewards* for good behavior—cookies, candy, key chains, pencils—although such rewards are used less in high school than in elementary school. For example, Donnie goes to a discount supermarket and buys a big supply of candy that she keeps in a back closet; when students have been especially cooperative, she'll break out the Twizzlers for an unexpected treat. Similarly, Fred sometimes gives prizes when students have to review factual information for tests, a task they usually find boring. He might have students play vocabulary bingo, telling them: "I have two prizes in my pocket for the winner—two tickets for an all-expense-paid trip to Hawaii or a piece of candy. You get whichever one I pull out of my pocket first." Every now and then, Fred also uses candy to show his appreciation for good behavior. In his words,

If someone has never given me grief, I may be moved to a spontaneous act of generosity. I'll say, "Here take this," and give them a Sugar Daddy or package of Sweet Tarts. It's amazing; kids go crazy over a little piece of candy.

PROBLEMS WITH REWARDS

The practice of providing extrinsic rewards has been the focus of considerable controversy. One objection is that giving students tangible rewards in exchange for good behavior or academic performance is tantamount to bribery. Proponents of this position argue that students should engage in appropriate behavior and activities for their own sake: They should be quiet during in-class assignments because that is the socially responsible thing to do; they should do their homework so that they can practice skills taught during class; they should learn verb conjugations in Spanish because they need to know them. Other educators acknowledge the desirability of such intrinsic motivation but believe that the use of rewards is inevitable in situations when people are not completely free to follow their own inclinations. Even Richard Ryan and Edward Deci, two psychologists who strongly endorse the importance of self-determination and autonomy, acknowledge that teachers "cannot always rely on intrinsic motivation to foster learning" because "many of the tasks that educators want their students to perform are not inherently interesting or enjoyable" (2000, p. 55).

Another objection to the use of rewards is the fact that they are attempts to control and manipulate people. When we dispense rewards, we are essentially saying, "Do this, and you'll get that"—an approach not unlike the way we train our pets. Indeed, Alfie Kohn (1993) contends that rewards and punishments are "two sides of the same coin" (p. 50). Although rewards are certainly more pleasurable, they are "every bit as controlling as punishments, even if they control by seduction" (p. 51). According to Kohn, if we want youngsters to become self-regulating, responsible, caring individuals, we must abandon attempts at external control and provide students opportunities to develop competence, connection, and autonomy in caring classroom communities. For more information on Kohn's work, see Box 9.1, Meet the Educators.

Another major concern is that rewarding students for behaving in certain ways actually *undermines their intrinsic motivation to engage in those behaviors.* This question was explored in an influential study conducted by Mark Lepper, David Greene, and Richard Nisbett (1973). First, the researchers identified preschoolers who showed interest in a particular drawing activity during free play. Then they met with the children individually. Some children were simply invited to draw with the materials (the "no-reward" subjects). Others were told they could receive a "good-player" award

---

BOX 9.1   MEET THE EDUCATORS

Meet Alfie Kohn

Alfie Kohn writes extensively on education, parenting, and human behavior. He is a frequent lecturer on topics such as "the deadly effects of 'tougher standards'"; the use of "A's, praise, stickers, and contests" to "bribe" students to learn; "the case against competition"; "teaching children to care"; and "the homework myth." *Time* magazine described Kohn as "perhaps the country's most outspoken critic of education's fixation on grades [and] test scores."

Some Major Ideas on Motivation

- "How do I get these kids motivated?" is a question that reflects a "paradigm of control," and external control "is death to motivation" (Kohn, 1993, p. 199).
- "Do rewards motivate people? Absolutely. They motivate people to get rewards" (Kohn, 1993, p. 67).
- People who are trying to earn rewards generally end up doing worse on many tasks than people who are not. Like punishment, rewards are a form of control, designed to bring about compliance.
- In contrast, the three Cs create the conditions for "authentic motivation": *collaboration* (learning together), *content* (things worth

knowing), and *choice* (autonomy in the classroom). When students have opportunities to work cooperatively on learning activities built around their interests, questions, and real-life concerns and when they share responsibility for deciding what gets learned and how, there is no need for rewards.

Selected Books and Articles

The homework myth: Why our kids get too much of a bad thing (Kohn, Philadelphia: De Capo Press, 2006)

The case against standardized testing: Raising the scores, ruining the schools (Kohn, Portsmouth, NH: Heinemann, 2000)

The schools our children deserve: Moving beyond traditional classrooms and "Tougher Standards" (Kohn, Boston: Houghton Mifflin, 1999)

Beyond discipline: From compliance to community (Kohn, Alexandria, VA: Association for Supervision and Curriculum Development, 1996/2006)

Punished by rewards: The trouble with gold stars, incentive plans, A's, praise, and other bribes (Kohn, Boston: Houghton Mifflin, 1993/1999)

Website: www.alfiekohn.org

for drawing (the "expected-reward" subjects). Still others were invited to draw and were then given an unexpected reward at the end (the "unexpected-reward" subjects). Subsequent observations during free play revealed that the children who had been promised a reward ahead of time engaged in the art activity half as much as they had initially. Children in the other two groups showed no change.

This study stimulated a great deal of research on the potentially detrimental effects of external rewards. Although the results were not always consistent, this research led educators to conclude that *rewarding people for doing something that is inherently pleasurable decreases their interest in continuing that behavior.* A common explanation for this effect is the *overjustification hypothesis.* It appears to work like this: Individuals being rewarded reason that the task must not be very interesting or engaging because they have to be rewarded (i.e., provided with extra justification) for undertaking it. In other words, what was previously considered "play" is now seen as "work" (Reeve, 2006). Another explanation focuses on the possibility that external rewards conflict with people's need for autonomy and self-determination. This explanation argues that interest in a task decreases if individuals perceive rewards as attempts to control their behavior.

The detrimental effect of extrinsic reward on intrinsic motivation has been—and continues to be—hotly debated. In fact, reviews of the research (Cameron, 2001; Cameron, Banko, & Pierce, 2001; Cameron & Pierce, 1994; Deci, Koestner, & Ryan, 1999, 2001) have reached contradictory conclusions about the effects of expected tangible rewards. According to one researcher, it's all right to say, "If you complete the assignment with at least 80 percent accuracy, you'll get a coupon for something at the school store at the end of the period" (expected reward contingent on completion and level of performance), but it's *not* all right to say, "Work on the assignment and you'll get a coupon for something at the school store at the end of the period" (noncontingent reward) (Cameron). In contrast, other researchers contend that expected "tangible rewards offered for engaging in, completing, or doing well at a task" are *all* deleterious to intrinsic motivation (Deci, Koestner, & Ryan, 1999, p. 656; 2001). With respect to verbal rewards and unexpected tangible rewards, the reviews are more consistent: Both sets of researchers conclude that verbal praise can enhance intrinsic motivation and that unexpected tangible rewards have no detrimental effect. Furthermore, most researchers acknowledge that external rewards can help develop intrinsic motivation when the initial interest level in the task is low (Williams & Stockdale, 2004). For example, if you are teaching Spanish verb conjugation, which high school students are not likely to find inherently interesting, providing rewards for successfully learning the conjugations at the beginning of the course can be phased out as students recognize the value of learning these conjugations in order to be successful in writing and reading assignments.

At the present time, caution in the use of external rewards is still in order. As you contemplate a system of rewards for your classroom, keep in mind the suggestions listed in the Practical Tips box.

PAUSE AND REFLECT

Galvanized by No Child Left Behind, schools across the country are trying to improve attendance by offering students the chance to win cars, computers, iPods, shopping sprees, groceries—even a month's rent (Belluck, 2006). Having just read the section on providing extrinsic rewards, what do you think about this practice? Do you think such rewards are likely to bring about an increase in attendance?

PRACTICAL TIPS FOR

Using Rewards

- *Use verbal rewards to increase motivation to engage in academic tasks.* It seems clear that praise can have a positive impact on students' motivation to learn. But remember that teenagers might be embarrassed by public praise, and they are good at detecting phoniness. To be reinforcing, praise should be specific, sincere, and contingent on the behavior you are trying to strengthen.

- *Reward students for improvement or effort.* Be careful about rewarding students for meeting somewhat arbitrary achievement goals (e.g., earning an exam score of 90 percent). Students who cannot achieve at that level will be ineligible for the reward. Instead, if you reward students for improvement or effort, all students potentially qualify for the reward. The reward should also include information about what the student did to earn it (Anderman & Anderman, 2010).

- *Save tangible rewards for activities that students find unattractive.* When students already enjoy doing a task, there's no need to provide tangible rewards. Save tangible rewards for activities that students tend to find boring and aversive.

- *If you're using tangible rewards, provide them unexpectedly after the task performance.* In this way, students are more likely to view the rewards as information about their performance and as an expression of the teacher's pleasure rather than as an attempt to control their behavior.

- *Be extremely careful about using expected tangible rewards.* If you choose to use them, be sure to make them contingent upon completion of a task or achieving a specific level of performance. If you reward students simply for engaging in a task, regardless of their performance, they are likely to spend less time on the task once the reward is removed.

- *Make sure that you select rewards that students like.* You might think that animal stickers are really neat, but if your high school students do not find them rewarding, using the stickers will not reinforce their behavior.

- *Keep your program of rewards simple.* An elaborate system of rewards is impossible to maintain in the complex world of the classroom. The fancier your system, the more likely that you will abandon it. Moreover, if rewards become too salient, they overshadow more intrinsic reasons for behaving in certain ways. Students become so preoccupied with collecting, counting, and comparing that they lose sight of why the behavior is necessary or valuable.

MOTIVATING UNDERACHIEVING AND DISAFFECTED STUDENTS

In *Building Community from Chaos* (2007), Linda Christensen, a high school teacher in Portland, Oregon, vividly portrays the challenge of motivating the academically unmotivated. Christensen writes about her fourth-block senior English class, a tracked class in which most of the students were short on credits to graduate but long on anger and attitude. Convinced that English class was a waste of time, her students made it clear that they didn't want "worksheets, sentence combining, reading novels and discussing them, writing about 'stuff we don't care about' " (p. 48). Christensen knew she needed to engage them "because they were loud, unruly, and out of control" (p. 48), but she didn't know how. She eventually decided to use the novel *Thousand Pieces of Gold* by Ruthann Lum McCunn, a book normally read by her college-level course in Contemporary Literature and Society:

> Students weren't thrilled with the book; in fact they weren't reading it. I'd plan a 90-minute lesson around the reading and dialogue journal they were supposed to be keeping, but only a few students were prepared. Most didn't even attempt to lie about the fact that they weren't reading and clearly weren't planning on it.
>
> In an attempt to get them involved in the novel, I read aloud an evocative passage about the unemployed peasants sweeping through the Chinese countryside pillaging, raping, and grabbing what was denied them through legal employment. Suddenly students saw their own lives reflected back at them through Chen, whose anger at losing his job and ultimately his family led him to become an outlaw. Chen created a new family with this group of bandits. Students could relate: Chen was a gang member. I had stumbled on a way to interest my class. The violence created a contact point between the literature and the students' lives.
>
> This connection, this reverberation across cultures, time and gender challenged the students' previous notion that reading and talking about novels didn't have relevance for them. They could empathize with the Chinese but also explore those issues in their own lives. (pp. 48–49)

As Christensen's story illustrates, finding ways to enhance students' motivation is particularly daunting when students are disaffected, apathetic, or resistant. Even when they know they could be successful, such students might find academic tasks meaningless and irrelevant to their lives. They could even fear that by engaging in learning activities, they will be acting in ways that are inconsistent with their self-image or objectionable to their peer group. This fear is apparent in some African Americans and other students of color who equate academic achievement with "acting White." In an influential paper published more than two decades ago, anthropologists describe how bright Black students might "put brakes" on their academic achievement by not studying or doing homework, cutting class, being late, and not participating in class (Fordham & Ogbu, 1986). Not surprisingly, the existence of "acting White" has been the subject of heated debate ever since, but a more recent study (Fryer, 2006) provides empirical evidence to support this phenomenon.

Motivating resistant, underachieving, or apathetic students requires "sustained efforts to resocialize such students' attitudes and beliefs . . ." (Brophy, 2010, p. 256). This means using the strategies described in this chapter in more sustained, systematic, and personalized ways. Extrinsic rewards might be especially useful in this regard (Hidi & Harackiewicz, 2000). By triggering engagement in tasks that students initially view as boring or irrelevant, "there is at least a chance" that real interest will develop (p. 159).

Resocialization also means combining high expectations for students with the encouragement and support needed to achieve those expectations—in short, showing students that you care about them as students and as people. As we mentioned in

Chapter 3, a substantial body of research exists on students' perceptions of school and teachers (see Hoy & Weinstein, 2006). This research consistently demonstrates that when students perceive their teachers as caring and supportive, they are more likely to be academically motivated, to engage in classroom activities, and to behave in prosocial, responsible ways (e.g., Murdock & Miller, 2003; Ryan & Patrick, 2001; Wentzel, 1997, 1998, 2006).

Perceiving that teachers care appears to be especially important for students who are alienated and marginalized and those who are at risk of school failure. For example, Anne Locke Davidson (1999) interviewed 49 adolescents representing diverse socioeconomic, cultural, and academic backgrounds. Data revealed not only students' appreciation and preference for teachers who communicated interest in their well-being but also students' willingness to reciprocate by being attentive and conscientious. This was particularly evident in the responses of "stigmatized" students who faced "social borders"—differences between their academic world (school) and their social world (home and community) in terms of values, beliefs, and expected ways to behave. Describing Wendy Ashton, a teacher who prodded students to achieve, one student commented, "She won't put you down, she'll talk to you and she'll go, 'Yeah, you know I love you. You know I want you to make something out of yourself, so stop messing around in class'" (Davidson, 1999, p. 361). Davidson speculates that students who do not face social borders might be more accepting of teachers who are relatively distant and impersonal because the students basically trust school as an institution; however, when students face the social divisions that can lead to alienation and marginalization, it is essential for teachers to be attentive, supportive, and respectful.

As the comment about Wendy Ashton suggests, this type of caring is less about being "warm and fuzzy" and more about being a "warm demander"—someone who provides a "tough-minded, no-nonsense, structured, and disciplined classroom environment for kids whom society has psychologically and physically abandoned" (Irvine & Fraser, 1998, p. 56). Researchers identified a small group of such teachers during a three-year study in two urban districts that served diverse student populations (Corbett, Wilson, & Williams, 2005). Both districts were desperately trying to find ways to close the achievement gap that existed between lower- and higher-income students. The researchers interviewed parents, students, teachers, and administrators and visited the classrooms of a sample of teachers from each grade level in each school. Their observations and interviews enabled them to identify a set of teachers who *simply refused to let students fail*. One of the teachers was Mrs. Franklin, an African American sixth-grade teacher whose school served mostly students of color. Mrs. Franklin believed that too many teachers had given up on students and didn't expect very much. As she put it: "Kids aren't the problem; adults are the ones finding the excuses" (p. 9). Mrs. Franklin didn't give her students an excuse not to do well. Her grading policy required any student work earning a grade lower than a C to be done over. Interestingly, interviews with students revealed that rather than resenting the strict grading policy, they appreciated it. As one student reported: "My teacher never let people settle for D or E; she don't let people get away with it. She give us an education. Other teachers don't care what you do. They pass you to be passing. Here, I pass my own self" (p. 10).

CONCLUDING COMMENTS

A while back, a colleague in educational psychology remarked that learning about classroom management would be unnecessary if prospective teachers understood how to enhance students' motivation. Although this argument struck us as naive and unrealistic, we understood—and agreed with—its underlying premise; *namely, that students who are interested and involved in the academic work at hand are less likely to daydream, disrupt, and defy.* In other words, management and motivation are inextricably linked.

As you contemplate ways to increase your students' expectations for success and the value they place on academic tasks, remember that motivating students doesn't happen accidentally. Fred emphasizes this point when he contends that "how I will motivate my students" should be an integral component of every lesson plan. Fortunately, the motivational strategies discussed in this chapter are consistent with current thinking about good instruction, which emphasizes students' active participation, collaborative group-work, and the use of varying assessments (Brophy, 2010).

Finally, remember the suggestions in Chapter 3 for creating a safer, more caring classroom. As we have stressed, students are more motivated when they perceive that teachers care about them. In Brophy's words: "You can become your own most powerful motivational tool by establishing productive relationships with each of your students" (2010, p. 312).

SUMMARY

Although teachers are responsible for enhancing motivation, this chapter began by questioning the belief that "good teachers should make learning fun." Such a goal seems unrealistic and inappropriate given the constraints of the secondary classroom—compulsory attendance, required curricula, class sizes that inhibit individualization, and the specter of high-stakes standardized testing. A more appropriate, realistic goal is to stimulate students' *motivation to learn,* moving them to pursue academic activities because they find them meaningful and worthwhile.

An Expectancy × Value Framework

- Motivation depends on:
    Students' expectation of success.
    The value they place on the task (or the rewards that it could bring).
- If either factor is missing, there will be no motivation.

Strategies for Increasing Expectations of Success

- Provide opportunities for success.
- Teach students to set reasonable goals and to evaluate their own performance.
- Help students recognize the relationship between effort and outcome.
- Provide informative feedback.
- Provide special motivational support to discouraged students.

Strategies for Increasing the Perceived Value of the Task

- Relate lessons to students' own lives.
- Provide opportunities for choice.

- Model interest in learning and express enthusiasm for the material.
- Include novelty/variety elements.
- Provide opportunities for students to respond actively.
- Allow students to create finished products.
- Provide opportunities for students to interact with peers.
- Provide extrinsic rewards:

> Keep in mind the different types of rewards: social rewards, special activities, tangible rewards.
>
> Be aware that rewarding people for doing something they already like to do can decrease their interest in continuing that behavior.
>
> Think carefully about when and how to use rewards.

Motivating Underachieving and Disaffected Students

- Be sensitive to the possibility that students of color could fear accusations of "acting White" if they strive to achieve academically.
- Recognize that resistant, apathetic students need to know you care about them. Research on students' perceptions of "good teachers" demonstrates that they want teachers who make sure they do their work, maintain order, offer help, explain assignments clearly, vary instruction, and take the time to get to know them as people.
- Demonstrate care by using the strategies described in this chapter in more sustained and systematic ways.

By working to ensure that students are engaged in learning activities, you can avoid many of the managerial problems that arise when students are bored and frustrated. Management and motivation are closely intertwined.

ACTIVITIES FOR SKILL BUILDING AND REFLECTION

In Class

1. In the following two vignettes, the teachers have directed the activity. In a small group, discuss ways they could have involved students in the planning, directing, creating, or evaluating.

   a. Mrs. Peters believed that the unit her seventh-grade class completed on folk tales would lend itself to a class play. She chose Paul Bunyan and Pecos Bill as the stories to dramatize. The students were excited as Mrs. Peters gave out parts and assigned students to paint scenery. Mrs. Peters wrote a script and sent it home for the students to memorize. She asked parents to help make the costumes. After three weeks of practice, the play was performed for elementary students and parents.

   b. Mr. Wilkins wanted his 10th-grade world civilization class to develop an understanding about ancient civilizations. He assigned a five-part project. Students had to research four civilizations (Egyptian, Mesopotamian, Indus Valley, and Shang); write a biography of Howard Carter, a famous archaeologist; describe three pyramids (step, Great Pyramid, Pyramid of Sesostris II); outline the reigns of five kings (Hammurabi, Thutmose III, Ramses II, David, and Nebuchadnezzar); and make a model of a pyramid. He gave the class four weeks to complete the projects and then collected them, graded them, and displayed them in the school library.

2. Working in small groups that are homogeneous in terms of discipline (i.e., English, world language, math, science), select a topic in your content area and design a lesson or activity that incorporates at least two of the strategies for increasing perceived value.

On Your Own

Interview an experienced, effective teacher about the motivational strategies he or she finds particularly effective with disaffected, resistant students.

For Your Portfolio

Design a "slanty rope assignment" in your content area that will enable students of varying achievement levels to experience success. For example, the task might vary in complexity; it might be open ended, allowing a variety of acceptable responses; it might require the use of different reference materials; or it might allow students to choose the format in which they demonstrate their understanding (e.g., a report, poster, or role-play).

FOR FURTHER READING

Brophy, J. E. (2010). *Motivating students to learn,* 3rd ed. New York: Routledge.
    This excellent book is written explicitly for teachers and offers principles and strategies to use in motivating students to learn. It is not a "bag of tricks" but the product of the author's comprehensive, systematic review of the motivational literature.

Curwin R. L. (2010). *Meeting students where they live: Motivation in urban schools.* Alexandria, VA: ASCD.
    This book contains strategies for engaging hard-to-teach students with lessons that build motivation and assessments that inspire effort. The strategies are applicable beyond the urban school setting.

Cushman, K. (2010). *Fires in the mind: What kids can tell us about motivation and mastery.* San Francisco: Jossey-Bass.
    The chapters in this book contain students' answers to the questions: What makes young people catch fire, work hard, and persist despite difficulties? What supports and structures do they need to thrive and contribute both in school and society? Students describe the conditions that ignite their curiosity and inspire them to strive for excellence. They also point out what practices support them through the necessary struggles in learning and those that destroy their desire to keep struggling.

Intrator, S. M. (2003). *Tuned in and fired up: How teaching can inspire real learning in the classroom.* New Haven: Yale University Press.
    Sam Intrator spent a year in Mr. Quinn's academically and ethnically diverse fourth-period English class. He observed and recorded class sessions, repeatedly interviewed the teacher and students, and collected student writing including "experience journals" in which students recorded the "peaks and valleys" of the school day. His goal: to capture "treasured moments" when teenagers "become immersed in their work" and experience a sense of energy and vitality. This book is about those moments of inspired learning.

Jackson, R. R. (2011). *How to motivate reluctant learners.* Alexandria, VA: ASCD.
    This how-to guide illustrates how master teachers motivate the most reluctant students by developing a plan to get students to invest in their own learning and shaping their classroom to make it more likely that students will make those investments.

Kohn, A. (1993). *Punished by rewards: The trouble with gold stars, incentive plans, A's, praise, and other bribes.* Boston: Houghton Mifflin.
    Kohn argues that our basic strategy for motivating students ("Do this and you'll get that") works only in the short run and actually does lasting harm. Instead of rewards, Kohn suggests that teachers provide the "three Cs": collaboration, content (things worth knowing), and choice. The result, he posits, will be "good kids without goodies."

Reeve, J. (2006). Extrinsic rewards and inner motivation. In C. M. Evertson & C. S. Weinstein (Eds.), *Handbook of classroom management.* Mahwah, NJ: Lawrence Erlbaum.

As Reeve notes, "Extrinsic rewards are ubiquitous in educational settings." For this reason, it's important for teachers to understand how rewards can be presented to students in ways that support rather than interfere with students' inner motivational resources. This chapter discusses the different types of extrinsic rewards, whether they work, what their side effects are, and how rewards can be used to support autonomy.

Sherer, M. (Ed.) (2012). *Educational Leadership, 70*(1).

This issue is devoted to the theme feedback for learning with articles on how to provide effective feedback to guide student learning.

ORGANIZATIONAL RESOURCES

The Institute of Play, www.instituteofplay.org. This nonprofit design studio was founded by a group of game designers to develop new models of learning and engagement through games. The Institute has developed several digital game design projects and is currently studying the potential of digital games for assessment of the Common Core Standards.

Persuasive Games, www.persuasivegames.com. This organization has created a wide variety of games designed to teach topics ranging from the flu virus to personal debt.

10 CHAPTER

Managing Independent Work, Recitations, and Discussions

Independent work, recitations (question-and-answer sequences), and discussions are three instructional activities commonly used in secondary classrooms. Each of these poses unique managerial "pitfalls" that make them particularly challenging to teachers. In this chapter, we examine these managerial pitfalls and suggest ways to structure each instructional approach to increase the probability of success. As always, we draw on the experiences and wisdom of our five teachers.

INDEPENDENT WORK: WHAT, WHY, AND HOW?

During an observation of one of Donna's eighth-grade language arts classes, she introduced a unit of study on Chinese culture designed to coincide with the Chinese New Year. She began by having students consider what they knew about western astrology. She handed out a "KWL" sheet divided into three columns labeled "What I **K**now"; "What I **W**ant to Know"; and "What I **L**earned." On a whiteboard was a list of astrological signs and the dates that each covered. Students were to determine what their zodiac sign was and jot down five things they already knew about it and five things they wanted to know. Then Donna gave students a packet of information about the zodiac that they were to read to complete the third column. Students were allowed to form groups if they wanted or to work alone. While students completed the task, Donna walked up and down the aisles, assisting, encouraging, and questioning.

This scenario describes the instructional situation known as *independent work.* In this situation, students are assigned to work at their desks with their own materials while the teacher is free to monitor the total class—to observe students' performance, provide support and feedback, engage in mini-conferences, and prepare students for homework assignments. Independent work is often used to provide students the chance to practice or review previously presented material.

Independent work is also referred to as *seatwork,* which has very negative connotations, particularly among educators who promote students' active participation and collaboration. In fact, when we sat down with Donna, Donnie, Sandy, Fred, and Christina to discuss their views, we found heated differences of opinion on this particular instructional format. On one hand, Sandy was vehemently negative: "I hate seatwork," she told us. "As far as I'm concerned, it's just a way of killing time." Similarly, Donnie claimed that she never used seatwork. We pointed out that we had frequently observed her using a pattern of direct instruction, beginning class with a review of the homework, then introducing a small segment of the new lesson, and having students do one or two problems at their seats while she circulated throughout the room. Donnie readily acknowledged her use of "guided practice" but argued that this was not seatwork:

> **It's not like elementary school, where you have different reading groups, and you have to find a way for kids to be busy for long periods of time while you're working with a small group. Most of my instruction is done with the whole group, so there's no need for all the kids to be sitting there quietly working on worksheets.**

Christina admitted some ambivalence. She acknowledged that whenever she heard the word *seatwork,* she immediately thought of "bad teachers who sit at their desks grading papers, writing lesson plans, or even reading the newspaper, while their students do boring work designed to keep them in their seats and quiet." But she also recognized that independent work was sometimes useful:

> **Realistically, there are times when I need to confer with individuals, so I need the rest of the class to be meaningfully occupied. Or I might want students to do something in class so I don't have to give them additional homework (especially if they're already working on a long-term assignment). Or I might want the work to be preceded by some instruction and to be followed by an interactive activity. This necessarily situates the seatwork in the middle of the class period, rather than for homework. But because I'm so leery about seatwork, I always try to ask myself, "Does this work need to be done in the classroom, or should it be done as homework?"**

Finally, Fred argued that seatwork could be a valuable activity:

> **I use seatwork to give kids the opportunity to practice skills like making predictions, valid inferences, generalizations. . . . Intellectual skills like these benefit from practice just like a backhand stroke in tennis. If**

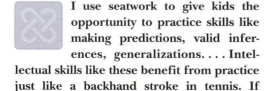

PAUSE AND REFLECT

The term *seatwork* has a negative connotation, and the question of whether or not to assign it often arouses debate. What has your experience as a student been with seatwork, and what types of seatwork have you observed in classrooms? What do you think about the contention that seatwork is a "necessary evil"?

I have 27 kids doing an assignment in class, I can walk around, see immediately what they're doing, give individual critiques, catch them if they're having a problem. I can't give that individual, immediate feedback if the work is done as homework.

In the end, we came to realize that there was no fundamental difference of opinion among us. We all agreed that teachers sometimes need to assign work for students to do on their own but in class with or without close teacher supervision. We also agreed that seatwork didn't have to mean silence; in fact, all the teachers felt strongly that students should generally be allowed to help one another. But we also agreed that seatwork is too often busywork, that it frequently goes on for too long, and that too many teachers use it as a substitute for active teaching. As Donnie put it, "Some teachers think of seatwork as 'give them something to do all period so I can do something else.' They'll teach for 10 minutes, then give their students 30 minutes of seatwork, and sit down. That's not seatwork—that's a free period."

Clearly, independent work can be useful, but it also poses significant challenges for both teachers and students. Consider the following description of a typical seatwork situation (adapted from Everhart, 1983). This scene takes place in Marcy's English class, where students are supposed to be learning how to write a persuasive essay.

First, Marcy asked the class to turn to the chapter on persuasive essays in their textbooks and read the first section. After five minutes Marcy asked the class, "How many have not yet finished?" Initially about one-third of the class raised their hands. Roy, sitting in the rear, nudged John. John then spoke up, "I'm not finished."

"I'm not finished either," Roy added, smiling. (Actually, they both had finished and closed their books a few minutes earlier and then proceeded to send text messages.)

"Well, I'll give you a few more minutes, but hurry up," said Marcy. Those not finished continued reading while the rest of the class began engaging in different activities: looking out the window, doodling, and looking at pictures on their phones. Roy pulled a copy of *Cycle World* magazine from beneath his desk and began leafing through it. After a few minutes Marcy went to the blackboard and began outlining the structure of the persuasive essay.

"Ok, what is the purpose of a persuasive essay?"

"To persuade," said one boy slouched in his chair and tapping his pencil.

"All right, comedian, that's obvious. What else?"

"To get out of doing something."

"Come on class, get serious! Why do you need to know how to write a persuasive essay? Larry?"

Marcy eventually gets through a description and explanation of the form of a persuasive essay. She then informs students that they will be writing their own persuasive essays, which will be due at the end of the following week. Today, they are to write the introductory paragraph:

After about 10 minutes of writing, Marcy asked, "How many are not finished with their paragraph?" About six students raised their hands. "OK, I'll give you a few minutes to finish up. The rest of you, I want you to read your paragraphs to each other because I want you to read them to the class tomorrow and they'd better be clear; if they aren't clear to you now they won't be clear to the class tomorrow."

One of the students at the back of the room seemed somewhat surprised at this. "Hey, you didn't say anything about having to read these in front of the class."

"Yeah, I don't want to read mine in front of the class," added Phil.

Marcy put her hands on her hips and stated emphatically, "Now come on, class, you'll all want to do a good job and this will give you a chance to practice and improve your paragraphs before they're submitted for grades. And you all want to get 'As', I'm sure." There was a chorus of laughs from most of the class and Marcy smiled.

"I don't care," said one girl under her breath.

"Yeah, I don't care either, just so I get this stupid thing done," said Don.

After saying that, Don turned to Art and said, "Hey, Art, what you writing your essay on?"

"On why we should be able to ditch school whenever we don't feel like coming."

"Wow," Ron replied.

"Don't think I'll write that though. Marcy will flip out."

"Yeah," Art replied.

The students continued talking to each other, which finally prompted Marcy to get up from her desk and say, "Class, get busy or some of you will be in after school."

Analysis of this scenario allows us to identify six problems that are frequently associated with seatwork. In the next section, we examine these problems and propose strategies for avoiding them. (These strategies are summarized in the Practical Tips box.)

PRACTICAL TIPS FOR

Designing and Implementing Effective Independent Work

- Assign work that is meaningful, useful, and relevant to students. Ask yourself:
  - What is the purpose of the task?
  - Does the task relate to current instruction? Are students likely to see the connection?
  - Are students likely to see the task as something worth doing or something boring and unrewarding?
  - Are the directions unambiguous and easy to follow?
  - Does the task provide students an opportunity to practice important skills or to apply what they are learning?
  - Does the task provide students the opportunity to think critically or to engage in problem solving?
  - Does the task require reading and writing, or does it simply ask students to fill in the blank, underline, or circle?
  - Does the task require higher-level responses or does it emphasize lower-level, factual recall and "drill and kill" practice of isolated subskills?
  - Is there a reason the task should be done in school (e.g., the need for coaching by the teacher) rather than at home?
  - Will students be able to accomplish the task without assistance? If not, how will assistance be provided?
- Match assignments to students' varying achievement levels.
- Make sure that written and oral directions are clear and thorough.
- Monitor behavior and comprehension.
- Plan for ragged endings.
- Teach students the norms for assisting peers.

Designing and Implementing Effective Independent Work

Donna's KWL assignment on astrological signs was clearly of interest to her students. We heard comments like, "Dude, you're a goat!" and "I'm a flying fish!" and "It says my lucky number is one, but it's really seven!" In contrast, one of Marcy's major problems is that *the assignment is not meaningful to students.* Don calls the persuasive essay a "stupid thing," Art jokes about writing that students should be allowed to ditch school, and an unnamed girl mumbles that she doesn't care about getting an A. In Fred's terms, Marcy has given her students the type of "garbage assignment" that is responsible for seatwork's bad reputation. "Garbage assignments" are not only a waste of precious learning time but also foster boredom, alienation, and misbehavior. If students do not perceive the value of a seatwork assignment, they are unlikely to become invested in it. That's when teachers have to resort to threats about detention or extrinsic incentives such as grades. Recall Marcy's words. First she tells her class, "And you all want to get 'As,' I'm sure." Later she warns, "Class, get busy or some of you will be in after school."

To avoid "garbage assignments," evaluating the activities you assign is essential. As Fred observes:

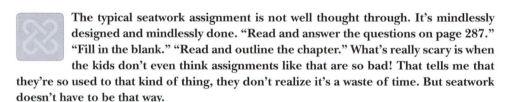 The typical seatwork assignment is not well thought through. It's mindlessly designed and mindlessly done. "Read and answer the questions on page 287." "Fill in the blank." "Read and outline the chapter." What's really scary is when the kids don't even think assignments like that are so bad! That tells me that they're so used to that kind of thing, they don't realize it's a waste of time. But seatwork doesn't have to be that way.

Donna, Donnie, Christina, Sandy, and Fred carefully evaluate the tasks they give students to complete during class. (The Practical Tips box lists some of the questions they ask themselves before they assign independent work.) Often our teachers create their own assignments rather than relying on commercially prepared materials. In this way, they are better able to connect the tasks with students' backgrounds and experiences, target particular problems that students are having, and provide increased individualization. For example, when Fred wants students to become familiar with the library resources, he asks them to do tasks such as these:

- Find two facts on a topic that interests you by using three different search engines to confirm the facts.
- Use the online CIA Factbook to find a country that begins with the first letter of your last name and list the population, type of government, and gross national product.
- Use *The New York Times* online electronic database to identify an important event that occurred on your last birthday.
- Locate a biography about a person whose last name begins with the same letter as your first name.

According to Fred, this simple way to individualize the assignment has a very positive effect on students' motivation. (And there's an added bonus: Students have to do their own work.) Fred acknowledges that he can't always "be creative and wonderful five days a week, week after week," but he always tries to ensure that the independent work he assigns has a valid purpose. It's worth keeping his comments in mind:

> **Look, I'm human. . . . There are times when I'll give kids seatwork assignments that are less than wonderful, assignments that I'm not especially proud of. But I really try to make that the exception, not the rule, and to come up with seatwork that's meaningful to kids and educationally useful.**

A second problem with Marcy's seatwork assignment is that it *does not match students' varying achievement levels.* For some students, the reading assignment seems too easy; they finish reading quickly and fill their time by doodling, looking out the window, and reading magazines. Others seem to find the reading more difficult and need "a few more minutes." Similarly, writing one paragraph in 10 minutes doesn't seem like a particularly challenging assignment for most of Marcy's students, yet six students indicate they are not finished when Marcy checks their progress. (Of course, it's possible that they have just been wasting time.)

In a large, heterogeneous class, creating multiple assignments on the same content can be difficult. One strategy is to use open-ended tasks that allow students working on a variety of levels to complete the work successfully. For example, when Donna's students read a chapter in their texts, she often forgoes the end-of-chapter questions (which often have one correct answer); instead, she might ask students to create their own questions and then answer them. At other times, she asks a question that is broad enough so that almost everyone in the class is able to respond—in some fashion—to the question, although answers obviously vary in terms of length, substance, and coherence. As mentioned in Chapter 9, Fred calls this the "slanty rope theory":

> **If we set a rope across a room at four feet, some kids can get over it and some can't. But if we slant the rope, then everyone can find their way over at some point. I firmly believe that people don't all want to go over at the lowest level. We can encourage kids to stretch—and once you teach kids to stretch, you've taught something more important than the subject matter.**

In the following example (Tomlinson, 1999), we see how a foreign language teacher has created a "slanty rope assignment" that allows her heterogeneous class to pursue the same general topic but at varying levels of difficulty and sophistication:

Mrs. Higgins's German 1 class is studying the formation of past-tense verbs. One group of students will work with pattern drills in which much of a German sentence is supplied. However, each sentence uses an English verb, and students must supply the correct form of the past-tense German verb. Mrs. Higgins has ensured that the missing verbs are regular.

A second, more proficient, group has a similar activity. But they will encounter a greater number and complexity of missing words, including a few irregular verbs. Another group of students works with the same sentences as the second group, but virtually all of the sentences are in English and must be translated into German. Two or three students don't need the skill drill at all; they are given a scenario to develop, with instructions about the sorts of grammatical constructions that must be included. (pp. 51–52)

For more about ways to differentiate assignments and respond to the needs of all learners, see Tomlinson (2001).

A third problem is that Marcy *does not provide her students clear, complete directions.* At the beginning of the period, she tells the students to start reading the chapter on persuasive essays, but she says nothing about why they are to read it, how long they have, or whether they should take notes. In other words, she merely tells them to "do it"—without explaining the purpose for reading or suggesting strategies that might be used. Nor does Marcy explain that they will be writing their own essays later in the period. Only after reviewing the form of the persuasive essay does Marcy instruct her students to write the introductory paragraph, and once again, she neglects to tell them what will be coming next—namely, that they will be reading the paragraphs aloud the following day. (Marcy might have made this decision at the last minute to provide an activity for students who finished early.) Not surprisingly, some of the students react with displeasure. One complains, "Hey, you didn't say anything about having to read these in front of the class," while another protests, "Yeah, I don't want to read mine in front of the class."

Obviously, Marcy could have avoided these negative reactions had she made sure that her oral directions were clear and complete. Contrast Marcy's directions with the way Donnie introduces a brief seatwork assignment on rearranging equations to solve for different variables. Even though the assignment will take just a few minutes, she explains what students are to do, how much time they will have, and what they will be expected to do when they're finished:

 What I need you to do now is turn to page 178. Get out some paper and a pencil or pen. We're going to look at the chapter review, up through #15. I'm going to begin by making an assignment to each person. Problem #1, Ernest; Problem #2, Damika; Problem #3, Latoya; Problem #4, Jerome. [She continues until everyone has been assigned a problem to do.] Now I want you to solve the problem you were assigned. These are just like the homework problems we just reviewed. You're going to be rearranging equations to solve for the different variables. . . . I'll give you approximately two minutes to do this. When we come back, make sure you can give us the answer and explain the problem to the rest of the class.

Christina is also careful about providing clear, complete directions, and she tries hard to avoid surprises (like having to read your letter aloud), especially because English class often involves having students write about personal experiences and feelings:

 Christina distributes copies of her own personal essay, which deals with her ethnic background. She explains that students should read her essay and then begin to jot down ideas and write a draft of their own personal essay on the topic of identity. They will have a total of 30 minutes. She cautions them to "select something that you will feel OK to share in small groups, and keep in mind that I'll be picking the groups." A girl in the front row nods and comments, "So we should write something we can share with anyone."

Sometimes teachers think they don't have to explain orally what students are to do because written instructions are in the textbook or on the worksheet. But don't assume that they'll read these automatically; this could be a skill you'll have to teach. Consider the lesson learned by this student teacher:

> *These kids don't instinctively read something when it is given to them: They wait to have it explained. . . . I know that I'm supposed to state all the objectives and explain things carefully, but there are times when I want them . . . to be curious enough to take a look at what's in front of them. I try to pepper my handouts with cartoons and some of my own spectacular drawings just to make them more attractive and engaging. I'm so used to the college mentality—something is passed out and you read it rather than listen to it being explained. I have to remember it's usually the opposite in high school.*

In addition to teaching students to read the directions, it is important to check that these are clear and precise. For example, one districtwide assignment that Christina gives requires students to read a book and write their reflections in a journal with at least 10 entries. Students are provided 10 guiding questions, but it's not clear from the directions whether students have to answer *one* question or *all* the questions for each journal entry. Actually, they have to do neither. So Christina adds a sentence specifying that students have to address each question *somewhere* in the journal but not in any specific order and not in every entry.

A fourth problem evident in Marcy's class is her *lack of monitoring.* Although the vignette doesn't explicitly describe what Marcy is doing while her students are reading and writing, the last paragraph does state that she gets up from her desk to admonish students who are talking. Furthermore, Marcy not only has to ask how many students have not yet finished but also seems unaware that students in the rear of the room are sending text messages. These are sure signs that Marcy is not circulating through the room, checking on students' progress, helping them with problems, and providing feedback. If Marcy is not going to provide this supervision and support, she might as well have her students do the assignment at home. As we mentioned in Chapter 8, our teachers rarely sit down while students are working unless they are having individual conferences. And even then, they continue to monitor the rest of the class. Donna often sets up her "editing table" in the center front of the classroom where she works with individual students while the rest of the class works on their writing assignment. She notes, "At the same time I am having a very in-depth conversation with a student, I am still monitoring what the rest are doing. My students say, '"She hears everything!"'"

In the following example, also taken from Donnie's lesson on rearranging equations, we see the way she circulates throughout the room while students are working. Notice how she is able to *overlap* (Kounin, 1970)—to monitor the behavior of students doing seatwork while she also works with an individual.

Students are working on the problems Donnie has just assigned. She walks around the room, peering over students' shoulders, commenting, helping, prodding them along. Then she heads over to three students who were absent and are making up the assignment that everyone else did the day before. She checks what they are doing and helps one girl who is having particular difficulty. While she is working with this student, she periodically looks up and scans the room to monitor the rest of the class. One boy appears to be doing nothing. "Jerome, are you finished with your problem?"

The purpose of circulating is not simply to monitor behavior. Roving around the room allows you to monitor students' *understanding of the assignment.* (Recall the distinction between *engaged time* and *productive learning time* discussed in Chapter 8.) Clearly, it's not enough for students to remain busy and on task. They must also understand what they are supposed to do and carry out their tasks successfully. Sandy comments:

> **When I give a seatwork assignment, I never sit at my desk doing paperwork. I give an assignment for an instructional reason, not just to keep kids busy while I grade papers. This means that I need to be moving around, seeing what they're doing. For example, at the end of the period, I might say, "Let's try problems 1, 2, and 3." I walk around and help. If I see that students are doing all right, then I know I can have them complete 4 through 6 for homework.**

Fifth, Marcy does not really plan for the fact that *students work at different paces.* They might *begin* seatwork at the same time, but they never *finish* at the same time. "Ragged" endings can upset a schedule that looked beautiful on paper. Students who cannot complete assignments in the allotted time might have to do them for homework. Students who complete their work earlier than you expected need something to keep them occupied; if they must sit and wait with nothing to do, they might distract students who are still working. In Marcy's class, students who finish earlier than their peers are actually quite well behaved: They text, read *Cycle World* magazine, look out the window, doodle, and look at pictures on their phones. Nonetheless, they are wasting time that could be spent on more profitable activities.

In the classrooms of our five teachers, ragged endings are rarely a problem because class activities are structured so that students rarely finish early. Listen to Sandy:

> **Not only do students have to understand what to do and why they're doing it, they need to know what's expected upon completion. If you don't do this, some kids may rush through, thinking I'll finish real fast and then I'll have time to do my homework. If they know they'll have a follow-up related assignment, they keep going. I never make it a closed assignment. I'll say, "Today you're going to do an analysis of knowns. Once you've completed the analysis, formulate the flow chart for your unknowns." I know it usually takes a complete double period to do this. When time is about to run out, I'll say, "If you're not done, do it tonight." If they know at the beginning that it's a homework assignment, they may relax, figure they'll just do it for homework. So I never let them know that they won't be able to finish. If they see that they have a lot to do, they'll say, "Wow, I really need to work." If it's a 10-minute task, they may drag it out.**

When students do finish a task early in Donna's classroom, she makes it clear what they are to do next.

> **I don't have students do coloring projects or puzzles. If they are done, I have them practice their writing. I only have them for a certain amount of time and their assessment has to reflect that they can meet the Language Arts standards. They will rush through their work if they have puzzles to do afterwards.**

Christina finds that ragged endings are a special challenge when students are doing writing workshop projects:

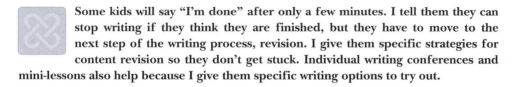 **Some kids will say "I'm done" after only a few minutes. I tell them they can stop writing if they think they are finished, but they have to move to the next step of the writing process, revision. I give them specific strategies for content revision so they don't get stuck. Individual writing conferences and mini-lessons also help because I give them specific writing options to try out.**

Finally, Marcy never makes it clear whether students can ask peers for assistance. In some classes, teachers encourage students to work collaboratively; in other classes, giving or receiving help is tantamount to cheating. This latter situation can present a real dilemma for students. On one hand is their need to follow the teacher's directions and to stay out of trouble. On the other hand is their need to complete the assignment successfully and to assist friends who are having difficulty.

Students' understanding and acceptance of the norms for helping peers can be influenced by culture. Providing assistance could be especially valued by students with cultural roots in collectivist societies (e.g., African, Asian, Hispanic, and Native American). In collectivist cultures, people assume responsibility for one another's welfare, and the focus is on working toward the common good (Cartledge with Milburn, 1996). Thus, students from these cultures might resist teachers' directives to work independently. In contrast, those from individualistic cultures (e.g., English-speaking countries) might value individual effort. Parents in these individualistic cultures might actually object to having their children help others, believing that it deprives them of learning time.

In general, all of our teachers not only allow but also *encourage* students to help one another. As Donnie puts it, "I can't possibly get around to everybody. The kids would constantly be calling me to come over and help them. For my own sanity, I have to have students help one another. But I think they learn better that way anyway." Christina agrees. When she circulates around the room monitoring students' progress, she'll frequently refer students who are having problems to individuals she's already assisted:

I do this for a few reasons. First, it's nice for the students I just helped to know that I now consider them to be "experts." Second, I think that having students teach others helps them to remember what I just explained. Third, it saves me having to repeat the same explanations. And finally I think it builds a helping community. But I always try to go back to the kids and check if the helpers were able to explain clearly and if the "helpees" now understand. I don't want kids to think I'm just pushing them off on others because I don't want to be bothered.

It's important to note that all the teachers work hard to explain what "helping" really means. They take pains to explain to students that simply providing the answer or doing the task for someone else is not helping, and they stress the futility of copying. Donnie says she has "parasites" in her geometry class who don't want to do anything on their own; they just want someone to give them the answer. To prevent this from happening, she'll sometimes assign different problems to students sitting next to each other; this allows them to help each other but not to copy.

Although all the teachers firmly believe in the value of peer assistance, there are also times when they do *not* allow students to help one another. In these situations, they are careful to explain that the ground rules are different. Listen to Sandy:

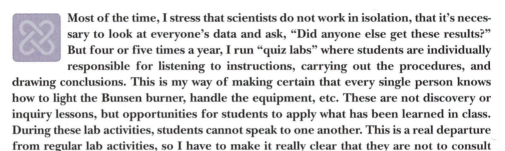

Most of the time, I stress that scientists do not work in isolation, that it's necessary to look at everyone's data and ask, "Did anyone else get these results?" But four or five times a year, I run "quiz labs" where students are individually responsible for listening to instructions, carrying out the procedures, and drawing conclusions. This is my way of making certain that every single person knows how to light the Bunsen burner, handle the equipment, etc. These are not discovery or inquiry lessons, but opportunities for students to apply what has been learned in class. During these lab activities, students cannot speak to one another. This is a real departure from regular lab activities, so I have to make it really clear that they are not to consult with one another—that the norms are different.

RECITATIONS AND DISCUSSIONS: WHAT, WHY, AND HOW?

Much of the talk that occurs between teachers and students is unlike the talk you hear in the "real world." Let's consider just one example. In the real world, if you ask someone the name of a particular author, we can assume that you really need to know that information and will be grateful for a reply. The conversation would probably go something like this:

"Who wrote *The Grapes of Wrath?*"

"John Steinbeck."

"Oh, yes, thank you."

In contrast, if a teacher asks this question during a lesson, the dialogue generally sounds like this:

"Who wrote *The Grapes of Wrath?*"

"John Steinbeck."

"Very good."

Here, the question is not a request for needed information but a way to find out what students know. The interaction is more like a quiz show (Roby, 1988) than a true conversation: The teacher *initiates* the interaction by asking a question, a student *responds,* and the teacher *evaluates* the response or *follows up* in some way (Abd-Kadir & Hardman, 2007; Mehan, 1979). This pattern of interaction (I-R-E or I-R-F) is called *recitation,* and several studies (e.g., Stodolsky, 1988) have documented the substantial amount of time that students spend in this instructional activity.

Recitation has been frequently denounced as a method of instruction. Critics object to the active, dominant role of the teacher and the relatively passive role of the student. They decry the lack of interaction among students. They condemn the fact that recitations often emphasize the recall of factual information and demand little higher-level thinking. They worry about the "negative interdependence" among students that recitations can generate (Kagan, 1989/90). In other words, if a student is unable to respond to the teacher's question, the other students have an increased chance to be called on and to receive praise; thus, students might actually root for their classmates' failure.

Despite the validity of these criticisms, recitation remains an extremely common feature of secondary classrooms. What is there about this instructional strategy that makes it so enduring in the face of other, more highly touted methods? We thought hard about this question during one visit to Donna's classroom, and our observation of a recitation session that she conducted provided some clues. Students had been learning about literary devices used in poetry, and now they were analyzing "Oh Captain, My Captain" by Walt Whitman, a poem in their literature anthology.

Donna: The authors give you a visual hint about who the subject of this poem is. What's the hint?

Student: The picture of Abraham Lincoln.

Donna: Right. What do we know about Abraham Lincoln?

Student: He got rid of slavery.

Donna: Yes, he abolished slavery.

Student: He was the president during the war.

Donna: What war?

Student: World War II.

Donna: [Looks skeptical] World War II was in the 1940s, and Abraham Lincoln lived in the 1800s. So is that possible?

Students: No.

Donna: So what war? What war took place when Abraham Lincoln was president?

Student: The Civil War.

Donna: Okay! Who was fighting in the Civil War?

Student: The U.S. It was between the North and the South.

Donna: Yes, right. And what finally happened to Abraham Lincoln?

Student: He was assassinated. He was at a play.

Donna: Yes, at Ford's Theater. Now what's interesting about this poem is that Walt Whitman never says straight out that it's about Abraham Lincoln, or the Civil War, or the North, or the South. He uses *metaphors*. Let's review what a metaphor is. Jason.

Student: Comparing two things without using like or as.

Donna: Yes! Awesome remembering. Okay, take a minute to re-read the first stanza and then we'll look at all the metaphors in just the first stanza. [She projects two columns on the smart board, one with the label "metaphor," under which are listed metaphors from the first stanza, and the other with the label "meaning." She gets a cup containing students' names so she can call on students randomly.] I'm going to call you up and ask you to write in the meaning of these metaphors. Let's start with "captain." Whitman is comparing Abraham Lincoln to a captain. Why do you think Whitman chose the metaphor of "captain?" [Silence.] Think for a minute about the way people traveled in 1865. If you wanted to go to England at that time, how would you get there?

Student: By ship.

Donna: Ahh. By ship. How would you probably go to England *now*?

Student: By plane.

Donna: So if Walt Whitman were writing the poem now, he'd probably use what metaphor for Lincoln?

Student: Pilot.

Donna: Good. But Whitman lived in the 1800s, so he knew that people would be familiar with ships' captains. So what's one meaning of "captain?" Katie.

Katie: Leader. [She goes up and writes "leader" across from "captain."]

Student: It could also mean an overseer, because Lincoln oversaw the war.

Donna: Great word. [She adds "overseer" to the graphic organizer.]

Donna: Okay, how about "fearful trip?" What was the "fearful trip?" Jorge.

Jorge: [Goes up to the smart board and writes "The Civil War.]

Donna: Yes, the Civil War was certainly a fearful trip. Alida, what about "rack?"

Alida: The rack was the battles. [Goes up to board and writes "battles".]

Donna: You people really understand these metaphors. You know, a lot of people don't like poetry because they don't know what's being compared, and then they just don't get the poem. Jason, what's the "prize?"

Jason: Winning the war.

Donna's question-and-answer session helped us to identify five very useful functions of classroom recitations. First, the recitation allowed Donna to assess students' recollection of metaphors and to check their background knowledge on Abraham Lincoln and the Civil War. Second, by asking students to think about what the metaphors stood for in the poem, she was able to prod her students to do some critical thinking and to guide them to some fundamental understandings. Third, the recitation permitted Donna to involve students in the presentation of material. Instead of telling students directly about the meaning of each metaphor, she brought out the information by asking questions. Fourth, the recitation provided the chance to interact individually with students even in the midst of a whole-group lesson. In fact, our notes indicate that Donna made contact with seven different students in just the brief interchange reported here. Finally, through her questions, changes in voice tone, and gestures, Donna was able to maintain a relatively high attention level; in other words, she was able to keep most of her students "with her."

During one of our meetings, Fred reflected aloud on some other useful functions of recitations:

 I'll use recitation a lot at the beginning of the year because it's a good way to get to know kids' names and to see how they handle themselves in class. It's also a tool for building self-confidence in a new class. They have a chance to speak in class, and I can provide them with opportunities for success early in the year. It's generally a pretty nonthreatening activity; since it doesn't ask for as much higher-level thinking as discussions, it's easier. I also try to emphasize that it's okay not to know, that we can figure out this stuff together. That's what education is.

TABLE 10.1 Differences between Recitations and Discussions		
Dimension	Recitation	Discussion
Predominant speaker	Teacher (2/3 or more)	Students (half or more)
Typical exchange	Teacher question; student answer, teacher evaluation (I-R-E)	Mix of statements and questions by mix of teacher and students
Pace	Many brief, fast exchanges	Fewer, longer, slower exchanges
Primary purpose	To check students' comprehension	To stimulate variety of responses, encourage students to consider different points of view, foster problem solving and critical thinking, examine implications
The answer	Predetermined right or wrong, same right answer for all students	No predetermined right or wrong, can have different answers for different students
Evaluation	Right or wrong, by teacher only	Agree or disagree, by student and teacher

Source: Adapted from Dillon, 1994.

As we can see, a recitation session does not have to be a "quiz show" in which passive students mindlessly recall low-level, insignificant facts. On the other hand, both the pattern of interaction (I-R-E or I-R-F) and the primary intent (to assess students' understanding of the reading) set it apart from another type of questioning session: the *discussion.* (Table 10.1 summarizes the differences between recitation and discussion.)

In contrast to recitation, *discussion* is a form of verbal interaction in which individuals work together to consider an issue or a question. The discussion is intended to stimulate a variety of responses, to encourage students to consider different points of view, to foster problem solving to examine implications, and to relate material to students' own personal experiences (Good & Brophy, 2008). In a discussion, individuals might offer their understandings, relevant facts, suggestions, opinions, perspectives, and experiences. These are examined for their usefulness in answering the question or resolving the issue (Dillon, 1994).

To make the distinction clear, let's consider an example from Fred's class. The topic was budget deficits, and Hope had just asked a key question: "Why can't the government just print more money to pay off a debt?" Fred noted that this was an important question, and he asked if students had any possible explanations.

Susan: I think maybe I know. You know how they say that everyone can't be a millionaire. There's got to be some poor people? It's like that.

John: Yeah, like when I play Monopoly. I buy every property, so I go into bankruptcy. So I take out a loan, and I'm ruining the game because I'm not playing with the money I'm supposed to have. It's like cheating.

   Lorie: **Yeah, that money doesn't really exist.**

   Hope: **What do you mean? If the government prints the money, it does exist. [A number of students begin talking at the same time.]**

   Fred: **Hold on. Stuart, then Roy, then Alicia.**

  Stuart: **The money's worth a lot because there's only a little. If there were a lot, it would only be worth a little.**

   Hope: **I still don't understand. So what, if it's only worth a little.**

   Roy: **Pretend there's this gold block sitting in Fort Knox and it's worth $10, but there's only one $10 bill. Now if we make up ten $10 bills, each will only be worth $1.**

   Hope: **So what? I can still use it to buy stuff. [A few students start to jump in, but Fred intervenes.]**

   Fred: **Alicia hasn't had her chance to talk.**

  Alicia: **I think I got it now. Let me try. There's this diamond, and we both want it. . . . [She continues to explain, but Hope is still confused.]**

   Fred: **Let's see if I can help out here. . . .**

As we can see from this excerpt, the predominant pattern in this interchange was not I-R-E, but I-R-R-R. Fred essentially stays out of the interaction, except for making sure that students have an opportunity to speak when the interaction gets excited. In contrast to the recitation, students speak directly to one another. They comment on one another's contributions, they question, they disagree, and they explain.

Providing opportunities for discussions means that teachers have to give up their role as *leader* and assume the role of *facilitator*. This can be difficult for teachers who are accustomed to dominating or at least directing the conversation. But acting as a facilitator rather than a leader does not mean abdicating responsibility for guiding the interaction. This became very clear during a conversation with Fred in which he described some of the problems that he tries to anticipate and avoid:

 First of all, a discussion like this can be an opportunity for some kids to show how smart they are and to get air time, so it's important to watch out that kids don't pontificate and monopolize. Second, you have to listen carefully and ask yourself, "Where is this going?" I often have an end goal in mind, and I try to make sure that the discussion doesn't get too far afield. Occasionally, I'll jump in and say something like, "I think we're losing the focus here" or "I think you're arguing over semantics." Also, a lot of times kids state opinions as fact, and I think it's important not to let them get away with that. I'll interject and ask them to provide supporting evidence. Or I'll ask for clarification: "Is that what you meant to say?"

Recitation and discussion are often confused. Teachers often say that they use discussion a great deal when in fact they are conducting recitations. For example, in an observational study (Alvermann, O'Brien, & Dillon, 1990), 24 middle school teachers reported using discussion. Yet only seven could actually be observed doing so; the others were using recitation or lecture interspersed with questions. These findings are consistent with observations of 1,000 elementary and secondary classrooms across the country in which discussion was seen only *4 to 7 percent of the time* (Goodlad, 1984). Almost 20 years later, the amount of discussion does not appear to have changed: A study of 64 English/language arts classes in 19 middle and high schools found that discussion occurred for only 1.7 minutes per 60 minutes of class time—or 3.8 percent of the time (Applebee, Langer, Nystrand, & Gamoran, 2003). It is clear that real discussion is very rarely used in classroom. As Sandy comments:

> **A lot of beginning teachers get these two mixed up. They've been told they're supposed to ask a lot of questions, so they do, but often the questions are yes/no questions or questions that elicit short answers without a lot of depth: What do all atoms have in common? How many protons are in this atom? In discussions, the majority of the questions are critical thought questions, and the response time is longer. You're trying to develop an idea or draw a conclusion. You're not just reviewing; you're working toward a conceptual goal.**

Although educational critics frequently decry the use of recitation and promote the use of discussion, both types of interaction have a legitimate place in the secondary classroom—if done well. The next section of this chapter considers the managerial challenges of recitations and suggests strategies for avoiding or minimizing these challenges. We then do the same for discussions.

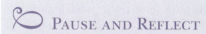

Pause and Reflect

Even if you are unfamiliar with the term *recitation,* you have most likely participated in many such question-and-answer sessions during your years in school. In contrast, your experiences with discussions could be far more limited. Reflecting on the differences between these two, consider the appropriateness of both instructional strategies for the content you plan to teach. Can you think of instances when a discussion would be appropriate? If so, how would you manage it?

Implementing Effective Recitations

The first challenge of recitations is *unequal participation among students.* Imagine yourself in front of a class of 25 students. You've just asked a question. A few individuals have their hands up, conveying their desire (or at least their willingness) to be called on. Others are sitting quietly, staring into space, their expressions blank. Still others are slumped down as far as possible in their seats; their posture clearly says, "Don't call on me."

In such a situation, it's tempting to call on an individual whose hand is raised. After all, you're likely to get the response you want—a very gratifying situation! You also avoid embarrassing students who feel uncomfortable speaking in front of the group or who don't know the answer, and you're able to keep up the pace of the lesson. But selecting only those who volunteer or those who call out could limit the interaction to a handful of students. This can be a problem. Students tend to learn more if they are actively participating. Furthermore, because those who volunteer are often high achievers, calling only on volunteers is likely to give you a distorted picture of how well everyone understands. Finally, restricting your questions to a small number of students can communicate negative attitudes and expectations to the others (Good & Brophy, 2008): "I'm not calling on you because I'm sure you have nothing to contribute." Negative attitudes like this can be communicated even if you have the best of intentions. Listen to Sandy recall a situation in which she made a practice of not calling on a student who seemed painfully shy:

> It was my second year of teaching, but I still remember it clearly. My kids did course evaluations at the end of the year, and one kid said I didn't care about students. I was devastated. I tracked her down and asked her why she thought I didn't care. She said it was because I hadn't required her to participate in class discussions. Here I had been trying to avoid causing her embarrassment. She seemed so afraid to talk, so I left her alone. And she interpreted my behavior as saying I didn't care. That taught me a good lesson!

Unequal participation can be a particular problem if you have English language learners (ELLs) in your classes. Although ELLs can become proficient in conversations with their peers after about two years of exposure to English, it can take five to seven years for them to acquire grade-level proficiency in academic discourse (Cummins, 2000). Thus, it could be difficult or intimidating for them to take an active role in either recitations or discussions.

During one visit to Donnie's classroom, we watched her distribute participation widely by specifying that each student should give only one possible answer to the problem:

Donnie: Today we start a new adventure—equations with two variables. Our answers are going to be ordered pairs. I'm going to put this up here, $x + y = 3$. [She writes the equation on the board.] Now, if I ask you to give me all the possible answers, what would you say? [There are lots of hands up.] Okay, give me one, Shameika.

Shameika: (0, 3).

Donnie: [She writes that on the board.] Okay, give me another. Sharif.

Sharif: (1, 2).

Donnie: Another. Tayeisha.

Tayeisha: (2, 1).

In another application of this strategy, we see Christina increase participation by not "grabbing" the first answer and moving on to a new question. She has just focused students' attention on a passage from Edith Wharton's *Ethan Frome* in which Ethan looks at a cushion his wife Zeena had made for him when they were engaged—"the only piece of needlework he had ever seen her do"—and then flings it across the room.

Christina: He throws it across the room. What does this suggest about his feelings for her?

Student 1: I think it shows that he really did hate her.

Student 2: I think he just felt so guilty. Guilt overpowered the hate. That's why he didn't leave her.

Student 3: He wouldn't know how to react to the freedom. I think he's afraid to leave.

Christina: Good point. Is he not leaving because he's used to the farm, or because of Zeena, or because he's afraid to be alone?

Student 5: Now that you said that, it made me think, maybe it's not Zeena who has the problem. Maybe it's Ethan. And maybe it would happen again with Mattie. . . .

Student 6: Yeah. He needs someone to rely on. First he relied on Zeena and his parents. Now she's getting sicker, and he can't rely on her, so he's turning to Mattie.

Student 7: But if he relied on her when he needed it, why can't she rely on him now that she needs it?

Student 8: He could slip something into her drink and get rid of her and marry Mattie.

Sometimes teachers use a "round-robin" technique, going around the room and calling on each student in order. You can also use a pattern that is more subtle than the round-robin so that students do not know exactly when they will be called on. Donnie uses this approach (described earlier in the section on interaction routines in Chapter 5):

 Sometimes I'll start in a front corner, and then go diagonally to the back of the room, then across, and down. I find that using a pattern like that helps me to keep track of who I call on, and it helps me make sure I get to everyone. And it's less obvious than just going up and down the rows.

Another strategy is to use the "popsicle stick system" (described in Chapter 5), pulling sticks labeled with students' names from a can or mug and placing the sticks on the side after the student has responded. You can also have each student write a response and share it with one or two neighbors. This allows everyone to participate actively. You might then ask some of the groups to report on what they discussed.

A second challenge of recitations is *balancing the need to maintain pace and involvement with the need to provide feedback and time to think.* When you ask your question, you might receive the response you have in mind. You might also get ill-timed remarks that have nothing to do with the lesson (e.g., "There's gum on my shoe."), answers that indicate confusion and misunderstanding, or complete silence. All of these threaten the smooth flow of a recitation and can cause it to become sluggish, jerky, or unfocused.

Threats like these require you to make instantaneous decisions about how to proceed. If a student's answer reveals confusion, for example, it's essential to provide feedback and assistance. But how can you provide appropriate feedback while maintaining the pace and momentum of your lesson? Rosenshine (1986) reviewed the research on effective teaching and developed a set of guidelines that might be helpful. According to Rosenshine, when students give correct, confident answers, you can simply ask another question or provide a brief verbal or nonverbal indication that they are correct. If students are correct but hesitant, however, a more deliberate affirmation is necessary. You might also explain *why* the answer is correct ("Yes, that's correct, because . . .") to reinforce the material.

When students provide an incorrect answer, the feedback process is trickier. If you think the individual has made a careless error, you can make a simple correction and move on. If you decide that the student can arrive at the correct answer with a little help, you can provide hints or prompts. Sometimes it's useful to backtrack to a simpler question that you think the individual can answer and then work up to your original question step by step. Watch Sandy:

> **Students are stuck on the question: "Given the following balanced equation, what volume of hydrogen gas can be produced from the decomposition of two moles of H_2O?" Their faces are blank, and there's absolute silence. Sandy asks: "Well, what is the volume of one mole of any gas at STP [standard temperature and pressure]?" All hands shoot up. Sandy calls on a student to respond. "22.4 liters." Sandy continues: "Do you know the relationship between moles of H_2O and moles of hydrogen gas produced?" Again, there are lots of hands, and a student replies: "It's a one-to-one relationship. The equation shows you that." Suddenly there is a lot of hand-waving, and students begin to call out, "Ooh, I see." "Oh, I got it." With a smile, Sandy motions for them to calm down and wait: "Okay, hold on, let's go back to the original question. Given the following balanced equation, what volume of hydrogen gas can be produced from the decomposition of two moles of H_2O?"**

Sometimes students are simply unable to respond to your question. When that happens, there's little point in belaboring the issue by providing prompts or cues; this will only make the recitation sluggish. Donnie sometimes allows students in this situation to "pass." This practice not only helps to maintain the pace, it also allows students to "save face." Meanwhile, she makes a mental note that she needs to reteach the material to the individuals having difficulty.

The most problematic situation for teachers is when students' answers are clearly incorrect. Saying "No, that's not right" can be uncomfortable, yet students deserve to have accurate feedback. As Sandy emphasizes: "It's really important to be clear about what's correct and what's not. The students have to know that the teacher will not leave them thinking the wrong thing." Rather than directly correcting students, however, Sandy prefers to help them discover their own errors:

> **I have difficulty saying "Your answer is wrong," but I usually don't have to. I can ask them to explain their reasoning. Or I can take the part of the answer that is correct and work with it. I can ask a question about their response. "How does the graph show that?" "So you're saying it would have to be like this. . . ." I like students to find their own mistakes and correct them.**

If recitations are losing momentum, our teachers often use "group-alerting" strategies to stimulate attention and to maintain the pace of the lesson (Kounin, 1970). Here are a few examples of statements to challenge students and keep them on their toes.

Fred: Please listen to this now . . . most Americans don't understand this at all; they don't have a clue. I want you to understand this.

Donnie: You need to fix this in your minds because we're going to use this later. . . . Now this is not really a trick question, but you'll have to think.

Donnie challenges students to think during a lesson on triangles.

Sandy: **This usually isn't covered in a first-year chemistry course. As a matter of fact, it's a problem that I asked on my honors chemistry test. But I know you guys can do it. I have confidence you can do it. Just take it apart, step by step.**

Although it's important to maintain pace, it's also important to provide time for students to think before responding. There is no point asking a well-formulated, higher-level question designed to stimulate critical thinking if you don't allow sufficient wait time. Yet even a few seconds of silence can seem like eternity. This helps to explain why Rowe (1974, 1986) found that many teachers wait *less than one second* before calling on a student. Rowe calls this interval "wait time 1." Similarly, Rowe found that the pause after a student responds ("wait time 2") is also only about a second. After that, teachers tend to jump in to repeat the student's answer, elaborate, or call on someone else. Not surprisingly, this has the effect of cutting off the possibility that students can give longer, higher-quality responses.

Remarkably, Rowe's research also showed that extending wait times to only *3 to 5 seconds* increases the quality and length of students' answers and promotes participation. Extending wait time is also beneficial for students with learning disabilities who tend to process information more slowly than their peers. Yet extending wait time appears to be extremely difficult for many teachers. One way to combat the desire to jump in is to tell students that you don't expect an immediate answer. This legitimates the silence and gives students an opportunity to formulate their responses. Allowing students to write an answer to your question is another way to provide them time to think. Written responses also help to maintain students' engagement because everyone has to construct a response. In addition, students who are uncomfortable speaking extemporaneously can read from their written papers. In the following example, we see Sandy use this strategy:

> **Sandy is introducing the concept of chemical equilibrium. She has drawn a diagram on the board showing the relative concentrations of A + B and C + D over time. She asks, "Where is equilibrium established? At Time 1, Time 2, or Time 3? Jot it down and write a sentence explaining why you chose T1, T2, or T3." She walks around the room, looking at students' papers. With a little laugh, she comments: "I see a lot of correct answers, and then the word *because*."**

During our conversation about her lesson, Sandy recalled an incident that underscored the value of having all students write a response to a question:

> **I had this girl in my honors class, who came to see me about the second week of school. She was obviously upset about how she was doing; she wanted to drop the class. She started to cry. "Everyone is so much smarter than I am." I asked her how she had come to that conclusion, and it was clear that she was equating response time with ability. I find that a lot of the girls do that. She says, "I'm just in the middle of figuring it out, and the other kids are already answering." She says, "I like it when you ask us to write our answers down first. But when I have to respond orally I'm intimidated."**

Once you have selected someone to respond, it's important to protect her or his opportunity to respond before allowing anyone else (you included) to jump into the interaction. Watch the way Donnie deals with this situation during a lesson on linear measurement:

Donnie: Okay, so how are you going to figure this out? (Pause) Eugene.
Eugene: You have to know how many inches are in a mile.
Donnie: And how are you going to figure that out? [Eugene is silent, but Ebony is waving her hand.]
 Ebony: Ooh, ooh, Miss, I know, I know how to do it.
Donnie: [very softly] Wait a minute, Ebony, give him a chance. Let him think.

A final challenge is to recognize that *the I-R-E format might be incompatible with the communication patterns that students bring to school.* Although the I-R-E format of recitations is a staple of schools, it stems from White, middle-class values and represents a way to communicate that does not match well with the discourse styles of many students from different cultural backgrounds (White, 2011). For example, recitation generally follows a "passive-receptive" discourse pattern: Students are expected to listen quietly during teacher presentations and then respond individually to teacher-initiated questions. African American students, however, could be accustomed to a more active, participatory discourse pattern ("call-response"). When they demonstrate their engagement by calling out prompts, comments, and reactions, European American teachers could interpret the behavior as rude and disruptive (Gay, 2000). Native Americans could also find the form of recitations unfamiliar and uncomfortable: "In Native-American culture, there is no naturally occurring situation in which a single adult authority regulates who speaks, when they speak, at what volume they speak, and to whom they speak" (Henning, 2008, p. 138). When Native American students are reluctant to participate, European American teachers could conclude that they are uninterested.

In addition to cultural and socioeconomic background, gender differences in discourse style could affect students' participation in recitations and discussions. As the linguist Deborah Tannen (1995) notes, boys and girls learn different ways to speak as they are growing up. Girls learn to downplay status differences and to stress the ways everyone is the same. They also learn that sounding too sure of themselves will make them unpopular. At the same time, boys generally recognize and expect differences in status; in fact, they learn to use language to negotiate their status in the group by displaying their abilities and knowledge. Boys in leadership positions give orders, challenge others, and "take center stage by telling stories or jokes" (Tannen, p. 140). When we consider these very different styles of communication, it is easy to see that the I-R-E pattern of discourse with its public display of knowledge and its inherent competition is more compatible with males' communication styles than with those of females (Arends, 2008).

Research on gender and classroom talk has also indicated that some teachers have a clear bias in favor of male participation (Grossman & Grossman, 1994). They could be more likely to call on a boy, listen to boys, respond to them in more helpful ways, and allow them to call out answers. Obviously, you need to be sensitive to gender differences in participation and use strategies to ensure that both males and females have opportunities to participate.

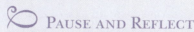

PAUSE AND REFLECT

Reflect on your own experiences with respect to communication patterns that students bring to school. Have you noticed any gender differences in communication styles or differences between students from different cultural backgrounds in any of your classes? How have these differences affected participation in class recitations or discussions?

By understanding and appreciating the fact that students' home patterns of discourse might be mismatched with the discourse pattern used in recitation, you are better able to ensure that all students in your class—regardless of cultural background or gender—will have equitable opportunities to participate. The Practical Tips box on implementing effective recitations lists some suggestions regarding this issue as well as others.

One important note: Although accommodation to students' discourse patterns could be possible and appropriate at times, some educators (e.g., Delpit, 1995) argue that teachers need to be explicit about the discourse patterns that are expected (and usually implicit) in school. Indeed, the explicit teaching of this knowledge is considered a teacher's "moral responsibility" because it enables individuals to participate fully in the classroom community and the larger society (Gallego, Cole, & Laboratory of Comparative Human Cognition, 2001, p. 979).

PRACTICAL TIPS FOR

Implementing Effective Recitations

- *Distribute chances to participate.*
   Pick names from a cup.
   Check off names on a seating chart.
   Use patterned turn taking.
- *Provide time to think.*
   Extend wait time to three seconds.
   Tell students you don't expect an immediate answer.
   Allow students to write a response.
- *Stimulate and maintain interest.*
   Inject mystery and suspense.
   Inject humor and novelty.
   Challenge students to think.
   Incorporate physical activity.
- *Provide feedback to students.*
   When answer is correct and confident, affirm briefly.
   When answer is correct but hesitant, provide more deliberate affirmation.
   When answer is incorrect but careless, make a simple correction.
   When answer is incorrect but student could get answer with help, prompt or back-track to simpler question.
   If student is unable to respond, don't belabor the issue.
- *Monitor comprehension.*
   Require overt responses (e.g., have students hold up response cards, physically display answers with manipulative materials, put thumbs up or down).
   Use a steering group (e.g., observe the performance of a sample of students, including low achievers, to know when to move on).
- *Support the participation of diverse learners.*
   Be conscious of your pattern of asking questions. Track whom you call on, how often you call on them, and how you respond to their answers.
   Become familiar with the discourse patterns characteristic of your culturally diverse students.
   Consider whether some accommodation to students' discourse style is possible.
   Teach explicitly about the discourse patterns that are expected in school.
   Incorporate "alternative response formats" designed to engage all students rather than just one or two.

Implementing Effective Discussions

As we indicated earlier in the chapter, both teachers and students have difficulty break-ing out of the teacher-dominated interaction pattern so characteristic of classrooms. For this reason, Christina has developed a strategy she calls "sticky note discussions." When students read an assigned text, they choose a passage that especially interests them—it can be a few words, a few pages, or anything in between. They place a sticky note near the passage they've chosen and write responses to questions that Christina constructed (e.g., Why did you choose this passage? What does it mean? What does it tell you about the rest of the text? What issues are raised here?) Then they take a second sticky note and write a question for discussion. The following exchange is from a sticky note discussion on *Ethan Frome:*

Student 1: **My passage is on page 95, beginning with "His impulses. . . ."
[Students turn to page 95, and she reads the paragraph aloud, while everyone follows along.] I chose this passage because I think it's the most important in the chapter. It shows how Ethan is finally deciding to tell Zeena how he feels, but then he begins to change his mind and he's thinking he can't do it. My question is, why do you think Ethan is having such a hard time about leaving Zeena?**

Student 2: **I think he feels it's wrong to leave her because she's sick and she's relying on him.**

Student 3: **I also think he's worried about the money, but it wouldn't stop him.**

Student 4: **But I do think it would stop him. He can't even afford the train ticket to leave her.**

Student 3: **But in the next sentence, he says he's sure he's going to get work.**

Student 5: **He's worried he won't be able to support Mattie.**

Student 6: **He wants to leave but he's afraid of change. . . .**

As we can see, the students' role is to pose the discussion questions and to call on classmates to respond—not a role to which students are accustomed. During the previous discussion, in fact, a girl asked her question and then seemed paralyzed in the face of her peers' raised hands. When she turned to Christina for assistance, Christina quietly reminded her, "You're in charge, Renata." The girl laughed, "I'm not used to this!"

Being "in charge" is certainly an unfamiliar role for students, but one that students gradually learn to assume with the sticky note strategy. After class, Christina shared her thoughts on the importance of having students take responsibility for class discussions:

> During my field experiences and student teaching, I often saw class "discussions," where the teachers did almost all the talking. I worried that I wouldn't be able to run an effective discussion because even the most experienced and talented teachers I observed were struggling to involve their students. It seemed like it would be torture to stand in front of a class and get no response. So I started thinking about how I could get students to take more responsibility for the discussion. I always write in the margins of my books when a passage interests me, but obviously kids can't do that with the school's books. So I hit upon the idea of sticky notes. I think it's working pretty well, and students' reactions have been overwhelmingly positive. This way, students really "own" the discussion. They talk about what interests them, rather than just what I think is important. They have to prepare for the discussion by putting their thoughts into writing, and that almost always makes it a better discussion. And all the students have to participate, at least to read their passage and ask their question. The hardest part is being quiet. I purposely sit on the outside of the group, so I'm less likely to dominate, but I still have to remind myself a lot to stay out of it as much as possible.

When you're learning to lead a discussion, keep in mind four basic suggestions. First, it is wise to *limit the size of the group.* It's difficult to have a student-centered discussion with a large number of participants. In his larger classes, Fred sometimes uses the "fishbowl" method, in which five or six students carry on the discussion in the middle of the room while the rest of the class sits in a large circle around them and acts as observers and recorders. Another solution is to divide the class into small discussion groups of five with one student in each group acting as a discussion leader. Second, *arrange students so they can make eye contact.* It's difficult to speak directly to someone if all you can see is the back of a head. If at all possible, students should move their desks into an arrangement that allows them to be face-to-face.

Third, *establish a structure that allows all students to participate in the discussion.* Some teachers are having students post their contributions on micro-blogging platforms such as Twitter, which the teachers monitor in real time (Gabriel, 2011; Simon, 2011). Teachers fold these contributions into the classroom discussion, allowing more students' voices to be heard. Noted a student in an English class, "It's made me see my peers as more intelligent, seeing their thought process and beginning to understand them on a deeper level" (Gabriel). Another student, normally shy and teased by others about his long hair, said that using Twitter has changed how his peers view him. "They see me as somebody now—as an equal" (Simon).

Finally, *prepare students for participating in a student-centered discussion by explicitly teaching the prerequisite skills:*

- Talk to each other, not just to the moderator.
- Don't monopolize.
- Ask others what they think.
- Don't engage in personal attacks.
- Listen to others' ideas.
- Acknowledge others' ideas.
- Question irrelevant remarks.
- Ask for clarification.
- Ask for reasons for others' opinions.
- Give reasons for your opinions.

Dillon (1994) also provides some extremely helpful guidelines for facilitating discussions. (See the Practical Tips box.) Note that Dillon advises against the teacher asking questions beyond the first one for fear of turning the discussion into a recitation. Although his concern is well founded, other discussion experts believe that questions can be an appropriate and effective way to keep conversation going. In fact, Brookfield and Preskill (1999) identify several types of questions that are especially helpful in maintaining momentum:

QUESTIONS THAT ASK FOR MORE EVIDENCE

How do you know that?

What data is that claim based on?

What does the author say that supports your argument?

Where did you find that view expressed in the text?

What evidence would you give to someone who doubted your interpretation?

QUESTIONS THAT ASK FOR CLARIFICATION

Can you put that another way?

What do you mean by that?

What's an example of what you're talking about?

Can you explain the term you just used?

LINKING OR EXTENSION QUESTIONS

Is there any connection between what you've just said and what Rajiv was saying a moment ago?

How does your comment fit in with Neng's earlier comment?

How does your observation relate to what the group decided last week?

Does your idea challenge or support what we seem to be saying?

HYPOTHETICAL QUESTIONS

What might have happened if Joey hadn't missed the school bus?

In the video we just saw, how might the story have turned out if Arnold had caught the ball?

If the author had wanted the teacher to be a more sympathetic figure, how might he have changed this conversation?

CAUSE-AND-EFFECT QUESTIONS

What is likely to be the effect of the name calling?

How might the rumor affect the school play?

SUMMARY AND SYNTHESIS QUESTIONS

What are the one or two most important ideas that emerged from this discussion?

What remains unresolved or contentious about this topic?

What do you understand better as a result of today's discussion?

Based on our discussion today, what do we need to talk about next time if we're to understand this issue better?

What key word or concept best captures our discussion today?

Although most discussions are focused around topics that don't have one correct answer or procedure, it is also possible to orchestrate a discussion on problem-solving processes in mathematics or science. For these discussions, students first work independently or in small groups to solve an intellectually challenging problem and then present their work to the class and participate in a discussion about the solution strategies. The key challenge for the teacher is how to build on and honor students' thinking while ensuring that the correct solution is presented. One way to do this is to adopt practices promoted by mathematics educators but that are applicable to other topics (Smith, Hughes, Engle, & Stein, 2009). These practices are to anticipate the

PRACTICAL TIPS FOR

Implementing Effective Discussions

- Carefully formulate the discussion question (making sure that it is not in a form that invites a yes/no or either/or answer) along with subsidiary questions, embedded questions, follow-up questions, and related questions.
- Create a question outline, identifying at least three subquestions and at least four alternative answers to the main question.
- Present the discussion question to the class, writing it on the board or on paper distributed to the class or projecting it on a screen. After reading the question aloud, go on to give the sense of the question, identifying terms, explaining the relevance of the question, connecting it to a previous discussion or class activity, and so on. End with an invitation to the class to begin addressing the question.
- Initially, help the class focus on the question rather than giving answers to it. For example, invite the class to tell what they know about the question or what it means to them.
- DO NOT COMMENT AFTER THE FIRST STUDENT'S CONTRIBUTION. (If you do, the interaction will quickly become I-R-E.) In addition, do not ask, "What does someone else think about that?" (If you do, you invite statements of difference or opposition to the first position, and your discussion turns into a debate.)
- In general, do not ask questions beyond the first question. Instead use nonquestion alternatives: statements (the thoughts that occurred to you in relation to what the speaker has just said; reflective statements that basically restate the speaker's contribution; statements indicating interest in hearing further about what the speaker has just said; statements indicating the relationship between what the speaker has just said and what a previous speaker has said); signals (sounds or words indicating interest in what the speaker has said); even silence. (Dillon acknowledges that deliberate silence is the hardest of all for teachers to do. To help teachers remain quiet, he recommends silently singing "Baa, baa, black sheep" after each student's contribution.)
- Facilitate the discussion by
  - Locating: "Where are we now? What are we saying?"
  - Summarizing: "What have we accomplished? Agreed on?"
  - Opening: "What shall we do next?"
  - Tracking: "We seem a little off track here. How can we all get back on the same line of thought?"
  - Pacing: "Just a minute, I wonder whether we're not moving a little too fast here. Let's take a closer look at this idea. . . ."
- When it's time to end the discussion, help students to summarize the discussion and identify the remaining questions.

different ways a problem can be solved, monitor students' thinking and solution strategies while they work on the problem, select particular students whose solutions are consistent with the learning goals of the lesson to present their work, sequence student presentations to build toward the learning goals, and help students draw connections between their solutions and other students' solutions.

CONCLUDING COMMENTS

This chapter began by highlighting the challenges associated with independent work and providing suggestions for avoiding, or at least minimizing, these problems. As you decide on the activities students will engage in during independent work time, remember the way you will introduce assignments and the rules and procedures you will establish to guide behavior.

It is important to note that the chapter focused almost exclusively on the situation in which the work is assigned to the entire class while the teacher circulates and assists students in accomplishing the tasks. But this is not the only way that seatwork can be used. Another option is to assign independent work to the majority of the class while you work with individuals who need additional help or a more challenging assignment. This format can be particularly useful if you have an extremely heterogeneous class. But take heed: If you are going to be unavailable for circulating and assisting, your assignments need to be even clearer and more meaningful than usual. You also need to hone the skill of overlapping. This is a situation that truly requires you to have "eyes in the back of your head."

The chapter then turned to recitations and discussions. It's important not to get them confused—to think that you're leading a discussion when you're actually conducting a recitation. Also keep in mind the criticisms that have been leveled against recitations, and reflect on how frequently you dominate the verbal interaction in your classroom. Ask yourself whether you also provide opportunities for true discussion during which you serve as a facilitator (rather than a questioner) and encourage direct student-student interaction. Reflect on the level of thinking that you require from students. As we have stressed, we believe that both recitations and discussions have a place in the secondary classroom, but they need to be managed thoughtfully by teachers who are cognizant of their pitfalls and potential.

SUMMARY

This chapter began by examining independent work or seatwork, the situation in which students work individually on a given task at their own desks. Seatwork provides teachers the opportunity to observe students' performance, to provide support and feedback, to engage in mini-conferences with individuals, and to prepare students for homework assignments. The chapter then considered two forms of teacher-student verbal interaction: the recitation and discussion. We examined some of the major criticisms of recitation as well as the useful functions it can serve and suggested a number of strategies for using recitations successfully. Finally, we looked at discussion and considered a number of guidelines for managing this type of verbal interaction.

Designing and Implementing Effective Independent Work

- Provide assignments that are meaningful, useful, and relevant.
- Match the work to varying achievement levels.
- Make sure oral and written directions are clear.
- Monitor behavior and comprehension.

- Plan for ragged endings.
- Teach students the norms for assisting peers

Characteristic Pattern of a Recitation

- I-R-E or I-R-F (teacher initiation, student response, teacher evaluation or follow-up).
- Quick pace.
- Intended use to review material, to elaborate on a text.

Characteristic Pattern of a Discussion

- I-R-R-R.
- Student-initiated questions.
- Student comments on contributions of peers.
- Slow pace.
- Intended use to stimulate thinking, foster problem solving, and examine implications.

Implementing Effective Recitations

- Distribute chances for participation.
- Provide time to think about answers before responding.
- Stimulate and maintain interest.
- Provide feedback without losing the pace.
- Monitor comprehension.
- Support the participation of diverse learners.

Implementing Effective Discussions

- Act as facilitator rather than questioner.
- Ensure that some students don't monopolize.
- Make sure the discussion stays on track.
- Ask students to provide supporting evidence for opinions.
- Limit group size.
- Arrange students so they have eye contact.
- Teach discussion skills.

When planning independent work, think carefully about the types of activities students will engage in, the way you will introduce assignments, and the rules and procedures you will establish to guide behavior. When planning recitations and discussions, think about the level of the questions that you ask: Are all of your questions low-level, factual questions that can be answered with a word or two, or are they designed to stimulate thinking and problem solving? Ask yourself whether you consistently dominate the interaction or whether you also provide opportunities for real discussion among students.

ACTIVITIES FOR SKILL BUILDING
AND REFLECTION

In Class

1. Select a workbook page or obtain a handout (preferably in your content area), and bring four copies of it to class. Working in a small group, examine the pages that students have brought to class. For each page, note the topic, describe the format of the worksheet, identify the skill being practiced or extended, and generate an alternative activity that would accomplish the same goal. An example is provided.

Topic	Description of Worksheet	Skill	Alternative
Who fired the first shot at Lexington and Concord	Three accounts by individuals who observed or participated in events at Lexington and Concord; students are to determine point of view for each account	Identifying point of view and bias	Choose two of the following characters (a British officer, an American militiaman, a French reporter, the minister's wife at Lexington, a maid at the inn in Concord) and tell the story of the events at Lexington and Concord from their respective points of view.

2. Your colleague has asked you to help him figure out why his students aren't paying attention in class. He would like you to observe him and offer feedback. What follows is a session you observed. In a small group, identify the trouble spots of his lesson and provide three specific suggestions for improvement. Use what you know about distributing participation, stimulating and maintaining interest, and monitoring comprehension.

MR. B.: Who remembers what photosynthesis is? [No response.] Do you remember yesterday when we looked at green plants and we discussed how a plant makes its own food? [Mr. B. notices that Thea is nodding.] Thea, do you remember about photosynthesis?

THEA: Yeah.

MR. B.: Well, can you tell the class about it?

THEA: It has something to do with light and chlorophyll.

MR. B.: Good. Tom, can you add to this? [Tom was drawing in his notebook.]

TOM: No.

MR. B.: Tom, Thea told us that photosynthesis had to do with light and chlorophyll. Do you recall our discussion from yesterday when we defined photosynthesis?

TOM: Sort of.

MR. B.: What do you mean? Didn't you write down the definition with the rest of the class? Look in your notebook and tell me the definition. [Tom starts to page through his notebook. Many of the students have begun to whisper and snicker. Some are looking in their notebooks.] How many of you have found the page where we defined photosynthesis? [Seven students raise their hands.] Good. Would somebody read to me that definition? Thea.

THEA: Photosynthesis is the process of forming sugars and starches in plants from water and carbon dioxide when sunlight acts upon chlorophyll.

MR. B.: Excellent. Does everyone understand? [A few students nod.] Good. Tomorrow we will be having a quiz about plants and photosynthesis. Tom, will you be ready for the quiz?

TOM: Sure, Mr. B.

MR. B.: Okay, now let's all turn to page 135 in our science texts and read about the uses of plants.

On Your Own

1. Observe a class, preferably in your content area, and note how much time is allocated to independent work during a typical period. During that time, observe three "target" students. Try to select a high-, average-, and low-achieving student. Note what activities each student is required to do during independent work time (for example, are the activities the same across achievement levels?). Every two or three minutes, record whether the students are on or off task. If possible, ask the students to explain what they are doing and why.

2. Visit a classroom and observe a recitation. On a seating chart, map the verbal interaction by placing a check or an x in the "seat" of each student who participates. (See the example in Figure 10.1.) Analyze your results and draw conclusions about how widely and fairly participation is distributed in this class.

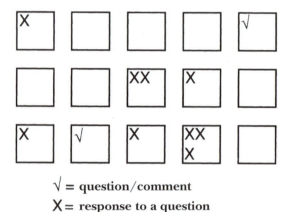

√ = question/comment

X = response to a question

FIGURE 10.1 Seating Chart Example

3. We know that recitations and discussions are often confused. Observe and record 10 minutes of a class "discussion." Then, using the following checklist, determine whether the verbal interaction actually meets the criteria for a discussion or whether it is more like a recitation.
   - Students are the predominant speakers.
   - The verbal interaction pattern is not I-R-E but a mix of statements and questions by a mix of teacher and students.
   - The pace is longer and slower.
   - The primary purpose is to stimulate a variety of responses, to encourage students to consider different points of view, to foster problem solving, and the like.
   - Evaluation consists of agree/disagree rather than right/wrong.

For Your Portfolio

1. Select a topic in your content area and identify an instructional objective (e.g., "Students will be able to describe the process of photosynthesis."). Then design three independent work activities that all target that objective. Differentiate the activities so that advanced students, average students, and struggling students can have an assignment well matched to their abilities. In a brief commentary, explain what the objective is and how you are differentiating.

2. Create two lesson plans, one that includes a recitation and one that includes a discussion. In sequence, list the questions that you will use for each. In a brief commentary, explain how these lessons differ from each other and why the chosen teaching strategy is appropriate for the content of the lesson.

FOR FURTHER READING

Henning, J. E. (2008). *The art of discussion-based teaching: Opening up conversation in the classroom.* New York: Routledge.

    This is a valuable text for K through 12 teachers who want to foster more student-centered discussion in their classrooms. The book provides practical advice for asking questions, guiding discussions, and keeping students involved. A particularly helpful section focuses on ways to support culturally and linguistically diverse students.

Little, C. A., Hauser, S. & Corbishley, J. (2009). Constructing complexity for differentiated learning. *Mathematics Teaching in the Middle School, 15*(1), 34–42.

    This article describes how to differentiate tasks to challenge learners at different levels by developing alternate versions that increase or decrease the task complexity. Although the specific examples involve mathematics tasks, the general principles can be applied to any content.

Rock, M. L,. & Thead, B. K. (2009). Promote student success during independent seatwork. *Intervention in School and Clinic, 44*(3), 179–184.

    Based on the theory that some students with learning and behavioral disorders lack the skills and self-control to remain engaged in seatwork activities, this article presents 20 approaches that can be used in classrooms to increase academic involvement during such tasks.

Tomlinson, C. A. (2001). *How to differentiate instruction in mixed ability classrooms,* 2nd ed. Alexandria, VA: Association for Supervision and Curriculum Development.

    Tomlinson explains what differentiated instruction is (and isn't), provides a look inside some differentiated classrooms, presents the "how-tos" of planning lessons differentiated by readiness, interest, and learning styles, and discusses the complex issues of grading and recordkeeping.

Walsh, J. A., & Sattes, B. D. (2005). *Quality questioning: Research-based practice to engage every learner.* Thousand Oaks, CA: Corwin Press.

    Based on the authors' questioning and understanding to improve learning and thinking (QUILT) framework, this book discusses preparing questions, presenting questions, prompting student response, processing student responses, teaching students to generate questions, and reflecting on questioning practice.

Managing Small-Group Work

Keep your eyes on your own paper.

Work without talking to your neighbor.

Pay attention to the teacher.

If you need help, raise your hand.

Do your own work.

These are the norms of the traditional classroom, a setting in which students have little opportunity to interact, assist one another, and collaborate on tasks. (See Figure 11.1.) Phrases such as these are so much a part of the way we view classrooms that four-year-olds who have never even attended kindergarten use them when playing school.

This lack of interaction is unfortunate, especially in today's heterogeneous classrooms. Letting students work together in pairs or small groups has many advantages. Donnie and Christina alluded to one advantage in Chapter 10: If students can help one another during classwork, they are less likely to "get stuck," to have to sit and wait for the teacher's assistance, and to become uninvolved and disruptive. In addition, working with peers on tasks can enhance students' motivation, especially for those students who have negative attitudes toward school and classroom work (Pell, Galton, Steward, Page, & Hargreaves, 2007). Small-group work can also have positive effects on achievement as students debate and discuss, ask questions, explain, and evaluate the work of others (Walters, 2000). It can allow students to generate new understandings within their small groups and then share those ideas with the entire class (Kendrick, 2010). Research that has focused specifically on middle school students confirms

"This class will stimulate your ideas and thoughts. And remember — no talking."

FIGURE 11.1   Reprinted by permission of Warren.

these advantages: Cooperative groups promote greater efforts to achieve, more positive relationships, and greater psychological health than competitive or individualistic efforts (Johnson, Johnson, & Roseth, 2010).

In addition, when students work in heterogeneous groups, they can develop relationships across gender, racial, and ethnic boundaries (Ginsburg-Block, Rohrbeck, & Fantuzzo, 2006; Kutnick, Ota, & Berdondini, 2008; Oortwijn, Boekaerts, Vedder, & Fortuin, 2008). Group work can also help to integrate students with disabilities into the general education classroom (Johnson & Johnson, 1980; Madden & Slavin, 1983). Finally, as Rachel Lotan (2006) observes, group work can help teachers build more caring, equitable classrooms in which "students serve as academic, linguistic, and social resources for one another and are accountable to each other individually and as members of a group" (p. 525).

Given all these benefits, why is there so little group work in secondary classrooms? Part of the answer has to do with the teacher's responsibility for keeping order and covering curriculum. In the crowded, complex world of the classroom, it's easier to keep order and cover curriculum when teachers do the talking and students do the listening. Furthermore, if the school culture equates orderly classrooms with quiet classrooms, teachers can feel uncomfortable when group work raises the noise level. Consider this student teacher's journal entry:

Every time I read about group work it sounds so great I'm ready to use it everyday. Then I attempt it in the classroom and I start having second thoughts. I love the learning that comes out of it, but I never feel in control when it is happening. The part that really upsets me is that I really do not mind if the class gets loud. It's the other teachers and the principal I worry about. There have been a few times when I was using cooperative learning and someone has come in to ask if I need any help or they will take it upon themselves to tell my class to be quiet. This really makes me angry. I feel like the only acceptable noise level is no noise at all.

Finally, like seatwork, group work has its own set of challenges and potential pitfalls that can make it difficult for teachers to manage. This chapter examines those special pitfalls. It then discusses ways they can be minimized, drawing on the experiences of our five teachers as well as the research on group work.

THE CHALLENGES OF SMALL-GROUP WORK

Let's begin by considering the recent experience of Ralph, a student teacher in social studies. During a recent meeting, Ralph recounted his first attempt to use group work with his U.S. history class:

We were working on sectional differences—the period from 1800 to 1850, when the Northeast, the West, and the South were like three different countries. I wanted my kids to research the views that each section of the country had on three topics—tariffs, slavery, and the role of the federal government. I didn't want to just lecture, or have them read out of the textbook and then discuss the material, and it seemed like this could be a great cooperative learning activity. My kids haven't had much experience working in groups, but my cooperating teacher is really good about letting me try new things, and he said, "Sure, go ahead and see what happens."

I decided to do this over two days. On the first day, I planned to divide the class into the three sections of the country and have each group learn about its section's position on the three topics. I only have 20 kids in this class, so I figured that would be about six or seven kids in each group, which seemed about right. At the end of the first day, they were supposed to pick someone to be their section's spokesman—Daniel Webster from the Northeast, John C. Calhoun from the South, and Henry Clay from the West. The second day, these three spokesmen would debate the issues.

So I come into class all fired up about this great thing we're going to do. It didn't seem important to have the groups be absolutely equal in size, and I figured if the kids could choose their own section they'd be more motivated. So I told them they could decide what section of the country they wanted to study. I told them, "If you want to do the Northeast move to this corner, and if you want to do the South move to that corner, etc. Ready, move." Well, it didn't work out. First of all, most of the kids wanted to be the West or the South—there were like nine people in the West and six people in the South and only four people in the Northeast. Plus—I couldn't believe it—the West was all girls (White and Asian American), the South was this really juvenile group of White boys (I just knew they would never get anything done), and the Northeast was my three African American kids and Rick Moore, this White basketball player! And this really quiet, insecure kid just kind of stood there in the middle of the room, not knowing where to go. I had to start asking people to switch and they weren't very happy about that and started making comments about how I didn't know what I was doing and when was Mr. M going to come back and do some "real teaching."

Well, I finally got some of the girls from the West to move into the Northeast group so the sections were about the same size, and I explained what they were going to do. I told them to use their text, and I showed them all the resource materials I had gotten from the library, and told them to use those too. I explained that they were all supposed to help one another research their section's views on tariffs, slavery, and the role of the federal government. Then they were to work together to write a position paper outlining these views and choose someone to be Webster, Calhoun, or Clay for tomorrow's debate. By this time there's only about 25 minutes left, so I tell them to get to work right away. Well, most of them just sat there and stared and kept saying things like, "I don't understand what we're supposed to do." A few kids got up and went back to their desks to get their textbooks and pencils (of course, I had forgotten to tell them to take their books and stuff with them when they moved), and I went around giving out paper, but a lot of the kids just sat there.

I kept going around and trying to get them to work. When I'd come over, they'd begin to jot down notes, but I think they were really just acting like they were working, to get me off their back. Finally, some of the kids in the West and the Northeast began looking up stuff in their texts and taking notes, but they weren't helping each other much. I just could not get them to work together! And some of the kids never did anything—they just sat and let the other kids do it. I even heard comments like, "Let Allison be Clay—she's the smartest one in history." Meanwhile, the guys in the South spent most of the time fooling around and laughing. And they kept putting each other down, saying things like, "He's too dumb to be Calhoun. . . . We don't have any smart kids in this group," and yelling, "Hey Mr. G, we need some smart kids in this group." I kept asking them to be quiet and get to work but they just ignored me.

At the end of the period I told them they'd have to finish looking up their section's views for homework. Then I told them to decide on their spokesman, and of course nobody wanted to do it. In the West, they decided that this one kid who's really conscientious should do it. In the South, they fooled around a lot and then finally this real wise-guy says OK, he'll do it. Well, he was absent the next day, so there was no Calhoun, which they seemed to think was really funny.

All in all, these were two of the worst days of my student teaching experience. After reading all these education theorists who say that cooperative learning is such great stuff, I had been real excited, but now I'm not so sure. Maybe if your class is really motivated to begin with, it would work, but my class is not all that great (the really smart kids are in Honors History), and maybe they just can't work together like this.

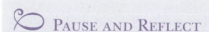

PAUSE AND REFLECT

You have just read Ralph's experiences and thoughts about group work. He began with great intentions and optimism. Where did the lesson begin to fall apart? What did he do that contributed to the problems with his lesson? What suggestions might you give to Ralph? Is group work only for honors-level students as Ralph suggests?

Unfortunately, Ralph's story is not unusual. It illustrates all too vividly what can happen when teachers don't understand the potential problems associated with group work and don't work to prevent them from occurring. Let's take a closer look at four of these problems.

First, as Ralph discovered, allowing students to form their own groups often leads to *segregation* among students in terms of gender, race, and ethnicity. Have you ever had lunch in the cafeteria of an ethnically diverse school? One glance is enough to see that members of each ethnic and racial group tend to sit together. It is important to recognize that strong forces operate against the formation of cross-ethnic friendships; left to their own devices, most students will choose to be with those whom they perceive as being similar. An even greater barrier to friendship exists between students with disabilities and their nondisabled peers (Slavin, 1991). As we discussed in Chapter 6, the Individuals with Disabilities Education Act (IDEA) requires the inclusion of students with disabilities in general education classrooms whenever possible, but mere physical presence is not enough to ensure that these individuals will be liked or even accepted.

A second problem of group work is the *unequal participation of group members.* Sometimes, this is due to the "freeloader" phenomenon that occurs when one or two students in the group end up doing all the work while the others sit back and relax. We saw this happen in Ralph's class when only a few of the students took the research assignment seriously, and one group decided to let Allison, the "smartest" history student, be her group's spokesperson. Although this might be an efficient approach to the task, it's not exactly a fair distribution of responsibility. And those who were freeloading were unlikely to learn anything about sectional differences.

Unequal participation can occur for other, more poignant, reasons as well. In a study of students' perceptions of doing mathematics in a cooperative learning group (King, Luberda, Barry, & Zehnder, 1998), Brett, an average achiever, reported that he often failed to understand the task; consequently, he either withdrew from participation or engaged in distracting, off-task behavior. Similarly, Peter, a low achiever, "was aware that the other students seldom asked for his ideas and if he suggested ideas they never listened to him" (p. 8). To save face, he engaged in "silly," "weird" behaviors.

Brett and Peter are good examples of the "discouraged" and "unrecognized" categories in Catherine Mulryan's (1992) typology of passive students (outlined in Table 11.1). These categories are worth keeping in mind. Although a desire to freeload might be at the root of some students' passivity, it is also possible that uninvolved students are feeling discouraged, despondent, unrecognized, bored, or superior.

Just as some individuals might be passive and uninvolved in the group activity, others might take over and dominate the interaction. Frequently, the dominant students are those with high academic status in the classroom—those who are recognized by their peers as successful, competent students. At other times, the dominant students are those who are popular because they are good athletes or are especially attractive. And sometimes dominance simply reflects the higher status our society accords to those who are white and male. Indeed, research has shown that in heterogeneous groups, males often dominate females (Webb, 1984) while Whites dominate African Americans and Hispanics (Cohen, 1972; Rosenholtz & Cohen, 1985).

TABLE 11.1 Six Categories of Passive Students		
Category	Description	Typical Achievement Level
Discouraged student	The student perceives the group task to be too difficult and thinks it better to leave it to others who understand.	Mostly low achievers
Unrecognized student	The student's initial efforts to participate are ignored or unrecognized by others, and he or she feels that it's best to retire.	Mostly low achievers
Despondent student	The student dislikes or feels uncomfortable with one or more students in the group and does not want to work with them.	High or low achievers
Unmotivated student	The student perceives the task as being unimportant or "only a game" with no grade being assigned to reward effort expended.	High or low achievers
Bored student	The student thinks the task is uninteresting or boring, often because it is seen as too easy or unchallenging.	Mostly high achievers
Intellectual snob	The student feels that peers are less competent and doesn't want to have to do a lot of explaining. Often ends up working on the task individually.	High achievers

Source: Mulryan, 1992.

A third pitfall of group work is *lack of accomplishment.* In Ralph's class, a significant amount of instructional time was wasted while students formed groups, and most people didn't get much done even once the groups had formed. A number of students, particularly those in the South group, seemed to view the opportunity to interact as an opportunity to fool around and socialize. Their behavior undoubtedly distracted students who were trying to work. Furthermore, the disruption was upsetting to Ralph, who repeatedly asked students to quiet down—without success.

Finally, a fourth problem associated with group work is students' *lack of cooperation* with one another. Ralph tells us that the students tended to work alone, and the boys in the "juvenile" group spent a lot of time "putting each other down." Although such behavior is certainly disappointing, it isn't surprising. As we have pointed out, most students have little experience working in cooperative groups, and the norms of the traditional classroom are dramatically different from the norms for successful group work.

Analysis of Ralph's experience demonstrates that *successful group work will not just happen.* If you want your students to work together productively, you must plan the groups and the tasks carefully, teach students new norms, and provide opportunities for them to practice the behaviors that are required. As Sandy comments:

Sometimes, when beginning teachers do group work, they think, "I'll divide my students into groups and that's it. That's all I have to do." They don't plan the groups and they don't plan the group work. That's where they get into trouble. You not only have to think about how you're going to get your kids into groups, but what you're going to do after they're in the groups. You have to plan it so carefully, and it's not an easy thing to do.

DESIGNING AND IMPLEMENTING EFFECTIVE GROUP WORK

This section of the chapter presents some general strategies for avoiding the pitfalls of group work based on research and the experiences of our five teachers. (These strategies are summarized in the Practical Tips box.)

 PRACTICAL TIPS FOR

Designing and Implementing Effective Group Work

- Decide on the type of group to use:
  - *Helping permitted:* Students are allowed to assist one another on individual assignments.
  - *Helping obligatory:* Students are expected to help one another.
  - *Peer tutoring:* A more skillful peer assists a less skillful peer.
  - *Cooperative:* Students share a common goal or end; some division of responsibilities can occur.
  - *Completely cooperative:* Students share a common goal and there is little or no division of labor; all members of the group work together to create the group product.
- Decide on the size of the group:
  - Partners are usually more appropriate for younger students.
  - Groups of four to five are generally recommended, and six is the upper limit.
- Decide on group composition:
  - Think carefully about achievement level, gender, cultural/linguistic background, race/ethnicity, ableness, and social skills.
- Structure the task for positive interdependence by having students:
  - Share materials.
  - Work toward a group goal, grade, or reward.
- Share information.

(continued on next page)

- Share talents and multiple abilities.
  - Fulfill different roles (materials person, timekeeper, recorder, facilitator, reporter, etc.).
- Ensure individual accountability:
  - Make sure that all group members are held responsible for their contribution to the goal.
  - Assess individual learning.
  - Differentiate responsibilities according to students' individual needs.
- Teach students to cooperate:
  - Help them to understand the value of cooperation.
  - Provide group skills training.
  - Provide the chance to evaluate their group work experiences.
- Monitor learning, involvement, and cooperative behavior:
  - Monitor groups and intervene when needed.

Decide on the Type of Group to Use

Students can work together in a variety of ways. Stodolsky (1984) has identified five different types of group work: helping permitted, helping obligatory, peer tutoring, cooperative, and completely cooperative (see the accompanying Practical Tips box). The first three types of groups can be considered "collaborative seatwork" (Cohen, 1994a). Each of them involves students assisting one another on individual assignments. In a *helping permitted* group, individuals work on their own tasks, and they are evaluated as individuals; however, they are allowed—but not required—to help one another. *Helping obligatory* situations differ only in that students are *expected* to offer mutual assistance. In *peer tutoring,* the relationship between the students is not equal: An "expert" is paired with a student who needs help, so assistance flows in only one direction. Peer tutoring is a particularly useful way to meet the needs of students with disabilities and those who are learning English as a second language.

Cooperative groups differ from these helping situations in that students in those groups share a common goal or end instead of working on completely individual tasks. In a *simple cooperative group,* some division of responsibilities can occur. For example, a group researching the Civil War might decide that one student will learn about the causes of the war, another will learn about famous battles, and a third learns about important leaders. Tasks are carried out independently, but everyone's assignment has to be coordinated at the end to produce the final joint product.

More complex is a *completely cooperative group.* Not only do students in it share a common goal but also there is little or no division of labor. All members of the group work together to create the group product. This was the type of group work that Ralph tried to implement when he directed his history students to research their section's views on tariffs, slavery, and the role of the federal government and then develop a position paper. (Of course, his students could have decided to divide up the research assignment and then coordinate their findings, but Ralph did not direct them to do so.)

Keeping these distinctions in mind is important as you plan group work. *Different types of groups are suitable for different types of activities, and they require different*

TABLE 11.2 Different Types of Groups

Type of Group	Skills Required	Activity Example
Helping permitted Helping obligatory	Ask for help Explain Provide support and encouragement	Creating clay sculptures: Students ask each other for assistance and opinions, but everyone completes an individual sculpture.
Peer tutoring	Ask for help Explain Provide support and encouragement	Having a tutor help a tutee to complete a set of chemistry problems.
Cooperative group	Divide group task into individual tasks Coordinate individual efforts to produce final group product	Taking survey on what students do after school: Each group member interviews students at one grade level and then all pool the data to make a group graph.
Completely cooperative	Take turns Listen to one another Coordinate efforts Share materials Collaborate on a single task Solve conflicts Achieve consensus	Determining political party affiliation: As a group, decide whether a hypothetical person is a Democrat or Republican.

types of skills. (See Table 11.2.) In helping situations, for example, students are ultimately responsible for completing individual tasks. Although these students need to know how to ask for help, how to explain and demonstrate (rather than simply providing the right answer), and how to provide support and encouragement, they do not need the more complex skills required in truly cooperative situations in which they share a common goal.

As an example of a helping situation, let's consider the following activity that we observed in Christina's class:

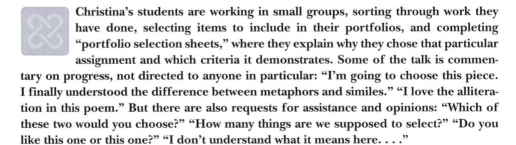

Christina's students are working in small groups, sorting through work they have done, selecting items to include in their portfolios, and completing "portfolio selection sheets," where they explain why they chose that particular assignment and which criteria it demonstrates. Some of the talk is commentary on progress, not directed to anyone in particular: "I'm going to choose this piece. I finally understood the difference between metaphors and similes." "I love the alliteration in this poem." But there are also requests for assistance and opinions: "Which of these two would you choose?" "How many things are we supposed to select?" "Do you like this one or this one?" "I don't understand what it means here. . . ."

In contrast to helping situations, cooperative groups require skills beyond requesting and giving appropriate assistance. Students must be able to develop a plan of action, to coordinate efforts toward a common goal, to evaluate the contributions of their peers and give feedback in a constructive way, to monitor individuals' progress toward the group goal, and to summarize and synthesize individual efforts. Consider the following example provided by Donnie:

> **In my basic skills class, I work on collecting, analyzing, and depicting data. I have the students work in groups of four. Each group has to create a survey designed to learn what high school kids do after school—for example, how much they play video games, watch TV, just hang around, play basketball, have an after-school job, do homework. Then, each group has to interview 80 students in the high school, and each person in the group is responsible for interviewing 20 students at one grade level (in other words, one person interviews all freshmen, one interviews all sophomores, and so on). Each person has to collect his or her own information, but then they have to come together to make a group graph showing how people at all four grade levels manage their time. Kids know that they can't complete the project unless everybody does their part, so they really get on each other's case if somebody isn't working.**

Completely cooperative groups with no division of labor present even greater challenges. Not only must students be able to take turns, listen to one another carefully, and coordinate efforts but also they must be able to collaborate on a single task, reconcile differences, compromise, and reach a consensus. During one visit to Fred's class, we observed a good example of a completely cooperative group activity. The class was divided into groups of four or five to consider profiles of eight hypothetical Americans (e.g., "A union member working in an American automobile plant in Kentucky. He is a college graduate"; "A bank executive in a small county seat in Colorado. She is concerned about her career, is unmarried, and is about to buy her own home"). For each profile, students had to determine the probable party affiliation (or lack of one), the types of issues that would be important to the individual in a campaign, and whether the individual was likely to be a voter or a nonvoter. Although students were required to carry out individual tasks, they had to coordinate their individual efforts if the groups were to be successful:

> **Fred hands out the worksheet describing the eight hypothetical American voters (or nonvoters). He explains that students will first do the task individually, taking notes for each profile. When everyone is finished, he divides the class into groups of four or five. Fred explains that students are to share their opinions, being sure to provide their reasoning. He encourages the groups to work toward consensus on each hypothetical voter and suggests that a different person serve as recorder for each voter. Each group will be expected to report on its results to the rest of the class.**
>
> **Students begin to go through the eight profiles, sharing their responses. Fred circulates, asking students to explain their reasoning ("Why do you think he's a Democrat?"), commenting on their responses ("I can't believe how confident you people are!"), and checking on group process ("What number are you on? Has everyone had a chance to be a recorder for at least one profile?").**
>
> **When the groups have finished, Fred announces that Group B will be the first group to report out. The four members of Group B stand in the front of the room. Sandra reports on the group's opinions about the first profile: "We think he's a Democrat. He definitely votes. We think he cares about auto safety." The reports continue with Fred interjecting questions and comments.**

Although this activity first required students to think through their responses as individuals, they then had to work together to construct a group report. They had to decide who would be the recorder and reporter for each profile, take turns explaining the reasons for their ideas, listen respectfully to one another, reject ideas without being destructive, and reach consensus on what to report. These are not easy skills to learn—even for adults.

As these three examples illustrate, the more interdependent students are, the more skills they need to cooperate successfully. It's a good idea to use simpler types of groups when you are just starting out. In Ralph's case, we can see that he began with the most complex type of group work. He set up a situation in which students who were not even accustomed to helping one another were expected to cooperate completely.

Spencer Kagan has developed a vast array of simple group structures that can be used at a variety of grade levels and in many content areas. Learn more about Kagan in Meet the Educator Box 11.1.

Decide on the Size of the Group

To some extent, the size of the group you use depends on the task you assign. Pairs are appropriate when foreign language students are preparing a dialogue to role-play or when home economics students are reviewing weights and measures in preparation for a test. Groups of two maximize students' opportunity to participate and are easier for beginning teachers to manage, and teachers of younger or less mature students often prefer pairs over larger groups that require more elaborate social skills. Even with high school students, Sandy makes sure to provide students experiences in pairs before using cooperative groups.

In the following vignette, we see Donnie use pairs of students in a helping situation:

Donnie is reviewing problems that involve different kinds of angles (supplementary, complementary, and vertical). After going through a number of problems on the board, Donnie announces that students will be doing the next set by themselves. She explains: "Please listen to what you're going to do next. On this assignment, you may confer with one other person. You're going to count off: one, two, three. [The students do so.] If you are a number one, you will start with problem number 19, and then go up by 3's (22, 25, 28, 31, 34, and 37). If you are a number two, your problems will start with 20, and go up by 3's. If you are a number three, your problems will start with 21, and go up by 3's. Pair yourself up with someone who has the same number that you have. Your job is to help one another understand the problems. You have 20 minutes to do these. Please have them ready to be passed in at the end of the period."

When the task is an ambitious one that requires a division of labor (e.g., the survey on what high school students do after school), it makes sense to form groups larger than two. Groups of three are still relatively easy to manage, but you need to make sure that two students don't form a coalition, leaving the third isolated and excluded.

In general, educators recommend cooperative groups of four or five (Cohen, 1994a), and six is usually the upper limit (Johnson, Johnson, Holubec, & Roy, 1984). Keep in mind that as group size increases, the "resource pool" also increases; in other

BOX 11.1 MEET THE EDUCATOR

Spencer Kagan

Spencer Kagan is a former clinical psychologist and professor of psychology and education. In 1989, he created Kagan Publishing and Professional Development, which offers materials, workshops, and graduate courses on topics such as cooperative learning, multiple intelligences, emotional intelligence, brain-friendly instruction, and classroom energizers. Dr. Kagan developed the concept of "structures," content-free ways to organize social interaction among students. His structures are used in classrooms worldwide.

Some Major Ideas about Cooperative Learning

1. In a traditional classroom, teachers use structures such as "whole-class question-answer." In this structure, the teacher asks a question, students raise their hands to respond, and the teacher calls on one person. This is a *sequential structure,* in which each person participates in turn, giving little time per pupil for active participation. This structure also leads to competition among students for the teacher's attention and praise.

2. Teachers can increase opportunity for student participation by following the *simultaneity principle.* For example, if all students pair up to discuss a question, half the class is talking at any given moment.

3. From a wide array, teachers select the structures that are most appropriate for their specific objectives. Some structures are useful for team building or for developing communication skills; others are most suitable for increasing mastery of factual material or for concept development.

- "Numbered Heads Together" is appropriate for checking on students' understanding of content. Students "number off" within teams (e.g., one through four). When the teacher asks a question, team members "put their heads together" to make sure that everyone on the team knows the answer. The teacher then calls a number, and students with that number may raise their hands to answer.

- In "Timed Pair Share," students pair up to share their responses to a question posed by the teacher. First Student A talks for a minute, and then Student B has a turn. This simultaneous interaction allows all students to respond in the same amount of time that it would have taken for just two students if the teacher had used the more traditional "whole-class question-answer" structure.

Selected Books and Articles

The structural approach to cooperative learning. *Educational Leadership, 47*(4), 14 (Kagan, 1989/90)

Cooperative learning and the gifted: Separating two questions. *Cooperative Learning, 14*(4), 26–28 (Kagan, 1994)

Teaching for character and community. *Educational Leadership, 59*(2), 50–55 (Kagan, 2001)

Kagan structures for English Language Learners. *ESL Magazine, 5*(4), 10–12 (Kagan & High, 2002)

Cooperative learning: The power to transform race relations. *Teaching Tolerance, 53* (Kagan, 2006)

Kagan Cooperative Learning (Kagan & Kagan, San Juan Capistrano, CA: Kagan, 2008)

Website: www.kaganonline.com

words, there are more heads to think about the task and more hands to share the work. It is also true, however, that the larger the group, the more difficult it is to develop a plan of action, allocate turns for speaking, share materials, and reach consensus.

Decide on Group Composition

In addition to deciding on the type and size of your groups, you must think carefully about group composition. As we mentioned earlier in this chapter, group work can provide opportunities for students to develop relationships with those who are different from themselves. For this reason, educators (e.g., Slavin, 1995) generally advise teachers to form groups that are heterogeneous with respect to gender, ethnicity, race, linguistic background, and ableness. On the other hand, it is important to be sensitive to the fact that trying to achieve heterogeneity can place a burden on students who must be separated from those with whom they feel most comfortable.

Let's consider a concrete example provided by Beth Rubin (2003), who studied two untracked ninth-grade classes in a diverse urban high school. The teachers of these classes were committed to using group work so that students could "learn about one another, appreciate differences, and develop the ability to work with others" (p. 553). However, because African American students were a racial minority, constructing groups that reflected the racial makeup of the class led to "one Black kid in each group" (p. 553). Thus, when Tiffany and Christie, two African American students, wanted to be placed in the same group, their teacher said no. Instead, each was assigned to a group with three European American students they did not know well. As Rubin comments, "having one African American student in each group usually meant that that student did not have any close friends in that group" (p. 553).

Teachers also need to consider whether small groups will be heterogeneous or homogeneous with respect to achievement level. At times, homogeneous groups can be useful; for example, you might want to form a helping group of several students who are all working on a particular mathematics skill. In general, however, educators recommend the use of groups that are heterogeneous in terms of academic performance (Cohen, 1994a; Slavin, 1995). One reason for this recommendation is that heterogeneous groups provide more opportunities for asking questions and receiving explanations. But keep in mind that creating academically heterogeneous groups does not guarantee that students will actually engage in these behaviors. Research indicates that students' interactions in groups appear to mirror the behavior of their teachers (Webb, Nemer, & Ing, 2006): If teachers model the role of the teacher as active problem solver with students as passive recipients of instruction, this is the behavior that students demonstrate in small groups. Research also suggests that the productivity of the group is more a function of the interactions among the students than their ability levels (Webb & Mastergeorge, 2003). Thus, preparing students for group work by modeling productive helping interactions is extremely important. And don't overlook the fact that students can model such behaviors for their peers. Donna touches on the beneficial influence of peers when she explains how she sometimes groups students:

I have assigned one non-performing student to a group of high-performing students because they will ignore his attempts to distract the group. And, underperforming kids will often try to perform at the same level as the rest of

the group. This doesn't always work, but the other students' modeling of group work and collaboration sometimes speaks louder than I do. At times, peers are better at teaching group skills than I am!

Another variable you need to consider when deciding on group composition is social skill. In fact, Fred focuses more on social skills and personalities than on academic ability:

> First I think about who can't be in the same group, and I say, "Okay, he goes in Group 1, and she goes in Group 2, etc." Then I think about who the nicest people in the class are—the people who can get along with everybody—and I spread them out too. Then I separate the loudmouths—the kids who are not good listeners and who tend to talk a lot. Finally, I think about the kids who need "special handling." Maybe somebody who doesn't speak English, or maybe someone who's very sensitive or shy. I think, "Which group will not destroy this person?" and I try to put that kid in a group that will be most supportive.

As Fred's comments indicate, groups work better when students' personalities and social skills are considered. Some students have difficulty working with others—they might be unusually volatile, or angry, or bossy—and it makes sense to distribute them across the groups. On the other hand, some students have unusual leadership abilities; others are particularly adept at resolving conflicts; still others are especially alert to injustice and can help to ensure that everyone in the group has a chance to participate. When forming groups, it generally makes sense to disperse students like these too so that each group has the benefit of their talents. All five teachers follow this practice; however, Sandy and Donnie occasionally find it useful to put all of the leaders in one group. Donnie explains:

> At first, the kids in the other groups say, "Oh, we don't have anybody good in our group. This isn't fair." They sort of sit there aimlessly, wondering what to do. But with encouragement, they begin to get their act together. It doesn't always work, of course, but sometimes this creates a chance for new leaders to emerge.

Teachers develop different systems for assigning students to groups. Some teachers write each student's name on a note card, along with information about achievement and interpersonal relationships (e.g., with whom the student doesn't get along). Then they rank students in terms of achievement level and assign a top-ranked student and a bottom-ranked student to each of the groups (although many teachers try to avoid extremes). Next the average students are distributed. Having each student's name on a note card allows you to shuffle students around as you try to form equivalent groups in which students will work well together.

Trying to create the perfect groups can be a daunting challenge for teachers. Lotan (2006) suggests another approach—*controlled randomness*—in which teachers make group assignments in the students' presence. Using pocket charts on the wall to display group assignments, teachers shuffle students' names like a deck of cards, and then place the cards in the pockets. After distributing all the cards, teachers review the groups that emerge and make necessary changes. For example, an English language learner might need someone to translate, or two close friends who socialize might need to be separated.

All five teachers use controlled (or uncontrolled) randomness every now and then when they are forming groups. As mentioned in Chapter 9, we once observed Donnie take a deck of playing cards from her desk, walk toward a student, and ask him to help her shuffle:

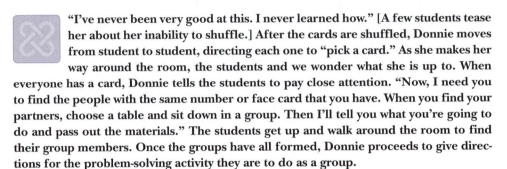

"I've never been very good at this. I never learned how." [A few students tease her about her inability to shuffle.] After the cards are shuffled, Donnie moves from student to student, directing each one to "pick a card." As she makes her way around the room, the students and we wonder what she is up to. When everyone has a card, Donnie tells the students to pay close attention. "Now, I need you to find the people with the same number or face card that you have. When you find your partners, choose a table and sit down in a group. Then I'll tell you what you're going to do and pass out the materials." The students get up and walk around the room to find their group members. Once the groups have all formed, Donnie proceeds to give directions for the problem-solving activity they are to do as a group.

After class, we talked about this strategy for forming groups:

This was the first time I ever tried this. My main reason was to get them talking and working with people other than their normal neighbors. They're in seats they chose on the first day, and some of them are very quiet and shy. They don't like to move around or interact with new people. This made them get up and form some new groups.

This year, Donna laminated six different colors of construction paper and cut them into small cards. She uses these to form groups, either by handing out the cards as students enter her classroom or by putting them on students' desks ahead of time. And sometimes, rather than have students put their desks together to work in groups, she has all the students with a given color move to one of six large sheets of laminated paper posted on the walls. During one observation, Donna used this procedure to review vocabulary homework. She wrote an exercise number, from two through seven, on the top of each laminated paper and then explained the task:

"When I call your color group, you'll go up to your poster and put the answers on it. Green will go here to Exercise #2; orange group, Exercise #3 here; pink Group, Exercise #4, over here." She continues on with purple, blue, and red groups. "Before writing anything down, I want you to make sure that everybody in the group has the same answer and, if not, help each other to figure out the correct answer. Then when you're done, you're going to sit down, and check your homework against the answers on the posters. You have 10 minutes."

Finally, all five teachers allow their students at times to form their own groups but only for certain types of tasks and not until the students have had substantial experience working in various types of groups with almost everyone in the class.

Donna's students work in small groups.

For example, Christina allows students to form their own groups for long-term assignments that require work to be done at home. As she comments, "It's just too difficult for students to get together with people other than their friends outside of school."

Structure Cooperative Tasks for Positive Interdependence

If you want to ensure that students cooperate on a task, you have to create a situation in which students perceive that they need one another to succeed. This is called *positive interdependence,* and it's one of the essential features that transforms a group work activity into true cooperative learning (Antil, Jenkins, Wayne, & Vadasy, 1998).

One simple strategy for promoting interdependence is to require group members to *share materials* (Johnson, Johnson, Holubec, & Roy, 1984). If one member of a pair has a page of math problems, for example, and the other member has the answer sheet, they need to coordinate (at least a little) if they are both to complete the problems and check their answers. By itself, however, sharing materials is unlikely to ensure meaningful interaction.

Another way to encourage interdependence is to create a *group goal.* For example, you might have each group produce a single product, such as a report, a science demonstration, a poem, or a skit. When Christina's students studied the play *Antigone,* she had students individually read Henry David Thoreau's essay, "Resistance to Civil Government," and then meet in groups to (1) define civil disobedience in their own words, (2) explain the purpose of civil disobedience, (3) list three to five real-life examples of civil disobedience, and (4) predict how the issue of civil disobedience is important in the play. Christina explained how group members were to discuss each part of the assignment, combine their ideas, and turn in one paper from the whole group. Although requiring a group product increases the likelihood that students will work together, Christina recognizes that this strategy is not foolproof: One person in the group can do all the work while the others remain uninvolved.

A stronger way to stress the importance of collaborating is to give a *group grade or group reward.* For example, suppose you want to encourage students to help one another with the symbols for chemical ions. You can do this by rewarding groups on the basis of the total number of ions correctly supplied by all the members of the group. You can also give bonus points to every group in which all students reach a predetermined level of accomplishment. Some teachers give each group member a number (e.g., one to four) at the beginning of class, and then spin a numbered spinner or toss a die to select the number of the group member whose homework or classwork paper will be graded (Webb & Farivar, 1994). Then everyone in the group receives that score. Such a practice clearly increases the pressure on group members to make sure that everyone's homework or classwork is complete and well done.

Another way to promote collaboration is to structure the task so that students depend on one another for *information* (Johnson, Johnson, Holubec, & Roy, 1984). In Donnie's lesson on collecting and displaying information, for example, group members had to pool their individual data on adolescents' after-school activities. Because each student was responsible for collecting data on one grade level, they needed each other to construct a graph depicting the activities of freshmen, sophomores, juniors, and seniors.

Jigsaw, one of the earliest cooperative learning methods (Aronson, Blaney, Stephan, Sikes, & Snapp, 1978), is a good example of a group-work situation in which students need one another if they are to complete the task successfully. In Jigsaw, heterogeneous teams are responsible for learning academic material (usually a narrative, such as a social studies chapter) that has been divided into sections. Each team member reads only one section of the material. The teams then disband temporarily, and students meet in "expert groups" with other people who have been assigned the same section. Working together, they learn the material in these expert groups and then return to their home teams to teach it to their teammates. Everyone is responsible for learning all the material, so successful task completion requires students to listen carefully to their peers. A note of caution is needed; one study (Souvignier & Kronenberger, 2007) found that students tended to learn the section they were assigned but were less inclined to learn the material their peers presented.

You can also foster interdependence by creating rich, complex tasks that require *multiple abilities* (e.g., reading, writing, computing, role-playing, building models, spatial problem solving, drawing, creating songs, public speaking). By convincing your students that *every* member of the group is good at *some* of these and that *no* member of the group is good at *all* of them, you can reduce the differences in participation between high- and low-status students and enable those who are often left out to contribute (Cohen, 1994a, 1994b, 1998). Listen to Donnie:

> **I have one girl who is not very good in math, but she's a great artist. When we were doing group projects on baking cookies, I put her in a group that I knew would be receptive and sensitive, and I structured the activity so there would be a need for artwork. I try to show them that we're not all good at the same things, but that we bring different strengths and weaknesses to the table.**

Finally, you can assign *different roles* to group members, requiring each role to be fulfilled if the group is to complete the task. For example, Fred sometimes designates a recorder, a timekeeper, an encourager (to facilitate participation), a taskmaster (to keep people on track), a summarizer (to report out at the end of the group session), and an observer (to monitor group process). In addition to getting the task completed, another benefit of assigning roles is that it sends the message to students that each of them has something to offer and this "can lay the groundwork for equity" (Esmonde, 2009, p. 1030).

Sometimes the roles that Fred assigns are integral to the activity itself. In a social studies simulation on reconstruction, students form "presidential advisory committees" to advise President Andrew Johnson on a program for the South after the Civil War. Groups have to provide guidance on weighty issues:

- Are the southerners who lately rebelled against us citizens? Should they have the same rights and privileges as other loyal Americans?

- What should we do with the leaders of the rebellion, especially General Lee and President Davis?

- What should we do about the former slaves? Should they be given citizenship? Should they be allowed to vote? Should we pay former slave owners for the loss of their slave "property"?

Each presidential advisory committee is composed of characters with very different backgrounds and points of view. Here are two examples:

- The Reverend Harry (Harriet) Stone, 43 years old, deeply religious, attended college in Virginia, not very active in the abolition movement. Believed slavery is immoral but felt John Brown took things "too far."

- William (Mary) Hardwick, 52, a rich mill owner from Delaware, two sons fought in the war, the youngest was killed in the Wilderness while serving under Grant. Manufactures shirts and has profited from government war contracts, which have been canceled since Lee's surrender at Appomattox. Southern distributors still owe him (her) $40,000 for purchases made before the war began.

Having a variety of roles ensures that everyone has a role to play and that all students have to participate if the group is to succeed.

Ensure Individual Accountability

As we discussed earlier in the chapter, one of the major problems associated with group work is unequal participation. Sometimes individuals refuse to contribute to the group effort, preferring to "freeload." Sometimes more assertive students dominate, making it difficult for others to participate. In either case, lack of participation is a genuine problem. Those who do not actively participate might not learn anything about the academic task; furthermore, the group is not learning the skills of collaboration.

One way to encourage the participation of all group members is to make sure that everyone is held responsible for his or her contribution to the goal and that each student's learning is assessed individually. *Individual accountability* is the second essential feature of cooperative learning—and it is one that teachers most often neglect (Antil, Jenkins, Wayne, & Vadasy, 1998).

There are several ways to establish individual accountability. You can require students to take individual tests on the material and receive individual grades; you can have each student complete an identifiable part of the total group project; or you can call on one or two students from each group to answer a question, explain the group's reasoning, or provide a demonstration. One morning in May, we watched Sandy explain that students were going to be working on understanding the idea of equilibrium. She divided the class into groups of three, explained the task, and reminded students that they needed to work together to discover the operative principle. Before she allowed them to begin work, however, she stressed that a group should not consider itself through until all group members understood because everyone would eventually be taking an individual quiz. In other words, Sandy made it very clear that every student would be accountable for explaining the process of equilibrium.

Ensuring accountability does not always mean that every student has to perform the same activity or be responsible for the same material. Within a heterogeneous cooperative group, it is sometimes desirable or necessary to differentiate tasks by complexity and quantity (Schniedewind & Davidson, 2000). In other words, students can engage in tasks at different levels of difficulty or learn different amounts of material. The important point is that "every student learns something that he or she doesn't already know" and can "contribute to a common goal" (p. 24). For example, each student in a heterogeneous group might be responsible for reading a segment of a biography of Harriet Tubman. Students who are struggling readers might be assigned a relatively short portion of the book and review it with a resource teacher or an aide before the class activity; more proficient readers have a more demanding section. But all students summarize their reading, report to one another, and are held accountable for knowing about all aspects of Tubman's life. According to Schneiedewind and Davidson, students do not appear to feel awkward or resentful about differentiated assignments such as these. Indeed, they are well aware of one another's capabilities and seem to "feel more comfortable when teachers acknowledge and engage them in discussion about the tension-producing subject of academic difference" (p. 25). One teacher, for example, explained to her students that differentiated assignments helped her to fulfill her responsibility to challenge each student.

Teach Students to Cooperate

Recently, one of us read the following entry in a reflective paper written by a student teacher in English:

> *I have tried to use cooperative learning activities as much as possible but I'm not at all sure it's been beneficial. . . . Students spend more time goofing off than getting anything done. I'm not convinced that cooperative learning can work unless (1) students are mature enough to work without a teacher breathing down their necks and (2) they have the social skills to interact with peers.*

This student teacher has come to understand the fact that students' social skills can make or break a group work activity. What he fails to understand, however, is the role of the teacher in *teaching* these skills. Indeed, one research study compared students in groups that were taught to work cooperatively to students who were just placed in groups (Gillies, 2008). The students in the groups given instruction on cooperative work demonstrated more cooperative behaviors during group work as well as more complex thinking and problem-solving skills, both during the group work and on a follow-up assessment of their learning.

As the classroom teacher, *it is your responsibility to teach students to work together.* This is not a simple process; students do not learn to cooperate in one 45-minute lesson. Indeed, we can think about the process in terms of three stages: learning to value cooperation, developing group skills, and evaluation. Let's consider each of these briefly.

VALUING COOPERATION

Before students can work together productively, they must understand the value of cooperation. Sandy introduces cooperative group work early in the year by setting up a situation that students are unable to do alone:

> **I tell the kids that they are to solve a particular chemical problem (it's different every year), and that they should go to the lab tables and get started. They look at me as if I'm crazy. They say, "But Ms. Krupinski, you didn't tell us what procedure to use." I tell them I forgot to write out the procedure for them. I say, "Let's see if you can come up with the procedure. You'll get five extra points if you can figure out a procedure by yourself. If you do it in pairs, you'll split the five points, etc." They all start out working alone—they want those five points for themselves. But as the period goes on, they begin to work in groups. They realize that they need each other, that they can really help one another and they don't care about the points. At the end of the period, I say, "Let's talk about what happened here. Why did you start out by yourself?" They tell me, "I wanted the five points, but I had to ask for help because I didn't know enough." We talk about how helpful it is to work together when you're learning something new, and how the points don't matter.**

When students are going to work in the same groups over a period of time, it's often helpful to have them engage in a nonacademic activity designed to build a team identity and to foster a sense of group cohesion. For example, when Christina introduces group work, the first task that groups have is to write a summary about the group members. Then Christina calls on someone in each group and asks that student to tell her what they learned about the members of the group. Another idea is to have each group create a banner or poster displaying a group name and a logo. To ensure that everyone participates in creating the banner, each group member can be given a marker of a different color; individuals can use only the marker they have been given, and the banner must contain all the colors.

GROUP SKILLS TRAINING

Teaching a group skill is much like teaching students how to balance equations or use a pipette. It requires systematic explanation, modeling, practice, and feedback. *It's simply not enough to state the rules and expect students to understand and remember.* And don't take anything for granted; even basic guidelines such as "don't distract others" and "speak quietly" might need to be taught. Introducing simple norms for group work (Cohen, 1994a) can give students helpful guidelines for what is expected of them:

Ask peers for assistance.

Help one another.

Explain material to other students.

Check that they understand.

Provide support.

Listen to your peers.

Give everyone a chance to talk.

It's helpful to begin by analyzing the group work task you have selected to determine the specific skills students need to know (Cohen, 1994a). Will students have to explain material? Will they have to listen carefully to one another? Will they have to reach a consensus? Once you have analyzed the task, select one or two key behaviors to teach your students. Resist the temptation to introduce all the required group skills at once; going too far too fast is sure to lead to frustration.

Next explain to your students that they will be learning a skill necessary for working in groups. *Be sure to define terms, discuss rationales, and provide examples.* Johnson and Johnson (1989/90) suggest that you construct a "T-chart" on which you list the skill and then—with the class—record ideas about what the skill would look like and what it would sound like. Figure 11.2 shows a T-chart for "encouraging participation."

Finally, you need to provide opportunities for students to practice the skill and to receive feedback. You might have students role-play, pair the skill with a familiar academic task so that students can focus their attention on using the social skill, or have students engage in exercises designed to teach particular skills.

Donnie sometimes teaches group skills in a more "devious" way. She secretly assigns individuals to act out different roles: the dictator, the nonparticipant, the person who tears down everybody else, and the facilitator who encourages participation and listens well. Students engage in some sort of nonacademic activity—perhaps the task of building a tower with pins and straws—and then debrief, sharing their reactions about the group process. An activity like this serves to heighten students' awareness of group skills—and they have fun at the same time.

Regardless of the type of practice you provide, you need to give students feedback about their performance. Fred has found that it's helpful to designate a "process

Encouraging Participation

Looks Like	Sounds Like
Make eye contact.	What do YOU think?
Look and nod in person's direction.	We haven't heard from you yet.
Gesture to a person to speak.	Do you agree?
Make sure everyone's chair is in the cluster (no one is physically left out).	Anyone else have something to say?
	I'd like to know what you think.
	Let's go around to see what each person thinks.

FIGURE 11.2   T-Chart for Encouraging Participation

person" or "observer" for each group. This individual is responsible for keeping track of how well the group is functioning; for example, he or she might monitor how many times each person speaks. At the end of the group work session, the process person is able to share specific data that the group can use to evaluate its ability to work together.

EVALUATION

To learn from their experiences, students need the chance to discuss what happened and to evaluate how successful they were in working together. This is especially important when norms for group work are first being established. For example, during one visit to Fred's classroom early in the year, we observed a lesson on U.S. policy toward Afghanistan. Students were working in groups of four or five, trying to reach consensus on a number of politically sensitive questions (e.g., What military and security presence should the United States maintain in Afghanistan after the official troop withdrawal in 2014? Should the United States contribute funds to support Afghanistan after 2014?). Before students began to work, Fred explained that students were to discuss each question and prepare a report for a special envoy advising the president on Afghanistan. The chairperson of each group was responsible for compiling the report and seeing that all members had an opportunity to participate. Fred made it clear that groups would not be evaluated solely on their reports but also on how well they worked together—specifically, how quickly they got to work; how involved and engaged they looked; how well group members listened to each other; whether members conducted themselves with maturity and decorum; and whether all group members had a chance to express their views. During the activity, Fred roamed the room, watching and listening; in addition, the school's media specialist videotaped the entire class.

The following day, Fred spent about half the period evaluating the group activity his students had done. First he talked about how difficult it is to work in groups and told a few horror stories about groups in which he had worked. Then he asked students to complete a self-evaluation of their group's interaction. (See Figure 11.3 for one

FIGURE 11.3   One Student's Evaluation of the Group Work Activity

student's evaluation.) Finally, he played the videotape, commenting on the things he had noticed:

> [The tape shows students getting into groups, getting organized, and getting to work.] The first thing I did was watch you getting started. I actually timed you, from the moment you entered class to the time the last group was seated and working. It was less than three minutes. I think that was pretty good. [The camera zooms in on each group.] I also looked at how people were seated. [The tape shows a group where four people are clustered and one person is sitting away.] Your physical placement in the group is very important; if you have someone sitting outside the group, it's a good bet that person's not participating. I also tried to watch the way you took turns participating. Look at this. [William's group is shown on the tape.] William was a very organized chairperson. He went around to each person, asking, "What do you think? What do you think?" It was very orderly, and everyone got a chance to speak. But what's a drawback? A drawback is you might be disengaged when you're not talking. [Camera shows Frank's group.] Now Frank here ran a more free-wheeling group. There was more arguing back and forth. What's a drawback here? [Student responds.] Yeah, someone can easily get left out. Now take a look at Jan's group. Jan really made an effort to draw people in. . . . I also tried to look at whether any people were dominating the discussion. It really ticks people off if you dominate the group. I'll say that again. It ticks people off. Now what did you people think about the composition of the groups? [Students comment.] I tried to put one person in each chair's group who I thought the chair could relate to. Instead of separating all the friends, I thought it might make it easier to chair. Did it? What do you think about having friends in the group?

The impact of sharing a videotaped lesson with students was demonstrated in a study of an eighth-grade mathematics classroom (Kotsopoulos, 2010). In spite of instruction in how to behave collaboratively, students were observed to take roles of "foreman" and "laborer" in their groups with the foreman telling the laborers what to do. In addition, some students were marginalized and then engaged in off-task behavior. When questioned about how well their groups had functioned, students told the researcher that they had collaborated well. It was only when they watched a videotape of the lesson and talked about their interactions that they began to recognize that they weren't actually cooperating and began to behave more collaboratively.

A far simpler approach to evaluation is to ask students to name three things their group did well and one thing the group could do better next time (Johnson & Johnson, 1989/90). You also can have students consider more specific questions, such as:

Did everyone carry out his or her job?

Did everyone get a chance to talk?

Did you listen to one another?

What did you do if you didn't agree?

For additional suggestions of questions that students could use to assess their own and their group members' work in small groups, see the Teamwork Skills Inventory (Strom & Strom, 2012).

After individual groups have talked about their experiences, you might want to have them report to the whole class. You can encourage groups to share and compare their experiences by asking, "Did your group have a similar problem?" "How many groups agree with the way they solved their problem?" "What do you recommend?"

Christina sometimes has students write letters to members of their group, noting the group's strengths and weaknesses, each member's contributions, and what areas need improvement. Afterward, students pass the letters around their group, read what everyone has written, and briefly discuss the sentiments that were expressed. They then respond in writing to Christina.

Sometimes this process can be very encouraging for individuals. One very bright senior, for example, was gratified to learn that her less-proficient peers appreciated her patience, encouragement, and explanations. On the other hand, the process can sometimes lead to rancor. During one observation, we saw Christina meet with four students to discuss how they felt about having Nathan—who was now working by himself—rejoin their group. We were curious about what had happened, and after class, Christina explained:

> **About a week ago, I had the students write letters to their group. Nathan's was really offensive; it was racist, sexist, and vulgar. The other kids were really upset, for good reason. He said it was all a joke, of course, but he got ISS [in-school suspension] for one day. I also removed him from the group for one week, and I told him we would then discuss whether or not he would go back. I know he's afraid to go back to the group. He knows they're mad. He asked me to check out how they feel about having him come back. They wanted to write their responses to me. Two said they don't want him, and two said they don't care. He's really bright and knows the material, but he's always telling everyone how great he is, and distracting everyone, and the kids get annoyed with him. And of course the letter was the last straw. But he's not learning any social skills sitting there by himself. I think I'm going to put him back in the group for a trial period and see what happens.**
>
> **Obviously, this process can be very sensitive and cause a lot of hard feelings. Things like this don't usually happen, though, because students know that I'm going to collect the letters and that I expect them to give constructive criticism.**

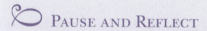

PAUSE AND REFLECT

Teachers sometimes use the terms *group work* and *cooperative learning* interchangeably. But although cooperative learning is a form of group work, group work is not always cooperative learning. It's important to be able to explain to students, parents, and, yes, administrators the type of learning opportunities you'll be using in your class. With this in mind, identify the key elements of cooperative learning that set it apart from other group work.

Monitor Learning, Involvement, and Cooperative Behavior

During cooperative learning activities, Donnie, Sandy, Christina, Donna, and Fred constantly circulate throughout the room, listening, assisting, encouraging, prodding, questioning, and in general, trying to ensure that students are involved, productive, and working collaboratively. For example, during the cooperative learning activity on equilibrium described earlier, Sandy was especially vigilant because she knew that the task was difficult and that students might become frustrated:

> Students are working in groups of three, trying to predict the molecular behavior of three chemical systems. Sandy notices that one group is particularly quiet. She moves over and places her hand on one boy's shoulder. He looks up and tells her: "I don't know what I'm doing." Sandy responds: "Why don't you talk to your group members?" He moves closer to the other individuals. As Sandy approaches another group, a girl indicates that she's "got it." Excitedly, she tries to explain the process to her group and to Sandy, but then collapses in confusion. "I'm just babbling," she says. Sandy decides it's time to intervene: "Okay, let's go back to the question. You have to understand what the question is asking first. What's the question?" In another group, a boy doesn't like the idea offered by a teammate: "I don't want to argue, but I don't think that's right." Sandy reaffirms his behavior: "That's okay. You're supposed to question one another." At one point, Sandy divides one group and sends its members to temporarily join two adjacent groups. "Mrs. K. says I should ask you my question," one boy says to his new group. While Sandy is working with a group on one side of the room, two groups on the other side begin to fool around. One boy has a bottle of correction fluid that he is tossing into the air with one hand and trying to catch with the other (which is behind his back). Sandy notices the disruption: "Excuse me, I don't think you're done, are you?" One group finally discovers the principle that is involved and erupts in a cheer. A girl in another group expresses frustration: "We're clueless over here and they're cheering over there." A few minutes later, Sandy joins this group to provide some assistance.

After class, during her free period, Sandy reflected on the importance of monitoring cooperative learning activities:

> Since this was a difficult activity, I expected that there would be some frustration, so it was really important to keep close tabs on what the groups were doing. You can tell a lot just by watching students' physical positions. If kids' heads are down, or if they're facing away, those are good signs that they're not participating or interacting with other group members. Today, I could tell that Richard was going to try the problem as an individual; he was off by himself—until he got frustrated and joined the other students. But that group never really worked well. I thought that Sylvia would help the group along, but she never got completely involved.
>
> I also try to listen closely to what they're saying to one another in terms of group process. Like Mark—he wasn't sure it was OK to disagree. I was glad I heard that so I could reassure him that he's supposed to do that. What's neat is to see how some kids begin to function as really good group leaders. For example, Sivan is really quiet, but she really listens, and she was able to bring in the other two boys she was working with.
>
> You also have to monitor students' progress in solving the problem and try to prevent them from getting completely off track. Today I could see that one group got stuck; the kids were really in a rut, saying the same words over and over. So I split the group up and sent the kids to explain what they were thinking or to ask their questions to two other groups. Sometimes having them talk to other kids can help to move them forward. In this case, it seemed to work. By interacting with a different group, Roy got out of the rut and then he was able to go back and help the kids in his own group.

Research confirms that teacher monitoring helps to promote a high level of student involvement in group activities (Emmer & Gerwels, 2002). By monitoring, you are able to discern when an intervention into the group's activities is necessary. Chiu (2004) studied the way that two 9th-grade algebra teachers monitored small-group problem-solving activities and the impact of their interventions. He found that teachers typically intervened when students were more off task than usual or had made little overall progress. In general, teacher interventions were beneficial to the group: Students were more likely to be on task after an intervention from the teacher than before and were more likely to recognize their errors, develop new ideas, and explain ideas to one another. Unfortunately, such positive effects persisted for only about five minutes; eventually, students' attention wandered to other topics, such as events in their personal lives. Such results underscore the importance of continuing to monitor students' progress.

Another way to monitor what groups are actually achieving is to build in "progress checkpoints." For example, after two days of having his students try to rewrite the district's "Human Dignity and Affirmative Action" policies, Fred stopped the groups' activity and asked students to report on what they had accomplished and what problems they were having. Similarly, you can divide large assignments into components that are due every few days. This allows you to keep track of how well groups are functioning.

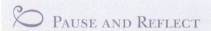

PAUSE AND REFLECT

Now that you've read about managing group work, go back to your original suggestions for Ralph. What additional ideas might you offer him? What are some key changes he could make to ensure that his next attempt at cooperative learning will be more successful?

Think about What to Do When a Student Doesn't Want to Join a Group

Sometimes a student will resist being part of a small group and want to work alone. What do you do then? Should you comply with the student's wishes? We posed this question to our teachers, and their initial response was revealing: *This doesn't happen very often.* Part of the reason is the fact that they lay the groundwork for small-group work at the very beginning of the year. That's when they set up rules and routines for small-group activities, discuss the value of collaboration, and begin to teach group work skills. In addition, because our teachers work hard to get to know their students, they are generally (but not always) able to tell which students will work together well, and this enables them to minimize problems with group composition.

We persisted: "But what would you do if it *did* happen?" Our discussion identified four ways to deal with this issue. First, assuming that the group work is meaningful and that the student's participation is important, they would try to find out why the student didn't want to join a group. As Fred put it:

 What I do depends on the student and why he or she doesn't want to work in the group. Perhaps I assigned him to a group in which there is someone who bullies him or a girl who has just rejected him. Just changing the group might solve the problem. On the other hand, if the student is just being uncooperative and is testing me, then I'd have an after-school meeting with him and his folks, explain the importance of the assignment and its value to their child, and work together to figure out how to handle the situation.

Second, our teachers talked about the need to change group composition on a regular basis so that students don't feel stuck with people they don't particularly like. They announce ahead of time how long the groups will be together. Depending on the activity, the group can last 15 minutes or four or five weeks. In any case, students know the group is temporary—and this helps them to accept what is perhaps an unappealing situation.

Third, our teachers continually emphasize the importance of learning to work with many different types of people. Christina commented:

Sometimes it's a lot easier just to allow the student not to join a group. But a part of education is developing the social skills needed to work with a variety of people. I try to stress that these are essential skills not just for school, but also for life.

When students are working in completely cooperative groups, Sandy allows individuals to submit a "minority report," a strategy that makes them more willing to work with people they perceive as less capable:

On any graded cooperative assignment students have the right to disagree with the group's final answer. In other words, if they have been trying to convince the group that their answer was the correct one and the group refused to listen or did not agree, that person can submit a separate answer.

Finally, our teachers agreed that they might occasionally allow students to opt out of a group activity if their reasoning was valid and if the activity did not require their participation. As Donna remarked: "There are times students just feel like working alone. Maybe they've had a bad day, or there's a problem at home, or they think they'd get more done working individually. In cases like this, forcing them to work in a group seems counterproductive."

CONCLUDING COMMENTS

Although this chapter is entitled "Managing Small-Group Work," we have seen that there are actually a number of different group-work situations, each with its own set of uses, procedures, requirements, and pitfalls. As you plan and implement group work in your classroom, it's important to remember these distinctions. Too many teachers think that cooperative learning is putting students into groups and telling them to work together. They select tasks that are inappropriate for the size of the group; they use heterogeneous groups when homogeneous groups would be more suitable (or vice versa); they fail to build in positive interdependence and individual accountability; they fail to appreciate the differences between helping groups and cooperative learning. The following example (O'Donnell & O'Kelly, 1994) would be funny—if it weren't true:

One of our colleagues recently described an example of "cooperative learning" in his son's school. The classroom teacher informed the students that [they] would be using cooperative learning. His son was paired with another student. The two students were required to complete two separate parts of a project but were expected to complete the work outside of class. A grade was assigned to each part of the project and a group grade was given. In this instance, one child received an "F" as he failed to complete the required part of the project. The other child received an "A." The group grade was a "C," thus rewarding the student who had failed to complete the work, and punishing the child who had completed his work. In this use of "cooperative learning," there was no opportunity for the students to interact, and the attempt to use a group reward (the group grade) backfired. Although this scenario is not recognizable as cooperative learning to most proponents of cooperation, the classroom teacher described it as such to the students' parents. (p. 322)

This example illustrates the need for teachers to acquire an understanding of the intricacies of group work in general and cooperative learning in particular. We hope that this chapter has sensitized you to some of the problems that can arise and has provided some strategies for minimizing these problems. Group work is an extremely challenging instructional approach, and successful management requires careful planning and implementation. Despite the potential pitfalls, we believe group work should be an integral part of secondary classrooms—particularly as you work to establish a caring, supportive community.

SUMMARY

This chapter began by talking about the potential benefits of group work and about some of the special challenges it presents. It then suggested strategies for designing and implementing effective group work.

Benefits of Group Work

- Decreased idle time while waiting for the teacher to help.
- Enhanced motivation.
- Increased achievement.
- Enhanced involvement in learning.
- Decreased competition among students.
- Increased interaction across gender, ethnic, and racial lines.
- Improved relationships among students with and without disabilities.

Pitfalls of Small-Group Work

- Segregation in terms of gender, ethnicity, and race.
- Unequal participation.
- Lack of accomplishment.
- Lack of cooperation among group members.

Designing and Implementing Effective Group Work

- Decide on the type of group to use (helping permitted, helping obligatory, peer tutoring, cooperative, completely cooperative).
- Decide on the size of the group.
- Decide on group composition.
- Structure the task for interdependence (e.g., create a group goal or reward).

- Ensure individual accountability.
- Teach students to cooperate.
- Monitor learning, involvement, and cooperative behavior.
- Think about what to do when a student doesn't want to join a group.

Group work offers unique social and academic rewards, but it is important to understand the challenges it presents and not to assume that, just because a task is fun or interesting, the lesson will run smoothly. Remember to plan group work carefully, prepare your students thoroughly, and allow yourself time to develop experience as a facilitator of cooperative groups.

ACTIVITIES FOR SKILL BUILDING AND REFLECTION

In Class

1. In small groups that are homogeneous in terms of content area (e.g., math, science, social studies), choose a topic that you will be teaching and work together to create a completely cooperative activity. As you design the activity, consider the following questions:

    How will you assign students to groups?
    How will you structure the activity to foster positive interdependence?
    What roles will you assign, if any?
    What forms of individual accountability will you incorporate?
    What are the social skills you need to teach, and how will you teach them?
    How will you monitor the group work?
    How will you provide an opportunity for students to evaluate the group process?

2. Consider the following situation: You regularly use small groups that are heterogeneous in terms of achievement because you believe that students can learn from one another. You also believe that learning to work cooperatively and to appreciate differences are important and valid goals. However, the parents of one of your high-achieving students contact you to complain that their son is not being appropriately challenged and is "wasting his time tutoring the slower kids." In a group, discuss what you might say in response.

3. In a group, read the following excerpt from a teacher-authored case on cooperative learning (Shulman, Lotan, & Whitcomb, 1998).

    Period 3 is one of the six eighth-grade social studies classes I teach each day. . . . [As an experienced proponent of cooperative groups,] I entered into group instruction this year with a good deal of confidence. I met my match with period 3. . . . This is one class in the district that merits a full time Resource Specialist Program teaching aide because we have nine—yes, nine—special education students. We also have 10 sheltered students who have recently left bilingual classes and are now making the transition to full-time English instruction. The makeup of this class creates a disturbing chemistry that is felt within 30 seconds of the starting bell. I usually place them in groups of four or five, then invariably watch in frozen amazement as they torment each other. I persist as I was trained to do, but find myself wondering whether group work is appropriate for this uncooperative class of 28 students, skewed with a disproportionate number of emotionally needy individuals. . . .

    To sum it up, after 42 minutes with period 3, I feel like a giant, emotion-filled ball being slammed from one side of the room to the other. . . . Whether it's because they lack experience in small-group interaction or they lack self-esteem, or some combination of the two, creating a cooperative atmosphere is not something the students of period 3 seem to be able to accomplish.

At the end of the day I find myself wondering why I don't switch to the more traditional teacher-controlled setting with which these students are more familiar. Perhaps group work is not meant for every class. "It's okay to give up," I tell myself. Yet deep down I tell myself, "It's not okay. I know I need to do something." (pp. 21–23)

In your group, discuss what that "something" might be.

On Your Own

1. Observe a cooperative learning activity. In what ways has the teacher tried to promote positive interdependence and individual accountability?

2. Consider when you might use each of the following types of group work. List an example of an activity from your own content area.
   a. Helping permitted
   b. Helping obligatory
   c. Peer tutoring
   d. Cooperative group
   e. Completely cooperative group

For Your Portfolio

Design a cooperative learning lesson on a topic of your choice. Write a brief commentary describing (1) the social skills that are required in this lesson and how you will teach them, (2) the way(s) in which you built in positive interdependence and individual accountability, and (3) how students will evaluate their group interaction.

FOR FURTHER READING

Gillies, R. M. (2007). *Cooperative learning: Integrating theory and practice.* Los Angeles: Sage.
    This book situates cooperative learning within the context of No Child Left Behind and high-stakes testing, arguing that cooperative learning has the potential to transform schools and lead to student success on standardized tests. Chapters in the book deal with establishing successful cooperative groups, promoting student discourse, and assessing small-group learning.

Lotan, R. (2006). Managing groupwork in the heterogeneous classroom. In C. M. Evertson & C. S. Weinstein (Eds.), *Handbook of classroom management: Research, practice, and contemporary issues.* Mahwah, NJ: Lawrence Erlbaum.
    This chapter posits that group work is not only a useful pedagogical strategy for academically and linguistically heterogeneous classrooms but also that it has the potential to help teachers build equitable classrooms. Lotan addresses the need to teach social skills, assign specific roles, delegate authority to students, and design interventions to combat unequal participation.

Rubin, B. C. (2003). Unpacking detracking: When progressive pedagogy meets students' social worlds. *American Educational Research Journal, 40*(2), 539–573.
    This article is based on a year-long study of two detracked ninth-grade classes, one in English and one in social studies, in a diverse urban high school. Rubin describes how the teachers used group work to facilitate both learning and social interaction across race and class lines.

Schniedewind, N., & Davidson, E. (2000). Differentiating cooperative learning. *Educational Leadership, 58*(1), 24–27.

This article provides "guiding tenets" and examples of how to differentiate assignments and responsibilities within heterogeneous cooperative groups.

Slavin, R. E. (1995). *Cooperative learning: Theory, research, and practice,* 2nd ed. Boston: Allyn & Bacon.

This book provides an excellent introduction to cooperative learning methods, describes various approaches (e.g., Student Team Learning methods, Learning Together, Jigsaw), and summarizes the research on the effects of cooperative learning on achievement and social-emotional outcomes.

ORGANIZATIONAL RESOURCES

Cooperative Learning Center at the University of Minnesota. www.co-operation.org. Co-directed by Roger T. Johnson and David W. Johnson, the CLC is a research and training center focusing on how students should interact with each other as they learn and the skills needed to interact effectively.

The International Association for the Study of Cooperation in Education (IASCE), www.iasce.net. Established in 1979, IASCE is the only international, nonprofit organization for educators interested in cooperative learning to promote academic achievement and democratic, social processes. The website provides an annotated list of web pages related to cooperative learning.

PART IV

Protecting and Restoring Order

Most of the misbehaviors that teachers encounter are relatively mundane: inattention, talking to neighbors, not having homework done, calling out, and forgetting to bring supplies and books. Nevertheless, behaviors such as these can be aggravating and wearing, can take precious time away from teaching and learning, and can threaten a caring community. Clearly, teachers must have a way to think about such problems and a repertoire of strategies for dealing with them effectively.

The two chapters in this section focus on strategies for responding effectively to instances of problem behavior. Chapter 12 begins with a set of principles to guide your thinking about how best to respond in a constructive fashion. We then consider a hierarchy of strategies for dealing with a variety of problem behaviors, starting with strategies that are minimally obtrusive and easy to implement and concluding with those that require considerable time and effort. In Chapter 13, we turn to the issue of school violence. First we look at its frequency and severity. Then we consider approaches for preventing and coping with hostile, aggressive, and dangerous behavior. Throughout the chapters, we hear the voices of our five teachers describing how they handle problem and aggressive behavior.

Both chapters echo themes heard in earlier chapters—namely, the importance of building community and fostering positive relationships. When students are inattentive, resistant, or disruptive, it's easy to fall back on punitive, authoritarian reactions: "Stop that or else!" "Because I said so!" "Go to the principal's office!" "That's three days of detention!" But such responses destroy relationships with students. Resentment builds, defiance escalates, and an atmosphere of "us against them" begins to take hold. Moreover, such responses are usually ineffective, leading teachers to conclude that "nothing can be done with these kids."

As we have stated in earlier chapters, research consistently indicates that students are more likely to engage in cooperative, responsible behavior and adhere to classroom norms when they perceive their teachers to be supportive and caring. Thus, teachers who have positive relationships with students are better able to *prevent* inappropriate behavior. But we believe that *teacher-student relationships also play a key role in a teacher's ability to respond effectively to problem behaviors.* If your students perceive you as fair, trustworthy, and "on their side," they are likely to comply more readily with your disciplinary interventions.

Responding Effectively to Inappropriate Behavior

Not too long ago, we read an entry in the journal of a student teacher whose fourth- and fifth-period English classes were disrespectful and disruptive. It was the middle of November, and Sharon was feeling frustrated: "They just won't sit still long enough to hear directions," she wrote. "I am spending more and more time on telling people to 'Shhh.' I don't understand why they are so rude, and I just don't know what to do." As we read more, it became clear that this student teacher's problem was not due to an absence of clear rules and routines or to boring, tedious instruction:

> On the first day that I took over, we reviewed the rules my cooperating teacher had established (just like you suggested!): Come to class on time, don't call out, treat each other with respect, etc. They were really cooperative; I thought this was going to be great, but I guess they were just "psyching me out." Now they argue with me all the time. I say "quiet" and they say, "But I was just telling him. . . ." I say, "Put the newspaper/magazine/cell phone away," and they say "Just let me look, I have to see. . . ." There doesn't seem much else to do

except repeat myself. Sometimes it works, sometimes it doesn't. . . . I'm really at my wits' end. If I can't gain some control, there's obviously no way I can teach anything. Sometimes I think I'd be better off if I just forgot about trying to have interesting discussions, projects, small groups, etc., and just gave out work-sheets every day, lectured, and didn't allow any talking. That's a far cry from the kind of classroom I wanted to have. I wanted to respect my students, to treat them like adults, but I found I can't. I've always gotten along great with kids, but not now. All these kids seem to understand is discipline referrals and detention.

This student teacher had learned a sad fact of classroom life: Having clear, reasonable rules and routines doesn't automatically mean that everyone will follow them. At the beginning of the school year, students work hard at figuring out the teachers—determining teachers' expectations and requirements, the amount of socializing they will tolerate, and how far they can be pushed. Most students pursue their agendas within the limits the teacher sets, but they need to know those limits. This underscores the importance of communicating your behavioral expectations to students (the topic of Chapter 5)—and then *enforcing those expectations.* Listen to Donnie:

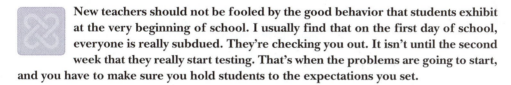

New teachers should not be fooled by the good behavior that students exhibit at the very beginning of school. I usually find that on the first day of school, everyone is really subdued. They're checking you out. It isn't until the second week that they really start testing. That's when the problems are going to start, and you have to make sure you hold students to the expectations you set.

In this chapter, we consider ways to respond to the problems that you might encounter—from minor, nondisruptive infractions to chronic, more serious misbehaviors.

PRINCIPLES FOR DEALING WITH INAPPROPRIATE BEHAVIOR

In Chapter 1, we presented a contrast between *authoritarian* teachers (who are dictatorial and unresponsive to students' needs) and *authoritative* teachers (who hold students to high standards but are also empathetic and supportive). Authoritative teachers are more able to establish respectful classroom climates and achieve better outcomes for students. Indeed, research indicates that an authoritarian approach to discipline is actually related to *more* student misbehavior (Way, 2011). Therefore, consistent with the importance of being a warm-demanding, authoritative teacher, six principles for dealing with inappropriate behavior guide our discussion. (See Table 12.1.)

First, *disciplinary strategies must be consistent with the goal of creating a safe, caring classroom environment.* You need to achieve order, but you also need to choose strategies that support your relationship with students, help them to become self-regulating, and allow them to save face in front of their peers. Curwin and Mendler (1988), authors of *Discipline with Dignity,* put it this way:

> Students will protect their dignity at all costs, even with their lives if pushed hard enough. In the game of chicken, with two cars racing at top speed toward a cliff, the loser is the one who steps on the brake. Nothing explains this bizarre reasoning better than the need for peer approval and dignity. (p. 27)

TABLE 12.1 Principles for Dealing with Inappropriate Behavior

1. Choose disciplinary strategies that are consistent with the goal of creating a safe, caring classroom environment.
2. Keep the instructional program going with a minimum of disruption.
3. Consider the context in deciding whether a particular action constitutes misbehavior.
4. Be timely and accurate when responding to inappropriate behavior.
5. Match the severity of the disciplinary strategy with the misbehavior you are trying to eliminate.
6. Be "culturally responsive" because differences in norms, values, and styles of communication can have a direct effect on students' behavior.

For more information about Curwin and Mendler, see Meet the Educators Box 12.1.

To protect students' dignity and preserve your relationship with them, it is important to avoid power struggles that cause students to feel humiliated and ridiculed. (Remember our discussion of "when school was awful" in Chapter 3.) Fred, Donnie, Sandy, Christina, and Donna make a real effort to speak with misbehaving students calmly and quietly. They don't bring up past sins. They take care to separate the student's *character* from the specific *misbehavior;* instead of attacking the student as a person ("You're lazy"), they talk about what the student has done ("You haven't handed in the last two homework assignments"). When more than a brief intervention is necessary, they try to meet with students privately.

During the first week of school, we witnessed a good example of disciplining with dignity in Sandy's classroom. Even though it was early in the school year, some students had already begun to test Sandy's adherence to the rules she had distributed a few days earlier:

 Sandy stands by the door, greeting students as they come in. The bell rings; Sandy begins to close the door, when William breathlessly rushes up. "You're late," she tells him quietly. "Does that mean I have to come after school?" he asks. "I'll talk to you later," she replies and moves to the front of the room to begin the lesson.

Later in the period, students are working in small groups on a lab experiment. Sandy circulates through the room, helping students with the procedure. She goes over to William and pulls him aside. She speaks softly: "You owe me 10 minutes. Today or tomorrow?"

"What's today?"

"Tuesday."

"Uh-oh." William looks worried.

"Is it better for you to come tomorrow?" Sandy asks.

"Yeah—but will you remind me?"

"I certainly will," she says with a rueful smile. Sandy goes over to her desk, makes a note in her grade book, and then continues circulating. A few minutes later, she stands beside William again, helping him with a problem and encouraging his progress.

In this vignette, we see how Sandy spoke to William privately to avoid embarrassing him; how she demonstrated concern for William by offering him a choice

BOX 12.1   MEET THE EDUCATORS

Richard Curwin and Allen Mendler

Richard Curwin and Allen Mendler are widely known authors, speakers, consultants, and workshop leaders who focus on issues of classroom management, discipline, and motivation. Curwin has been a seventh-grade teacher, a teacher of emotionally disturbed children, and a college professor. Mendler is a school psychologist who has worked extensively with children of all ages in general and special education settings. Together they developed the *Discipline with Dignity* program, first published in 1988.

Some Major Ideas about Classroom Management

- Dealing with student behavior is part of the job.
- Management strategies must maintain the dignity of each student.
- Discipline plans should focus on teaching responsibility rather than obtaining compliance.
- In a typical classroom, 80 percent of the students rarely break rules and don't really need a discipline plan; 15 percent break rules on an occasional basis and need a clear set of expectations and consequences; 5 percent are chronic rule breakers. A good discipline plan controls the 15 percent without backing the 5 percent into a corner.
- Consequences for rule violations are not punishments. Punishment is a form of retribution; the goal is to make the violator pay for misconduct. Consequences are directly related to the rule; their purpose is instructional rather than punitive because they are designed to teach students the effects of their behavior. Consequences work best when they are clear, specific, and logical.
- Teachers should have a range of alternative consequences so they can use discretion in choosing the best consequence to match the particular situation.
- Teachers need to teach the concept that "fair is not always equal."

Publications

Discipline with dignity (2nd ed.) (Curwin & Mendler; Alexandria, VA: Association for Supervision and Curriculum Development, 1999)

Discipline with dignity for challenging youth (Mendler & Curwin; Bloomington, IN: National Educational Service, 1999)

Connecting with students (Mendler; Alexandria, VA: Association for Supervision and Curriculum Development, 2001)

Making good choices: Developing responsibility, respect, and self-discipline in grades 4–9 (Curwin; Thousand Oaks, CA: Corwin Press, 2003)

Website: www.tlc-sems.com

about when to come for detention; how she avoided accusations, blame, and character assassination; and how she showed William that she held no grudge by helping with the lab a few minutes later. In short, the vignette demonstrates the way a teacher can communicate clear expectations for appropriate behavior while preserving a positive teacher-student relationship.

The second principle emphasizes the need to *keep the instructional program going with a minimum of disruption.* Achieving this goal requires a delicate balancing act.

On one hand, you cannot allow inappropriate behavior to interrupt the teaching-learning process. On the other hand, you must realize that disciplinary strategies themselves can be disruptive. As Doyle comments, interventions are "inherently risky" because they call attention to misbehavior and can actually pull students away from a lesson (1986, p. 421). To avoid this situation, you must try to anticipate potential problems and head them off; if you decide that a disciplinary intervention *is* necessary, you need to be as unobtrusive as possible.

Watching the five teachers in action, it is clear that they recognize the importance of protecting the instructional program. In the following incident, Donna sizes up a potentially disruptive situation and is able to maintain the flow of her lesson:

Donna is leading a discussion on an article students have read on New York City's proposed ban on large soft drinks. In the back of the room, two students do not have the article out and are talking quietly. Donna continues asking questions about the article while she moves up the aisle. Between comments, she gives the two students a quizzical look, as if to say, "What are you folks doing?" They both take the article out of their folders and put them on their desks.

The third principle is that *whether or not a particular action constitutes misbehavior depends on the context in which it occurs* (Doyle, 1986). There are obvious exceptions to this notion—punching another person and stealing property are obvious violations that always require a teacher response. But other behaviors are not so clear cut. For example, in some classes, wearing a hat, sitting on your desk, chewing gum, and listening to your MP3 player while doing independent work are all misbehaviors, but in other classes, these are perfectly acceptable. What constitutes misbehavior is often a function of a particular teacher's tolerance level or the standards set by a particular school. Even within a class, the definition of misbehavior depends on the context. A teacher can decide that talking out of turn is acceptable during a class discussion as long as students' comments contribute to the lesson and the situation doesn't turn into a free-for-all; at other times, this same teacher could feel that a more structured lesson is needed.

When determining a course of action, you need to ask yourself, "Is this behavior disrupting or benefiting the ongoing instructional activity? Is it hurtful to other students? Does it violate established rules?" If the answer to these questions is no, disciplinary interventions might not be necessary.

"I've got no control today," Fred announces with a grin. A glance around the room seems to confirm his assessment. Some students are sitting on their desks; others are standing in the aisles, leaning over other students who are writing. In the back of the room, four students are turned around in their seats and are having an animated discussion. One girl is standing by Fred's desk, loudly debating with a girl seated nearby. Just about everyone is talking. After a few moments, the topic of all this heated conversation becomes clear. Because of severe winter storms, the school district has exceeded the normal allotment of snow days. To meet the state mandate for 180 days of school, the board of education must now decide whether to eliminate spring break or extend the school year. Fred has seized the

opportunity to teach a lesson on political activism. His students are to think about the issue, consider whether there should be a waiver from the 180-day mandate, and write to their state legislators. Today's assignment is to construct the first draft of the letter. After class, Fred thinks about the atmosphere in the class: "I know I could have exerted a lot more control over the situation. I could have told them to sit quietly, to jot down ideas, and then silently write a first draft. But what would I have gained?"

The fourth principle is to *be timely and accurate when responding to inappropriate behavior.* Kounin (1970) identified two common errors that teachers make when attempting to handle misbehavior in the classroom: timing and target mistakes. A timing mistake occurs when a teacher waits too long to correct a misbehavior. For example, a teacher might not realize (or has ignored the fact) that several students have called out responses without raising their hands and sternly reprimands the next student to do so. Not only is this timing mistake unfair to that particular student but also calling out could have already become a habit for the students and much more difficult to curb than if it had been corrected immediately.

Similar to timing mistakes, target mistakes call attention to one particular student when in fact one or more others are at fault. A student might kick the backpack of the girl in front of him and the girl gets reprimanded for yelling in class. The student who threw the paper airplane that hit the teacher could go unnoticed while a student closer to the teacher is blamed for the incident. Similar mistakes are understandable because instances of inappropriate behavior are often ambiguous and occur when the teacher is looking elsewhere. For this reason, care must be taken to respond accurately and in a timely manner.

The fifth principle emphasizes the importance of *making sure the severity of the disciplinary strategy matches the misbehavior you are trying to eliminate.* It is helpful to think about misbehavior in terms of three categories: *minor misbehaviors* (noisiness, socializing, daydreaming), *more serious misbehaviors* (arguing, failing to respond to a group directive), and *never tolerated misbehaviors* (stealing, intentionally hurting someone, destroying property). You also need to consider whether the misbehavior is part of a pattern or an isolated event.

When deciding how to respond to a problem, it is useful to think in terms of these categories and to select a response that is congruent with the seriousness of the misbehavior. This is easier said than done, of course. When misbehavior occurs, teachers have little time to assess its seriousness, decide whether it's part of a pattern, and select an appropriate response. Nonetheless, you don't want to ignore or react mildly to misbehavior that warrants a more severe response, nor do you want to overreact to behavior that is relatively minor. For example, a firm reminder to the class to lower the noise level is an appropriate response to this minor misbehavior, and your response to a student who has disrupted the class for the third time today might be to have a private conference with him.

Finally, the sixth principle stresses the need to be *"culturally responsive" because differences in norms, values, and styles of communication can have a direct effect on students' behavior.* Being culturally responsive means reflecting on the types of behaviors you judge to be problematic and considering how these might be related to race and ethnicity. For example, Gail Thompson (2004), an African

American educator whose research focuses on the schooling experiences of students of color, notes that African American children are often socialized to talk loudly at home—a behavior that gets them into trouble at school. Listen to the mother of an eighth-grader who was starting to be labeled as a discipline problem at school for this reason:

> She's a loud person. My husband is a loud person, and when they get to explain themselves, they get loud. Their voices go up. Then, the teachers think she's being disrespectful. She's gotten a referral for that once. (G. Thompson, p. 98)

Similarly, African American youngsters tend to be more intense and confrontational than European American youngsters; they are more likely to challenge school personnel because they see leadership as a function of strength and forcefulness (rather than as a function of position and credentials); and they could jump into heated discussion instead of waiting for their turn (Irvine, 1990). Teachers who subscribe to the dominant culture are likely to see these behavioral patterns as examples of rudeness and disruptiveness, to respond with anger, and to invoke punitive measures. Alternatively, teachers who view the behaviors as reflections of cultural norms are better able to remain calm and nondefensive and to consider a variety of more constructive options (e.g., discussing classroom norms and the need for turn taking in large groups). Indeed, they might actually come to see the benefits of allowing intensity and passion to be expressed in the classroom and broaden their definition of what is acceptable student behavior.

In addition, culturally responsive classroom managers are aware of the ways that race and ethnicity influence the use of disciplinary consequences. Research conducted over 30 years repeatedly shows that African American and Latino students, particularly males, are disproportionately referred for inappropriate behavior compared to their majority counterparts (Peguero & Shekarkhar, 2011; Shirley & Cornell, 2011; Skiba et al., 2008). Data collected by the U.S. Department of Education's Office for Civil Rights (2012) indicate that Latino students are one and a half times more likely to be expelled from their schools than are white students. In districts reporting at least one expulsion, African American students represented 19 percent of the enrollment but 33 percent of the students expelled.

What accounts for this disproportionality? One obvious explanation is that African American and Latino students violate class and school norms more often than their White peers. If this is the case, disproportionate punishment is an appropriate response to inappropriate behavior rather than an indicator of bias. Research on student behavior, race, and discipline, however, has yielded no evidence to support this explanation. In fact, studies suggest that African American students tend to receive harsher punishments for less severe behaviors (Skiba & Rausch, 2006). In addition, White students appear to be referred to the office more frequently for "objective" offenses, such as vandalism, leaving without permission, and obscene language, while Black students are referred more often for "subjective" offenses: disrespect, excessive noise, and threat (Skiba, Michael, Nardo, & Peterson, 2002; Skiba et al., 2011). One study of female students (Blake, Butler, Lewis, & Darensbourg, 2011) found that African American girls were more likely to receive disciplinary sanctions that removed them from the classroom than were other girls. Furthermore, many of the offending behaviors of the African American girls in this study seemed to defy traditional standards of femininity (e.g., inappropriate and "unlady-like" dress). In sum, it does not appear that racial disparities in school discipline are due to higher rates of misbehavior on the part of African American students. Instead, the evidence indicates that African American students are sent to the office and given punitive disciplinary consequences for less serious or more subjective reasons (Skiba & Rausch). Moreover, schools with a greater number of special education students, underachieving students, and students living in poverty were more likely to take severe disciplinary actions even when the incidence of inappropriate behavior was the same as other schools (Han & Akiba, 2011).

The implication is clear: To be a culturally responsive classroom manager, teachers need to acknowledge their biases and values and think about how these affect their interactions with students. Some useful questions to ask yourself are listed here (Weinstein, Curran, & Tomlinson-Clarke, 2003):

- Am I more patient and encouraging with some students?
- Am I more likely to reprimand other students?
- Do I expect certain students to be disruptive based on their race or ethnicity?
- Do I use hairstyle and dress to form stereotypical judgments of my students?
- When students violate norms, do I recommend equal treatment of all students?

With these six principles in mind—preserving a safe, caring classroom environment; protecting the instructional program; considering the context; responding in a timely and accurate manner; selecting a disciplinary strategy that matches the misbehavior; and being culturally responsive—we turn now to specific ways to respond to inappropriate behavior.

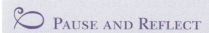

PAUSE AND REFLECT

Before reading about specific disciplinary interventions, think back to your own years as a student in elementary and high school. What disciplinary strategies did your most effective teachers use? What strategies did your least effective teachers use?

DEALING WITH MINOR MISBEHAVIOR

As mentioned in Chapter 5, Kounin's (1970) classic study of orderly and disorderly classrooms gave research support to the belief that successful classroom managers have eyes in the back of their heads. Kounin found that effective managers knew what was going on all over the room; moreover, *their students knew they knew* because the teachers were able to spot minor problems and "nip them in the bud." Kounin called this ability *withitness,* a term that has since become widely used in discussions of classroom management.

How do "with it" teachers deal with minor misbehavior? How do they succeed in nipping problems in the bud? This section discusses both nonverbal and verbal interventions and then considers the times when it might be better to do nothing at all. (Suggestions are summarized in the Practical Tips box.)

PRACTICAL TIPS FOR

Dealing with Minor Misbehavior

- Use a nonverbal intervention such as:
  Make facial expressions.
  Make eye contact.
  Use hand signals.
  Move closer to the misbehaving student (proximity).
- Use a nondirect verbal intervention:
  State the student's name.
  Incorporate the student's name into the lesson.
  Call on the student to participate.
  Use gentle humor.
  Use an I-message.
- Use a direct verbal intervention:
  Give a succinct command.
  Remind students about a rule.
  Give a choice between behaving appropriately or receiving a penalty.
- Choose deliberate nonintervention (but only if the misbehavior is minor and fleeting).

Nonverbal Interventions

A while back, an 11-year-old we know announced that she could be a successful teacher. When we asked why she was so confident, she replied: "I know how to make *the look.*" She proceeded to demonstrate: her eyebrows slanted downward, her forehead creased, and her lips flattened into a straight line. She definitely had "the look" down pat.

The "teacher look" is a good example of an unobtrusive, nonverbal intervention. Making eye contact, using hand signals (e.g., thumbs down; pointing to what the individual should be doing), and moving closer to the misbehaving student are other nonverbal ways to communicate withitness. Nonverbal interventions all convey the message, "I see what you're doing, and I don't like it," but because they are less directive than verbal commands, they encourage students to assume responsibility for getting back on task. Watch Donnie:

> **Donnie is at the board demonstrating how to construct congruent segments and congruent angles. Students are supposed to be following along, constructing congruent segments with rulers and compasses. Instead of working, two boys sit twirling their rulers on their pencils. Donnie notices what they are doing but continues with her explanation. While she's talking, she gives the two boys a long, hard stare. They put down the rulers and get to work.**

Nonverbal strategies are most appropriate for behaviors that are minor but persistent: frequent or sustained whispering, staring into space, calling out, putting on makeup, and sending text messages. The obvious advantage of using nonverbal cues is that you can deal with these misbehaviors without distracting other students. In short, nonverbal interventions enable you to protect and continue your lesson with minimum disruption.

A nonverbal cue is sometimes all that's needed to stop a misbehavior and get a student back "on task." In fact, a study of six middle school teachers (Lasley, Lasley, & Ward, 1989) found that the *most successful responses to misbehavior were nonverbal.* These strategies stopped misbehavior 79 percent of the time; among the three "more effective managers," the success rate was even higher—an amazing 95 percent.

Verbal Interventions

Sometimes you find yourself in situations in which it's just not possible to use a nonverbal cue. Perhaps you can't catch the student's eye, or you're working with a small group, and it would be too disruptive to get up and walk across the room to the misbehaving individual. At other times, you're able to use a nonverbal cue, but it's unsuccessful in stopping the misbehavior.

In such cases, you might use a *nondirective verbal intervention.* This allows you to prompt the appropriate behavior but leave the responsibility for figuring out what to do with the misbehaving student. For example, *simply saying the student's name* might be enough to get the student back on task. Sometimes it's possible to *incorporate the student's name* into the ongoing instruction:

> **Shaheed is slouching down in his seat and appears inattentive. As Fred talks about respect for the elderly in China, he moves closer to him. "Let's say Shaheed was my son, and I beat him up because he was getting a failing grade in class. What happens to me?" Shaheed sits up and "tunes in."**

If the misbehavior occurs during a group discussion or recitation, *you can call on the student to answer a question.* Consider the following example:

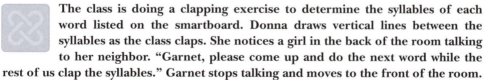

> **The class is doing a clapping exercise to determine the syllables of each word listed on the smartboard. Donna draws vertical lines between the syllables as the class claps. She notices a girl in the back of the room talking to her neighbor. "Garnet, please come up and do the next word while the rest of us clap the syllables." Garnet stops talking and moves to the front of the room.**

Calling on a student allows you to communicate that you know what's going on and to capture the student's attention—without even citing the misbehavior. But keep in mind what we said earlier about preserving students' dignity. If you are obviously trying to "catch" students and to embarrass them, the strategy might well backfire by creating resentment (Good & Brophy, 2008). One way to avoid this problem is to alert the student that you will be calling on him or her to answer the *next question:* "Sharon, what's the answer to number 18? Taysha, the next one's yours."

The *use of humor* can provide another "gentle" way to remind students to correct their behavior. Used well, humor can show them that you are able to understand the funny sides of classroom life. But you must be careful that the humor is not tinged with sarcasm that can hurt students' feelings.

It's near the end of the year, and Fred's students obviously have a case of "senioritis." They have just entered the room, and Fred is trying to get them to settle down. "Ladies and gentlemen, I know it's almost the end of the year, but could we make believe we're students now?"

A student in Donna's classroom shouts out that he needs a pencil. Donna responds: "Please don't tell me you need a pencil the way you order when you drive up to a Jack in the Box. How do you ask for a pencil?" The boy amends his request: "May I please have a pencil?"

An *"I-message"* is another way to verbally prompt appropriate behavior without giving a direct command. I-messages generally contain three parts. First, the teacher *describes the unacceptable behavior in a nonblaming, nonjudgmental way.* This phrase often begins with "when": "When people talk while I'm giving directions. . . ." The second part describes the *tangible effect on the teacher:* "I have to repeat the directions and that wastes time. . . ." Finally, the third part of the message states the *teacher's feelings* about the tangible effect: "and I get frustrated." Consider these examples of I-messages:

> "When you come to class without your supplies, I can't start the lesson on time, and I get really irritated."

> "When you leave your book bag in the middle of the aisle, I can trip over it, and I'm afraid I'll break a leg."

Although I-messages ideally contain all three parts in the recommended sequence, I-messages in any order, or even with one part missing, can still be effective. We've witnessed the five teachers use "abbreviated" I-messages. For example, Fred communicates how strongly he feels about paying attention when he tells his class: "If you pass notes while I'm lecturing, I'll become suicidal." On the first day of school, Donna states, "I don't want to speak over you because then I will be very hoarse by the end of the day." Using this approach has several benefits. In contrast to typical "you-messages" (e.g., "You are being rude"; "You ought to know better"; "You're acting like a baby"), I-messages minimize negative evaluations of the student. They make it easier to avoid using extreme (and usually inaccurate) words such as "always" and "never" (as in "You *always* forget to do your homework" or "You're *never* prepared for class"). For these reasons, they foster and preserve a positive relationship between people. Because I-messages leave decisions about changing behavior up to students, this approach is also likely to promote a sense of responsibility and autonomy. In addition, I-messages show students that their behavior has consequences and that teachers are people with genuine feelings. Unlike you-messages, I-messages don't make students defensive and stubborn; thus, they might be more willing to change their behavior.

Most of us aren't accustomed to speaking this way, so I-messages can seem awkward and artificial. With practice, however, using them can become natural. We once heard a 4-year-old girl (whose parents had consistently used I-messages at home) tell her nursery school peer: "When you poke me with that pencil, it really hurts, and I feel bad 'cause I think you don't want to be my friend."

In addition to these nondirective approaches, there are also *more directive strategies* that you can try. Indeed, several African American educators contend that these could be particularly well matched to the communication patterns of African American students (e.g., Delpit, 1995; G. Thompson, 2004). For example, Lisa Delpit, author of *Other People's Children: Cultural Conflict in the Classroom,* observes that framing directives as questions (e.g., "Would you like to sit down now?") is a particularly mainstream, middle-class (and female) way to speak that is designed to foster a more egalitarian and nonauthoritarian climate. According to Delpit,

> Many kids will not respond to that structure because commands are not couched as questions in their home culture. Rather than asking questions, some teachers need to learn to say, "Put the scissors away" and "Sit down now" or "Please sit down now." (Valentine, 1998, p. 17)

As Delpit suggests, the most straightforward approach is to *direct students to the task at hand.* Donna often uses this approach. When a girl was going through her cosmetic case, for example, Donna approached her and quietly directed her to "put all the mirrors and stuff away and start on the assignment." You can also *remind students about the rule* or behavioral expectation that is being violated (e.g., "When someone is talking, everyone else is supposed to be listening"). Sometimes, if inappropriate behavior is fairly widespread, it's useful to review rules with the entire group. This is often true after a holiday, a weekend, or a vacation.

Another strategy is to *give students a choice between behaving appropriately or receiving a penalty* for continued inappropriate behavior (e.g., "If you can't handle working in your group, you'll have to return to your seats"; "You either choose to raise your hand instead of calling out, or you will be choosing not to participate in our discussion"). Such statements not only warn students that a penalty will be invoked if the inappropriate behavior continues but also emphasize that students have real choices about how to behave and that penalties are not imposed without reason. In the following example, we see how Fred embellishes this strategy with a little humor:

 The bell rings; Fred moves to the front of the room and tries to get his students' attention. They continue talking. "Ladies and gentlemen, if you want a zero for life, talk now. If you don't, listen." Students laugh and settle down.

Deliberate Nonintervention

During an observation in Donna's class, we noticed a student lightly tapping a pencil on his desk while Donna was calling roll. It was obvious that Donna was aware of the tapping but chose not to respond, and the boy stopped once she began the lesson. As this incident illustrates, when misbehavior is extremely brief and unobtrusive, the best course of action can be *deliberate nonintervention.* For example, during a discussion, a student could be so eager to comment that she forgets to raise her hand, or someone becomes momentarily distracted and inattentive, or two boys quietly exchange a comment while you're giving directions. In these cases, an intervention can be more disruptive than the students' behavior.

One risk of overlooking minor misbehavior is that students might conclude that you're unaware of what's going on. Suspecting that you're not "with it," they might decide to see how much they can get away with, and then problems are sure to escalate. You need to monitor your class carefully to make sure this doesn't happen.

Another problem is that occasional ignoring can turn into full-fledged "blindness." This was vividly demonstrated in a study of a student teacher named Heleen (Créton, Wubbels, & Hooymayers, 1989). When Heleen was lecturing, her students frequently became noisy and inattentive. In response, Heleen talked more loudly and looked more at the chalkboard, turning her back on her students. She did not allow herself to see or hear the disorder—perhaps because it was too threatening and she didn't know how to handle it. Unfortunately, Heleen's students seemed to interpret her "blindness" as an indication that noise was allowed, and they became even more disorderly. Heleen eventually recognized the importance of "seeing" and responding to slight disturbances to prevent them from escalating.

DEALING WITH MORE SERIOUS MISBEHAVIOR

Sometimes, nonverbal cues or verbal reminders are not enough to convince students that you're serious about the behavioral expectations that you've established. And sometimes misbehavior is just too serious to use these types of low-level responses. In such cases, it might be necessary to use more substantial interventions to enforce your expectations for appropriate behavior.

In some cases, teachers discuss penalties when they teach rules and procedures, so students understand the consequences of violating a rule from the very beginning. We saw Sandy do this with her students in Chapter 5 when she laid out the penalties for coming late to class. This practice prevents unpleasant "surprises" and should minimize protests of blissful ignorance—"But you didn't *tell* me that would happen!"

Selecting Penalties

It's often difficult for beginning teachers to decide on appropriate penalties. One student teacher in social studies vented his frustration in this way:

> These two kids come to class every day and sit and do absolutely nothing. They don't create a big disturbance, and they're not really nasty or belligerent; they just won't do any work. They prefer to sit there and talk, and draw cartoons, and goof off. I keep telling them they're getting a zero for each day they just sit, and that they're going to fail for the marking period, but they just don't care. I've told them I'm going to call their parents, but they just laugh. I don't want to send them to the disciplinarian's office, because my cooperating teacher says I could get a reputation as a teacher who can't control the class, and I'd really like to get a job in this district. So I'm really at a loss. These kids are really smart, and I hate to see them fail. But what can I do?

We posed this question to all five of our teachers and learned about the types of penalties that they typically use. As a general rule of thumb, our teachers try to implement penalties that are logically related to the misbehavior. For example, when a student in Christina's class failed to work constructively in his small group, he had to work by himself until he indicated a readiness to cooperate. Similarly, if students make a mess in Sandy's chemistry lab, a logical penalty would be to make them clean it up. If an individual forgets her book and can't do the assignment, she must borrow someone's book and do the assignment during a free period. A student who hands in a carelessly done paper has to rewrite it.

Logical consequences differ from traditional punishments, which bear no relationship to the misbehavior involved. Examples are as follows: A student who continually whispers to her neighbor has to do an additional homework assignment (instead of being isolated). A student who forgets to get his parents' permission to go on a field trip has to serve detention (rather than writing a letter home to parents about the need to sign the permission slip). A student who continually calls out during a whole-class discussion gets an F for the day (instead of making a cue-card to post on his desk saying "I won't call out" or not being allowed to participate in the discussion).

We describe the specific penalties our teachers use next. As you read about each one, keep in mind that these five teachers have worked hard to build caring, trusting relationships with students. Undoubtedly, these relationships increase the likelihood that students will interpret the penalties not as punishments imposed by a hostile, dictatorial adversary but as reasonable consequences enacted by a teacher who cares enough to insist that students behave the best they can (Bondy & Ross, 2008; Gregory & Ripski, 2008).

MANDATORY PRIVATE CONFERENCES

When students do not respond to nonverbal cues or verbal reminders, our teachers generally call a private conference, often after school or during a free period. During these conferences, they express their disappointment in the student's behavior. We normally don't think of this as a penalty, but because students in these classes really like their teachers, they feel bad when their teachers are upset. In serious, almost sorrowful tones, our teachers express their disappointment and surprise at the inappropriate behavior and direct students to think about the consequences of their actions. Sometimes they negotiate a plan for change, trying to get the students to take responsibility for their behavior. For example, when a student in Donna's class continually goofed off, failed to do his homework, and then loudly announced that he hated this class, Donna held a private conference with him after school:

DONNA: Tell me, do you think teachers have feelings?

STUDENT: Yes.

DONNA: Why do you think that?

STUDENT: Because they're people.

DONNA: Yes, so I want you to understand that when I hear you say, "I hate this class," it really hurts my feelings. My job is to teach you as much as I can and I really love my job, so I need you to work with me. Next year when you go to high school, you'll have a whole new batch of teachers, but until then, you're stuck with me, so we've got to find a way to work together. [Student nods and murmurs that he understands.]

DONNA: What do you understand?

STUDENT: You said. . . . You want me to. . . . Well, I'll just get to the bottom line. I need to cooperate with you and get my work done. [They continue to discuss exactly what he needs to do.]

Later Donna told us that the boy's father had recently gotten out of jail after 10 years and then died while sitting in front of the television. The funeral was a week before this conference. In addition, the boy was being raised by a great aunt who had made it clear that she wanted somebody else to take him. Donna concluded by saying, "He doesn't need me yelling in his face, but I had to talk with him about his behavior."

LOSS OF PRIVILEGES

Sometimes students lose the right to sit wherever they like, particularly if their behavior is having a negative impact on other students. Other privileges that can be taken away include working with a friend, having free time, chewing gum, freely moving around the room, and joining in a class popcorn party.

ISOLATION FROM THE GROUP

All five teachers will move students to an isolated or secluded area of the room if they are unable to work productively, but they try to be positive rather than negative about the move. Fred will signal a student to move to a place that's "less distracting." When Sandy covered a seventh-grade class, she sometimes had to tell a student, "Come with me. Let's go to the back of the class and see what you can do back here where you can concentrate better. This will be your own private office." This strategy can be particularly effective with students who suffer from attention-deficit/hyperactivity disorder (ADHD). These students have trouble dealing with the distraction and stimulation of the typical classroom environment; moving temporarily to a secluded area of the room can provide a much needed opportunity to refocus.

EXCLUSION FROM CLASS

All five teachers believe that "kicking kids out" is a strategy that should be reserved for major disruptions. As Donnie points out, "Some students *want* to get out; they'll provoke a teacher just so they can leave the room. I know teachers who throw kids out all the time, but what's the point? Kids can't learn if they're in the office."

Despite their preference for handling problems within the room, our teachers recognize that there are times when this is just not possible. Sandy remembers how she sent a student to the "time-out" room when his behavior was so infuriating that she couldn't discuss it calmly: "I was so mad, I knew I was losing it. I was yelling, and the kid was yelling. So it was better for him to be out of the room. But 10 minutes later, I called and told him to come back. By then we had both cooled down and we were able to talk." Sandy has also worked out a system with another teacher so that she can send a student to his classroom if necessary. In the other room, the student must sit quietly, ignored by both teacher and students, and do chemistry work.

Fred also sends students to the office if their behavior is really out of control. He recalls one student who was severely disturbed:

 I had it worked out with the office, so they knew what to do with him when he showed up. In the beginning, I had to kick him out three times a week, but slowly he got better about controlling his behavior, and we got it down to once every two weeks. But this only worked because class was a good place to be. He had friends there, we laughed every day, he got to do good stuff. If he hadn't liked it—and me—getting to leave would have been a reward.

DETENTION

For routine violations of rules (e.g., coming late to class), Donnie, Sandy, and Fred use regular school detention as a penalty. However, they are cautious about using this for "big" problems. As Sandy puts it, "If students are disrespectful, or really having problems controlling themselves, I prefer to talk privately with them. What's going to be learned from 45 minutes of detention?"

WRITTEN REFLECTIONS ON THE PROBLEM

Sometimes a situation is so complex that it warrants serious reflection in writing. Fred recalls this incident:

 My senior honors class was supposed to do a short research paper. When I began to grade the papers, it seemed to me that a lot of the citations were suspicious. I did some checking and found that some students had simply lifted material from the Web and made up the references. I went into class and told them how serious this was, and how they would all get zeros for their papers if they couldn't validate their references. But I gave them a way out: They could write a letter to me explaining what they had done and why, and they had to make "reparation" by doing two additional research papers with valid citations. The letters were really revealing. A lot of these kids were absolutely clueless about why it's important to reference accurately. One kid came in and thanked me for making a big deal about this. He said he really didn't know that what he was doing was dishonest.

CONTACTING PARENTS

Our five teachers all contact parents or guardians if a student shows a pattern of consistent misbehavior. For example, when a student in Sandy's class repeatedly "forgot" to do his homework, Sandy told him she would be calling his parents to discuss the problem. She tried to make it clear that she was calling not in anger but out of serious concern. She also wanted to convey the idea that "between all of us, maybe we can help you get it together."

These penalties illustrate the ways Christina, Donnie, Fred, Donna, and Sandy choose to deal with problems when they have a degree of flexibility. In addition, there are times when they are required to follow school policies mandating particular responses to specific misbehaviors. Consider the example of cutting class. In Christina's school, two instances of cutting a class result in no credit earned for that course. In Fred's school, one cut requires parental notification and a warning letter; two cuts result in "student/counselor contact" and "administrator/parent contact," a possible conference, and a warning letter. The third cut requires removal from class with a grade of AW (administrative withdrawal) and placement in study hall.

It's also important to note that under No Child Left Behind, schools must have a plan for keeping schools safe and drug free. These plans must include discipline policies that prohibit disorderly conduct; the illegal possession of weapons; and the illegal use, possession, distribution, and sale of tobacco, alcohol, and other drugs. As a result, almost all schools now have *zero-tolerance* policies with predetermined consequences for such offenses. Zero tolerance might also be applied to other problems, such as bullying and threatening. These policies usually result in automatic suspension or expulsion although there can still be wide variation in severity. Be sure to familiarize yourself with the zero-tolerance policies in your school.

In recent years, a number of studies have raised concerns about zero-tolerance policies. The American Psychological Association (APA) Zero Tolerance Task Force (2006) examined the outcomes of zero-tolerance policies across the nation and concluded that removing students who violated rules did not improve the climate for learning. In fact, rather than acting as a deterrent to future disruptions, suspension was actually positively correlated with future disruptions. The report concludes by recommending that schools focus instead on preventing disruptions and helping students feel connected to the school community. These sentiments are echoed by other researchers (Gregory & Cornell, 2009) who contend that zero-tolerance policies are inconsistent with adolescents' developmental need for support and structure (i.e., authoritative rather than authoritarian discipline).

If you have students with disabilities in your classes, it's also essential that you consult a special educator or a member of the student study team about appropriate intervention strategies. Serious behavior problems require a team effort, and parents, special education teachers, psychologists, social workers, and administrators can all provide valuable insights and suggestions. Also be aware that IDEA 2004 includes several stipulations about the rights of students with disabilities with respect to disciplinary procedures. For example, if the problematic behavior is "caused by" or has a "direct and substantial relationship" to the child's disability, removing the student for more than 10 school days might not be allowed.

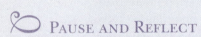 **PAUSE AND REFLECT**

Review the various penalties that our five teachers generally use when dealing with inappropriate behavior. Which ones would you be most inclined to implement? Are there any with which you disagree?

Imposing Penalties and Preserving Relationships

It's frustrating when students misbehave, and sometimes we let our frustration color the way we impose penalties. We've seen teachers scream at students from across the room, lecture students on their history of misbehavior, insinuate that they come from terrible homes, and attack their personalities. Clearly, such behavior destroys students' dignity and ruins the possibility of a good relationship. How can you avoid creating a situation like this?

First, if you're feeling really angry at a student, *delay the discussion.* You can simply say to the individual, "Sit there and think about what happened. I'll talk to you in a few minutes." During one observation in Fred's room, it was clear that he was becoming really annoyed at two students who were talking while he was introducing a film the class was about to watch. Twice during his comments he turned and told them to stop talking, but their conversation would begin again. We watched with curiosity to see whether he would do anything else, but he continued the lesson. At the end of the period, however, he promptly went over and quietly spoke with the two offending students. Later, he reflected on their conversation:

 I told them I couldn't talk while they were talking, that it distracted me and made me really mad—especially since I was talking about Gandhi, who's one of my favorite guys. They apologized; they said they had been talking about

some of the ideas that had come up in class. I told them I was really glad they were so excited, but they had to share their thoughts with the whole class, or wait until after class to talk. I think they got the message. Talking with them after class had three advantages: It allowed me to continue with my lesson, it gave me a chance to calm down, and it made it possible to talk to them privately.

As Fred's comments point out, by delaying discussion, you have a chance to calm down and to think about what you want to say. You'll also be more able to separate the student's character from the student's behavior. Your message must be: "*You're* okay, but your *behavior* is unacceptable."

Second, it's a good idea to *impose penalties privately, calmly, and quietly.* Despite the temptation to yell and scream, the softer your voice and the closer you stand to the student, the more effective you tend to be. Remember that students are very concerned about saving face in front of their peers. Public sanction might have the advantage of "making an example" out of one student's misbehavior, but it has the disadvantage of creating resentment and embarrassment. Numerous studies have found that students view public reprimand as the *least acceptable method* of dealing with problems (Hoy & Weinstein, 2006). Furthermore, the ability to be firm without using threats and public humiliation appears to be particularly important for students who are already disaffected or alienated from school. For example, interviews conducted with 31 "marginal" junior high school students judged to be at risk of school failure found that teachers were perceived as uncaring and unfair adversaries if they "engaged in public acts intended to convey an impression of authority: making examples of specific students, sending students from the room, and ordering compliance" (Schlosser, 1992, p. 135).

Our five teachers agree. Sandy observes:

Let's say you've just given back some paper you graded. A student looks at his or her paper, crumples it up, and throws it on the floor. If you yell, "Pick that paper up," you've created a confrontational situation. It's a lot better to go over and talk privately and calmly. If you say something like, "If you have a problem with your grade, we can talk about it," then the kid doesn't lose face. It's really important not to back students into a corner; if you do, they'll come out fighting and create an even bigger problem than before.

Finally, after imposing a penalty, it's important to get back to the student and *reestablish a positive relationship.* At the beginning of this chapter, we saw how Sandy made a point of helping William with his lab experiment after giving him detention. Similarly, complimenting a student's work or patting a back communicates that there are no hard feelings.

Another way to reestablish a positive relationship is to implement the Two-by-Ten strategy (Wlodkowski, 1983). For two minutes each day for 10 days in a row, have a personal conversation with the misbehaving student (or any one of your most difficult students) about anything of interest to the student. Teachers who have tried this strategy report a remarkable improvement in the behavior of the target student as well as the entire class. In fact, the most difficult students can become your allies when there is a strong personal connection.

Being Consistent

Beginning teachers are constantly told to "be consistent," and research certainly supports this advice. Recall Evertson and Emmer's (1982) study of effective classroom management on the junior high level (discussed in Chapter 5). This study showed that more successful managers responded in a consistent, predictable fashion, often invoking the rules or procedures to stop the disruptive behavior. In contrast, the ineffective managers were more likely to act inconsistently: Sometimes they ignored the behavior; sometimes they invoked a prestated consequence (e.g., detention); sometimes they warned students of penalties but then didn't act on their warnings. Inevitably, inappropriate behavior increased in frequency and severity.

Although the importance of being consistent is obvious, teachers sometimes feel trapped by the need for consistency. (See the discussion in Chapter 3 about being fair.) When a normally conscientious student forgets a homework assignment, it seems unreasonable to send the same note home to parents that you would send if a student repeatedly missed assignments. To get out of this bind, it's desirable to develop a *hierarchy of consequences* that can be invoked if rules are violated. Some teachers develop a graduated list of generic consequences that can be applied to all misbehaviors. The following hierarchy is an example:

> First violation: Verbal warning
>
> Second violation: Name is written down
>
> Third violation: Conference with teacher
>
> Fourth violation: Call parents

Another approach is to develop a graduated list of consequences for individual classroom rules. For example, teachers might have a graduated list of consequences just for coming late (e.g., 5 minutes of detention the first time; 10 minutes of detention the second time). This makes it easier to enforce the consequences no matter who is involved. Sandy tells us:

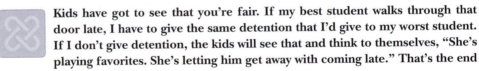 **Kids have got to see that you're fair. If my best student walks through that door late, I have to give the same detention that I'd give to my worst student. If I don't give detention, the kids will see that and think to themselves, "She's playing favorites. She's letting him get away with coming late." That's the end of my relationship with them.**

Although all five teachers are absolutely consistent when dealing with straightforward behaviors such as coming late, they consider these the "little problems." With the "big things," they prefer to talk privately with students and to develop a plan of action that is tailored to the individual student. By holding "mandatory private conferences," the five teachers can show students they are consistent in terms of enforcing class rules and dealing with inappropriate behavior, but they can remain flexible with respect to the solution.

Penalizing the Group for Individual Misbehavior

Sometimes teachers impose a consequence on the whole class even if only one or two individuals have been misbehaving. The hope is that other students will be angry at receiving a penalty when they weren't misbehaving and will exert pressure on their peers to behave. Our five teachers are unanimous in their negative response to this practice. Donnie observes, "If you even attempt to do this, students will be furious. You'll alienate the whole class." And Fred puts it this way: "I do this when I'm teaching about the causes of revolutions. It's a great way to foment a rebellion!"

DEALING WITH CHRONIC MISBEHAVIOR

Some students with persistently inappropriate behavior fail to respond to the routine strategies we have described so far: nonverbal cues, verbal reminders, and penalties. What additional strategies are available? In this section, we consider two basic approaches. First, we examine a *problem-solving strategy,* which views inappropriate behavior as a conflict to be resolved through discussion and negotiation. Second, we take a look at strategies *based on principles of behavioral learning.* We examine *self-management approaches* (self-monitoring, self-evaluation, self-instruction, and contingency contracting) and then turn to *positive behavioral supports* (PBS), interventions designed to replace inappropriate behaviors with new behaviors that serve the same purpose for the student.

Using a Problem-Solving Approach

Most teachers think in terms of winning or losing when they think about classroom conflicts. According to Thomas Gordon, author of *T.E.T.—Teacher Effectiveness Training* (2003),

> This win–lose orientation seems to be at the core of the knotty issue of discipline in schools. Teachers feel that they have only two approaches to choose from: They can be strict or lenient, tough or soft, authoritarian or permissive. They see the teacher–student relationship as a power struggle, a contest, a fight. . . . When conflicts arise, as they always do, most teachers try to resolve them so that they win, or at least don't lose. This obviously means that students end up losing, or at least not winning. (2003, p. 185)

A third alternative is a "no-lose" problem-solving method of conflict resolution (Gordon, 2003) consisting of six steps. In Step 1, the teacher and the student (or students) *define the problem.* In Step 2, everyone *brainstorms possible solutions.* As in all brainstorming activities, suggestions are not evaluated at this stage. In Step 3, *evaluate the solutions:* "Now let's take a look at all the solutions that have been proposed and decide which we like and which we don't like. Do you have some preferences?" Stating your own opinions and preferences is important. Don't permit a solution to stand if it isn't really acceptable to you. In Step 4, you and the student(s) involved *decide on the solution that you will try.* If more than one student is involved, it is tempting to vote on the solution, but that's probably not a good idea. Voting always produces winners and losers unless the vote is unanimous, so some people leave the discussion feeling dissatisfied. Instead, try to work for consensus.

Once you have decided which solution to try, move to Step 5 and *determine how to implement the decision:* who will do what by when. Finally, in Step 6, *evaluate the solution.* You might want to call everybody together again and ask, "Are you still satisfied with our solution?" It is important that everyone realize that decisions are not chiseled in granite and that they can be discarded in search of a better solution to the problem.

During one meeting, Donnie explained how she used problem solving when some of her students weren't sitting in their assigned places during assemblies:

Whenever there's an assembly program, we're supposed to walk together to the auditorium and sit together. But it's crowded in the halls on the way to the auditorium, and everyone "loses" kids; someone has darted here or there, joined another class, faded into the crowd. By the time we get to the auditorium, the kids are scattered all over. They sit with other classes, and they act up. The teachers don't really know who they are, and sometimes the kids even give wrong names when the teachers ask. The behavior in assembly programs can be really bad. I decided this was a problem that we had to deal with before another assembly program was held.

I told the class that I felt this was a problem, and they agreed. Then I explained that we were going to brainstorm solutions. Boy, these kids can really be hard on each other! They came up with about eight different solutions:

- Kick the offenders out of the assemblies.
- Don't let past offenders go to assemblies at all.
- Suspend them.
- Kids have to get permission to sit with another class.
- Bring your friend to sit with you and your class (your friend would have to have special permission from his/her teacher).
- Invite parents to assemblies (kids would act better).
- Take attendance once you get to the assembly.
- Have a buddy system.

The next day, we talked about each of these possible solutions, focusing on how they would affect everyone. I told them I didn't like the one about kicking people out of the assemblies because assembly programs were part of their education. I also explained that teachers don't have the right to suspend students, and if we chose that one, we'd have to get the disciplinarian involved. The kids said they could live with getting permission, and they also liked the buddy system. They said buddies should also have the responsibility of telling the person next to them to stop if he or she was disruptive. So we agreed to try those two. We also agreed that I would use the "teacher look" technique if I saw kids acting up and then write up a referral to the disciplinarian if they didn't stop.

We haven't had an assembly program yet, so I don't know how this is going to work, but I think it was good to get the kids involved in trying to solve the problem. Maybe they'll be more interested in trying to improve the situation.

Using a Behavioral Learning Approach

Behavioral learning principles emphasize external events (rather than thinking or knowledge) as the cause of changes in behavior (Woolfolk, 2007). Applied behavior analysis (also known as *behavior modification*) involves the application of behavioral learning principles to change behavior and the systematic use of reinforcement to strengthen desired behavior. Probably more research has focused on the effectiveness of applied behavior analysis than on any other classroom management approach, and dozens of books are available for teachers (e.g., Alberto & Troutman, 2006; Zirpoli, 2005).

Because traditional behavior modification techniques emphasize external control by the teacher rather than trying to foster internal control by the student, some educators recommend behavioral approaches that involve the student in *self-management:* self-monitoring, self-evaluation, self-instruction, and contingency contracting. Self-management strategies have been reported to be effective with children with and without identified disabilities from preschool through secondary school and for a wide variety of inappropriate behaviors, both academic and social (Shapiro, DuPaul, & Bradley-Klug, 1998; Smith & Sugai, 2000). The goal of self-management is to help students learn to regulate their own behavior. The perception of control is crucial in this process: When we feel in control, we are much more likely to accept responsibility for our actions.

In the next sections of the chapter, we describe these self-management strategies. Then we turn to a behavioral approach that focuses on teaching students appropriate behavior through positive behavioral intervention and supports.

SELF-MONITORING

Some students might not realize how often they're out of their seats or how frequently they sit daydreaming instead of focusing on their work. Others could be unaware of how often they call out during class discussions or how many times they make nasty comments to other members of their small group. Such students might benefit from a self-monitoring program in which they learn to observe and record a targeted behavior during a designated period of time. Interestingly, self-monitoring can have positive effects even when students are *inaccurate* (Graziano & Mooney, 1984).

Before beginning a self-monitoring program, you need to make sure that students can identify the behaviors targeted for change. For example, some students might not be able to accurately describe all the component parts of "working independently." You might have to model, explicitly noting that, "When I work independently, I am sitting down (without tilting back in my chair), I am looking at the paper on my desk, and I am holding my pencil in my hand."

Students then learn how to observe and record their own behavior. They can record in two ways. The first approach has individuals tally each time they engage in the targeted behavior. For example, students can learn to chart the number of math problems they complete during an in-class assignment, the number of times they blurt out irrelevant comments during a discussion, or the number of times they raise their hand to speak. For middle school students, the tally sheet might contain pictures of the appropriate and inappropriate behaviors. In the second approach, individuals observe and record the targeted behavior at regular intervals. At the designated time, for instance, students can mark a recording sheet with a "1" or a "2," depending on whether they are engaged in appropriate or inappropriate behavior.

There has been some debate about whether self-management can be helpful for students diagnosed with ADHD because "the lack of self-management skills can be viewed as a core deficit among individuals with this disorder" (Shapiro, DuPaul, & Bradley-Klug, 1998). Research, however, supports the use of these strategies. For example, researchers investigated the practicality and efficacy of self-monitoring for five middle school students with ADHD (Barry & Messer, 2003). According to their teacher, all five boys had limited attention spans, rarely completed in-class assignments, frequently wandered around the room, and engaged in loud, disruptive behavior. Students were taught to ask themselves a series of questions written on a data-collection sheet: "Was I in my seat or where I needed to be to complete my classwork? Was I paying attention by working on the assignment or listening to the teacher? Did I complete my assignments? Did I play or fight with my classmates in the classroom? Did I talk loudly or make noise in class?" In individual conferences, the teacher went over each question and asked the student to describe an example of his behavior that would indicate occurrence or nonoccurrence. The teacher also modeled the on-task behaviors that were described and had the students practice recording data. Initially, the boys had to respond to the questions every 15 minutes, but this interval was gradually increased. Goals were set (e.g., 75 percent or more 15-minute intervals on task), and students earned simple reinforcers from the teacher such as snacks and increased computer time. The researchers reported that the use of self-monitoring was effective in increasing students' on-task behaviors and academic performance and decreasing disruptive behaviors. Moreover, the intervention was relatively easy to implement. The teacher's initial meeting with each student took only about 20 minutes; although some additional time was spent checking for accuracy and providing feedback to students, this time was gained back as students' behavior and academic work improved.

SELF-EVALUATION

This self-management approach goes beyond simple self-monitoring by requiring individuals to judge the quality or acceptability of their behavior (Hughes, Ruhl, & Misra, 1989). Sometimes self-evaluation is linked with reinforcement so that an improvement in behavior brings points or rewards.

A study of three 7th-grade inclusive language arts classrooms provides a good example of how self-evaluation strategies can be used to reduce off-task, disruptive behavior in a general education classroom (Mitchem, Young, West, & Benyo, 2001). Using lesson plans and materials provided by the investigators, the teacher taught all students procedures for a ClassWide Peer-Assisted Self-Management (CWPASM) program for which students evaluated their behavior using a rating system based on the school's citizenship grades: "H" (honors), "S" (satisfactory), "N" (needs improvement), and "U" (unsatisfactory). Training required from two to three periods, depending on the class. The teacher also assigned every student a partner based on her knowledge of students' personalities and preferences. During the implementation of the CWPASM program, students rated their own behavior and that of their partner every 10 minutes. Partners then compared their ratings and earned points for perfect or near-perfect ratings. The initial 10-minute interval was later lengthened to 20 minutes; eventually students did the ratings just once at the end of the period. The CWPASM program had an immediate and marked effect on all three classes. The researchers write:

> Before CWPASM was introduced, it was rare to see the entire group on task at the same time for even one minute during the entire period. The teacher spent a substantial portion of the class period managing students, redirecting them to get on task, and repeating instructions. After CWPASM was introduced, group on-task behavior across all target classes increased from near zero levels to almost 80 percent. In practical terms, this meant that all students were on task at the same time for approximately 32 minutes of the 40 minute observation. Group on-task behavior continued to increase the longer the intervention was in effect. (Mitchem, Young, West, & Benyo, 2001, p. 133)

WHAT DID YOU DO IN CLASS?

1. How well did you behave?

   Were you attentive?

   Did you complete assignments?

   Did you contribute to class discussion?

   Did you think?

   Did you learn something?`

2. What score would be accurate?   1   2   3   4
                                     (Excellent)   (Poor)

Monday:

Tuesday:

Wednesday:

Thursday:

Friday:

FIGURE 12.1   Daniel's Self-Evaluation Form

Recently, Fred decided to try a self-evaluation procedure with a boy in his contemporary world issues class. Daniel was in serious danger of failing the course; although he was not disruptive, he was consistently inattentive and rarely completed assignments. Fred and Daniel discussed self-evaluation, and Daniel was enthusiastic about trying it. Together, they designed a simple sheet, which they agreed that Fred would keep and give to Daniel to fill out at the end of each class period. As you can see from Figure 12.1, the form required Daniel to describe and evaluate his behavior. Fred describes how the self-evaluation procedure worked out:

 We did it faithfully for three weeks, and it really worked. Sometimes I forgot to give Daniel the self-evaluation sheet at the end of the period, and he actually reminded me. I took that as a sign of his commitment. His behavior really improved; he started paying attention and completing assignments for the first time all year. At the end of three weeks, Daniel was out for several days. When he got back, we didn't pick it up again, and I didn't push it. He was doing what he was supposed to be doing, without any monitoring.

SELF-INSTRUCTION

The third self-management approach is self-instruction in which students learn to give themselves silent directions about how to behave. Most self-instruction strategies are based on a five-step process of cognitive behavior modification: (1) An adult performs a task while talking aloud about it, carefully describing each part, (2) the student performs the task while the adult talks aloud (overt, external guidance),

(3) the student performs the task while talking aloud to self (overt self-guidance), (4) the student performs the task while whispering (faded, overt self-guidance), and (5) the student performs the task while thinking the directions (covert, self-instruction) (Meichenbaum, 1977). This approach has been used to teach impulsive students to approach tasks more deliberately, to help social isolates initiate peer interaction, to teach aggressive students to control their anger, and to teach defeated students to try problem solving instead of giving up (Brophy, 1983).

There is evidence that even seriously emotionally disturbed adolescents can learn to engage in self-instruction. In a study conducted in a self-contained special education class (Ninness, Fuerst, Rutherford, & Glenn, 1991), three teenage males who displayed high rates of off-task and inappropriate behaviors (running, fighting, fondling, spitting, throwing objects, jumping, or inappropriate language) were given formal instruction in social skills and self-management for one hour a day. These students were taught to raise their hands to ask questions, to avoid distractions of other students, and to talk politely to teachers and students. While others played the role of distractors, students rehearsed overt statements such as, "I'm not going to let him or her bother me. I'm going to keep doing my work," and they practiced avoiding eye contact with those who annoyed them. In addition, students were taught to evaluate their own on-task and socially appropriate behavior, using a scale ranging from one to four. A bonus point was awarded on any occasion in which a student's self-assessment was within one point of the teacher's assessment.

The results of the study demonstrated that training in self-management can dramatically improve students' behavior. Prior to the training, off-task and socially inappropriate behavior in the classroom averaged 92 percent, 95 percent, and 76 percent for subjects 1, 2, and 3, respectively. All three subjects improved substantially during the course of the five-week self-management training—and all three demonstrated *near-zero off-task or socially inappropriate behavior during the experimental situations.*

Before we leave the discussion of self-monitoring, self-evaluation, and self-instruction, it is important to note that these strategies hold particular promise for students with disabilities in general education settings. Only a few studies have been conducted in inclusive secondary classrooms, but they indicate that students with disabilities can be taught to use self-management to improve both their social and academic performance (McDougall, 1998). On the other hand, this training requires time and expertise that general education teachers might not have (McDougall). If you decide to try one of these self-management strategies, you should consult with your school's psychologist, a counselor, or a special education teacher.

CONTINGENCY CONTRACTING

A contingency or behavior contract is an agreement between a teacher and an individual student that specifies what the student must do to earn a particular reward. Contingency contracts are negotiated with students; both parties must agree on the behaviors students are to exhibit, the period of time involved, and the rewards that will result. To be most effective, contracts should be written and signed. And, of course, there should be an opportunity for review and renegotiation if the contract is not working. An example of a typical contract appears in Figure 12.2.

Date_____

After discussion between Mr. Schroeder (social studies teacher) and Justin Mayer (student), the following decisions were reached:

During the next marking period, I, Justin Mayer, agree to:

1. Be on time for U. S. History I, with book, notebook, and writing utensil.

2. To complete all homework assignments and to turn them in on time.

3. To meet with Mr. Schroeder after school on Thursdays to check on the progress of my quarterly project.

4. To sit on the other side of the room from Sam Holloway.

5. To pay attention during class.

If I meet these conditions, I will pass this class with a C or better for this marking period.

Student_____

Teacher_____

Parent_____

FIGURE 12.2   Example of a Contract

Donna used a contingency contract with a girl who was going through a very difficult time in her life:

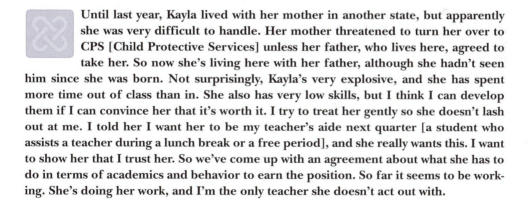

Until last year, Kayla lived with her mother in another state, but apparently she was very difficult to handle. Her mother threatened to turn her over to CPS [Child Protective Services] unless her father, who lives here, agreed to take her. So now she's living here with her father, although she hadn't seen him since she was born. Not surprisingly, Kayla's very explosive, and she has spent more time out of class than in. She also has very low skills, but I think I can develop them if I can convince her that it's worth it. I try to treat her gently so she doesn't lash out at me. I told her I want her to be my teacher's aide next quarter [a student who assists a teacher during a lunch break or a free period], and she really wants this. I want to show her that I trust her. So we've come up with an agreement about what she has to do in terms of academics and behavior to earn the position. So far it seems to be working. She's doing her work, and I'm the only teacher she doesn't act out with.

POSITIVE BEHAVIORAL INTERVENTIONS AND SUPPORTS (PBIS) AND FUNCTIONAL BEHAVIORAL ASSESSMENT (FBA)

More of a framework than a specific set of prescriptions, PBIS emphasizes research-based, positive, and preventive strategies to enhance the behavior of all students. PBIS is based on the premise that most students will succeed when a positive school culture is promoted, informative corrective feedback is provided, academic success is maximized, and the use of prosocial skills is recognized and reinforced (Sugai & Simonsen, 2012).

Although PBIS is typically implemented on a schoolwide basis (SWPBS), individual teachers can apply the basic principles. PBIS calls for a three-tiered approach. At the *primary* or universal level, a set of behavioral expectations is taught to all students, modeled, and consistently reinforced. At the *secondary* or group level, students whose behaviors are not responsive to the primary tier strategies receive more structured intervention practices, more frequent behavioral feedback, and more active support and monitoring. Finally, the *tertiary* or individual level provides intensive, specialized supports for students with frequent and severe behavior problems. At this level, information about the student's behavior is gathered to understand why the problem behavior is occurring and to strengthen more acceptable alternative behaviors. This process is known as *functional behavior analysis* (FBA).

FBA procedures have historically been used in cases of severe behavior disorders; in fact, IDEA 2004 mandates schools to conduct FBAs of a student with disabilities if he or she is to be removed more than 10 consecutive school days or if the removal constitutes a change in placement. In recent years, however, FBA has also been widely recommended for use in general education classrooms with typically developing students and those with mild disabilities (Robinson & Ricord Griesemer, 2006).

FBA is based on the behavioral principle that behavior occurs for one of two reasons. It either enables individuals to obtain something they desire (positive reinforcement) or it enables individuals to avoid something they find unpleasant (e.g., negative reinforcement). In other words, behavior happens for a reason although the individual might not be conscious of this. Given this principle, FBA begins by investigating *why* an inappropriate behavior occurs (i.e., what *function* or purpose does it serve); teachers can then design an intervention to eliminate the challenging behavior and replace it with a socially acceptable behavior that serves the same purpose.

FBA comprises several steps. First, it is necessary to *describe the inappropriate behavior* in precise, measurable, observable terms so that two or more persons could agree on the occurrence. This means that instead of saying that "Michael is aggressive," you need to say "Michael curses at other kids, puts his foot out to trip people, and throws his books on the floor when angry." In the second step, *information is collected regarding the environmental events that occur before and after the student's behavior.* This is generally referred to as an A-B-C assessment: A represents the antecedents of the behavior, B represents the behavior, and C represents the consequences. (Figure 12.3 shows a sample ABC recording sheet.) Because it's generally not feasible to collect this information while you're teaching, you will probably have to arrange for someone else to do the assessment while you provide instruction). Ideally, this would be an FBA specialist, but it might also be done by a collaborating teacher or a school counselor. It's also essential to conduct observations across several days so that you can be confident you are getting a representative sample of the student's behavior. Finally, make sure to observe times when the target behavior typically occurs and times when it typically does *not* occur. If you carry out

Student Ronald   Date 10/11

Observer Mr. Green   Time 9:15

Setting/Activity Language Art Class

Target Behavior(s) Noncompliance/Aggression

Time	Antecedents (What happened before the behavior?)	Behavior (What did the student do?)	Consequences (What happened after the behavior?)
9:15	Teacher tells class to take out the stories they are writing and work on revising them.	Ronald sits slumped in seat. He doesn't open his notebook to work on his story. He starts to make comments about other students' stories.	Teacher tells Ronald to get to work. He continues to sit slumped in seat. He pushes several books off his desk onto the floor.
9:17	Teacher goes over to Ronald; quietly tells him to settle down and get to work.	Ronald says he doesn't want to write a "stupid" story.	Teacher tells Ronald that he needs to work on his story or he will need to move to the back of the room. She walks away. Ronald starts to make noises but doesn't open his notebook.
9:20	The teacher tells Ronald to move to the back of the room and think about how he is supposed to behave during writing workshop.	Ronald throws his notebook on the floor, yells at teacher: "Who cares about a f_____story?!" and walks toward the door.	Teacher follows Ronald; tells him to go with her out into the hallway where they can talk.

FIGURE 12.3   Sample ABC Recording Sheet

this step carefully, you should then be able to answer the following questions (Kerr & Nelson, 2006):

Does the behavior occur in the presence of certain persons?

During what activities is the behavior more likely to occur?

During what activities is the behavior less likely to occur?

What happens to the student following the behavior?

How do others respond to the behavior?

Does the surrounding environment change in any way following the behavior?

In the third FBA step, *hypotheses are developed about the purpose of the behavior;* in other words, this is when you try to figure out what the student stands to gain. For example, let's assume that as a result of gathering information in step 2, it has become clear that Ronald, a student in a middle school English/language arts class, is disruptive only during writing workshop (the antecedent) when he annoys the students sitting nearby by uttering silly comments, making noises, and dropping books on the floor (the behavior). In response to this behavior, the teacher repeatedly tells him to "settle down and get to work" (one consequence). When this doesn't bring about a positive change, the teacher tells him to take a seat in the back of the room and think about how students are supposed to behave during writing workshop (another consequence). On the basis of this information, we can hypothesize that Ronald's behavior enables him to avoid something he seems to find aversive—namely, writing workshop.

The fourth step is to *test the hypotheses you have developed* by creating a behavior intervention plan (BIP). This involves modifying some aspect of the environment and observing the effect. In Ronald's case, because the writing task appears to be frustrating, the teacher might provide him additional support such as his own personal dictionary, allow him to seek assistance from a "writing buddy," and provide encouragement and additional instructional guidance as needed. In addition, the teacher might stop responding to the inappropriate behavior and instead respond to appropriate behavior with smiles and praise. If *monitoring* (the fifth step) shows the BIP is successful (i.e., the inappropriate behavior ceases), then the FBA is finished. If the inappropriate behavior continues, you need to go back to the third step and develop some new hypotheses. Remember, however, that long-standing behavior does not change overnight; you might need to follow the plan for two or three weeks before deciding whether it is making a difference (Friend & Bursuck, 2002).

Although FBA is an extremely useful tool, it is not simple, and identifying the underlying function of a behavior could require the assistance of well-trained observers (Landrum & Kauffman, 2006). Therefore, teachers need to consult with special services personnel.

DEALING WITH THORNY PROBLEMS

Some behaviors seem to plague teachers regardless of where they are teaching. It's impossible to generate recipes for dealing with these problems because every instance is unique in terms of key players, circumstances, and history. Nonetheless, it is helpful to reflect on ways to deal with them *before* they occur and to hear some of the thinking that guides the actions of our five teachers. In this section of the chapter, we consider four behaviors that keep teachers awake at night wondering what to do.

Defiance

Some years ago, Claire came to seminar looking shaken and upset. When we inquired what was wrong, she shared this story:

> *My ninth-graders were really rowdy today. I'm not sure what was going on, but they just wouldn't stop talking and laughing and calling out. One boy in particular, Jamal, was really annoying me. He wouldn't stay in his seat; he kept going to the back corner of the room where his buddies sit. I kept telling him to sit down, and he'd slowly saunter over to his desk. But then a few minutes later, I'd see he was up again. Finally, I got so mad, I just yelled across the room, "Jamal, I've had it with you. Get out! Go to the office!" And he looked at me and in this real slow, mocking voice he said, "Make me." I just froze. This kid is more than six feet tall and really strong.*

He towers over me. I had no idea what to do. Finally, I said something stupid like, "I'm not going to make you, but you just better sit down." Then I just ignored him for the rest of the period. I felt like a complete jerk, and he knew it.

Claire's interaction with Jamal was traumatic for her and unfortunate for him, but it gave our seminar group an opportunity to examine ways to deal with defiance. As we pondered alternative strategies, it became obvious that *the best course of action would have been to avoid the situation in the first place.* For example, after she had repeatedly told him to sit down without success, she might have approached him and quietly, but firmly, let him know that he had the choice of getting to work or facing one of the consequences for inappropriate behavior (e.g., "Jamal, here are your choices. You can sit down and begin working or you can go to Ms. Rosen's classroom for time-out"; "Jamal, you can sit down and begin working now or you can work on it after school"). Unfortunately, by shouting across the room, Claire created a public power struggle. She backed Jamal into a corner with no "graceful exit," and Jamal was forced to challenge her if he wanted to save face with his peers.

Having said that, we still need to consider Claire's options once Jamal defied her order to get out. When we recounted this episode to our five teachers, they gave several suggestions for dealing with defiance. (These are listed in the Practical Tips box.)

Interestingly, as the teachers discussed ways to respond to defiance, we began to understand that this was not a major problem for any of them. When Sandy commented that she could "count on one hand the cases of insubordination" she had

PRACTICAL TIPS FOR

Handling Defiance

- *Don't lose your cool.* Stay in control of yourself. Even though your first inclination is to shout back, don't. (It can help to take a few deep breaths and to use self-talk: "I can handle this calmly. I'm going to speak quietly.")
- *Direct the rest of the class to work on something* (e.g., "Everyone do the next three problems" or "Start reading the next section").
- *Move the student away from peers.* Talk to the student in an area where you can have more privacy. This eliminates the need for the student to worry about saving face.
- *Stand a few feet away from the student (i.e., don't get "in his face").* A student who is feeling angry and defiant might interpret closing in on him as an aggressive act (Wolfgang, 1999).
- *Acknowledge the student's feelings.* "I can see that you're really angry. . . ."
- *Avoid a power struggle.* Do not use assertions such as "I'm the boss in here and I'm telling you to. . . ."
- *Offer a choice.* In Jamal's case, the confrontation was no longer about doing the work but about going to the office. So the choices should focus on this issue: "Jamal, I can see that you're really upset, and we'll have to talk later. But meanwhile, here are the choices. You can go to the office, or I'll have to send for someone to come to get you."

encountered in a lifetime of teaching, the others nodded in agreement. So we asked why they thought that students in their classes were rarely defiant. The teachers were unanimous in their response: They don't allow minor problems to escalate into major ones. Donnie put it this way:

I sometimes see students in the office, and I ask them, "Why are you down here?" They'll tell me, "I was thrown out for chewing gum." But you know that couldn't be the whole story. It probably started out with gum chewing, but escalated into a real power struggle. And for what? We need to make sure that we don't blow up situations way out of proportion.

And Fred had one last suggestion for new teachers: "If defiance is *not* a rare thing in your classroom, then it's time to think seriously about what you're doing with those kids. Some examination of your own practice is clearly in order." (See Chapter 13 for a related discussion of defusing potentially explosive situations.)

Failure to Do Homework

When students consistently fail to do homework assignments, you need to consider just how valuable those assignments are and whether you have communicated that value to students. Fred comments:

I am convinced that if teachers were evaluated on the basis of the amount and quality of their homework assignments, students would have much less homework and would do more of it! I never give homework assignments unless I can explain the reason to my students. Having students understand the importance of doing a particular task at home cuts down dramatically on the number of missing assignments.

In a similar vein, Sandy tells her students "there's a reason for every assignment I give":

I tell them, "I will not insult your intelligence by giving you garbage assignments that waste your time. Every assignment is necessary for what we're currently working on; you have to do it to meet with success."

It's also important to reflect on how much homework you're assigning, whether it's too difficult for students to complete independently, and whether the time allotted is sufficient. Recall that in Chapter 3, Christina talked about an instance when students had been disgruntled by the amount and difficulty of the homework she had assigned: "They kept saying it was like college work and . . . they were only 15!" Together, Christina and her students forged an agreement that was mutually satisfactory. Some due dates were postponed, in-class time was provided so that students could work in groups on some of the work, and Christina made sure she was available for help after school.

In addition to monitoring the amount and difficulty of homework, you need to make sure that your students will be able to understand the assignments. One way to ensure this is to ask a colleague to review the assignment and give you feedback

(Darling-Hammond & Ifill-Lynch, 2006). Another way is to have students start the homework in class under your supervision so you can address any confusion before students attempt the assignment at home.

The accompanying Practical Tips box lists some additional strategies that can help increase the likelihood of students completing homework.

PRACTICAL TIPS FOR

Increasing the Likelihood That Students Will Do Their Homework

- *Review, collect, or grade assignments.* If you assign homework and then fail to check that students have done it, you're conveying the message that the homework just wasn't that important. Not all homework has to be graded, or even collected, but it's wise to check that students have done it and to record that fact in your grade book.
- *Give "homework quizzes."* Because Donnie finds that getting some students to do homework is a "constant struggle," she gives students a daily quiz with one or two problems that are just like those assigned the night before for homework. In addition, she gives a "homework quiz" every week or two. She selects five problems that were previously given for homework and allows students to refer to their homework papers but not their books.
- *Require a "product" in addition to reading.* When Christina assigned 17 pages of *The Martian Chronicles* for homework, she discovered that fully one-half of the class had not done the reading—despite the fact that she had warned them about having a quiz. According to Christina, "Students just don't count reading as homework." She has learned that they are far more likely to do the reading if she also has them do something *with* it (e.g., use sticky notes to mark your three favorite passages; list 10 words or phrases the author uses to give clues about the protagonist's character; generate three questions about the reading to ask your classmates).
- *Accept no excuses.* Sandy warns new teachers: "There are valid reasons for not doing homework. But if you start judging what's valid and what's not, that leads to a host of problems. My students know that I don't accept late homework. Period. If they don't have it, they come in and do it after school, because it's necessary for going on. But they get no credit for it."
- *Provide in-school support.* Sometimes students' home circumstances could interfere with doing homework. They might be in the midst of a family crisis, living in an abusive situation, or have after-school jobs or other responsibilities that leave little time for schoolwork. Donnie shares this incident: "Just last week I was visiting a friend in the hospital and ran into one of my students—a girl who often dozed off in class and frequently didn't have her homework. It turned out that she worked at the hospital every day from 3:00 to 11:00! This explained a lot! She's got a full-time job in addition to going to high school." In such situations, you might work with the student to develop a plan for getting homework done in school. Perhaps the student can do her homework during lunch or during a study hall. (If lunch is 40 minutes, a student can eat in 20 minutes and still have time to get started on homework.) Perhaps she can stop by your room before or after school for 15 minutes.

Despite your best efforts, some students will still not turn in homework. In this case, you need to meet individually to discuss the problem, generate possible solutions, and decide on an action plan. This might include contacting parents and asking for their cooperation and assistance, writing a contingency contract, or assigning a "homework buddy" to help the student remember and complete homework. Listen to Fred:

 Many teachers have hard and fast rules about homework, with serious consequences if homework is not turned in on time. But I've come to believe that this kind of rigidity often does more harm than good. I try to work individually with kids who seem to be "irresponsible" with regard to homework. Together, we develop a plan for improving in this area.

Cheating

A number of studies suggest that cheating is more prevalent than we like to think. A 2012 national survey conducted by the Josephson Institute of Ethics asked 23,000 high school students about their behavior during the last 12 months. Just over half (51 percent) reported that they had cheated on a test, 32 percent said they'd copied an Internet document, and 75 percent admitted they'd copied a classmate's homework. Despite these admissions, 93 percent said they were "satisfied with my own ethics and character," and 81 percent agreed with the statement, "When it comes to doing what is right I am better than most people I know."

Obviously, smart phones, e-mail, and online searches make it easier than ever before to distribute information to friends and to plagiarize. Websites offer research papers for sale or give them away; often the papers are not well written and contain spelling and grammatical errors—a fact that can actually help students avoid suspicion (Ditman, 2000). Furthermore, many students don't consider copying and pasting from a website to be cheating (Ma, Lu, Turner, & Wan, 2007).

Once again, it's better to prevent the problem than to deal with it after the fact. This means finding ways to *diminish the temptation to cheat.* Research indicates that students are more likely to report cheating when they perceive the teacher as emphasizing performance over mastery (i.e., when it's more important to get an A on a test than to really learn the material) (Anderman, Griesinger, & Westerfield, 1998). Similarly, students report more cheating when the teacher relies on extrinsic incentives to stimulate motivation (e.g., giving homework passes to students who get As on a test) rather than trying to foster genuine interest in academic tasks. In light of this research, you need to make sure that the work you assign and the tests you give are fair and worthwhile and that you use the information they provide to help students master the material (Savage, 1999). You can also help students avoid the temptation to cheat by not basing students' grades on one or two "high-stakes" tasks (Savage). Although students might complain about frequent testing or assignments, they are less likely to cheat if they know that no one task will determine success or failure in the course.

It is also important to discuss issues of academic dishonesty with your students and help them develop an ethical approach to their schoolwork (Thomas & Sassi, 2011). At the beginning of the year, our five teachers take the time to define cheating and to discuss how they feel about it. As we mentioned in Chapter 5, Sandy elaborates on the distinction between helping one another with homework and cheating. She emphasizes that cheating is "the ultimate disrespectful behavior," talks about the numerous behaviors that constitute cheating, gives students strategies for resisting peer pressure to cheat, and reviews the school's academic integrity policy, which students and parents have to sign. Similarly, Fred gives what he calls his "cheating sermonette": "Listen, you can lie and cheat and you may not be caught. . . . But if you don't cheat, you will be admirable."

In addition to reducing temptation, you can also take a number of simple precautions to *minimize opportunity*. When giving tests, for example, it's helpful to circulate throughout the room, use new tests each year, and create different forms of the same test for students seated in different rows. (With the help of a computer program, Donnie actually makes up four different forms for each test she administers.) We recently heard about a teacher who let four students take a makeup test out in the hallway. Not only was the test the same as the one the rest of the class had taken two days before (and which these students had heard about), but also the four students were allowed to sit together—unsupervised—to complete the test. Even the most ethical of students would find it hard to resist such an opportunity!

If you are assigning papers, make sure that you give realistic deadlines and provide enough preparation so that students feel comfortable. Make it clear to students that you know about websites that offer papers for sale or for free; also make it clear that you know how to detect plagiarism by using a search engine such as Google to search for words and phrases that don't sound like student writing. (You might even demonstrate!) It's also important to teach students how to write from sources, that is, how to understand and summarize material in their own words (Howard & Davies, 2009). Christina has students turn in bits and pieces of their research papers all along the way (e.g., notes, an outline, the first paragraph, a first draft), making it far more difficult for students to use a research paper obtained from a website.

Obviously, despite all your precautions, incidents of cheating will occur. It then becomes necessary to confront the students involved. The accompanying Practical Tips box lists some suggestions for handling those encounters.

 PRACTICAL TIPS FOR

Dealing with Cheating

- *Talk privately.* Once again, avoid creating a situation in which the student could be publicly humiliated. This is likely to lead to a series of accusations and denials that get more and more heated.
- *Present your reasons for suspecting cheating.* Present your evidence calmly and firmly, even sorrowfully. (If you suspect plagiarism, get help from www.plagiarism.org.)
- *Express concern.* Make it clear that you do not expect this type of behavior from this student. Try to find out why students cheated (e.g., Were they simply unprepared? Are they under a lot of pressure to excel?)

(continued on next page)

- *Explain consequences.* A common response to cheating is to give the student a low grade or a zero on the assignment or test. This seems to be a sensible solution at first glance, but it confounds the act of cheating with the student's mastery of the content (Cangelosi, 1993). In other words, a person looking at the teacher's grade book would be unable to tell whether the low grade meant that the student had violated the test-taking procedures or had failed to learn the material. We prefer using a logical consequence; namely, having the student redo the assignment or test under more carefully controlled conditions. But some schools have predetermined consequences for cheating, such as detention and parental notification. If so, you need to follow your school's policy.
- *Discuss the consequences for subsequent cheating.* Alert the student to the consequences for additional cheating incidents. Emphasize that you are available for assistance if cheating was the result of academic difficulties (i.e., there is no need to cheat because of problems with the material). If the student is under pressure at home to succeed, you might want to talk with parents. If students have no appropriate place to study at home, you might explore alternatives (e.g., studying at school or the public library).

As you deal with the issue of cheating, consider this perspective from a professional development specialist: "If my students are cheating, then I know I am not doing my job. I know I have not engaged, challenged, or presented my students with an assignment that demands legitimate effort and work" (O'Brien, 2010, p. 10).

Inappropriate Use of Electronic Devices

As we discussed in Chapter 5, cellphones and MP3 players are ubiquitous on school campuses, and students feel entitled to carry them. Thus, the inappropriate use of these devices during classes can become an issue. Students send and receive text messages (many can send messages without even looking at their phones!) or try to hide their earphone buds under a hood so they can listen to their MP3 players. Many schools such as Sandy's are adopting schoolwide policies to deal with this issue:

 Students can have cellphones at school as long as you don't see them and they're turned off. They can't be used during the school day (not even between classes in the halls). If a cellphone goes off in a classroom, the teacher confiscates it, and a parent has to come pick it up. If a cellphone goes off during a test, the student earns a zero for the test. Sometimes kids don't know what turning off a cellphone means; they think that silencing your cellphone means it's off. I say to my students, "If you don't trust your cellphone, put it on my desk. If it beeps while it's there, it's okay." So today I had 24 cellphones on my desk!

If your school does not have a policy regarding cellphone use, you will want to have a clear classroom policy. As Christina commented, "Cellphones are just electronic note passing. If you always watched your students to make sure they aren't passing notes, it's the same thing." The teachers we've worked with state the need for a clear and consistent expectation that phones will be silenced during class and stored in a backpack unless they are being used in classwork. To discourage students from taking their cellphones out during class, these teachers require that backpacks be placed on the floor, and they continually move around the classroom. Moving around also allows them to spot headphones, and they can quietly remind students to turn off MP3 players if they aren't doing independent work.

In addition to having a classroom policy, don't underestimate the value of a school-wide reputation. A teacher we know shared this story:

> *My school has a strict "no cellphones in the building" policy but it is difficult to enforce. I try to handle the issue in my classroom and not get the administration involved. I found a hammer in my room a few years ago and I joke with my kids that it is my "phone fixer." Not long after I found the hammer, a student gave me an old cellphone and we "fixed" it, leaving the pieces lying on my desk for my classes to discover. Within about a week and a half there was a wonderful rumor going around the school that I smash cellphones when I see them. It was pretty easy to keep the rumor going because it was a student's phone and I did smash it with a hammer. Just before the holiday break, I had a student approach me about staging a scene to take his old phone during my third hour and smash it in front of the class. The performance was Oscar worthy! I have been meaning to hang my hammer on the wall with a sign above it that reads "PHONE FIXER" and the pieces of a broken phone next to it with the sign "FIXED PHONE."*

Inappropriate Behavior Outside of School

The widespread use of social media by students makes it likely that, sooner or later, you will run across a photo or video of one of your students doing something dangerous or even illegal. If the behavior occurs when the student is not in school or at a school-sponsored event, what do you do? Are you obligated to report the behavior? Donna's school district addresses this in its student discipline policy: "The principal is authorized to take administrative action when a student's misconduct away from school has a detrimental effect on the other students or on the orderly educational process."

Sometimes it isn't completely clear whether a behavior meets the criteria in the policy. For example, does getting drunk at a party have a "detrimental effect" on other students? A school superintendent we know provided this advice:

In my judgment, even in non-reportable matters, if something relates to the health and welfare of a student, sound practice would be to at least sensitively communicate with the family. Even if something does not have a significant connection to the school, this practice supports working together with families in shared support of the best interests of students.

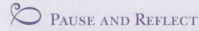 **PAUSE AND REFLECT**

Before reading the next section, consider the following scenario: A student in one of your classes comes to school wearing a T-shirt with a picture of former President Bush above the caption "International Terrorist." You tell him to turn the shirt inside out or to cover it with a jacket because it's inappropriate for school and because other students think it is disrespectful. Are you acting within your rights—or are you violating your student's freedom of expression? Reflect, and then read on.

WHEN DISCIPLINE VIOLATES STUDENTS' CONSTITUTIONAL RIGHTS

Before leaving the topic of disciplinary interventions, it's important to examine three types of situations in which well-meaning teachers could unknowingly violate students' constitutional rights.

The first situation involves students' *freedom of expression.* Consider the case of Tim Gies, a sophomore at a Michigan high school when the United States was preparing to go to war in Iraq. Passionately antiwar and anti-Bush, Gies painted symbols and slogans onto T-shirts and sweatshirts. School administrators repeatedly told him to remove the clothing, but Gies refused; as a result, he was suspended for weeks at a time and eventually threatened with expulsion. That's when he called the local American Civil Liberties Union (ACLU) chapter, which notified the school that it was infringing on Gies's First Amendment rights (Juarez, 2005). In April 2005, right before graduation, administrators rescinded their prohibition on his antiwar clothing.

Such conflicts occur on all points of the political spectrum. In 2001, Elliot Chambers, a high school student in Minnesota, wore a T-shirt to school bearing the slogan, "Straight pride." The principal prohibited his wearing the shirt, and Chambers's parents filed a lawsuit on his behalf. A federal judge ruled in their favor. And in 2005, Daniel Goergen's Minnesota high school refused to allow him to wear his sweatshirt with the words "Abortion is homicide." When a Christian law center warned of legal action, the school retreated (Juarez, 2005).

According to David Schimmel (2006), an expert on law and education, "Despite decades of judicial decisions reaffirming the free speech rights of students, teachers and administrators continue to restrict controversial expression that they think might be offensive" (p. 1007). In 1969, the U.S. Supreme Court ruled that the First Amendment applies to public schools and that a student's right to freedom of expression "does not stop at the schoolhouse gate" (*Tinker v. Des Moines,* 1969, p. 506; cited by Schimmel). In that groundbreaking case, schools in Des Moines, Iowa, fearing disruption, had forbidden students to wear black armbands protesting the Vietnam War. The Court rejected the schools' argument, concluding that schools cannot prohibit expression just "to avoid the discomfort and unpleasantness that always accompany an unpopular viewpoint" (p. 509). Although subsequent Supreme Court decisions have narrowed *Tinker,* the basic principle remains intact: "that is, a student's nondisruptive personal expression that occurs in school is protected by the First Amendment even if the ideas are unpopular and controversial" (Schimmel, p. 1006). Given these judicial rulings, you need to be careful about disciplining students for controversial expression, whether in speech or writings or on clothing. The Court acknowledged that schools can prohibit student expression that causes "substantial disruption or interferes with the rights of others" (Schimmel), but this judgment is not easy to make. Without question, you need to consult a school administrator or the district's legal counsel before taking disciplinary action.

Courts have ruled that students' free-speech rights also extend to electronic media; in 1997, the Supreme Court ruled that speech on the Internet (just like speech in print) is entitled to the highest degree of protection under the First Amendment (Haynes, Chaltain, Ferguson, Hudson, & Thomas 2003). The courts are still in the early stages of exploring limits on free-speech rights related to social media. In one case, a high school student set up a Facebook page on which she complained about one of her teachers. When her school principal found out, he removed her from Advanced Placement classes and suspended her for three days. The ACLU filed suit against the principal on the student's behalf, asking that the suspension be ruled unconstitutional and reversed. A federal magistrate ruled that the lawsuit could proceed through the court system (Simpson, 2010). In two other cases, an appeals court ruled that students who created MySpace profiles that made fun of their school principals were protected by the First Amendment and could not be punished by their schools (Nereim & Rosenthal, 2011). The U.S. Supreme Court subsequently declined to hear the two cases, leaving the appeals courts' decisions in effect.

The second situation occurs when educators' actions conflict with students' Fourth Amendment rights against search and seizure. For example, suppose you suspect that a student possesses drugs or alcohol in school (e.g., in a purse or backpack). Do you have the right to search the student's belongings or not? The answer derives from a landmark case (*New Jersey v. T.L.O.,* 1985), in which the U.S. Supreme Court ruled that a school official may properly conduct a search of a student "when there are reasonable grounds for suspecting that the search will turn up evidence that the student has violated or is violating either the law or the rules of the school" (Fischer, Schimmel, & Kelly, 1999). In other words, students in school have fewer protections than are normally afforded to citizens under the stricter "probable cause" standard (Stefkovich & Miller, 1998).

Although the Supreme Court ruling in *T.L.O.* was issued some 30 years ago, searches are still a subject of debate and litigation. A few years ago, the Supreme Court issued a ruling in the case of *Safford Unified School District v. Redding* (Liptak, 2009a). In this case, an assistant principal ordered the school nurse and a secretary to strip-search an eighth-grade honor student suspected of possessing prescription-strength ibuprofen tablets. No drugs were found, and the girl's mother, represented by the ACLU, filed suit against the school district. Although a district court in Arizona ruled *for* the school district, stating that the search was justified, a Court of Appeals in San Francisco ruled that the school had violated the student's Fourth Amendment rights. The Supreme Court subsequently ruled that the strip search *did* violate the student's constitutional rights (Liptak, 2009b). Writing for the majority opinion, Justice Souter stated that "the pills in question . . . did not justify an embarrassing, frightening and humiliating search" (p. A16). However, the Court's decision did not provide clear guidance to school personnel on searches, instructing them only to consider the danger of the suspected contraband and the likelihood for it to be hidden on the student's person. The majority opinion in this case noted that school personnel needed only "a moderate chance of finding evidence of wrongdoing" to justify a search (p. A16). Given the difficulty of determining what constitutes a "moderate chance" of finding evidence, it's best to leave that determination up to the school personnel who are familiar with the subtleties of the law.

Finally, another situation involving students' Fourth Amendment rights involves a form of time-out called "seclusion time-out" in which a student is removed from the classroom environment and placed alone in a room designated for this purpose. In recent years, parents have brought several lawsuits contending that school districts had violated their children's rights by improperly using seclusion time-out. In the *Peters v. Rome City School District* (2002) decision, for example, a jury in New York awarded $75,000 to a family whose second-grade child had been placed in a time-out room for more than an hour with the door held shut (Ryan, Peterson, & Rozalski, 2007). In May 2013, a bill (H.R. 1893, 2013) was proposed in the U.S. House of Representatives and has been referred to a committee for review; it would prevent and restrict the use of physical restraint and seclusion in schools. If current advocacy efforts are successful, this form of time-out could be entirely prohibited; meanwhile, seclusion time-out should be used only as a last resort and only after checking carefully on school or district policies and procedures.

CONCLUDING COMMENTS

As real human beings working in different school contexts, our five teachers sometimes differ in terms of the strategies they select for dealing with problem behaviors. Fred, for example, uses pointed humor more often than the other teachers; Sandy more readily imposes detention for lateness; Donnie more frequently uses proximity and a gentle touch on a student's shoulder; Donna uses short directives. Nonetheless, these teachers share two important characteristics of effective classroom managers. *First, they are clearly willing to take responsibility for the behavior of their students.* They rarely refer students to the office. They recognize that they are "in charge" and that they are accountable for what happens in their classrooms. This willingness to take responsibility distinguishes more effective managers from less effective ones who tend to disclaim responsibility and refer problems to other school personnel, such as the principal or the guidance counselor (Brophy & Rohrkemper, 1981).

Second, all five teachers have an authoritative style of classroom management and can be characterized as "warm demanders" (Bondy & Ross, 2008). They have deliberately built supportive, trusting relationships with their students. At the same time, they insist that students meet high expectations for behavior (as well as academics). Our teachers accept the fact that problem behaviors will occur, but they believe in students' ability to improve. They make it clear that they demand appropriate, respectful behavior not to be mean but because they care about their students. As Fred says: "It's important to remember that the goal of a penalty is not to hurt kids, but to help them change their behavior. It's not to put kids down; it's to bring them up."

SUMMARY

This chapter discussed ways to respond to a variety of problems—from minor, nondisruptive infractions to chronic, more serious misbehaviors.

Guidelines for Dealing with Misbehavior

- Use disciplinary strategies that are consistent with the goal of creating a safe, caring classroom environment.
- Keep the instructional program going with a minimum of disruption.
- Consider the context of students' actions. Behavior that is acceptable in one context could be unacceptable in another.
- Be timely and accurate when responding to inappropriate behavior.
- Match your disciplinary strategy to the misbehavior.
- Be culturally responsive because differences in norms, values, and styles of communication can have a direct effect on students' behavior.

Strategies for Dealing with Minor Misbehavior

- Nonverbal interventions.
- Verbal interventions.
- Deliberate nonintervention for misbehavior that is fleeting.

Strategies for Dealing with More Serious Misbehavior

- Select penalties:
    Mandatory private conferences.
    Loss of privileges.
    Isolation from the group.
    Exclusion from the group.
    Detention.
    Written reflection on the problem.
    Parental contact.
- Impose penalties while preserving relationships.
- Be consistent.
- Don't penalize the group for individual misbehavior.

Strategies for Dealing with Chronic Misbehavior

- Use a problem-solving approach:
    Step 1: Define the problem.
    Step 2: Brainstorm possible solutions.
    Step 3: Evaluate solutions.
    Step 4: Decide on a solution to try.
    Step 5: Determine how to implement the decision.
    Step 6: Evaluate the solution.
- Use a behavioral learning approach:
    Self-monitoring.
    Self-evaluation.
    Self-instruction.
    Contingency contracting.
    Positive behavioral interventions and supports and functional behavioral assessment.

Dealing with Thorny Problems

- Defiance.
- Failure to do homework.
- Cheating.
- Inappropriate use of electronic devices.
- Inappropriate behavior outside of school.

When Discipline Violates Students' Constitutional Rights

- The First Amendment protects students' freedom of expression unless it causes substantial disruption or interferes with the rights of others.
- The Fourth Amendment protects students from unreasonable search and seizure; however, school searches are permitted if there are "reasonable grounds" for suspecting that the student violated the law or school rules.
- Be very cautious about using "seclusion time-out" because it is a very restrictive, controversial intervention that might also violate students' Fourth Amendment rights against unreasonable seizure.

Effective teachers are willing to take responsibility for managing students' behavior. They can also be characterized as "warm demanders"—teachers who establish trusting, supportive relationships with students but also insist on respectful, appropriate behavior.

ACTIVITIES FOR SKILL BUILDING
AND REFLECTION

In Class

1. When a misbehavior occurs, there usually isn't much time for careful consideration of logical consequences. We've listed a few typical misbehaviors for your practice. In a small group, think of two logical consequences for each example.

    a. As part of a small group, Lou monopolizes the discussion and tells everyone what to do in an authoritarian manner.
    b. At the end of the year, Arianna returns her book with ripped pages and the cover missing.
    c. Shemeika yells out answers throughout your class discussion even though you have instructed students to raise their hands.
    d. Whenever you're not looking, Tom practices juggling with three small beanbags he has brought to school.
    e. Instead of working on the class activity, Tanya examines the contents of her cosmetic kit.

2. In a small group, discuss what you would do in the following situation. You are reviewing homework from the night before. You call on James to do number 5. He slumps in his seat and fidgets with the chain around his neck. You tell him the class is waiting for his answer to number 5. Finally he mutters, "I didn't do the f_____ homework."

On Your Own

1. Beginning teachers sometimes overreact to misbehavior or take no action at all because they simply don't know what to do or say. First, read the examples. Then consider the situations that follow and devise a nonverbal intervention, a verbal cue, and an I-message.

Example	Nonverbal	Verbal	I-Message
A student writes on the desk.	Hand the student an eraser.	"We use paper to write on."	"When you write on the desk, the custodian complains to me and I get embarrassed."
A student makes a big show of looking through her book bag for her homework, distracting other students and delaying the start of the lesson.	Give the "look."	"We're ready to begin."	"When you take so long to get your things out, I can't begin the lesson, and I get very frustrated about the lost time."

    a. A student is copying from another student's paper.
    b. A student takes another student's notebook.
    c. A student sharpens his pencil during your presentation.
    d. A student calls out instead of raising her hand.

2. One common misbehavior in many classrooms is students being off task (e.g., talking to other students while the teacher is presenting a lesson or trying to distract other students).

    a. What might be some of the reasons for the students' off-task behavior?
    b. What might you conclude about the classroom norms or the classroom activities if this misbehavior is common?
    c. Given your responses to parts a. and b., what would be a reasonable teacher response?

For Your Portfolio

Develop a behavior modification plan (such as self-monitoring or a contingency contract) to deal with the following problems:

a. Arthur is a seventh-grader who exhibits aggressive behavior. Hardly a day goes by that another student hasn't come to you complaining of Arthur's pushing, teasing, or name-calling. You've talked to his parents, but they are at a loss about what to do.
b. Cynthia, an 11th-grader, rarely completes her work. She daydreams, socializes with others, misunderstands directions, and gets upset when you speak to her about her incomplete work. The problem seems to be getting worse.

FOR FURTHER READING

Bear, G. G. (1998). School discipline in the United States: Prevention, correction, and long-term social development. *School Psychology Review, 27*(1), 724–742.

   This article reviews strategies used by highly effective classroom teachers to achieve the short-term goal of order and the long-term goal of self-discipline. Bear argues that effective teachers can be characterized by an authoritative style that combines strategies for preventing behavior problems, operant learning strategies for short-term management, and decision-making and social problem-solving strategies to achieve the long-term goal of self-discipline.

Colvin, G. (2010). *Defusing disruptive behavior in the classroom.* Thousand Oaks, CA: Corwin.

   This book written by a long-time teacher focuses on what teachers can do in the moment to defuse disruptive behavior. All the strategies are grounded in principles of effectively managing interactions between the teacher and student so that the situation doesn't escalate.

Gordon, T. (2003). *Teacher effectiveness training: The program proven to help teachers bring out the best in students of all ages.* New York: Three Rivers Press.

   In this updated edition of his 1974 classic, Gordon contends that both authoritarian and permissive approaches to dealing with young people in schools are destructive, "win-lose," power-based approaches. Instead, he advocates a "no-lose" approach to solving problems that protects the teacher-student relationship and promotes communication and caring. He explains the concept of "problem-ownership" so that teachers can respond in appropriate ways.

Kottler, J. A., & Kottler, E. (2009). *Students who drive you crazy: Succeeding with resistant, unmotivated, and otherwise difficult young people* (2nd ed.). Thousand Oaks, CA: Corwin Press.

   This book gives teachers a model to assess, understand, and respond to challenging students. The authors cover a range of potential misbehaviors that are prevalent in teaching and provide advice and support from teachers, counselors, and administrators who have had previous experience in handling such issues in practice.

Mendler, A. (2012, November 12). Defusing power struggles: It's not about getting the last word. Dr. Allen Mendler's Blog on Edutopia retrieved from www.edutopia.org/blog/defusing-power-struggles-last-word-allen-mendler.

This short article contains advice for teachers on avoiding power struggles with students.

Scherer, M. (Ed.) (2012). *Educational Leadership, 70*(2).

This special issue is devoted to articles about "students who challenge us." Topics include focusing on students' strengths, building relationships with students, and deciphering reasons for students' behaviors.

Thompson, G. L. (2004). *Through ebony eyes: What teachers need to know but are afraid to ask about African American students.* San Francisco: Jossey-Bass.

Written in lively, conversational language, this book provides information and strategies to help teachers increase their effectiveness with African American students. Thompson talks about why some African American students misbehave in class and how teachers often unwittingly contribute to their misbehavior.

ORGANIZATIONAL RESOURCES

Technical Assistance Center on Positive Behavior Interventions and Supports, www.pbis.org.

This site, maintained by the Office of Special Education Services of the U.S. Department of Education, contains resources for teachers and schools on enacting PBIS.

CHAPTER 13

Preventing and Responding to Violence

In the wake of the horrific school shootings that have occurred in recent years, school officials all across the country have reexamined their safety and security measures. Schools have installed metal detectors and surveillance cameras, stationed police officers or security guards in high schools, introduced photo identification cards, practiced "lock-downs" and safety drills, and required clear plastic backpacks or banned them completely. By the 2009–2010 school year, 92 percent of schools controlled access to buildings during the school day, 61 percent used security cameras to monitor campuses, and 63 percent required faculty and staff to wear ID badges (Robers, Kemp, & Truman, 2013). Additionally, 43 percent employed one or more security guards, and 28 percent of those security personnel carried a firearm. (See Figure 13.1.)

Although enhanced security is a logical reaction to the threat of violent crime, studies suggest that these measures can actually make students feel *less* safe and might not reduce incidents of violent crime (Bracy, 2011; Gastic, 2011; Portner, 2000). Furthermore, some educators worry that security measures create a negative environment, turning schools into prisonlike, oppressive institutions (Astor, Meyer, & Behre, 1999; Berreth & Berman, 1997; Noguera, 1995). A study of data from Pennsylvania public schools determined that school staff found 3.6 times as many weapons as did the metal detectors in schools, and students found twice as many (Gastic, 2010).

Enhanced security systems alone clearly will not solve the problem of school violence, nor will they allay students' fears and anxieties. Creating safer schools—and

$$250 \times 4 \qquad 28.3 \times 6$$

"GOOD MORNING. I'M MR. ELTON, YOUR TEACHER-SECURITY GUARD."

FIGURE 13.1   www.cartoonstock.com. Reprinted with permission.

schools that *feel* safer—requires a collaborative effort to reach out to students (especially those on the margins) and build a climate of tolerance.

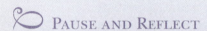

PAUSE AND REFLECT

With the issue of school violence so prevalent in the media, anxiety concerning this issue is normal for all teachers, particularly novices. What are your fears associated with school violence? Talk to teachers in the school where you are observing or teaching about the procedures in place to deal with issues of violence. Knowing what to do in a crisis situation will not only ease anxieties but also could make a significant difference in the outcome.

Many strategies for preventing violence have already been addressed in earlier chapters of this book. Getting to know your students, building respectful relationships, establishing orderly classrooms, curbing peer harassment and bullying, and working to meet students' learning needs all reduce the potential for violence. In this chapter, we discuss additional strategies for preventing violence and then examine ways to react to it if it occurs. Note that this chapter addresses violence by students directed at other students or teachers, *not* violent incidents by intruders.

STRATEGIES FOR PREVENTING VIOLENCE

Build Supportive School Communities

Although we focused on creating safer, more caring classrooms in Chapter 3, it's important to revisit this topic in relation to violence prevention. Numerous educators argue that violence prevention has to focus on the creation of environments in which students are known and feel supported and where rules are clear and consistently applied (Akiba, 2010; Astor, Meyer, & Behre, 1999; Bosworth, Ford, & Hernandez, 2011; Browne-Dianis, 2011). The superintendent of Sandy's district echoes this sentiment:

A safe school is one that is responsive to students, where the staff knows the kids, where you can get help for troubled kids right away. . . . We don't talk much about metal detectors or security measures here. Our approach to violence prevention emphasizes connecting to kids and addressing their social–emotional needs. We try hard to make sure that one group isn't elevated over another . . . and to respect differences among kids.

Creating a supportive school community isn't easy, especially in large high schools, in which feelings of anonymity, alienation, and apathy are leading causes of problems. Doing so, however, is perhaps more important than ever. Given the changing nature of families and economic conditions that require both parents to work outside the home, many students spend more time in the company of peers than adults. Because these peer relationships are not an adequate substitute for adult attention, it is critical that teachers develop and nurture caring relationships with their students (Laursen, 2008). Recent research has also shown that students perceive schools that are high in both support and structure (authoritative management) as safe with less student-reported victimization and less student- and teacher-perceived bullying among students (Gregory et al., 2010).

BE ALERT TO SIGNS OF HATE

According to a report from the Southern Poverty Law Center (2004), the number of hate crimes by youth has risen sharply since 9/11:

> [A] disproportionate number of assaults on Muslim-Americans were committed by teenagers. The same appears to be true for attacks against sexual and gender minorities, Hispanics and the homeless. And hate activity is no longer the province of white boys, though they are still the main offenders. Not only are more Hispanic and African-American kids getting involved in hate, but more girls as well. . . . [Furthermore,] in another demographic shift, the bulk of hate activity now bubbles up in the suburbs—among reasonably well-off youth. (p. 1)

As a teacher, you need to note messages of hate or violence in book reports, essays, or journal entries and report your concerns to the principal, a school counselor, or the district's affirmative action officer. Be aware of online hate sites and recruitment by hate groups. (The Southern Poverty Law Center's Intelligence Project can help you stay informed about this.) Help students to recognize hate literature containing swastikas, derogatory references to race or ethnicity, and caricatures of racial/ethnic groups and discuss what students can do if they find or someone gives them a hate flier. At Halloween, discourage costumes that involve negative stereotyping (e.g., "Gypsy" costumes or "homeless person" outfits) or organizations that promote hate (e.g., Ku Klux Klan robes).

EXAMINE THE WAYS YOUR SCHOOL RECOGNIZES STUDENT ACHIEVEMENT

Traditions that contribute to a sense of superiority among some students could lead to feelings of frustration or inadequacy in others. Are athletes disciplined less severely for offenses? Are their achievements highlighted more than the achievements of other students? Do honors students and student leaders enjoy special privileges? Recognition and special privileges might seem far removed from the issue of school violence. However, an investigation of conditions at Columbine High School prior to the 1999 shooting revealed rampant favoritism toward student athletes (Adams & Russakoff, 1999). Athletes convicted of crimes were allowed to continue participating in their sports, and they were not disciplined for physically abusing other students. Sports trophies were displayed in the front hallway but student artwork was relegated to a back hallway. Although this certainly does not excuse the actions taken by the two shooters, there was ample evidence that the school's "cult of the athlete" contributed to their actions. Given this, it's important that teachers take action to avoid institutionalized favoritism and find ways to recognize and celebrate different types of achievement.

ASK STUDENTS TO CONTRIBUTE TO VIOLENCE PREVENTION EFFORTS

Learning what students' views are with respect to violence and violence prevention strategies is critical—not just of the "good ones," but also of "the toughies, the gangbangers, the disruptive, the withdrawn, and the unmotivated" (Curwin, 1995, p. 75). Encourage students to organize their own antiviolence events. Solicit their perceptions of the school's high-conflict areas (e.g., hallways, cafeterias, restrooms) and their ideas about how to make these safer. Invite students to develop an anti-bullying campaign.

A good example of the way students can become meaningfully involved is by becoming peer mediators. As discussed in Chapter 4, these programs are becoming increasingly popular in schools across the country. Sandy's school has had a peer mediation program for many years, and a counselor there believes that it has definitely helped to reduce incidents of violence:

> Before we had peer mediation, we had lots of kids getting suspended for fighting; now we rarely have fights. Kids will tell the peer mediators when something is brewing, and the mediators can prevent the problem from erupting into a physical fight. Peer mediation gives kids a structure they may not have developed yet for dealing with emotional issues.

Thus far, anecdotal evidence supports this counselor's conviction that peer mediation programs can substantially reduce violent incidents. Some researchers contend that peer mediation actually has more impact on the *mediators* than on the disputants because they acquire valuable conflict resolution skills and earn the respect of their peers (Bodine & Crawford, 1998; Miller, 1994). If this is so, it means that high-risk students—not just the "good kids"—must be trained and used as mediators.

Know the Early Warning Signs of Potential for Violence

In 1998, the U.S. Department of Education and the Department of Justice published a guide to assist schools in developing comprehensive violence prevention plans (Dwyer, Osher, & Warger, 1998). The guide contains a list of "early warning signs" that can alert teachers and other school staff to students' potential for violence as well as signs that violence is imminent. These appear in Tables 13.1 and 13.2.

It's important to remember that the early warning signs are not an infallible predictor that a child or youth will commit a violent act toward self or others (Dwyer, Osher, & Warger, 1998). Also keep in mind that potentially violent students typically exhibit

TABLE 13.1 Early Warning Signs of Potential for Violence

- Social withdrawal
- Excessive feelings of isolation and being alone
- Excessive feelings of rejection
- Being a victim of violence
- Feelings of being picked on and persecuted
- Low school interest and poor academic performance
- Expression of violence in writings and drawings
- Uncontrolled anger
- Patterns of impulsive and chronic hitting, intimidating, and bullying behaviors
- History of discipline problems
- Past history of violent and aggressive behavior
- Intolerance for differences and prejudicial attitudes
- Drug use and alcohol use
- Affiliation with gangs
- Inappropriate access to, possession of, and use of firearms
- Serious threats of violence

TABLE 13.2 Imminent Signs of Violence

- Serious physical fighting with peers or family members
- Severe destruction of property
- Severe rage for seemingly minor reasons
- Detailed threats of lethal violence
- Possession and/or use of firearms and other weapons
- Other self-injurious behaviors or threats of suicide

multiple warning signs. Thus, be careful about overreacting to single signs, words, or actions, and don't be biased by a student's race, socioeconomic status, academic ability, or physical appearance. A counselor in Fred's school acknowledges the tension between needing to identify students who might pose a risk for violence and *social profiling:*

> *We have kids who wear the gothic look, and after shootings at Columbine, we wanted to reach out to them. But you have to be so careful about stereotyping, thinking that everyone who dresses in gothic must be potentially violent or alienated. It really made us think about our process. At what point does identifying kids who might be violent become social profiling?*

A 2000 federal court ruling in Washington state (Walsh, 2000) underscores the difficulty of distinguishing between a real threat to safety and harmless student expression. In this case, a high school junior submitted a poem to his English teacher about a lonely student who roamed his high school with a pounding heart. The poem contained this passage:

> As I approached the classroom door,
> I drew my gun and threw open the door.
> Bang, Bang, Bang-Bang.

> When it was all over, 28 were dead,
> and all I remember was not felling [sic] any remorce [sic],
> for I felt, I was, cleansing my soul.

The student's teacher alerted administrators, and the poem was reviewed by a psychologist, who determined that the student was unlikely to cause harm to himself or others. Nonetheless, the district decided to expel him on an emergency basis. After a psychiatrist examined the student, the district rescinded the expulsion, and the student completed his junior year. The boy's parents then sued the district, claiming that the school had violated his First Amendment right to free speech and asking that the expulsion be removed from their son's record. A federal district judge ruled for the family, maintaining that the district had overreacted in expelling the student. She suggested that there were less restrictive ways the district could have ensured the safety of students and school personnel, such as imposing a temporary suspension pending psychiatric examination.

Such stories can discourage teachers from reporting essays or artwork that contains threatening messages or behavior that suggests a potential for violence. But it's better to alert school officials about what you have learned than to ignore indicators and be sorry later. Find out what the reporting procedures are in your school: Do you report your concerns to the principal? The school nurse? A counselor? Do you notify parents? Remember that parental involvement and consent are required before sharing personally identifiable information with agencies outside the school (except in case of emergencies or suspicion of abuse). The Family Educational Rights and Privacy Act (FERPA), a federal law that addresses the privacy of educational records, must be observed in all referrals to community agencies (Dwyer, Osher, & Warger, 1998).

Be Observant in "Unowned" Spaces

In addition to knowing the early warning signs, teachers can help prevent violence by being observant in hallways, cafeterias, stairwells, and locker rooms—"unowned" spaces where violence is most likely to erupt (Astor, Meyer, & Behre, 1999). Chester Quarles, a criminologist who specializes in crime prevention, suggests that teachers attempt to make eye contact whenever they pass students in the halls:

> The subliminal message being exchanged is that "I know who is here and I know who you are. I can remember your features. I can identify you." The influence of careful observation is a strong criminal deterrent for everyone that you observe. . . . Observant teachers . . . can decrease the probability that any of the people they encounter will commit a delinquent act against another that day. (1989, pp. 12–13)

Be Attentive to Whispers and Rumors

The high-profile school shootings that we have witnessed in the last several years are what the Secret Service calls *targeted violence*—incidents in which the attacker selects a particular target prior to the violent attack. As part of the Safe School Initiative of the U.S. Secret Service and the U.S. Department of Education, researchers studied 37 school shootings involving 41 attackers who were current or recent students at the school (Vossekuil, Fein, Reddy, Borum, & Modzeleski, 2002). Here are some of their findings:

- Incidents of targeted violence at school are rarely sudden or impulsive. Typically, the attacker *planned* the attack in advance.

- In most of the cases, other people knew about the attack before it occurred. In more than three-quarters of the cases, at least one person knew; in nearly two-thirds, more than one person knew. Some peers knew details of the attack; others just knew that something "big" or "bad" was going to happen in school on a particular day.

- Most attackers engaged in some behavior prior to the incident that caused others concern or indicated a need for help.

These findings contradict the common perception that students who commit targeted acts of violence have simply "snapped." Nor are they loners who keep their plans to themselves. In a follow-up study, researchers interviewed 15 students who had known about potential threats of violence at their schools (Pollack, Modzelski, & Rooney, 2008). They found that the school climate affected whether or not these students reported the threats of violence. One student who knew of a weapon on school property was reluctant to come forward because he expected a negative reaction "When you say something, you get in trouble or interrogated by teachers" (Pollack, Modzelski, & Rooney, p. 7). Additionally, many of the bystanders did not believe that the threats would be carried out, and so told no one. This means that school staff must be attentive to whispers that something is afoot and create a climate that encourages students to report rumors of potential violence. In a recent study, ninth-grade students who perceived their teachers as caring and respectful were more likely to claim that they would report it if a classmate brought a gun to school or threatened another student (Eliot, Cornell, Gregory, & Fan, 2010).

De-Escalate Potentially Explosive Situations

Explosive situations often begin benignly. You make a reasonable request ("Would you join the group over there?") or give an ordinary directive ("Get started on the questions at the end of this section"). But the student is feeling angry—maybe he has just been taunted and humiliated in the hallway; maybe her mother has just grounded her for a month; maybe the teacher in the previous class has ridiculed an answer. The anger could have nothing to do with you at all, but it finds its outlet in your class. In a hostile mood, the student fails to comply immediately and could even respond defiantly. Unfortunately, at this point, teachers often contribute to the escalation of a conflict by becoming angry and impatient. They issue an ultimatum: "Do what I say or else." And now teacher and student are combatants in a potentially explosive situation neither of them wanted.

Let's consider an example (adapted from Walker, Colvin, & Ramsey, 1995) of a teacher-student interaction that begins innocuously enough but quickly escalates into an explosive situation:

> Students are working on a set of math problems the teacher has assigned. Michael sits slouched in his seat staring at the floor, an angry expression on his face. The teacher sees that Michael is not doing his math and calls over to him from the back of the room where she is working with other students.

Teacher: Michael, why aren't you working on the assignment?

Michael: I finished it.

Teacher: Well, let me see it then. [She walks over to Michael's desk and sees that he has four problems completed.] Good. You've done 4 but you need to do 10.

Michael: Nobody told me that!

Teacher: Michael, I went over the assignment very clearly and asked if there were any questions about what to do!

Michael: I don't remember that.

Teacher: Look at the board. I wrote it there. See, page 163, numbers 11–20.

Michael: I didn't see it. Anyway, I hate this boring stuff.

Teacher: OK, that's enough. No more arguments. Page 163, 11–20. Now.

Michael: It's dumb. I'm not going to do it.

Teacher: Yes you are, mister.

Michael: Yeah? Make me.

Teacher: If you don't do it now, you're going to the office.

Michael: F_____ you!

Teacher: That's enough!

Michael: You want math? Here it is! [He throws the math book across the room.]

At first glance, it appears that the teacher is being remarkably patient and reasonable in the face of Michael's stubbornness, defiance, and abuse. On closer examination, however, we can detect a chain of successive escalating interactions in which Michael's behavior moves from questioning and challenging the teacher to defiance and abuse and for which the teacher is also responsible (Walker, Colvin, & Ramsey, 1995). Could the teacher have broken this chain earlier? The probable answer is yes.

First, the teacher should have been sensitive to Michael's angry facial expression and the fact that he was slouching in his seat. Facial expression, flushing, squinty eyes, clenched fists, rigid body posture, pacing, and stomping—these all suggest an impending eruption (Hyman, 1997). Second, teachers can usually avoid defiant situations if they do not corner a student, do not argue, do not engage in a power struggle ("I'm the boss in this classroom, and I'm telling you to. . . ."), and do not embarrass the student in front of peers. The accompanying Practical Tips box summarizes specific recommendations.

 PRACTICAL TIPS FOR

Managing Potentially Explosive Situations

- Move slowly and deliberately toward the problem situation.
- Speak privately, quietly, and calmly. Do not threaten. Be as matter-of-fact as possible.
- Be as still as possible. Avoid pointing or gesturing.
- Keep a reasonable distance. Do not crowd the student. Do not get "in the student's face."
- Speak respectfully. Use the student's name.
- Establish eye-level position.

(continued on next page)

- Be brief. Avoid long-winded statements or nagging.
- Stay with the agenda. Stay focused on the problem at hand. Do not get sidetracked. Deal with less severe problems later.
- Avoid power struggles. Do not get drawn into "I won't, you will" arguments.
- Inform the student of the expected behavior and the negative consequence as a choice or decision for the student to make. Then withdraw from the student and allow some time for the student to decide. ("Michael, you need to return to your desk, or I will have to send for the principal. You have a few seconds to decide." The teacher then moves away, perhaps attending to other students. If Michael does not choose the appropriate behavior, deliver the negative consequence. "You are choosing to have me call the principal.") Follow through with the consequence.

Source: Adapted from Walker, Colvin, & Ramsey, 1995.

With this background, let's go back to Michael and see how the teacher might have dealt with the situation to prevent it from escalating.

> Students are working on a set of math problems the teacher has assigned. Michael sits slouched in his seat staring at the floor, an angry expression on his face. The teacher notices Michael's posture and realizes that he is feeling upset about something. She goes over, bends down so that she is on eye-level with Michael, and speaks very quietly.
>
> Teacher: Are you doing OK, Michael? You look upset. [Teacher demonstrates empathy.]
> Michael: I'm OK.
> Teacher: Well, good, but if you'd like to talk later, let me know. [Teacher invites further communication.] Meanwhile, you need to get going on this assignment.
> Michael: I already did it.
> Teacher: Oh, good. Let me see how you did. [She checks the paper.] OK, you've done the first four, and they're fine. Now do the next four problems and let me see them when you're finished. [She walks away, giving the student space.]

Be Alert for the Presence of Gang Activity

A report issued by the U.S. Departments of Education and Justice (Chandler, Chapman, Rand, & Taylor, 1998) found that the presence of gangs in schools nearly doubled between 1989 and 1995 when approximately one-third of the 10,000 students surveyed (aged 12 to 19) reported gang presence. In 2011, 18 percent of 6,500 students surveyed reported that there were gangs at their schools (Robers, Kemp, & Truman, 2013). Because gang presence is strongly linked to the presence of guns, drugs, and violence (Howell & Lynch, 2000), teachers need to be alert to the presence of gang activity in schools.

 PAUSE AND REFLECT

How prevalent is gang activity in the school where you are observing or teaching? What schoolwide rules are in place to restrict gang activity on campus? Think about how the presence of gangs in a school could impact your classroom. How might you attempt to defuse any tension between rival gang members who happen to be in one of your classes?

TABLE 13.3 Signs of Gang Presence	
Gathering or hanging out	Gang members could establish territory (e.g., in the lunch room, on playing fields, and in bleachers). Once these areas are claimed, other students will stay away.
Nonverbal and verbal signs	Gang members often have special ways of signaling one another and conveying messages: "Flashing"—the use of finger and hand signs. "Monikers"—nicknames emphasizing a member's particular attribute.
Graffiti	Signs, symbols, and nicknames on notebooks, papers, clothing, and walls; graffiti advertises the gang and its members and could contain challenging messages to other gangs; crossed out graffiti constitutes a direct challenge from a rival gang.
Stance and walk	Unique ways of standing and walking that set members apart.
Symbols	Tattoos, earrings, colors, scarves, bandannas, shoelaces, caps, belts (change over time).

Source: Adapted from Lal, Lal, & Achilles, 1993.

It's not easy to identify a gang because teenagers frequently "run in packs" and try to look and act just like everyone else. However, a group of teenagers does not constitute a gang. A widely accepted definition of gangs includes these variables: group, permanence, symbols of membership, acknowledgement of membership, and involvement in crime (Naber, May, Decker, Minor, & Wells, 2006). Kenneth Trump, president of the National School Safety and Security Services, reminds us that the key to gang activity is negative behavior:

> Kids who sit together in the lunch room don't constitute a gang. But when groups start assaulting other students or creating an atmosphere of fear and intimidation, they become a gang. In short, groups of students reach gang status when their behavior, either individually or collectively, is disruptive, antisocial, or criminal. (1993, p. 40).

To determine the extent to which gangs are present in your school, you need to be familiar with the indicators summarized in Table 13.3. Keep in mind, however, that indicators of gang affiliation such as clothing style or colors change frequently, especially as school personnel learn what signifies gang affiliation and outlaw those clothing items (Struyk, 2006). Gang members simply adopt subtler indicators, such as belt buckles engraved with gang symbols or earrings worn in combination with other accessories.

According to Donna, several gang families attend her school:

At times the tension is evident and explosive, and other times the factions just agree to keep their distance from each other. Being alert is difficult because a lot of the issues take place in the neighborhood or apartments, away from school. The police and school safety officer keep us aware of what we should look for: things like clothes, hand signs, or slang. Staff members are informed of potential gang-related problems by e-mail.

In my years of dealing with gang problems, the root problem seems to be that parents, older siblings, and other relatives involve younger family members to keep gang-related issues alive. And since most middle school kids want to fit in, they go along with the gang activities.

The presence of gang activity in schools can seem to be a problem too complex for a classroom teacher to address. Remember, however, as Donna notes, that students join gangs to satisfy needs that aren't being met elsewhere—namely, to belong to a group that is powerful and whose members stick up for each other. Although you might not be able to influence the "hard-core" members of gangs, you might be able to provide potential gang members the personal connection and sense of belonging that they need to resist gang membership.

RESPONDING TO VIOLENCE

Coping with Aggressive Behavior

Despite your best efforts at prevention, there are times when students erupt in hostile, aggressive behavior. A girl screams profanities and knocks a pile of dictionaries to the floor. A boy explodes in anger and throws a chair across the room. Someone yells, "I'll kill you," and hurls a notebook at another student. In such situations—every teacher's nightmare—it's easy to lose self-control and lash out. As Fred puts it,

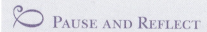 **Pause and Reflect**

Imagine an incident of aggressive behavior occurring in your classroom (e.g., a student explodes in anger and throws a book at another student). Think about the steps you would take to stop the aggression from escalating and to restore calm. What words would you use? Then continue to the next section and see how Sandy handled an outburst that occurred in her classroom.

 The *normal* reaction is to become angry and aggressive and to get in the kid's face. But *teachers can't react normally.* That will only make things worse, and your responsibility is *to make things better.*

To "make things better," you need to think carefully about what you will do to defuse the aggression and protect yourself and your students. Let's consider an episode that occurred in Sandy's classroom.

As usual, I was standing at the doorway as the kids were coming into the classroom. I noticed Robert come in without his backpack or any books. That didn't look right, and I watched him cross the room and go over to Daniel, who was sitting at his desk. Robert picked up the desk and the leg of Daniel's chair and overturned them, cursing and screaming the whole time. I ran over. The first thing I said was, "Daniel, don't raise your hands." He was on the floor on his back, and Robert was standing over him screaming. I kept saying, "Robert, look at me, look at me, look at me." Finally, he made eye contact. Then I said, "You need to come with me." We began to walk toward the door, but he turned back and started cursing again. Very quietly and firmly I told him, "You need to come with me now." He followed me to the door, and as I reached the door I picked up the phone and called the office and said there was a problem and to send someone up. Then we stepped out into the hallway. Robert was angry and was going to leave, and I asked him to please stop and talk to me about what was going on, what was bothering him. I didn't yell, I didn't say, "How could you do something so stupid?" (even though that's what I felt like saying). I said, "Obviously you're upset about something. Tell me about it." It turns out that these two were friends, but Robert found out that Daniel was sleeping with his [Robert's] girlfriend. I heard a lot I didn't really want to hear, but it kept him occupied until the vice-principal arrived.

Once the vice-principal took Robert, I got Daniel out into the hallway and asked him if he was OK, and if he needed to go to the nurse, or needed to be out of the classroom. He said no, he was OK. I told him, "You were very smart for not raising your hands against Robert." He returned to his seat, and all the kids started saying, "Daniel, are you OK?" and crowding around him. I told them, "Robert's in the office. Daniel's OK. Let's get started on chemistry." At the end of the period, the office called for Daniel to go to the peer mediation room to have the dispute mediated.

In addition to going to peer mediation, Robert was suspended for three days. But the day he was suspended, he came back after school hours (something he wasn't supposed to do) to apologize for his language. I accepted his apology, but I said that there were other ways to handle the situation and to express anger. It was a very low-key discussion. I didn't make light of what had happened, but I told him I was glad he realized the danger of the situation.

After the suspension, Daniel came to me before homeroom to say he was feeling frightened about coming to class that day. It was going to be his first meeting with Robert, and Robert sits right in front of him. I said that I had already changed both their seats. I told him, "Don't worry, I'll be watching." When they came in, I told them each "You have a new seat," and showed them where to sit. There was no problem from that point on.

Analysis of Sandy's response to Robert's outburst reveals some important guidelines for dealing with aggression in the classroom. Let's examine her behavior more closely and consider the lessons to be learned.

1. Although Sandy admits that she wanted to respond with anger ("What is wrong with you?!"), she remained outwardly calm and in control. By doing so, she was able to *prevent the situation from escalating.* She lowered the level of emotion in the class and decreased the chance of becoming a victim herself. She then directed Daniel not to raise his hands against Robert. This prevented Robert's aggressive actions from escalating into a full-scale physical fight. Next, she issued quiet, firm, repetitive instructions for Robert to look at her. This created a lull in the altercation, during which she was able to separate the two boys ("You need to come with me"). Because Daniel was lying on the floor under the desk, it was easier for her to have Robert move away. In other cases, however, it could be advisable to remove the targets of the aggression. You can direct them to go to a nearby teacher's classroom, preferably with a friend because they are bound to be angry and upset ("Take Scott and go to Ms. Thomson's room so we can get this sorted out") or have them move to a far corner of the room, out of the aggressor's line of sight.

2. Sandy's next action was to report that there was a problem in her room and *to summon help*. Never send angry, aggressive students to the office alone: You can't be certain they will actually get there, nor do you know what they will do on the way. If you don't have a telephone or intercom, quietly instruct a responsible student to go for assistance. Donna actually identifies two "trusted students" in each of her classes who can be trusted to get help for any sort of disruption when Donna isn't in her classroom.

   Who should be summoned will vary, so it's important for you to check on the procedures in your own school. Fred would call one of the two SROs—security resource officers—who patrol the hallways. Christina, Donna, and Sandy would call the main office. Donnie would contact one of the security guards.

3. While Sandy waited for someone from the office to provide assistance, she spoke privately and quietly with Robert in an attempt to *defuse the aggression*. She did not rebuke or threaten punishment. Instead, she acknowledged his anger and showed her willingness to listen.

   Again, it's critical that you resist the temptation to "react normally" and lash out at the student. You need to speak slowly and softly and to minimize the threat by not invading the student's space and keeping your hands by your side. Allow the student to relate facts and feelings, even if it involves profanity, and use active listening ("So you were really furious when you found out what was happening. . . ."). Do not disagree or argue.

   If, despite your efforts to restore calm, the student's aggression escalates, it's best to move away unless you are trained in physical restraint techniques. Even then, don't use restraint unless you are strong enough and there are no other options. As Hyman (1997) emphasizes, "The last thing you ever want to do is to physically engage an enraged student who may be out of control" (p. 251).

4. When Robert came to see Sandy after school, he gave her the opportunity to discuss what had happened, to reinforce alternative ways to handle anger, and to accept his apology. He also gave her the chance to *reestablish a positive relationship*. Fred emphasizes how important this is:

 Suspending a violent kid isn't the end of the situation. At some point, the kid is going to come back, and then it's your job to rebuild the relationship. You need to reassure them that they're still a member of the class. You need to tell them, "OK, you messed up. But I'm on your side. You can learn from this."

5. Once Robert was on his way to the office and Daniel was back in his seat, Sandy scanned the room to *determine how the other students were feeling* and what to do next. She decided that her best course of action was to provide them with the basic facts ("Robert is in the office. Daniel's OK") and to begin the lesson ("Let's get started on chemistry"). She certainly did not want to explore with her class the reasons behind Robert's aggressive actions.

Sometimes, however, your students might be so upset and frightened that it's impossible to continue working. A counselor at Sandy's school suggests that it's important to allow them to express their feelings:

If the students are upset, you have to give them the opportunity to talk about what happened and to acknowledge their fear. You don't want to pretend nothing happened and then send them on to the next class all churned up inside.

Responding Effectively to Physical Fights

Physical fights are more likely to occur in hallways and cafeterias than in classrooms. But what do you do if you're on the scene when a fight erupts? We asked our teachers that question one evening as we talked about the problem of violence in schools. They were unanimous in their response, which is listed in the accompanying Practical Tips box. As we discussed the issue of fighting in school, the teachers repeatedly stressed the fact that fights are fast. They can erupt quickly—so you don't have a lot of time to think through a response—and they're usually over in less than 30 seconds (although that can seem like a lifetime). There was also amazing unanimity among the teachers on the issue of fights among girls versus boys. As Donnie put it: "Teachers shouldn't think that fighting is only going to happen among boys. Girls fight too—and girl fights are terrible. Girls kick, pull earrings, bite, scratch, and when you try to stop it, they turn on *you.*"

It's important to remember that you must report violent acts. Every school system needs to have a violent incident reporting system that requires teachers to report what happened, when and where it happened, who was involved, and what action was taken.

 PRACTICAL TIPS FOR

Responding Effectively to Physical Fights

- *Quickly appraise the situation.* Is this a verbal altercation? Is there physical contact? Does anyone have a weapon?
- *Send a responsible student for help.* Send for the nearest teacher and for the principal or vice-principal. Once other people are there to help, it's easier—and safer—to get the situation under control.
- *Tell students to stop.* Often students don't want to continue the fight, and they'll respond to a short, clear, firm command. If you know the combatants' names, use them.
- *Disperse other students.* There's no need for an audience, and you don't want onlookers to become part of the fray. If you're in the hallway, direct students to be on their way. If you're in the classroom, send your students to the library or some other safe place.
- *Do not intervene physically*—unless the age, size, and number of combatants indicates that it's safe to do so, there are three or four people to help, or you have learned physical restraint.

Responding Effectively to Schoolwide Emergencies

Although not mandated by law, most school districts have developed emergency management plans. It is important that you are familiar with the plans at your school, which should cover fires, intruders on campus, and weather emergencies. Many schools review their emergency plans at the beginning of each school year and schedule drills to practice. Donna describes a recent incident at her school:

> **One day last week, a parent said she saw a student showing other students a weapon in front of the school. The parent called the school office to report this, and the school immediately went into lockdown. We had about 100 police here, and they searched every part of the school. As per the school's plan for this type of emergency, teachers and students had to remain in their classrooms, sitting on the floor, away from the windows, during the search. After two hours, they found the student with the weapon (a high-powered BB gun) and arrested him.**
>
> **For the rest of the day, I greeted each student at the door to my classroom. I wanted them to see me immediately, and know that I was calm and happy to see them. (Inside my head, I was a mess too!) I continued with a Daily Oral Language question on the board, and I took attendance in my usual manner. I allowed time for questions about the lockdown, and then we played a trivia game, which allowed them to be "silly." That seemed to calm them down and it encouraged some smiling and laughing. I never discounted their fears nor my own; I just tried to be the adult who was in control of my classroom. The next school day, the district did send a counseling team to the school to talk to students.**

It's important that you know your school's plans well enough that you can calmly and accurately direct students in what to do in the event of an emergency. As always, your focus should be on providing support and structure and on keeping your students with you and calm.

CONCLUDING COMMENTS

Using data from the National Longitudinal Study of Adolescent Health, the largest study ever conducted of teenagers in the United States, researchers set out to identify factors that predict whether adolescents will commit acts of violence (Resnick, Ireland, & Borowsky, 2004). They identified several factors, such as carrying a weapon, experiencing problems at school, and using alcohol and marijuana, that make violence more likely. They also identified factors that decrease the likelihood of involvement in violence. Of particular relevance to this chapter is their finding that *feeling connected to school is a key protective factor;* in other words, both males and females are less likely to perpetrate violence when they feel part of the school community.

Installing metal detectors and state-of-the-art security systems can go only so far in creating a more peaceful school. The challenge for teachers and administrators is to reach out to young people and help them feel connected. In the final analysis, the presence of caring adults holds the greatest promise for preventing school violence.

SUMMARY

Although data on the frequency and severity of school violence indicate a decrease, violence is still a serious problem. This chapter presented a variety of strategies for preventing and responding to violence.

Prevention Strategies

■ Build supportive school communities:
    Be alert to signs of hate.
    Examine the ways your school recognizes student achievement.
    Ask students to contribute to violence prevention efforts.
■ Know the early warning signs of potential for violence.
■ Be observant in "unowned" spaces.
■ Be attentive to whispers and rumors.
■ De-escalate potentially explosive situations.
■ Be alert for the presence of gang activity.

Responding to Violence

■ Coping with aggressive behavior to:
    Prevent escalation.
    Summon help.
    Defuse the aggression.
    Reestablish a positive relationship with the aggressor.
    Determine how the other students are feeling.
■ Responding effectively to physical fights:
    Quickly appraise the situation.
    Send a responsible student for help.
    Tell the students to stop.
    Disperse onlookers.
    Do not intervene physically unless doing so is safe.

   Metal detectors and security systems can go only so far. It's essential to build connections with students. In the final analysis, the presence of caring adults holds the greatest promise for preventing violence.

ACTIVITIES FOR SKILL BUILDING
AND REFLECTION

In Class

Consider the following situations. In small groups, discuss what you would do in each case.

1. As students enter your classroom, you overhear a girl teasing Annamarie about the boy Annamarie's dating. They go to their seats, but the taunts continue. Suddenly, Annamarie stands up, turns to the girl, and shouts, "You shut up, bitch. Just shut up, or I'll get you!"

2. Your students are taking a brief quiz on the homework. Those who have finished already are reading. As you circulate throughout the room, collecting the finished papers, you notice that James is looking at a catalog of weapons. He makes no attempt to conceal it.

3. Jesse comes to your first-period class wearing a T-shirt with a Celtic cross surrounded by the words "White Pride World Wide."

4. You ask Carla where her textbook is. She mutters something under her breath. When you tell her you didn't hear what she said, she shouts, "I left the f_____ book in my locker!"

On Your Own

Interview an experienced teacher, the student assistance counselor, the school nurse, or a guidance counselor about the school's efforts to prevent violence. Find out answers to the following questions:

1. If you think a student exhibits some of the early warning signs of potential for violence, to whom do you report?

2. Is there an official form to file?

3. Do you contact parents?

4. Are school personnel aware of gang activity?

5. What are the indicators of gang membership and gang activity?

For Your Portfolio

Document how you will establish a classroom climate in which students are comfortable telling you about threats of violence at school. Modify any of the artifacts you created at the end of Chapter 5 to incorporate this chapter's material. Write a brief commentary explaining how you will help your students understand the importance of reporting threats.

FOR FURTHER READING

Colvin, G. (2004). *Managing the cycle of acting-out behavior in the classroom.* Eugene, OR: Behavior Associates.

This book provides practical strategies for managing and preventing acting-out behavior such as defiance, tantrums, threats, resistance, avoidance, and classroom disruption at various levels. It presents a model of acting-out behavior that consists of seven phases. The characteristics of each phase are described using examples and case studies. It then presents strategies for interventions that can be used for each phase.

Teaching Tolerance

This is a magazine mailed twice a year at no charge to educators. Published by the Southern Poverty Law Center (www.teachingtolerance.org), a nonprofit legal and educational foundation, the magazine provides a wealth of information and resources on all aspects of promoting tolerance and respect and eliminating bias, oppression, and bullying.

ORGANIZATIONAL RESOURCES

The Anti-Defamation League (ADL), www.adl.org. Dedicated to combating hate crime and promoting intergroup cooperation and understanding.

National School Safety Center, www.schoolsafety.us. Resource for school safety information, training, and violence prevention.

Office of Safe and Drug-Free Schools, www.ed.gov/offices/OESE/SDFS/news.html. Provides reports and articles on school safety and school violence.

The Southern Poverty Law Center, www.teachingtolerance.org. The Teaching Tolerance project provides teachers at all levels ideas and free resources for building community, fighting bias, and celebrating diversity.

Students against Violence Everywhere (SAVE), www.nationalsave.org. This student-driven organization helps students learn about alternatives to violence and encourages them to practice what they have learned through school and community projects.

REFERENCES

Abd-Kadir, J., & Hardman, F. (2007). Whole class teaching in Kenyan and Nigerian primary schools. *Language and Education, 21*(1), 1–15.

Adams, L., & Russakoff, D. (1999, June 12). Dissecting Columbine's cult of the athlete. *Washington Post,* p. A-1.

Adams, R. S., & Biddle, B. J. (1970). *Realities of teaching: Explorations with video tape.* New York: Holt, Rinehart, & Winston.

Akiba, M. (2010). What predicts fear of school violence among U.S. adolescents? *Teachers College Record, 112*(1), 68–102.

Akin-Little, K. A., Little, S. G., & Laniti, M. (2007). Teachers' use of classroom management procedures in the United States and Greece: A cross-cultural comparison. *School Psychology International, 28*(1), 53–62.

Albert, D., Chein, J., & Steinberg, L. (2013). The teenage brain: Peer influences on adolescent decision making. *Current Directions in Psychological Science, 22*(2), 114–120.

Alberto, P. A., & Troutman, A. C. (2006). *Applied behavior analysis for teachers* (7th ed.). Upper Saddle River, NJ: Pearson Prentice Hall.

Alfi, O., Assor, A., & Katz, I. (2004). Learning to allow temporary failure: Potential benefits, supportive practices, and teacher concerns. *Journal of Education for Teaching, 30*(1), 27–41.

Allard, H., & Marshall, J. (1977). *Miss Nelson is missing.* Boston: Houghton Mifflin.

Allen, J. (2008). Family partnerships that count. *Educational Leadership, 66*(1), 22–27.

Allen, K. P. (2011). Off the radar and ubiquitous: Text messaging and its relationship to "drama" and cyberbullying in an affluent, academically rigorous U.S. high school. *Journal of Youth Studies, 15*(1), 99–117.

Alvermann, D., O'Brien, D., & Dillon, D. (1990). What teachers do when they say they're having discussions of content area reading assignments. *Reading Research Quarterly, 25,* 296–322.

American Association of University Women [AAUW]. (2011). *Crossing the line: Sexual harassment at school.* Washington, DC: Author.

American Psychiatric Association (2013). *Diagnostic and statistical manual of mental disorders* (5th ed.). Washington, DC: Author.

Anderman, E. M., & Anderman, L. H. (2010). *Classroom motivation.* Upper Saddle River, NJ: Pearson.

Anderman, E. M., Griesinger, T., & Westerfield, G. (1998). Motivation and cheating during early adolescence. *Journal of Educational Psychology, 90*(1), 84–93.

Anderman, E. M., & Mueller, C. E. (2010). Middle school transition and adolescent development. In J. L. Meece & J. S. Eccles (Eds.), *Handbook of research on schools, schooling and human development.* New York: Routledge.

Anderson, K. J., & Minke, K. M. (2007). Parent involvement in education: Toward an understanding of parents' decision making. *Journal of Educational Research, 100*(5), 311–323.

Antil, L. R., Jenkins, J. R., Wayne, S. K., & Vadasy, P. F. (1998). Cooperative learning: Prevalence, conceptualizations, and the relation between research and practice. *American Educational Research Journal, 35*(3), 419–454.

APA Zero Tolerance Task Force. (2006). *Are zero tolerance policies effective in the schools? An evidentiary review and recommendations.* Washington, DC: American Psychological Association.

Applebee, A. N., Langer, J. A., Nystrand, M., & Gamoran, A. (2003). Discussion-based approaches to developing understanding: Classroom instruction and student performance in middle and high school English. *American Educational Research Journal, 40*(3), 685–730.

Arends, R. I. (2008). *Learning to teach* (8th ed.). New York: McGraw-Hill.

Arlin, M. (1979). Teacher transitions can disrupt time flow in classrooms. *American Educational Research Journal, 16,* 42–56.

Aronson, E., Blaney, N., Stephan, C., Sikes, J., & Snapp, M. (1978). *The Jigsaw classroom.* Beverly Hills, CA: Sage.

Astor, R. A., Meyer, H. A., & Behre, W. J. (1999). Unowned places and times: Maps and interviews about violence in high schools. *American Educational Research Journal, 36*(1), 3–42.

Ayers, W. (2010). *To teach: The journey of a teacher.* New York: Teachers College Press.

Bailey, J. M., & Guskey, T. R. (2001). *Implementing student-led conferences.* Thousand Oaks, CA: Corwin.

Barry, L., & Messer, J. J. (2003). A practical application of self-management for students diagnosed with attention-deficit/hyperactivity disorder. *Journal of Positive Behavior Interventions, 5*(4), 238–248.

Baumrind, D. (1978). Parental disciplinary patterns and social competence in children. *Youth and Society, 9,* 239–276.

Belluck, P. (2006, February 5). And for perfect attendance, Johnny gets a car. *The New York Times,* pp. A1, A20.

Berreth, D., & Berman, S. (1997). The moral dimensions of schools. *Educational Leadership, 54*(8), 24–26.

Bigelow, M. L. (2012). You're the top card. *Educational Leadership, 69*(5), 88.

Blake, J. J, Butler, B. R., Lewis, C. W., & Darensbourg, A. (2011). Unmasking the inequitable discipline experiences of urban black girls: Implications for urban educational stakeholders. *Urban Review, 43,* 90–106.

Bodine, R. J., & Crawford, D. K. (1998). *The handbook of conflict resolution education: A guide to building quality programs in schools.* San Francisco: Jossey-Bass.

Bolick, C. M., & Cooper, J. M. (2006). Classroom management and technology. In C. M. Evertson & C. S. Weinstein (Eds.), *Handbook of classroom management: Research, practice, and contemporary issues* (pp. 541–558). Mahwah, NJ: Lawrence Erlbaum.

Bomer, R., Dworin, J. E., May, L., & Semingson, P. (2008). Miseducating teachers about the poor: A critical analysis of Ruby Payne's claims about poverty. *Teachers College Record, 110*(12), 2497–2531.

Bondy, E., & Ross, D. D. (2008). The teacher as warm demander. *Educational Leadership, 66*(1), 54–58.

Bosworth, K., Ford, L., & Hernandez, D. (2011). School climate factors contributing to student and faculty perceptions of safety in select Arizona schools. *Journal of School Health, 81*(4), 194–201.

Bottge, B. J., Gugerty, J. J., Serlin, R., & Moon, K. (2003). Block and traditional schedules: Effects on students with and without disabilities in high school. *NASSP Bulletin, 87,* 2–14.

Brackett, M. A., Reyes, M. R., Rivers, S. E., Elbertson, N. A., & Salovey, P. (2011). Classroom emotional climate, teacher affiliation, and student conduct. *Journal of Classroom Interaction, 46*(1), 27–36.

Bracy, N. L. (2011). Student perceptions of high-security school environments. *Youth & Society, 43*(1), 365–395.

Brady, K., Forton, M. B., Porter, D., & Wood, C. (2003). *Rules in school.* Greenfield, MA: Northeast Foundation for Children.

Brekelmans, M., Mainhard, T., den Brok, P., & Wubbels, T. (2011). Teacher control and affiliation: Do students and teachers agree? *Journal of Classroom Interaction, 46*(1), 17–26.

Brendgen, M., Wanner, B., Vitaro, F., Bukowski, W. M., & Tremblay, R. E. (2007). Verbal abuse by the teacher during childhood and academic, behavioral, and emotional adjustment in young adulthood. *Journal of Educational Psychology, 99*(1), 26–38.

Brenner, J., & Rainie, L. (2012, December 9). *Pew Internet: Broadband.* Retrieved from www. pewinternet.org/Commentary/2012/May/Pew-Internet-Broadband.aspx.

Brodey, D. (2005, September 20). Blacks join the eating-disorder mainstream. *The New York Times,* p. F5.

Brookfield, S. D., & Preskill, S. (1999). *Discussion as a way of teaching: Tools and techniques for democratic classrooms.* San Francisco: Jossey-Bass.

Brooks, D. M. (1985). The teacher's communicative competence: The first day of school. *Theory Into Practice, 24*(1), 63–70.

Brophy, J. (2010). *Motivating students to learn.* New York: Routledge.

Brophy, J. E. (1983). Classroom organization and management. *The Elementary School Journal, 83*(4), 265–285.

Brophy, J., & Rohrkemper, M. (1981). The influence of problem ownership on teachers' perceptions of and strategies for coping with problem students. *Journal of Educational Psychology, 73,* 295–311.

Brown, C. G., Rocha, E., & Sharkey, A. (2005). *Getting smarter, becoming fairer: A progressive education agenda for a stronger nation.* Washington, DC: Institute for America's Future. Retrieved from www.ourfuture.org.

Browne-Dianis, J. (2011). Stepping back from zero tolerance. *Educational Leadership, 69*(1), 24–28.

Bush, M. J., & Johnstone, W. G. (2000, April). *An observation evaluation of high school A/B block classes: Variety or monotony?* Paper presented at the annual meeting of the American Educational Research Association, New Orleans.

Cameron, J. (2001). Negative effects of reward on intrinsic motivation—A limited phenomenon: Comment on Deci, Koestner, and Ryan (2001). *Review of Educational Research, 71*(1), 29–42.

Cameron, J., Banko, K. M., & Pierce. W. D. (2001). Pervasive negative effects of rewards on intrinsic motivation: The myth continues. *The Behavior Analyst, 24*(1), 1–44.

Cameron, J., & Pierce, W. D. (1994). Reinforcement, reward, and intrinsic motivation: A meta-analysis. *Review of Educational Research, 64,* 363–423.

Campbell, L., Campbell, B., & Dickinson, D. (1999). *Teaching and learning through multiple intelligences* (2nd ed.). Boston: Allyn & Bacon.

Cangelosi, J. S. (1993, April). Cheating: Issues in elementary, middle, and secondary school classrooms. Paper presented during the symposium "Psychometric Taboo: Discussions on Cheating" at the annual meetings of the American Educational Research Association and the National Council for Measurement in Education, Atlanta.

Carbone, E. (2001). Arranging the classroom with an eye (and ear) to students with ADHD. *Teaching Exceptional Children, 34*(2), 72–81.

Cartledge, G., with Milburn, J. E. (1996). *Cultural diversity and social skills instruction: Understanding ethnic and gender differences.* Champaign, IL: Research.

Cary, S. (2007). *Working with second language learners: Answers to teachers' top ten questions* (2nd ed.). Portsmouth, NH: Heinemann.

Catalano, R. F., Haggerty, K. P., Oesterle, S., Fleming, C. B., & Hawkins, J. D. (2004). The importance of bonding to school for healthy development: Findings from the social development research group. *Journal of School Health 74*(7), 252–261.

Centers for Disease Control and Prevention (2005). *Mental health in the United States: Prevalence of diagnosis and medication treatment for attention-deficit/hyperactivity disorder—United States, 2003.* Retrieved from www.cdc.gov/mmwr/preview/mmwrhtml/mm5434a2.htm.

Centers for Disease Control and Prevention (2012, March 30). Prevalence of Autism Spectrum Disorders—Autism and Developmental Disabilities Monitoring Network, 14 Sites, United States, 2008. *Surveillance Summaries, 61*(SS03); 1–19.

CHADD. (1993). *Attention deficit disorders: An educator's guide (CHADD Facts #5).* Plantation, FL: Children and Adults with Attention Deficit Disorders.

Chandler, K. A., Chapman, C. D., Rand, M. R., & Taylor, B. M. (1998). *Students' reports of school crime: 1989 and 1995.* Washington, DC: U.S. Department of Education, Office of Educational Research and Improvement, National Center for Education Statistics, and U.S. Department of Justice, Office of Justice Programs, Bureau of Justice Statistics.

Charles, C. M., & Charles, M. G. (2004). *Classroom management for middle-grades teachers.* Boston: Pearson/Allyn & Bacon.

Chiu, M. M. (2004). Adapting teacher interventions to student needs during cooperative learning: How to improve student problem solving and time on-task. *American Educational Research Journal, 41*(2), 365–399.

Chrispeels, J. H., & Rivero, E. (2000, April). Engaging Latino families for student success: Understanding the process and impact of providing training to parents. Paper presented at the annual meeting of the American Educational Research Association, New Orleans.

Christensen, L. (2007). Building community from chaos. In W. Au, B. Bigelow, & S. Karp (Eds.), *Rethinking our classrooms: Teaching for equity and justice.* Milwaukee, WI: Rethinking Schools Limited, pp. 47–52.

Cody, A. (2013, February 14). How can teachers overcome depression and strife? [Education Week Teacher Blog: Living in Dialogue]. Retrieved from http://blogs.edweek.org/teachers/living-in-dialogue/2013/02/how_can_teachers_overcome_depr.html.

Cohen, E. G. (1972). Interracial interaction disability. *Human Relations, 25,* 9–24.

Cohen, E. G. (1994a). *Designing groupwork: Strategies for the heterogeneous classroom* (2nd ed.). New York: Teachers College Press.

Cohen, E. G. (1994b). Restructuring the classroom: Conditions for productive small groups. *Review of Educational Research, 64*(1), 1–35.

Cohen, E. G. (1998). Making cooperative learning equitable. *Educational Leadership, 56,*(1) 18–21.

Coles, A. D. (2000, June 14). Lately, teens less likely to engage in risky behaviors. *Education Week,* 6.

Connolly, L. C. (2012). Anti-gay bullying in schools—Are anti-bullying statutes the solution? *New York University Law Review, 87*(1), 248–283.

Copeland, S. R., McCall, J., Williams, C. R., Guth, C., Carter, E. W., & Fowler, S. E., et al. (2002). High school peer buddies: A win-win situation. *Teaching Exceptional Children, 35*(1), 16–21.

Corbett, D., Wilson, B., & Williams, B. (2005). No choice but success. *Educational Leadership, 62*(6), 8–12.

Cornelius-White, J. (2007). Learner-centered teacher-student relationships are effective: A meta-analysis. *Review of Educational Research, 77*(1), 113–143.

Corpus, J. H., McClintic-Gilbert, M. S., & Hayenga, A. O. (2009). Within-year changes in children's intrinsic and extrinsic motivational orientations: Contextual predictors and academic outcomes. *Contemporary Educational Psychology, 34,* 154–166.

Cothran, D. J., Kulinna, P. H., & Garrahy, D. A. (2003). "This is kind of giving a secret away . . .": Students' perspectives on effective class management. *Teaching and Teacher Education, 19,* 435–444.

Cotton, K. (2001). *New small learning communities: Findings from recent literature.* Portland, OR: Northwest Educational Research Library.

Créton, H. A., Wubbels, T., & Hooymayers, H. P. (1989). Escalated disorderly situations in the classroom and the improvement of these situations. *Teaching & Teacher Education, 5*(3), 205–215.

Cummins, J. (2000). Language, power and pedagogy: Bilingual children in the crossfire. Clevedon, UK: Multilingual Matters.

Curwin, R. L. (1995). A humane approach to reducing violence in schools. *Educational Leadership, 52*(5), 72–75.

Curwin, R. L., & Mendler, A. N. (1988). *Discipline with dignity.* Alexandria, VA: Association for Supervision and Curriculum Development.

Darling-Hammond, L., & Ifill-Lynch, O. (2006). If they'd only do their work! *Educational Leadership, 63*(5), 8–13.

Davidson, A. L. (1999). Negotiating social differences: Youths' assessments of educators' strategies. *Urban Education, 34*(3), 338–369.

Davis, H. A., Gabelman, M. M., & Wingfield, R. D. (2011). She let us be smart: Low-income African-American first-grade students' understandings of teacher closeness and influence. *Journal of Classroom Interaction, 46*(1), 4–16.

Deci, E. L., Koestner, R., & Ryan, R. M. (1999). A meta-analytic review of experiments examining the effects of extrinsic rewards on intrinsic motivation. *Psychological Bulletin, 125*(6), 627–668.

Deci, E. L., Koestner, R., & Ryan, R. M. (2001). Extrinsic rewards and intrinsic motivation in education: Reconsidered once again. *Review of Educational Research, 71*(1), 1–27.

Delpit, L. (1995). *Other people's children: Cultural conflict in the classroom.* New York: The New Press.

Delpit, L. (2002). No kinda sense. In L. Delpit & J. K. Dowdy (Eds.), *The skin that we speak: Thoughts on language and culture in the classroom* (pp. 31–48). New York: The New Press.

Deslandes, R., & Bertrand, R. (2005). Motivation of parent involvement in secondary-level schooling. *Journal of Educational Research, 98*(3), 164–175.

Diaz-Rico, L. T., & Weed, K. Z. (2009). *The crosscultural, language, and academic development handbook. A complete K-12 reference guide* (4th ed.). Boston: Allyn and Bacon.

Dieker, L. A. (2001). What are the characteristics of "effective" middle and high school co-taught teams for students with disabilities? *Preventing School Failure, 46*(1), 14–23.

Dillon, J. T. (1994). *Using discussion in classrooms.* Philadelphia: Open University Press.

Ditman, O. (2000, July/August). Online term-paper mills produce a new crop of cheaters. *Harvard Education Letter, 16*(4), 6–7.

Dotger, B. H. (2010). "I had no idea": Developing dispositional awareness and sensitivity through a cross-professional pedagogy. *Teaching and Teacher Education, 26,* 805–812.

Dowd, J. (1997). Refusing to play the blame game. *Educational Leadership, 54*(8), 67–69.

Doyle, W. (1983). Academic work. *Review of Educational Research, 53*(2), 159–200.

Doyle, W. (1985). Recent research on classroom management: Implications for teacher preparation. *Journal of Teacher Education, 36*(3), 31–35.

Doyle, W. (1986). Classroom organization and management. In M. C. Wittrock (Ed.), *Handbook of research on teaching* (pp. 392–431). New York: Macmillan.

Doyle, W. (2006). Ecological approaches to classroom management. In C. M. Evertson & C. S. Weinstein (Eds.), *Handbook of classroom management: Research, practice, and contemporary issues* (pp. 97–126). Mahwah, NJ: Lawrence Erlbaum.

Durlak, J. A., Weissberg, R. P., Dymnicki, A. B., Taylor, R. D., & Schellinger, K. B. (2011). The impact of enhancing students' social and emotional learning: A meta-analysis of school-based universal interventions. *Child Development, 82*(1), 405–432.

Dwyer, K., Osher, D., & Warger, C. (1998). *Early warning, timely response: A guide to safe schools.* Washington, DC: U.S. Department of Education.

Eccles, J. S., Wigfield, A., & Schiefele, U. (1998). Motivation to succeed. In W. Damon (Series Ed.) & N. Eisenberg (Vol. Ed.), *Handbook of child psychology: Vol. 3, Social, emotional, and personality development* (5th ed., pp. 1017–1095). New York: John Wiley.

Edwards, J. (2012). *Mapping the field: A report on expanded-time schools in America.* Boston, MA: National Center on Time and Learning.

Elias, M. (2011). Student pledges: Preventing harassment and bullying at your school. *Edutopia.* Retrieved from www.edutopia.org/blog/student-pledges-against-bullying-harrassment-maurice-elias.

Elias, M. J., & Schwab, Y. (2006). From compliance to responsibility: Social and emotional learning and classroom management. In C. M. Evertson & C. S. Weinstein (Eds.), *Handbook of classroom management: Research, practice, and contemporary issues* (pp. 309–342). Mahwah, NJ: Lawrence Erlbaum.

Eliot, M., Cornell, D., Gregory, A., & Fan, X. (2010). Supportive school climate and student willingness to seek help for bullying and threats of violence. *Journal of School Psychology, 48,* 533–553.

Elmore, R. F. (2002). The limits of "change." *Harvard Education Letter.* Retrieved from www.hepg.org/hel/article/195.

Emmer, E. T., & Evertson, C. M. (2013). *Classroom management for middle and high school teachers.* Boston: Pearson.

Emmer, E. T., & Gerwels, M. C. (2002). Cooperative learning in elementary classrooms: Teaching practices and lesson characteristics. *The Elementary School Journal, 102*(1), 5–91.

Emmer, E. T., & Gerwels, M. C. (2006). Classroom management in middle and high school classrooms. In C. M. Evertson & C. S. Weinstein (Eds.), *Handbook of classroom management: Research, practice, and contemporary issues* (pp. 407–438). Mahwah, NJ: Lawrence Erlbaum.

Epstein, J. L., & Dauber, S. L. (1991). School programs and teacher practices of parent involvement in inner-city elementary and middle schools. *The Elementary School Journal, 91*(3), 289–305.

Epstein, J. L., Sanders, M. G., Simon, B. S., Salinas, K. C., Jansorn, N. R., & Van Voorhis, F. L. (2002). *School, family, and community partnerships: Your handbook for action* (2nd ed.). Thousand Oaks, CA: Corwin.

Erikson, E. H. (1963). *Childhood and society* (2nd ed.). New York: W. W. Norton.

Esmonde, I. (2009). Ideas and identities: Supporting equity in cooperative mathematics learning. *Review of Educational Research, 79*(2), 1008–1043.

Everhart, R. B. (1983). *Reading, writing, and resistance: Adolescence and labor in a junior high school.* Boston: Routledge and Kegan Paul.

Evertson, C. M., & Emmer, E. T. (1982). Effective management at the beginning of the school year in junior high classes. *Journal of Educational Psychology, 74*(4), 485–498.

Evertson, C. M., & Weinstein, C. S. (2006). Classroom management as a field of inquiry. In C. M. Evertson & C. S. Weinstein (Eds.), *Handbook of classroom management: Research, practice, and contemporary issues* (pp. 3–16). Mahwah, NJ: Lawrence Erlbaum.

Farrington, D., & Tfoti, M. (2009). *School based programs to reduce bullying and victimization.* Washington, DC, & Oslo, Norway: Campbell Collaboration.

Finders, M., & Lewis, C. (1994). Why some parents don't come to school. *Educational Leadership, 51*(8), 50–54.

Fischer, L., Schimmel, D., & Kelly, C. (1999). *Teachers and the law.* New York: Longman.

Fisher, C. W., Berliner, D. C., Filby, N. N., Marliave, R., Cahen, L. S., & Dishaw, M. M. (1980). Teaching behaviors, academic learning time, and student achievement: An overview. In C. Denham & A. Lieberman (Eds.), *Time to learn* (pp. 7–32). Washington, DC: U.S. Department of Education.

Fisher, D. (2009). The use of instructional time in the typical high school classroom. *The Educational Forum, 73,* 168–176.

Fleming, D. S., Olenn, V., Schoenstein, R., & Eineder, D. (1997). *Moving to the block: Getting ready to teach in extended periods of learning time.* (An NEA Professional Library Publication.) Washington, DC: National Education Association.

Fleming, N. (2012). Districts deploy digital tools to engage parents. *Education Week, 32*(11), 15–17.

Flowerday, T., & Schraw, G. (2000). Teacher beliefs about instructional choice: A phenomenological study. *Journal of Educational Psychology, 92*(4), 634–645.

Fordham, S., & Ogbu, J. U. (1986). Black students' school success: Coping with the "burden of 'acting white.'" *The Urban Review, 18*(3), 176–206.

Friend, M., & Bursuck, W. D. (2002). *Including students with special needs: A practical guide for classroom teachers.* Boston: Allyn & Bacon.

Fryer, R. G., Jr. (2006, Winter). Acting white. *Education Next,* 52–59.

Fuller, M. L., & Olsen, G. (1998). *Home–school relations: Working successfully with parents and families.* Boston: Allyn & Bacon.

Gabriel, T. (2011, May 12). Speaking up in class, silently, using social media. *The New York Times.* Retrieved from www.nytimes.com/.

Gallego, M. A., Cole, M., & Laboratory of Comparative Human Cognition (2001). Classroom cultures and cultures in the classroom. In V. Richardson (Ed.), *Handbook of research on teaching* (4th ed., pp. 951–997). Washington, DC: American Educational Research Association.

Gardner, H. (1993). *Multiple intelligences: The theory in practice.* New York: Basic Books.

Gardner, H. (1995). Reflections on multiple intelligences: Myths and messages. *Phi Delta Kappan, 77*(3), 200–209.

Gastic, B. (2010). Students and school adults: Partners in keeping schools safe. *Journal of School Health, 80*(6), 269–270.

Gastic, B. (2011). Metal detectors and feeling safe at school. *Education & Urban Society, 43*(4), 486–498.

Gay, G. (2000). *Culturally responsive teaching: Theory, research, and practice.* New York: Teachers College Press.

Gay, G. (2006). Connections between classroom management and culturally responsive teaching. In C. M. Evertson & C. S. Weinstein (Eds.), *Handbook of classroom management: Research, practice, and contemporary issues* (pp. 343–370). Mahwah, NJ: Lawrence Erlbaum.

Gearheart, B. R., Weishahn, M. W., & Gearheart, C. J. (1992). *The exceptional student in the regular classroom* (5th ed.). New York: Macmillan.

Gest, S. D., & Rodkin, P. C. (2011). Teaching practices and elementary classroom peer ecologies. *Journal of Applied Developmental Psychology, 32*(5), 288–296.

Giangreco, M. F., & Doyle, M. B. (2002). Students with disabilities and paraprofessional supports: Benefits, balance, and band-aids. *Focus on Exceptional Children, 34*(7), 1–12.

Gillies, R. M. (2008). The effects of cooperative learning on junior high school students' behaviours, discourse, and learning during a science-based learning activity. *School Psychology International, 29*(3), 328–347.

Ginott, H. G. (1972). *Teacher and Child: A book for parents and teachers.* New York: Macmillan. (Re-issued by Scribner Paper Fiction, 1993.)

Ginsburg-Block, M. D., Rohrbeck, C. A., & Fantuzzo, J. W. (2006). A meta-analytic review of social, self-concept, and behavioral outcomes of peer-assisted learning. *Journal of Educational Psychology, 98*(4), 732–749.

Gonet, M. M. (1994). *Counseling the adolescent substance abuser: School-based intervention and prevention.* Thousand Oaks, CA: Sage.

Good, T. L., & Brophy, J. E. (2008). *Looking in classrooms* (10th ed.). Boston: Pearson Education.

Goodlad, J. I. (1984, 2004). *A place called school.* New York: McGraw-Hill.

Gordon, J. A. (1998). Caring through control: Reaching urban African American youth. *Journal for a Just and Caring Education, 4*(4), 418–440.

Gordon, R. L. (1997). How novice teachers can succeed with adolescents. *Educational Leadership, 54*(7), 56–58.

Gordon, T. (2003). *Teacher effectiveness training: The program proven to help teachers bring out the best in students of all ages.* New York: Three Rivers.

Grandin, T. (2007). Autism from the inside. *Educational Leadership, 64*(5), 29–32.

Graue, E., & Brown, C. P. (2003). Preservice teachers' notions of families and schooling. *Teaching and Teacher Education, 19,* 719–735.

Graziano, A. M., & Mooney, K. C. (1984). *Children and behavior therapy.* New York: Aldine.

Green, C. L., Walker, J. M. T, Hoover-Dempsey, K. V., & Sandler, H. M. (2007). Parents' motivations for involvement in children's education: An empirical test of a theoretical model of parental involvement. *Journal of Educational Psychology, 99,* 532–544.

Greenwood, G. E., & Hickman, C. W. (1991). Research and practice in parent involvement: Implications for teacher education. *The Elementary School Journal, 91*(3), 279–288.

Gregg, K., Rugg, M., & Souto-Manning, M. (2011). Fostering family-centered practices through a family-created portfolio. *The School Community Journal, 21*(1), 53–70.

Gregory, A., & Cornell, D. (2009). "Tolerating" adolescent needs: Moving beyond zero tolerance policies in high school. *Theory Into Practice, 48*(2), 106–113.

Gregory, A., Cornell, D., & Fan, X. (2011). The relationship of school structure and support to suspension rates for black and white high school students. *American Educational Research Journal, 48*(4), 904–934.

Gregory, A., Cornell, D., Fan, X., Sheras, P., Shih, T.-H., & Huang, F. (2010). Authoritative school discipline: High school practices associated with lower bullying and victimization. *Journal of Educational Psychology, 102*(2), 483–496.

Gregory, A., & Ripski, M. (2008). Adolescent trust in teachers: Implications for behavior in the high school classroom. *School Psychology Review, 37*(3), 337–353.

Grossman, H. (2004). *Classroom behavior management for diverse and inclusive schools* (3rd ed.). Lanham, MD: Rowman & Littlefield.

Grossman, H., & Grossman, S. H. (1994). *Gender issues in education.* Boston: Allyn & Bacon.

Gruber, C. D., & Onwuegbuzie, A. J. (2001). Effects of block scheduling on academic achievement among high school students. *The High School Journal, 84*(4), 32–42.

Gump, P. V. (1982). School settings and their keeping. In D. L. Duke (Ed.), *Helping teachers manage classrooms* (pp. 98–114). Alexandria, VA: Association for Supervision and Curriculum Development.

Gump, P. V. (1987). School and classroom environments. In D. Stokols & I. Altman (Eds.), *Handbook of environmental psychology* (pp. 691–732). New York: John Wiley.

Gutman, L. M., & McLoyd, V. G. (2000). Parents' management of their children's education within the home, at school, and in the community: An examination of African-American families living in poverty. *The Urban Review, 32*(1), 1–24.

Han, S., & Akiba, M. (2011). School safety, severe disciplinary actions, and school characteristics: A secondary analysis of the school survey on crime and safety. *Journal of School Leadership, 21*(2), 262–292.

Hansen, P., & Mulholland, J. A. (2005). Caring and elementary teaching: The concerns of male beginning teachers. *Journal of Teacher Education, 56*(2), 119–131.

Harmon, A. (2004, August 26). Internet gives teenage bullies weapons to wound from afar. *The New York Times,* pp. A1, A23.

Harrison, M. M. (Fall 2005). Bully on the bus. *Teaching Tolerance, 28,* 39–43.

Haynes, C. C., Chaltain, S., Ferguson, J. E., Jr., Hudson, D. L., Jr., & Thomas. O. (2003). *The first amendment in schools.* Alexandria, VA: Association of Supervision and Curriculum Development.

Henning, J. E. (2008). *The art of discussion-based teaching.* New York: Routledge.

Hidi, S., & Harackiewicz, J. M. (2000). Motivating the academically unmotivated: A critical issue for the 21st century. *Review of Educational Research, 70*(2), 151–179.

Holt, C., Hargrove, P., & Harris, S. (2011). An investigation into the life experiences and beliefs of teachers exhibiting highly effective classroom management behaviors. *Teacher Education and Practice, 24*(10), 96–113.

Hoover, J., & Oliver, R. (2008). *The bullying prevention handbook: A guide for teachers, principals and counselors.* Bloomington, IN: Solution Tree.

Hoover-Dempsey, K. V., & Sandler, H. M. (1997). Why do parents become involved in their children's education? *Review of Educational Research, 67*(1), 3–42.

Hoover-Dempsey, K. V., Walker, J. M. T., Reed, R. P., & Jones, K. P. (2002). Teachers Involving Parents (TIP): Results of an in-service teacher education program for enhancing parental involvement. *Teaching and Teacher Education, 18,* 843–867.

Horowitz, P., & Otto, D. (1973). *The teaching effectiveness of an alternate teaching facility.* Alberta, Canada: University of Alberta. Retrieved from ERIC database (ED 083242).

Howard, R. M., & Davies, L. J. (2009). Plagiarism in the Internet age. *Educational Leadership, 66*(6), 64–67.

Howell, J. C., & Lynch, J. P. (2000). *Youth gangs in schools.* Washington, DC: Office of Juvenile Justice and Delinquency Prevention, U.S. Department of Justice.

Hoy, A., & Weinstein, C. S. (2006). Student and teacher perspectives on classroom management. In C. M. Evertson and C. S. Weinstein (Eds.), *Handbook of classroom management: Research, practice, and contemporary issues* (pp. 181–219). Mahwah, NJ: Lawrence Erlbaum.

H.R. 1893—113th Congress: Keeping All Students Safe Act. (2013). Retrieved from www.govtrack.us/congress/bills/113/hr1893.

Hu, W. (2008, November 12). A school district asks: Where are the parents? *The New York Times,* p. A25.

Hughes, C. A., Ruhl, K. L., & Misra, A. (1989). Disordered students in school settings: A promise unfulfilled? *Behavioral Disorders, 14,* 250–262.

Hullena, T., & Hullena, V. (2010). Student-teacher relationships: A pathway for at-risk youth. In V. Green & S. Cherrington (Eds.), *Delving into diversity* (pp. 9–20). Hauppauge, NY: Nova Science.

Hyman, I. A. (1997). *School discipline and school violence: The teacher variance approach.* Boston: Allyn & Bacon.

Hyman, I., Kay, B., Tabori, A., Weber, M., Mahon, M., & Cohen, I. (2006). Bullying: Theory, research, and interventions. In C. Evertson & C. Weinstein (Eds.), *Handbook of classroom management: Research, practice, and contemporary issues* (pp. 855–884). Mahwah, NJ: Lawrence Erlbaum.

Irvine, J. J. (1990). *Black students and school failure: Policies, practices, and prescriptions.* New York: Greenwood.

Irvine, J. J., & Fraser, J. (1998, May 13). Warm demanders: Do national certification standards leave room for the culturally responsive pedagogy of African-American teachers? *Education Week, 17*(35), 56.

Jackson, P. W. (1990). *Life in classrooms.* New York: Teachers College Press.

Jennings, P. A., & Greenberg, M. T. (2009). The prosocial classroom: Teacher social and emotional competence in relation to student and classroom outcomes. *Review of Educational Research, 79*(1), 491–525.

Jeynes, W. H. (2007). The relationship between parental involvement and urban secondary school student academic achievement: A meta-analysis. *Urban Education, 42*(1), 82–110.

Johnson, D. W., & Johnson, R. T. (1980). Integrating handicapped students into the mainstream. *Exceptional Children, 47*(2), 90–98.

Johnson, D. W., & Johnson, R. T. (1989/90). Social skills for successful groupwork. *Educational Leadership, 47*(4), 29–33.

Johnson, D. W., & Johnson, R. T. (1999). The three Cs of school and classroom management. In H. J. Freiberg (Ed.), *Beyond behaviorism: Changing the classroom management paradigm* (pp. 119–144). Boston: Allyn & Bacon.

Johnson, D. W., & Johnson, R. T. (2004). Implementing the "Teaching Students to be Peacemakers Program." *Theory Into Practice, 43*(1), 68–79.

Johnson, D. W., & Johnson, R. T. (2005). *Teaching students to be peacemakers* (3rd ed.). Edina, MN: Interaction.

Johnson, D. W., Johnson, R. T., Holubec, E. J., & Roy, P. (1984). *Circles of learning: Cooperation in the classroom.* Alexandria, VA: Association for Supervision and Curriculum Development.

Johnson, D. W., Johnson, R. T., & Roseth, C. (2010). Cooperative learning in middle schools: Interrelationship of relationships and achievement. *Middle Grades Research Journal, 5*(1), 1–18.

Jones, F. H., Jones, P., Jones, J. L., Jones, F., & Jones, B. T. (2007). *Tools for teaching: Discipline, instruction, motivation.* Santa Cruz, CA: Fredric H. Jones.

Jones, V. F., & Jones, L. S. (2010). *Comprehensive classroom management: Creating communities of support and solving problems.* Upper Saddle River, NJ: Pearson.

Josephson Institute. (2010). *Josephson Institute's 2010 report card on the ethics of American youth.* Los Angeles: Author. Retrieved from http://charactercounts.org/programs/reportcard/2010/index.html.

Josephson Institute. (2012). *Josephson Institute's 2012 report card on the ethics of American youth.* Los Angeles: Author. Retrieved from http://charactercounts.org/programs/reportcard/2012/index.html.

Juarez, V. (2005, October 4). They dress to express. *Newsweek.* Retrieved from www.newsweek.com/they-dress-express-129581.

Kagan, S. (1989/90). The structural approach to cooperative learning. *Educational Leadership, 47*(4), 12–15.

Karweit, N. (1989). Time and learning: A review. In R. E. Slavin (Ed.), *School and classroom organization* (pp. 69–98). Hillsdale, NJ: Lawrence Erlbaum.

Katz, M. S. (1999). Teaching about caring and fairness: May Sarton's *The Small Room.* In M. S. Katz, N. Noddings, & K A. Strike (Eds.), *Justice and caring: The search for common ground in education* (pp. 59–73). New York: Teachers College Press.

Katz, S. R. (1999). Teaching in tensions: Latino immigrant youth, their teachers, and the structures of schooling. *Teachers College Record, 100*(4), 809–840.

Kazdin, A., & Rotella, C. (2009, August 11). Bullies: They can be stopped, but it takes a village. *Slate.* Retrieved from www.slate.com/id/2249424.

Keith, S., & Martin, M. E. (2005). Cyber-bullying: Creating a culture of respect in a cyber world. *Reclaiming Children and Youth, 13*(4), 224–228.

Kendrick, M. (2010). Using student collaboration to foster progressive discourse. *English Journal, 99*(5), 85–90.

Kerr, M. M., & Nelson, C. M. (2006). *Strategies for addressing behavior problems in the classroom* (5th ed.). Upper Saddle River, NJ: Pearson Prentice Hall.

Kidder, T. (1989). *Among schoolchildren.* Boston: Houghton Mifflin.

King, J. R. (1998). *Uncommon caring: Learning from men who teach young children.* New York: Teachers College.

King, L., Luberda, H., Barry, K., & Zehnder, S. (1998, April). *A case study of the perceptions of students in a small-group cooperative learning situation.* Paper presented at the Annual Conference of the American Education Research Association, San Diego, CA.

Klein, P. D. (1997). Multiplying the problems of intelligence by eight: A critique of Gardner's theory. *Canadian Journal of Education, 22*(4), 377–394.

Kleinfeld, J. (1975). Effective teachers of Eskimo and Indian students. *The School Review, 83,* 301–344.

Kline, M., & Silver, L. B. (Eds.). (2004). *The educator's guide to mental health issues in the classroom.* Baltimore: Paul H. Brookes.

Kohn, A. (1993). *Punished by rewards: The trouble with gold stars, incentive plans, As, praise, and other bribes.* Boston: Houghton Mifflin.

Kohn, A. (1996). *Beyond discipline: From compliance to community.* Alexandria, VA: Association for Supervision and Curriculum Development.

Kosciw, J. G., Greytak, E. A., Bartkiewicz, M. J., Boesen, M. J., & Palmer, N. A. (2012). *The 2011 national school climate survey: The experiences of lesbian, gay, bisexual and transgender in our nation's schools.* New York: Gay, Lesbian, and Straight Education Network. Retrieved from www.glsen.org.

Kotsopoulos, D. (2010). When collaborative is not collaborative: Supporting student learning through self-surveillance. *International Journal of Educational Research, 49,* 129–140.

Kottler, E. (1994). *Children with limited English: Teaching strategies for the regular classroom.* Thousand Oaks, CA: Corwin.

Kottler, J. A., & Kottler, E. (1993). *Teacher as counselor: Developing the helping skills you need.* Newbury Park, CA: Corwin.

Kounin, J. S. (1970). *Discipline and group management in classrooms.* New York: Holt, Rinehart & Winston.

Kralovec, E., & Buell, J. (2000). *The end of homework: How homework disrupts families, overburdens children, and limits learning.* Boston: Beacon.

Kriete, R. (2002). *The morning meeting book* (2nd ed.). Greenfield, MA: Northeast Foundation for Children.

Kutnick, P., Blatchford, P., Clark, H., McIntyre, H., & Baines, E. (2005). Teachers' understandings of the relationship between within-class (pupil) grouping and learning in secondary schools. *Educational Research, 47*(1), 1–24.

Kutnick, P., Ota, C., & Berdondini, L. (2008). Improving the effects of group working in classrooms with young school-aged children: Facilitating attainment, interaction and classroom activity. *Learning and Instruction, 18,* 83–95.

Ladson-Billings, G. (1994). *The dreamkeepers: Successful teachers of African American children.* San Francisco: Jossey-Bass.

Lal, S. R., Lal, D., & Achilles, C. M. (1993). *Handbook on gangs in schools: Strategies to reduce gang-related activities.* Newbury Park, CA: Corwin.

Landrum, T. J., & Kauffman, J. M. (2006). Behavioral approaches to classroom management. In C. M. Evertson & C. S. Weinstein (Eds.), *Handbook of classroom management: Research, practice, and contemporary issues* (pp. 47–72). Mahwah, NJ: Lawrence Erlbaum.

Landsman, J. (2006). Bearers of hope. *Educational Leadership, 63*(5), 26–32.

Lasley, T. J., Lasley, J. O., & Ward, S. H. (1989, April). Activities and desists used by more and less effective classroom managers. Paper presented at the annual meeting of the American Educational Research Association, San Francisco.

Laursen, E. K. (2008). Respectful alliances. *Reclaiming Children and Youth, 17*(1), 4–9.

Lawrence-Lightfoot, S. (2003). *The essential conversation: What parents and teachers can learn from each other.* New York: Random House.

Lee, J., & Bowen, N. K. (2006). Parent involvement, cultural capital, and the achievement gap among elementary school children. *American Educational Research Journal, 43*(2), 193–215.

Leinhardt, G., & Greeno, J. G. (1986). The cognitive skill of teaching. *Journal of Educational Psychology, 78*(2), 75–95.

Leinhardt, G., Weidman, C., & Hammond, K. M. (1987). Introduction and integration of classroom routines by expert teachers. *Curriculum Inquiry, 17*(2), 135–175.

Lepi, K. (2013). Texting in the classroom: 3 tools to do it right. *Edudemic.* Retrieved from http://www.edudemic.com/texting-in-the-classroom/.

Lepper, M., Greene, D., & Nisbett, R. E. (1973). Undermining children's intrinsic interest with extrinsic rewards: A test of the "overjustification" hypothesis. *Journal of Personality and Social Psychology, 28,* 129–137.

Lewis, C. W., Dugan, J. J., Winokur, M. A., & Cobb, R. B. (2005). The effects of block scheduling on high school academic achievement. *NASSP Bulletin, 89*(645), 72–87.

Lindeman, B. (2001). Reaching out to immigrant parents. *Educational Leadership, 58*(6), 62–66.

Lindle, J. C. (1989). What do parents want from principals and teachers? *Educational Leadership, 47*(2), 12–14.

Liptak, A. (2009a, March 23). Strip-search of girl tests limit of school policy. *The New York Times,* pp. A1, A19.

Liptak, A. (2009b, June 25). Supreme court says child's rights violated by strip search. *The New York Times,* p. A16.

Lisante, J. E. (2005, June 6). *Cyber bullying: No muscles needed.* Retrieved from sparkaction. org/content/cyber-bullying-no-muscles-needed.

Loera, G., Rueda, R., & Nakamoto, J. (2011). The association between parental involvement in reading and schooling and children's reading engagement in Latino families. *Literacy Research and Instruction, 50*(2), 133–155.

Lopez, G. R. (2001). The value of hard work: Lessons on parent involvement from an (im) migrant household. *Harvard Educational Review, 71*(3), 416–437.

Lotan, R. (2006). Managing groupwork in the heterogeneous classroom. In C. M. Evertson & C. S. Weinstein (Eds.), *Handbook of classroom management: Research, practice, and contemporary issues* (pp. 711–731). Mahwah, NJ: Lawrence Erlbaum.

Luckner, A. E., & Pianta, R. C. (2011). Teacher–student interactions in fifth grade classrooms: Relations with children's peer behavior, *Journal of Applied Developmental Psychology, 32*(5), 257–266.

Ma, H., Lu, E. Y., Turner, S., & Wan, G. (2007). An empirical investigation of cheating and digital plagiarism among middle school students. *American Secondary Education, 35*(2), 69–82.

Madden, N. A., & Slavin, R. E. (1983). Cooperative learning and social acceptance of mainstreamed academically handicapped students. *Journal of Special Education, 17,* 171–182.

Mamlin, N., & Dodd-Murphy, J. (2002). Minimizing minimal hearing loss in the schools: What every classroom teacher should know. *Preventing School Failure, 46*(2), 86–93.

Marschall, M. (2006). Parent involvement and educational outcomes for Latino students. *Review of Policy Research, 23*(5), 1053–1076.

Martin, S. H. (2002). The classroom environment and its effects on the practice of teachers. *Journal of Environmental Psychology, 22,* 139–156.

Marwick, A., & boyd, d. (2011, September 22). *The drama! Teen conflict, gossip, and bullying in networked publics.* Paper presented at Oxford Internet Institute's "A Decade in Internet Time: Symposium on the Dynamics of the Internet and Society."

Marzano, R. J., Marzano, J. S., & Pickering, D. J. (2003). *Classroom management that works: Research-based strategies for every teacher.* Alexandria, VA: Association for Supervision and Curriculum Development.

Maslow, A. H., & Mintz, N. L. (1956). The effects of esthetic surroundings: I. *Journal of Psychology, 41,* 247–254.

Mastropieri, M. A., & Scruggs, T. E. (2001). Promoting inclusion in secondary classrooms. *Learning Disability Quarterly, 24,* 265–274.

Matthews, K. (2012, April 19). *Arizona Daily Star,* p. A16.

McDougall, D. (1998). Research on self-management techniques used by students with disabilities in general education settings: A descriptive review. *Remedial and Special Education, 19*(5), 310–320.

McGarity, J. R., Jr., & Butts, D. P. (1984). The relationship among teacher classroom management behavior, student engagement and student achievement of middle and high school science students of varying aptitude. *Journal of Research in Science Teaching, 21*(1), 55–61.

McIntosh, K., Herman, K., Sanford, A., McGraw, K., & Florence, K. (2004). Teaching transitions: Techniques for promoting success *between* lessons. *Teaching Exceptional Children, 37*(1), 32–38.

McNaughton, D., & Vostal, B. R. (2010). Using active listening to improve collaboration with parents: The LAFF don't CRY strategy. *Intervention in School and Clinic, 45,* 251–256.

Meadan, H., & Monda-Amaya, L. (2008). Collaboration to promote social competence for students with mild disabilities in the general classroom: A structure for providing social support. *Intervention in School and Clinic, 43*(3), 158–167.

Mehan, H. (1979). *Learning lessons: Social organization in a classroom.* Cambridge, MA: Harvard University.

Meichenbaum, D. (1977). *Cognitive behavior modification.* New York: Plenum.

Miller, E. (1994). Peer mediation catches on, but some adults don't. *Harvard Education Letter, 10*(3), 8.

Minke, K. M., & Anderson, K. J. (2003). Restructuring routine parent-teacher conferences: The family-school conference model. *The Elementary School Journal, 104*(6), 49–69.

Mitchem, K. J., Young, K. R., West, R. P., & Benyo, J. (2001). CWPASM: A classwide peer-assisted self-management program for general education classrooms. *Education & Treatment of Children, 24*(2), 111–140.

Morrell, E., & Duncan-Andrade, J. M. R. (2002). Promoting academic literacy with urban youth through engaging hip-hop culture. *English Journal, 91*(6), 88–92.

Morrell, E., & Duncan-Andrade, J. (2004). What they do learn in school: Using hip-hop as a bridge between youth culture and canonical poetry texts. In J. Mahiri (Ed.), *What they don't learn in school: Literacy in the lives of urban youth* (pp. 247–268). New York: Peter Lang.

Motz, L. L., Biehle, J. T., & West, S. S. (2007). *NSTA guide to planning school science facilities.* Arlington, VA: NSTA.

Mulryan, C. M. (1992). Student passivity during cooperative small groups in mathematics. *Journal of Educational Research, 85*(5), 261–273.

Murawski, W. W., & Dieker, L. A. (2004). Tips and strategies for co-teaching at the secondary level. *Teaching Exceptional Children, 36*(5), 52–58.

Murdock, T. B., & Miller, A. (2003). Teachers as sources of middle school students' motivational identity: Variable-centered and person-centered analytic approaches. *The Elementary School Journal, 103*(4), 383–399.

Murray, C. (2004). Clarifying collaborative roles in urban high schools: General educators' perspectives. *Teaching Exceptional Children, 36*(5), 44–51.

Myles, B. S., Gagnon, E., Moyer, S. A., & Trautman, M. L. (2004). Asperger syndrome. In F. M. Kline & L. B. Silver (Eds.), *The educator's guide to mental health issues in the classroom* (pp. 75–100). Baltimore: Paul H. Brookes.

Naber, P. A., May, D. C., Decker, S. H., Minor, K. I., & Wells, J. B. (2006). Are there gangs in schools? *Journal of School Violence, 5*(2), 53–72.

National Coalition of Homeless Children and Youth. (2007). *Fact Sheet #10, August 2007.*

National Commission on Excellence in Education. (1983). *A nation at risk: The imperative for educational reform.* Washington, DC: Government Printing Office.

National Crime Prevention Council. (2009). *What parents can do about cyberbullying.* Retrieved from www.ncpc.org/topics/cyberbullying/stop-cyberbullying.

National Dissemination Center for Children with Disabilities. (2010). *Pervasive developmental disorders.* Fact Sheet 20. Retrieved from http://nichcy.org/disability/specific/autism.

National Education Commission on Time and Learning. (1994). *Prisoner of time.* Washington, DC: Government Printing Office.

National Research Council, Committee on Increasing High School Students' Engagement and Motivation to Learn. (2004). *Engaging schools: Fostering high school students' motivation to learn.* Washington, DC: National Academies Press.

Nereim, V., & Rosenthal, L. (2011, June 14). Court backs students' rights to parody principals online. *Pittsburgh Post-Gazette.*

New Jersey v. T.L.O., 105 S. Ct. 733 (1985).

Newby, T. (1991). Classroom motivation: Strategies of first-year teachers. *Journal of Educational Psychology, 83,* 195–200.

Newsam, B. S. (1992). *Complete student assistance program handbook.* West Nyack, NY: The Center for Applied Research in Education.

Nichols, J. D. (2005). Block-scheduled high schools: Impact on achievement in English and language arts. *Journal of Educational Research, 98*(5), 299–309.

Nieto, S. (2002). *Language, culture, and teaching: Critical perspectives for a new century.* Mahwah, NJ: Lawrence Erlbaum.

Nieto, S., & Bode, P. (2008). *Affirming diversity: The sociopolitical context of multicultural education* (5th ed.). Boston: Allyn & Bacon.

Ninness, H. A. C., Fuerst, J., Rutherford, R. D., & Glenn, S. S. (1991). Effects of self-management training and reinforcement on the transfer of improved conduct in the absence of supervision. *Journal of Applied Behavior Analysis, 24*(3), 499–508.

Noguera, P. A. (1995). Preventing and producing violence: A critical analysis of responses to school violence. *Harvard Educational Review, 65*(2), 189–212.

Nucci, L. (2006). Classroom management for moral and social development. In C. M. Evertson & C. S. Weinstein (Eds.), *Handbook of classroom management: Research, practice, and contemporary issues* (pp. 711–731). Mahwah, NJ: Lawrence Erlbaum.

Oakes, J., & Lipton, M. (2007). *Teaching to change the world.* Boston: McGraw-Hill.

O'Brien, T. (2010, Winter). Learning to cheat. *Ed.: Harvard Graduate School of Education Alumni Magazine.* Retrieved from www.gse.harvard.edu/news-impact/2010/01/a-to-b-why-i-got-into-education-3/?issue=9.

O'Donnell, A., & O'Kelly, J. (1994). Learning from peers: Beyond the rhetoric of positive results. *Educational Psychology Review, 6*(4), 321–349.

Olweus, D. (2003). A profile of bullying at school. *Educational Leadership, 60*(6), 12–17.

Oortwijn, M. B., Boekaerts, M., Vedder, P., & Fortuin, J. (2008). The impact of a cooperative learning experience on pupils' popularity, non-cooperativeness, and interethnic bias in multiethnic elementary schools. *Educational Psychology, 28*(2), 211–221.

Osterman, K. F. (2000). Students' need for belonging in the school community. *Review of Educational Research, 70*(3), 323–367.

Ostrander, R. (2004). Oppositional defiant disorder and conduct disorder. In F. M. Kline & L. B. Silver (Eds.), *The educator's guide to mental health issues in the classroom* (pp. 267–286). Baltimore: Paul H. Brookes.

Pastor, P. N., & Reuben, C. A. (2008). Diagnosed attention deficit hyperactivity disorder and learning disability: United States 2004–2006. *National Center for Health Statistics, Vital Health Statistics, 10*(237).

Patall, E. A., Cooper, H., & Robinson, J. C. (2008). Parent involvement in homework: A research synthesis. *Review of Educational Research, 78*(4), 1039–1101.

Patall, E. A., Cooper, H., & Wynn, S. R. (2010). The effectiveness and relative importance of choice in the classroom. *Journal of Educational Psychology, 102*(4), 896–915.

Patrick, H., Ryan, A. M., & Kaplan, A. (2007). Early adolescents' perceptions of the classroom social environment, motivational beliefs, and engagement. *Journal of Educational Psychology, 99*(1), 83–98.

Patrikakou, E. N., & Weissberg, R. P. (2000). Parents' perceptions of teacher outreach and parent involvement in children's education. *Journal of Prevention and Intervention in the Community 20,* 103–119.

Payne, R. K. (2005). *A framework for understanding poverty* (4th rev. ed.). Highlands, TX: aha! Process.

Payne, R., (2008). Nine powerful practices. *Educational Leadership, 65*(7), 48–52.

Peariso, J. F. (2008). Multiple intelligences or multiply misleading: The critic's view of the multiple intelligences theory. *Educational Resources Information Center.* Retrieved from ERIC database (ED500515).

Peguero, A. A., & Shekarkhar, Z. (2011). Latino/a student misbehavior and school punishment. *Hispanic Journal of Behavioral Sciences, 33*(1), 54–70.

Pelco, L. E., & Ries, R. (1999). Teachers' attitudes and behaviors towards family-school partnerships: What school psychologists need to know. *School Psychology International, 20*(3), 265–278.

Pell, T., Galton, M., Steward, S., Page, C., & Hargreaves, L. (2007). Promoting group work at key stage 3: Solving an attitudinal crisis among young adolescents? *Research Papers in Education, 22*(3), 309–322.

Peters v. Rome City School District, 7M N.Y.S. 2d 867 (N.Y. AD4 Dept. 2002).

Phillips, M. (2013, May 23). A curriculum of concerns. *Edutopia.* Retrieved from www.edutopia.org/blog/a-curriculum-of-concerns-mark-phillips.

Pollack, W. S., Modzelski, W., & Rooney, G. (2008). *Prior knowledge of potential school-based violence: Information students learn may prevent a targeted attack.* U.S. Secret Service and Department of Education. Washington, DC: U.S. Government Printing Office.

Portner, J. (2000, April 12). School violence down, report says, but worry high. *Education Week, 3.*

Powell, R. R., Zehm, S. J., & Kottler, J. A. (1995). *Classrooms under the influence: Addicted families/addicted students.* Thousand Oaks, CA: Corwin.

Powers, K. M. (2006). An exploratory study of cultural identity and culture-based educational programs for urban American Indian students. *Urban Education, 41*(1), 20–49.

Preidt, R. (2013a, February 1). School bullies often popular, survey finds. *HealthDay.* Retrieved from http://consumer.healthday.com/Article.asp?AID=672882.

Preidt, R. (2013b, May 5). 16 percent of U.S. high schoolers victims of cyberbullying: Study. HealthDay. Retrieved from http://consumer.healthday.com/Article.asp?AID=676059.

Proshansky, E., & Wolfe, M. (1974). The physical setting and open education. *School Review, 82,* 557–574.

Quarles, C. L. (1989). *School violence: A survival guide for school staff, with emphasis on robbery, rape, and hostage taking.* Washington, DC: National Education Association.

Queen, J. A. (2000). Block scheduling revised. *Phi Delta Kappan, 82*(3), 214–222.

Reeve, J. (2006). Extrinsic rewards and inner motivation. In C. M. Evertson & C. S. Weinstein (Eds.), *Handbook of classroom management: Research, practice, and contemporary issues* (pp. 645–664). Mahwah, NJ: Lawrence Erlbaum.

Resnick, M. D., Ireland, M., & Borowsky, I. (2004). Youth violence perpetration: What protects? What predicts? Findings from the National Longitudinal Study of Adolescent Health. *Journal of Adolescent Health, 35*(5), 424.e1–424.e10.

Ridley, D. S., & Walther, B. (1995). *Creating responsible learners: The role of a positive classroom environment.* Washington, DC: American Psychological Association.

Rief, S. F. (1993). *How to reach and teach ADD/ADHD children.* West Nyack, NY: The Center for Applied Research in Education.

Rioux, J. W., & Berla, N. (1993). *Innovations in parent and family involvement.* Princeton Junction, NJ: Eye on Education.

Robers, S., Kemp, J., & Truman, J. (2013). *Indicators of School Crime and Safety: 2012* (NCES 2013-036/NCJ 241446). National Center for Education Statistics, U.S. Department of Education, and Bureau of Justice Statistics, Office of Justice Programs, U.S. Department of Justice. Washington, DC.

Robinson, S., & Ricord Griesemer, S. M. (2006). Helping individual students with problem behavior. In C. M. Evertson & C. S. Weinstein (Eds.), *Handbook of classroom management: Research, practice, and contemporary issues* (pp. 787–802). Mahwah, NJ: Lawrence Erlbaum.

Roby, T. W. (1988). Models of discussion. In J. T. Dillon (Ed.), *Questioning and discussion—A multidisciplinary study* (pp. 163–191). Norwood, NJ: Ablex.

Roeser, R. W., Eccles, J. S., & Sameroff, A. J. (2000). School as a context of early adolescents' academic and social–emotional development: A summary of research findings. *The Elementary School Journal, 100*(5), 443–471.

Rolland, R. G. (2012). Synthesizing the evidence on classroom goal structures in middle and secondary schools: A meta-analysis and narrative review. *Review of Educational Research, 82*(4), 396–435.

Romero, M., Mercado, C., & Vasquez-Faria, J. A. (1987). Students of limited English proficiency. In V. Richardson-Koehler (Ed.), *Educators' handbook: A research perspective* (pp. 348–369). New York: Longman.

Roorda, D. L., Koomen, H. M. Y., Spilt, J. L., & Oort, F. J. (2011). The influence of affective teacher-student relationships on students' school engagement and achievement: A meta-analytic approach. *Review of Educational Research, 81*(4), 493–529.

Rosenholtz, S. J., & Cohen, E. G. (1985). Status in the eye of the beholder. In J. Berger & M. Zelditch, Jr. (Eds.), *Status, rewards, and influence* (pp. 430–444). San Francisco: Jossey Bass.

Rosenshine, B. (1980). How time is spent in elementary classrooms. In C. Denham and A. Lieberman (Eds.), *Time to learn* (pp. 107–126). Washington, DC: U.S. Department of Education.

Rosenshine, B. V. (1986). Synthesis of research on explicit teaching. *Educational Leadership, 43*(7), 60–69.

Ross, R. P. (1985). *Elementary school activity segments and the transitions between them: Responsibilities of teachers and student teachers* (Unpublished doctoral dissertation). University of Kansas.

Rothstein-Fisch, C., & Trumbull, E. (2008). *Managing diverse classrooms.* Alexandria, VA: ASCD.

Rowe, M. B. (1974). Wait-time and rewards as instructional variables, their influence on language, logic, and fate control: Part 1: Wait time. *Journal of Research in Science Teaching, 11,* 291–308.

Rowe, M. B. (1986). Wait time: Slowing down may be a way of speeding up! *Journal of Teacher Education, 37*(1), 43–50.

Rubin, B. C. (2003). Unpacking detracking: When progressive pedagogy meets students' social worlds. *American Educational Research Journal, 40*(2), 539–573.

Ryan, A., & Patrick, H. (2001). The classroom social environment and changes in adolescents' motivation and engagement during middle school. *American Educational Research Journal, 38*(2), 437–460.

Ryan, J. B., Peterson, R. L., & Rozalski, M. (2007). State policies concerning the use of seclusion timeout in schools. *Education and Treatment of Children, 30*(3), 215–239.

Ryan, R. M., & Deci, E. L. (2000). Intrinsic and extrinsic motivations: Classic definitions and new directions. *Contemporary Educational Psychology, 25,* 54–67.

Sadker, D., Sadker, M., & Zittleman, K. (2009). *Still failing at fairness: How gender bias cheats girls and boys in school and what we can do about it.* New York: Simon & Schuster.

Sapon-Shevin, M. (2010). *Because we can change the world: A practical guide to building cooperative, inclusive classroom communities.* Thousand Oaks, CA: Corwin.

Savage, T. V. (1999). *Teaching self-control through management and discipline* (2nd ed.). Boston: Allyn & Bacon.

Scarcella, R. (1990). *Teaching language minority students in the multicultural classroom.* Upper Saddle River, NJ: Prentice Hall Regents.

Schaps, E. (2003). Creating a school community. *Educational Leadership, 60*(60), 31–33.

Schimmel, D. (2006). Classroom management, discipline, and the law: Clarifying confusions about students' rights and teachers' authority. In C. M. Evertson & C. S. Weinstein (Eds.), *Handbook of classroom management: Research, practice, and contemporary issues* (pp. 1005–1020). Mahwah, NJ: Lawrence Erlbaum.

Schlosser, L. K. (1992). Teacher distance and student disengagement: School lives on the margin. *Journal of Teacher Education, 43*(2), 128–140.

Schlozman, S. C. (2001). Too sad to learn? *Educational Leadership, 59*(1), 80–81.

Schmollinger, C. S., Opaleski, K. A., Chapman, M. L., Jocius, R., & Bell, S. (2002). How do you make your classroom an inviting place for students to come back to each year? *English Journal, 91*(6), 20–22.

Schniedewind, N., & Davidson, E. (2000). Differentiating cooperative learning. *Educational Leadership, 58*(1), 24–27.

Schultz, S. (2012). Your story is important. *Educational Leadership, 69*(5), 88.

Schumm, J. S., & Vaughn, S. (1992). Planning for mainstreamed special education students: Perceptions of general classroom teachers. *Exceptionality, 3,* 81–98.

Scruggs, T. E., & Mastropieri, M. A. (1996). Teacher perceptions of mainstreaming/inclusion, 1958–1995: A research synthesis. *Exceptional Children, 63,* 59–74.

Shakeshaft, C., Mandel, L., Johnson, Y. M., Sawyer, J., Hergenroter, M. A., & Barber, E. (1997). Boys call me cow. *Educational Leadership, 55*(2), 22–25.

Shanley, M. (1999, October 22). Letter to the editor. *The New York Times,* A26.

Shapiro, E. S., DuPaul, G. J., & Bradley-Klug, K. L. (1998). Self-management as a strategy to improve the classroom behavior of adolescents with ADHD. *Journal of Learning Disabilities, 31*(6), 545–555.

Shariff, S. (2004). Keeping schools out of court: Legally defensible models of leadership. *The Educational Forum, 68,* 222–232.

Sheets, R. H. (1996). Urban classroom conflict: Student-teacher perception: Ethnic integrity, solidarity, and resistance. *Urban Review, 28*(2), 165–183.

Shernoff, D. J., Czikszentmihalyi, M., Schneider, B., & Shernoff, E. S. (2003). Student engagement in high school classrooms from the perspective of flow theory. *School Psychology Quarterly, 18*(2), 158–176.

Shirley, E. L. M., & Cornell, D. G. (2011). The contributions of student perceptions of school climate to understanding the disproportionate punishment of African American students in a middle school. *School Psychology International, 33*(2), 115–134.

Shortt, T. L., & Thayer, Y. V. (1998/99). Block scheduling can enhance school climate. *Educational Leadership, 56*(4), 76–81.

Shulman, J. H., Lotan, R. A., & Whitcomb, J. A. (Eds.). (1998). *Groupwork in diverse classrooms: A casebook for educators.* New York: Teachers College Press.

Sifferlin, A. (2012, March 30). *"Cinnamon challenge," popular with teens, proves risky.* Retrieved from http://healthland.time.com.

Sileo, T. W., & Prater, M. A. (1998). Creating classroom environments that address the linguistic and cultural backgrounds of students with disabilities: An Asian Pacific American perspective. *Remedial and Special Education, 19*(6), 323–337.

Simon, D. (2011, June 8). Twitter finds a place in the classroom. *CNN Tech.* Retrieved from www.cnn.com/TECH/.

Simpson, H. (2010, February 16). Judge: Students' Facebook rant "protected speech." *Miami Herald.*

Skiba, R., Horner, R., Gung, C. G., Rausch, M. K., May, S. L., & Tobin, T. (2008, March). *Race is not neutral: A national investigation of African American and Latino disproportionality in school discipline.* Paper presented at the Annual Meeting of the American Educational Research Association, New York.

Skiba, R., Horner, R., Gung, C. G., Rausch, M. K., May, S. L., & Tobin, T. (2011). Race is not neutral: A national investigation of African American and Latino disproportionality in school discipline. *School Psychology Review, 40*(1), 85–107.

Skiba, R. J., Michael, R. S., Nardo, A. C., & Peterson, R. (2002). The color of discipline: Sources of racial and gender disproportionality in school punishment. *Urban Review, 34,* 317–342.

Skiba, R. J., & Rausch, M. K. (2006). Zero tolerance, suspension, and expulsion: Questions of equity and effectiveness. In C. M. Evertson & C. S. Weinstein (Eds.), *Handbook of classroom management: Research, practice, and contemporary issues* (pp. 1063–1089). Mahwah, NJ: Lawrence Erlbaum.

Slavin, R. (1991). *Student team learning: A practical guide to cooperative learning* (3rd ed.). Washington, DC: National Education Association.

Slavin, R. E. (1995). *Cooperative learning: Theory, research, and practice* (2nd ed.). Boston: Allyn & Bacon.

Smith, B. W., & Sugai, G. (2000). A self-management functional assessment-based behavior support plan for a middle school student with EBD. *Journal of Positive Behavior Interventions, 2*(4), 208–217.

Smith, E. (2002). Ebonics: A case history. In L. Delpit & J. K. Dowdy (Eds.), *The skin that we speak: Thoughts on language and culture in the classroom* (pp. 15–30). New York: The New Press.

Smith, M. S., Hughes, E. K., Engle, R. A., & Stein, M. K. (2009). Orchestrating discussions. *Mathematics Teaching in the Middle School, 14*(9), 548–556.

Sobel, A., & Kugler, E. G. (2007). Building partnerships with immigrant parents. *Educational Leadership, 64*(6), 62–66.

Sommer, R., & Olson, H. (1980). The soft classroom. *Environment & Behavior, 12*(1), 3–16.

Soodak, L. C., & McCarthy, M. R. (2006). Classroom management in inclusive settings. In C. M. Evertson & C. S. Weinstein (Eds.), *Handbook of classroom management: Research, practice, and contemporary issues* (pp. 461–490). Mahwah, NJ: Lawrence Erlbaum.

Southern Poverty Law Center. (2004, September). Hate among youth becomes widespread. *SPLC Report, 34*(3), 1.

Souvignier, E., & Kronenberger, J. (2007). Cooperative learning in third graders' jigsaw groups for mathematics and science with and without questioning training. *British Journal of Educational Psychology, 77*, 755–771.

Steele, F. I. (1973). *Physical settings and organization development.* Reading, MA: Addison-Wesley.

Stefkovich, J. A., & Miller, J. A. (1998, April). *Law enforcement officers in public schools: Student citizens in safe havens?* Paper presented at the conference of the American Educational Research Association, San Diego, CA.

Sterzing, P. R., Shattuck, P. T., Narendorf, S. C., Wagner, M., & Cooper, B. P. (2012, November). Bullying involvement and autism spectrum disorders: Prevalence and correlates of bullying involvement among adolescents with an autism spectrum disorder. *JAMA Pediatrics,* 1–7. Retrieved from http://archpedi.jamanetwork.com/article.aspx?articleid=1355390&resultClick=3.

Stipek, D. J. (2002). *Motivation to learn: Integrating theory and practice* (4th ed.). Boston: Allyn & Bacon.

Stodolsky, S. S. (1984). Frameworks for studying instructional processes in peer work groups. In P. L. Peterson, L. C. Wilkinson, & M. Hallinan (Eds.), *The social context of instruction* (pp. 107–124). New York: Academic Press.

Stodolsky, S. S. (1988). *The subject matters: Classroom activity in math and social studies.* Chicago: University of Chicago Press.

Strauss, S., with Espeland, P. (1992). *Sexual harassment and teens: A program for positive change.* Minneapolis, MN: Free Spirit.

Strom, P. S., & Strom, R. D. (2005). Cyberbullying by adolescents: A preliminary assessment. *The Educational Forum, 70*(1), 21–36.

Strom, P. S., & Strom, R. D. (2012). Teamwork skills assessment for cooperative learning. *Educational Research and Evaluation: An International Journal on Theory and Practice, 17*(4), 233–251

Strong-Wilson, T., & Ellis, J. (2007). Children and place: Reggio Emilia's environment as third teacher. *Theory Into Practice, 46*(1), 40–47.

Struyk, R. (2006). Gangs in our schools: Identifying gang indicators in our school population. *Clearing House, 8*(1), 11–13.

Sugai, G., & Simonsen, B. (2012, June 19). *Positive behavioral interventions and supports: History, defining features, and misconceptions.* Retrieved from www.pbis.org/school/pbis_revisited.aspx.

Swap, S. M. (1993). *Developing home–school partnerships: From concepts to practice.* New York: Teachers College Press.

Tannen, D. (1995). The power of talk: Who gets heard and why. *Harvard Business Review, 73*(5), 138–148.

Tarr, P. (2004). Consider the walls. *Young Children, 59*(3), 88–92.

Telem, M., & Pinto, S. (2006). Information technology's impact on school-parents and parents-student interrelations: A case study. *Computers & Education, 47*(3), 260–279.

Thomas, E. E., & Sassi, K. (2011). An ethical dilemma: Talking about plagiarism and academic integrity in the digital age. *English Journal, 100*(6), 47–53.

Thomas, K. M., & McGee, C. D. (2012). The only thing we have to fear is . . . 120 characters. *TechTrends, 56*(1), 19–33.

Thompson, B. (2008). Characteristics of parent-teacher e-mail communication. *Communication Education, 57*(2), 201–223.

Thompson, G. L. (2004). *Through ebony eyes: What teachers need to know but are afraid to ask about African American students.* San Francisco: Jossey-Bass.

Thornburg, D. D. (2007). *Campfires in cyberspace: Primordial metaphors for learning in the 21st century.* Retrieved from http://www.usdla.org/html/journal/JUN01_Issue/article01.html.

Tomlinson, C. A. (1999). *The differentiated classroom: Responding to the needs of all learners.* Alexandria, VA: Association for Supervision and Curriculum Development.

Tomlinson, C. A. (2001). *How to differentiate instruction in mixed-ability classrooms* (2nd ed.). Alexandria, VA: Association for Supervision and Curriculum Development.

Trueba, H. T., Cheng, L. R. L., & Ima, K. (1993). *Myth or reality: Adaptive strategies of Asian Americans in California.* Washington, DC: Falmer.

Trumbull, E., Rothstein-Fisch, C., Greenfield, P. M., & Quiroz, B. (2001). *Bridging cultures between home and school: A guide for teachers.* Mahwah, NJ: Lawrence Erlbaum.

Trump, K. (1993). Tell teen gangs: School's out. *American School Board Journal, 180*(7), 39–42.

U.S. Department of Education, Office for Civil Rights. (2012). *Title VI enforcement highlights.* Washington, DC: Author.

Urdan, T., & Schoenfelder, E. (2006). Classroom effects on student motivation: Goal structures, social relationships, and competence beliefs. *Journal of School Psychology, 44*(5), 331–349.

Valentine, G. (1998, Fall). Lessons from home (interview with Lisa Delpit). *Teaching Tolerance, 7*(2), 15–19.

Valenzuela, A. (1999). *Subtractive schooling: U.S.–Mexican youth and the politics of caring.* Albany: State University of New York.

Valli, L., Croninger, R. G., & Walters, K. (2007). Who (else) is the teacher? Cautionary notes on teacher accountability systems. *American Journal of Education, 113*(4), 635–662.

Vaughn, S., Bos, C. S., & Schumm, J. S. (2003). *Teaching exceptional, diverse, and at-risk students in the general education classroom.* Boston: Allyn & Bacon.

Vaughn, S., Gersten, R., & Chard, D. J. (2000). The underlying message in LD intervention research: Findings from research syntheses. *Exceptional Children, 67*(1), 99–114.

Villa, R. A., Thousand, J. S., & Nevin, A. I. (2008). *A guide to co-teaching: Practical tips for facilitating student learning* (2nd ed.). Thousand Oaks, CA: Corwin.

Villegas, A. M., & Lucas, T. (2007). The culturally responsive teacher. *Educational Leadership, 64*(6), 28–33.

Vossekuil, B., Fein, R., Reddy, M., Borum, R., & Modzeleski, W. (2002). *The final report and findings of the Safe School Initiative: Implications for the prevention of school attacks in the United States.* Washington, DC: U.S. Secret Service and the U.S. Department of Education. Retrieved from www.secretservice.gov/ntac/ssi_final_report.pdf.

Walker, C. O., & Greene, B. A. (2009). The relations between student motivational beliefs and cognitive engagement in high school. *Journal of Educational Research, 102*(6), 463–471.

Walker, H. M., Colvin, G., & Ramsey, E. (1995). *Antisocial behavior in school: Strategies and best practices.* Pacific Grove, CA: Brooks/Cole.

Walker, J. M. T. (2008). Looking at teacher practices through the lens of parenting style. *The Journal of Experimental Education, 76*(2), 218–240.

Walker, J. M. T. (Ed.) (2009). Authoritative classroom management: How control and nurturance work together. *Theory Into Practice, 48*(2), 122–129.

Walker, J. M. T., & Dotger, B. H. (2012). Because wisdom can't be told: Using comparison of simulated parent-teacher conferences to assess teacher candidates' readiness for family-school partnership. *Journal of Teacher Education, 63*(1), 62–75.

Walker, J. M. T., & Hoover-Dempsey. K. V. (2008). Parent involvement. In T. L Good (Ed.), *21st century education: A reference handbook* (pp. 383–392). Thousand Oaks, CA: Sage.

Walker, J. M. T., Ice, C. L., & Hoover-Dempsey, K. V. (2011). Latino parents' motivations for involvement in their children's schooling: An exploratory study. *The Elementary School Journal, 111*(3), 409–429.

Walkington, C. A. (2012, April). *Context personalization in algebra: Supporting connections between relevant stories and symbolic representations.* Paper presented at the annual meeting of the American Educational Research Association, Vancouver, British Columbia.

Wallace, T., Anderson, A. R., Bartholomay, T., & Hupp, S. (2002). An ecobehavioral examination of high school classrooms that include students with disabilities. *Exceptional Children, 68*(3), 345–359.

Walsh, M. (1999, June 2). Harassment ruling poses challenges. *Education Week, 18*(38), 1, 22.

Walsh, M. (2000, March 8). Law update: A fine line between dangerous and harmless student expression. *Education Week,* 14.

Walters, L. S. (2000). Putting cooperative learning to the test. *Harvard Education Letter, 16*(3), 1–6.

Ware, F. (2006). Warm demander pedagogy: Culturally responsive teaching that supports a culture of achievement for African American students. *Urban Education, 41*(4), 427–456.

Watson, M., & Battistich, V. (2006). Building and sustaining caring communities. In C. M. Evertson and C. S. Weinstein (Eds.), *Handbook of classroom management: Research, practice, and contemporary issues* (pp. 253–280). Mahwah, NJ: Lawrence Erlbaum.

Way, S. M. (2011). School discipline and disruptive classroom behavior: The moderating effects of student perceptions. *The Sociological Quarterly, 52*(3), 346–375.

Webb, N. M. (1984). Sex differences in interaction and achievement in cooperative small groups. *Journal of Educational Psychology, 76,* 33–44.

Webb, N. M., & Farivar, S. (1994). Promoting helping behavior in cooperative small groups in middle school mathematics. *American Educational Research Journal, 31*(2), 369–395.

Webb, N. M., & Mastergeorge, A. M. (2003). The development of students' helping behavior and learning in peer-directed small groups. *Cognition and Instruction, 21*(4), 361–428.

Webb, N. M., Nemer, K. M., & Ing, M. (2006). Small group reflections: Parallels between teacher discourse and student behavior in peer-directed groups. *The Journal of the Learning Sciences, 15*(1), 63–119.

Weiner, L. (1999). *Urban teaching: The essentials.* New York: Teachers College Press.

Weinstein, C. S. (1982). Privacy-seeking behavior in an elementary classroom. *Journal of Environmental Psychology, 2,* 23–35.

Weinstein, C. S., Curran, M., & Tomlinson-Clarke, S. (2003). Culturally responsive classroom management: Awareness into action. *Theory Into Practice, 42*(4), 269–276.

Weinstein, C. S., Tomlinson-Clarke, S., & Curran, M. (2004). Toward a conception of culturally responsive classroom management. *Journal of Teacher Education, 55*(1), 25–38.

Weissbourd, R., & Jones, S. (2012). Joining hands against bullying. *Educational Leadership, 70*(2), 26–31.

Wentzel, K. R. (1997). Student motivation in middle school: The role of perceived pedagogical caring. *Journal of Educational Psychology, 89*(3), 411–419.

Wentzel, K. R. (1998). Social relationships and motivation in middle school: The role of parents, teachers, and peers. *Journal of Educational Psychology, 90*(2), 202–209.

Wentzel, K. R. (2006). A social motivation perspective for classroom management. In C. M. Evertson & C. S. Weinstein (Eds.), *Handbook of classroom management: Research, practice, and contemporary issues* (pp. 619–644). Mahwah, NJ: Lawrence Erlbaum.

Wheldall, K., & Lam, Y. Y. (1987). Rows versus tables. II. The effects of two classroom seating arrangements on classroom disruption rate, on-task behaviour and teacher behaviour in three special school classes. *Educational Psychology, 7*(4), 303–312.

White, J. W. (2011). Resistance to classroom participation: Minority students, academic discourse, cultural conflicts, and issues of representation in whole class discussions. *Journal of Language, Identity and Education, 10*(4), 250–265.

Wigfield, A., & Eccles, J. S. (2000). Expectancy-value theory of achievement motivation. *Contemporary Educational Psychology, 25*(1), 68–81.

Williams, M. (1993). Actions speak louder than words: What students think. *Educational Leadership, 51*(3), 22–23.

Williams, R. L., & Stockdale, S. L. (2004). Classroom motivation strategies for prospective teachers. *The Teacher Educator, 39*(3), 212–230.

Wlodkowski, R. J. (1983). *Motivational opportunities for successful teaching (Leader's guide).* Phoenix, AZ: Universal Dimensions.

Wodrich, D. L. (2000). *Attention-deficit/hyperactivity disorder: What every parent wants to know* (2nd ed.). Baltimore: Paul Brookes.

Wolfgang, C. H. (1999). *Solving discipline problems: Methods and models for today's teachers* (4th ed.). Boston: Allyn & Bacon.

Woolfolk, A. E. (2007). *Educational Psychology* (10th ed.). Boston: Pearson Education/Allyn & Bacon.

Wubbels, T., Brekelmans, M., den Brok, P., & van Artwijk, J. (2006). An interpersonal perspective on classroom management in secondary classrooms in the Netherlands. In C. M. Evertson & C. S. Weinstein (Eds.), *Handbook of classroom management: Research, practice, and contemporary issues,* Mahwah, NJ: Lawrence Erlbaum.

Wubbels, T., & Levy, J. (1993). *Do you know what you look like?* London: Falmer.

Xu, J., & Corno, L. (2003). Family help and homework management reported by middle school students. *The Elementary School Journal, 103*(5), 503–517.

Zeidner, M. (1988). The relative severity of common classroom strategies: The student's perspective. *British Journal of Educational Psychology, 58,* 69–77.

Zepeda, S. J., & Mayers, R. S. (2006). An analysis of research on block scheduling. *Review of Educational Research, 76*(1), 137–170.

Zirpoli, T. J. (2005). *Behavior management: Applications for teachers* (4th ed.). Upper Saddle River, NJ: Pearson Education.

NAME INDEX

SUBJECT INDEX